THE PURCHASE
OF FLORIDA

ITS HISTORY AND DIPLOMACY

BY

HUBERT BRUCE FULLER, A. M., LL. M.

A FACSIMILE REPRODUCTION
of the 1906 EDITION
with
INTRODUCTION
by WEYMOUTH T. JORDAN

QUADRICENTENNIAL EDITION
of the
FLORIDIANA FACSIMILE & REPRINT SERIES

University of Florida Press
GAINESVILLE, 1964

QUADRICENTENNIAL EDITION

of the

FLORIDIANA FACSIMILE & REPRINT SERIES

FACSIMILE REPRODUCTION

of the 1906 EDITION

WITH PREFATORY MATERIAL & INTRODUCTION

ADDED

NEW MATERIAL COPYRIGHT © 1964

BY THE

BOARD OF COMMISSIONERS

OF

STATE INSTITUTIONS OF FLORIDA

Library of Congress Catalog Card No. 64-19826

LITHOPRINTED BY DOUGLAS PRINTING COMPANY, INC.
BOUND BY UNIVERSAL-DIXIE BINDERY, INC.
JACKSONVILLE, FLORIDA

THE CABINET

FARRIS BRYANT
Governor

TOM ADAMS
Secretary of State

JAMES W. KYNES
Attorney General

RAY E. GREEN
State Comptroller

J. EDWIN LARSON
State Treasurer

DOYLE E. CONNER
Commissioner of Agriculture

THOMAS D. BAILEY
Superintendent of Public Instruction

THE BOARD OF CONTROL

BAYA M. HARRISON, JR.
Chairman
St. Petersburg

GERT H. W. SCHMIDT
Vice Chairman
Jacksonville

CHARLES R. FORMAN, D.V.M.
Ft. Lauderdale

JOHN C. PACE
Pensacola

WAYNE C. MCCALL, D.D.S.
Ocala

CHESTER E. WHITTLE
Orlando

JAMES LAWRENCE KING
Miami

J. B. CULPEPPER
Executive Director, Tallahassee

THE QUADRICENTENNIAL EDITION
of the
FLORIDIANA FACSIMILE & REPRINT SERIES

CARPETBAG RULE IN FLORIDA by John Wallace. 1888. Edited by Allan Nevins.

THE CIVIL WAR AND RECONSTRUCTION IN FLORIDA by William Watson Davis. 1913. Edited by Fletcher M. Green.

THE EXILES OF FLORIDA by Joshua R. Giddings. 1858. Edited by Arthur W. Thompson.

FLORIDA FOR TOURISTS, INVALIDS, AND SETTLERS by George M. Barbour. 1882. Edited by Emmett B. Peter, Jr.

HISTORICAL MEMOIR OF THE WAR IN WEST FLORIDA AND LOUISIANA IN 1814-15 by A. L. Latour. 1816. Edited by Jane Lucas de Grummond.

HISTORY OF JACKSONVILLE, FLORIDA, AND VICINITY, 1513 to 1924 by T. Frederick Davis. 1925. Edited by Richard A. Martin.

NOTICES OF FLORIDA AND THE CAMPAIGNS by M. M. Cohen. 1836. Edited by O. Z. Tyler, Jr.

THE ORIGIN, PROGRESS, AND CONCLUSION OF THE FLORIDA WAR by John T. Sprague. 1848. Edited by John K. Mahon.

PEDRO MENENDEZ de AVILES by Gonzalo Solís de Merás. 1567. (The Florida State Historical Society edition, edited and translated by Jeannette Thurber Connor.) Edited by Lyle N. McAlister.

THE PURCHASE OF FLORIDA by Hubert Bruce Fuller. 1906. Edited by Weymouth T. Jordan.

SKETCHES, HISTORICAL AND TOPOGRAPHICAL, OF THE FLORIDAS by James Grant Forbes. 1821. Edited by James W. Covington.

THE WHOLE & TRUE DISCOUERYE OF TERRA FLORIDA by Jean Ribaut. 1563. (The Florida State Historical Society edition, including a biography of Ribaut by Jeannette Thurber Connor.) Edited by David L. Dowd.

The Quadricentennial Coat-of-Arms

Surmounted by the Crest symbolizing our National Emblem and underlined by the Scroll, the Shield — with the Tower of Spain in the Heraldic quarter of honor, followed by the Fleur-de-lis of France, the Lion Rampant of Britain, and the Mullets and Saltier of the Confederacy — depicts the four-hundred-year cultural heritage of our Florida of today.

The Florida Quadricentennial Commission acknowledges its deepest gratitude to Chase D. Sheddan, distinguished scholar, and A. Vernon Coale, noted Heraldic Artist, for their conception and portrayal of the official Florida Quadricentennial Coat-of-Arms.

FLORIDA'S QUADRICENTENNIAL

 LORIDA *enjoys a unique position among the fifty states of the Union. Her city of St. Augustine antedates Jamestown, the second oldest European settlement within the present boundaries of the United States, by forty-two years. But it was not until 1950 that Florida entered the select circle of the ten most populous states of the nation. Since 1950 she has passed Massachusetts in population and is challenging New Jersey for eighth place. Within the South only Texas with more than four and one-half times the area of Florida has a larger population.*

Neither number nor age is necessarily a distinction, but most Americans are impressed by the former and revere the latter. Floridians view the recent and rapid increase in their state's population as an indication of youthful vigor. In 1860 eleven states of the Union had a million or more inhabitants, a status symbol not attained by Florida until the mid-1920's. At the turn of the century Florida ranked thirty-third in a nation of forty-six commonwealths; today she is ninth in population among the fifty states. In contrast to the national increase of less than 20 per cent from 1950 to 1960, Florida's population increased by more than 78 per cent. The number of people living in the state in 1964 is more than twice that of 1950.

While boasting of their state's recent surge, Floridians are also proud of their four-hundred-year-old origin. In 1957 the Florida Quadricentennial Commission was

*established. With the approval of its members local or-
ganizations have celebrated the quadricentennials of
several historic events. The attempt of Tristán de Luna
to found a colony on the western tip of Santa Rosa Island
in 1559 was observed in Pensacola by reconstructing the
Spanish village settlement. In 1962 Jacksonville noted
the Quadricentennial of Jean Ribault's explorations with
a colorful drama. Even before this tribute to the French
explorer, a museum was built near the spot where in
1564 another Frenchman, René de Laudonnière, brought
the first Protestant colonists to an area within the present-
day United States. These and other quadricentennial
celebrations will culminate in 1965 with state, national,
and international observance of the founding of St.
Augustine.*

*There are many ways to celebrate quadricentennials—
parades, speeches, pageants, the re-creation of villages and
forts, and the restoration of buildings. Some of these are
spectacular but fleeting; others, including the restoration
of buildings, will remain for our descendants to see and
feel. More enduring than any of these are ideas. For this
reason the Governor, the Cabinet, and the Florida Quadricentennial Commission gave priority to the reprinting
of rare and valuable books relating to Florida. These reproductions will endure. They will enable many Americans to share in the state's past, and will provide source
material for the historian.*

*Until recently few authors or publishers were inter-
ested in Florida. Englishmen brought the first printing
press to Florida in 1783 and from it came a newspaper
and two books. But for a century and a half the books*

on Florida were rare and the number of copies printed was small. In cooperation with the University of Florida Press the Quadricentennial Commission is reprinting twelve rare or semi-rare books. The subject matter in these volumes covers a period of more than three hundred years of Florida's history—the French and Spanish settlements, the War of 1812, the purchase by the United States, the Seminole War, the Civil War and Reconstruction, and the modern period. In addition to textual reproductions, these facsimile editions contain introductions by businessmen, journalists, and professors. The Quadricentennial Commission hopes these twelve books will stimulate the production of other reprints and encourage students to write original manuscripts which describe and interpret Florida's past.

The Florida Quadricentennial Commission

THE COMMISSION

FRED H. KENT, *Chairman*—Jacksonville
DOYLE E. CARLTON, SR.—Tampa
WILSON CARRAWAY—Tallahassee
JEAN ANN CONE—Tampa
CLARENCE M. GAY—Orlando
HAROLD W. GOFORTH—Ocala
HERBERT GRAY—Tampa
JOHN MARSHALL GREEN—Ocala
KATHRYN ABBEY HANNA—Winter Park
MALLORY HORNE—Tallahassee
CHARLES H. OVERMAN—Pensacola
JOHN D. PENNEKAMP—Miami
JOHN FITE ROBERTSON—Sarasota
GERT H. W. SCHMIDT—Jacksonville
H. E. WOLFE—St. Augustine

EDITORIAL PREFACE.

NEVER in American history have the terms of an international agreement been as incorrectly reported and as misinterpreted as were those of the Adams-Onís Treaty. As a consequence, students and most textbook writers "know" that in 1819 the United States purchased Florida from Spain for $5,000,000. The date, the purchase, and the $5,000,000 are myths, persistent myths that are repeated year after year in encyclopedias and general histories.

Throughout the Second Spanish Period of Florida, 1784-1821, the United States kept her eyes steadfastly on the desirable Florida provinces. Along with independence in 1783, the United States won from Great Britain a vast land lying between the Appalachian Mountains and the Mississippi River. Not satisfied, the acquisitive Americans demanded from Spain the area of West Florida between the line 32° 28' and the 31st parallel. Spain resisted for a decade, but in 1795 gave the United States clear title to the disputed territory which now comprises parts of Louisiana, Mississippi, and Alabama. On learning that Spain had retroceded Louisiana to France and thinking that West Florida was included in the transfer, President Jefferson attempted to buy it and the island of Orleans from Napoleon I. Jefferson's ministers secured Louisiana in 1803 and claimed West Florida as a part of the Louisiana Purchase. On the basis of this claim, military forces of the United States occupied sections of West Florida in 1810 and 1813. Furthermore, a fundamental purpose of the War of 1812 was the acqui-

sition of the rest of Florida. Recalcitrant senators defeated
the attempt of the Madison administration to acquire Florida, but the Spanish-owned province was invaded in 1816
by forces commanded by Colonel Duncan L. Clinch and in
1818 by forces commanded by General Andrew Jackson.
The latter action helped to convince Spain that the United
States was determined to possess an area needed to complete her southern boundary and to protect the interests of
her people in the Mississippi Valley.

This problem was only one of the territorial disputes between the United States and Spain. In addition to boundaries, the two nations had claims against each other for
property losses sustained by their citizens. After prolonged
negotiations, Secretary of State John Quincy Adams and
Spanish Minister Louis de Onís reached an agreement in
1819. The United States Senate ratified the treaty, but the
Spanish Cortes rejected it. In 1821 the Spanish legislature
ratified, and after a second confirmation by the American
Senate, the treaty was promulgated.

By its provisions, Spain gave the United States title to
the Floridas in exchange for American relinquishment of
all claims to Texas. Spain also assigned to the United States
all Spanish rights to the Oregon area, leaving eventual
ownership of the Pacific northwest country to negotiation
among Great Britain, Russia, and the United States. As
Samuel Flagg Bemis has determined, the Adam-Onís agreement was a "Transcontinental Treaty." Besides territorial
boundaries, the claims of American and Spanish citizens
were settled by separate and distinct provisions in the
treaty.

The date of the Adams-Onís Treaty was 1821, not 1819.
Instead of buying the Floridas, the United States acquired
the territories and Spanish claims to Oregon in exchange
for relinquishing vague rights to Texas. Not a penny was
paid to Spain for the Floridas, or to Americans claiming

indemnity for property losses suffered by Spanish acts, or to Spaniards demanding payment for American depredations. These claims were adjusted by provisions of the treaty other than those relating to territorial boundaries. By the Adams-Onís Treaty, ratified by Spain and the United States in 1821, the latter country gained the Floridas and Spanish claims to Oregon in return for giving Spain a clear title to Texas.

Hubert Bruce Fuller failed to give the complete account of the acquisition of the Floridas. His title, *The Purchase of Florida,* is inaccurate; but as Professor Jordan points out, Fuller's study was a pioneer one. It stimulated other investigators to delve into the Florida question. Weymouth T. Jordan is head of the Department of History at the Florida State University and the author of a number of books. The University of Florida Press acknowledges its indebtedness to Stanley L. West, Director of Libraries, and Elizabeth Alexander, Librarian of the Yonge Memorial Library, at the University of Florida, for the use of an original copy of Fuller's book in producing this facsimile.

University of Florida
May, 1964

REMBERT W. PATRICK
General Editor of the
FLORIDIANA SERIES

INTRODUCTION.

HUBERT Bruce Fuller was born on June 15, 1880, in East Derby, Connecticut, and was the son of Robert Bruce Fuller, a school principal, and Harriet A. (Prentice) Fuller. He married Florence B. Dennis, daughter of James H. and Harriet I. (Batty) Dennis, on May 25, 1910, in Chanute, Kansas, and was the father of two children, Harriet Lois and Florence Esther. He was descended from William Brewster, the Pilgrim leader, and from Benjamin Franklin's sister, Ann.

Fuller obtained a good education. He prepared for college at Central High School, Washington, D. C., and entered Columbian University (now George Washington University) as a member of the class of 1900. He left Columbian University before graduating in order to attend Yale University as a senior in the class of 1901. After graduating from Yale he returned to Columbian University Law School, where he received the LL.B. and LL.M. degrees in 1903. While in law school he was awarded prizes in insurance and corporation law, an essay on "The Regulation of Corporations by Taxation" winning first prize in a class of one hundred and ten men. He began practicing law in Cleveland, Ohio, in 1903. He had earlier started work on the manuscript which was to be published as *The Purchase of Florida*. This manuscript won for him the M.A. degree from Yale University in 1904, as well as the George Washington Eggleston Prize in American History.

As Fuller reported to Yale University for publication in

the 1917 issue of the *Quindecennial Record,* he had by that time become a member of the Cleveland Chamber of Commerce, the Sons of the American Revolution, and the Western Reserve Historical Society. He said for the *Record*: "Here I am not troubled with modesty but I suffer from lack of having led a very thrilling career. I have won no Carnegie medals, been swept into no public offices on waves of popular approval or enthusiasm, and have kept out of the police records. I am merely a lawyer specializing in insurance law, railroad rate law, and food and drug legislation. I was secretary to Senator Theodore E. Burton of Ohio (Republican) during his term in the United States Senate from 1909 to 1915." He reported that he had been "stumping" Cleveland and northern Ohio each fall in behalf of municipal and state candidates of the Republican Party.

His publication record was anything but modest. His major historical excursion, *The Purchase of Florida* (1906), was behind him. *Tax Returns in Ohio* was printed the following year, in 1909 his *Speakers of the House* was released, in 1913 he brought out *The Law of Accident and Employers' Liability Insurance,* and 1915 saw the publication of *The Act to Regulate Commerce.* He also contributed articles on historical, legal, and sociological subjects to such magazines as the *North American Review, World's Work, McClure's Magazine, The Review of Reviews, Century, Scribner's,* and *Munsey's Magazine.* He was interested in subjects which were of concern to persons of the Progressive persuasion of his day. He would become more conservative in later years.

Following World War I, Fuller concentrated on his law practice and Republican politics in the Cleveland area. In 1922 he was a member of the law firm of Chamberlin and Fuller. He was, for a time, associated with William S. Fitzgerald, a former Cleveland mayor. For many years, he was a member of Cull, Fuller and Laughlin, perhaps the leading law office in Cleveland. In his later years he operated his own law firm. Specializing in legal matters relating to the petroleum industry, he became an officer in the Cleveland Petroleum Club and a member of the American Petroleum Institute. He was for thirty years general counsel for the Ohio Petroleum Marketers Association, this being his chief activity. He belonged to the Cleveland, Ohio, and American Bar Associations, and continued his membership in the Western Reserve Historical Society, the Chamber of Commerce, and the Sons of the American Revolution. He also joined the New England Society and the Sons of Mayflower Descendants. He died on February 9, 1957, in Cleveland, a highly respected man of his community.

Fuller is best noted as a successful lawyer. History was not his profession. When one goes looking for information on him, one will not find it among the usual biographical accounts of authors in the field of history. At his death, the leading historical magazines did not carry obituary notices, and he is not listed in the volume of the *Dictionary of American Biography* which contains sketches of deceased historians. More appropriately, he is to be found in such compilations as *The Book of Clevelanders* (Cleveland, 1914) and *Who's Who in Law* (New York, 1937). Yale University is also justly proud of Fuller and records his outstanding accomplishments in *Sexennial Records, Class of 1901* (New Haven, 1909), in *Quindecennial Record* (Norwood, Massachusetts, 1917), and in *Vicennial Record* (New Haven, 1922).

Fuller's one large endeavor in the field of history was *The Purchase of Florida*, published in Cleveland in 1906. He begins with a few paragraphs describing Spanish Florida in the years before 1763, when Spain was forced to cede the territory to England. This is followed by brief accounts of the period 1763 to 1783, when the region was under English control, and of the retrocession to Spain at the close of the American Revolution. As Fuller aptly describes Florida's next period of importance, 1783 to 1795, two problems came to the front: the boundary between Georgia and Florida and American commercial use of the Mississippi River. An abortive effort was made to solve these two problems with the ill-starred Jay-Gardoqui negotiations of the mid-1780's. They were solved, in part, in 1795 by the Spanish-American Treaty of San Lorenzo, by which the boundary was placed at the 31st parallel, the United States was accorded free navigation of the lower Mississippi River, and Americans were allowed to deposit goods at New Orleans for transshipment to ocean-going vessels. England had just made an agreement (the Jay Treaty) with the United States. Spain signed her treaty because she wanted the United States as a friend in case of trouble with England. As Fuller says, Spain was afraid that England might "excite the United States against her."

Before and after the Treaty of San Lorenzo, many Americans wanted ownership of Florida. This was the rub—and the United States would be satisfied with nothing less. Settlers in the Kentucky-Tennessee area were especially hopeful of gaining the region. These Westerners believed that Florida should belong to the United States by "moral right," by manifest destiny. More particularly, they wanted to ship their goods to the east by water rather than overland through the Appalachian Mountains. They insisted that the leaders of the Jeffersonian political party push their cause. The political leaders—from Jefferson to Monroe—did not fail them. They were elated with the Louisiana Purchase of 1803 for its own sake, as well as because it would add pressure on Spain in regard to Florida.

As Fuller points out, over and over, the rise of the United States after 1789 and the weakening of Spain at home and abroad as a result of the wars brought on by the French Revolution, meant that Spain would be unable to maintain control of her possessions in America. Spain thus lost most of her New World possessions including the Floridas, her "fairest provinces." Put another way, this meant that Spain's troubles worked to the advantage of the United States.

In 1793 Thomas Jefferson had predicted that "time" would bring independence to "our neighbors," that "free commerce" would come, and that the United States would obtain Florida without fighting for it. Fuller tells how these predictions materialized and how various American Presidents urged them along. He emphasizes that Florida was surrounded by American territory after the purchase of Louisiana in 1803. He also tracks through the many conspiracies of Americans to take Florida, that is, the intrigues of John Sevier, William Blount, James Wilkinson, Thomas Jefferson, Alexander Hamilton, and George Matthews. Special attention is given to Andrew Jackson's invasion of Florida in 1818 and to Secretary of State John Quincy Adams' role in the final acquisition.

Fuller closes his story with an appraisal of the negotiation of the Adams-Onís treaty. He says, "The United States received the Floridas in return for an agreement to settle the disputed claims of certain of her citizens against Spain to an amount not more than $5,000,000." The United States also relinquished its trumped-up claims to Texas. Fuller leaves no doubt as to his sentiments about American annexation of Florida: "No sooner were we a nation than we cast our eyes about. We coveted Florida, and we talked of manifest destiny, and the falling of ripened fruit, and eased our conscience by like casuistry. Spain was weak, she was entangled in the Herculean grasp of European complications—all of which materially assisted this ever favorable manifest destiny. . . . It was the right of might—the triumph of force."

Fuller said this at a time just after the United States had

moved against Spain in the Spanish-American War of
1898 and had deprived Spain of Cuba, the Philippines,
Guam, and Puerto Rico. He wrote his book precisely at the
time President Theodore Roosevelt was "taking" Panama.
Perhaps Fuller was showing that American sanction of
"the white man's burden" of the day was a rebirth of the
continental "manifest destiny" of the United States during
the first half of the nineteenth century. Perhaps Fuller, the
staunch Republican, was trying to demonstrate that the Republicans of his time were acting in much the same way as
Democrats had acted under Jefferson, Madison, and Monroe. Also, although not a part of his main story, he had
managed some sharp side-swipes at another Democrat,
James K. Polk, for "despoiling Mexico." He had, however,
also censured a few members of the old Federalist political
party. However this may be, it is an established truism
among historians that every generation writes its own version of history. Fuller certainly added to the story of the
acquisition of Florida as presented by nineteenth century
American historians. He was, of course, a product of his
times—and he wrote his *Purchase of Florida* as he saw it.
His version was neither altogether pleasant nor complete.
He said his piece—on occasion as a lawyer pleading a case.
He used many an oratorical flourish in his writing—in a
style which is no longer practiced. He was a representative
of his time and place.

The *Purchase of Florida* was variously received by contemporary reviewers during the last three months of 1906.
The *New York Times* concluded that "Mr. Fuller's account
of this whole affair is the best we know of," while the *Review of Reviews* called it "a scholarly monograph." The
Literary Digest stated, "For his material Mr. Fuller has
gone direct to original sources" in preparing his "elaborate
monograph," adding that his "investigation has enabled
him to present a new light on many momentous episodes in

the early diplomatic history of the nation." But all was not rosy. The *Outlook* said that the book gave "ready access to much documentary information hitherto not generally available," but that a closely revised second edition was needed. The *Nation* offered "two serious criticisms" of the study: "The material upon which it is based is inadequate, and the knowledge which it displays of European diplomatic situations is insufficient." In January, 1907, the *American Historical Review* carried a caustic appraisal of the book. The reviewer, whose name was withheld, wrote that a reader would not find much that was new in Fuller's work, that he had "left large and fatal gaps in his narrative," and that the study did not give enough attention to the Texas boundary question or to contemporary events in Europe and South America. It was admitted, however, that the book had some merits: "The discussions as to West Florida, the events of the War of 1812, and Jackson's exploits in 1818 are fully treated. Here the author is more at home, and these chapters are distinctly the best. . . ."

For many years the work of Fuller was considered the standard account of the acquisition of Florida; but historians recognized that it did not cover all of the subject and, as is the way of historians, they delved deeper and deeper into it. They naturally benefited from new techniques and the greater availability of materials, as well as from the changing interpretations of history itself. Reference only to the major new studies and revisions must suffice here. Three books may be examined for general information on Florida: Kathryn A. Hanna, *Florida, Land of Change* (1941) ; Charles L. Mowat, *East Florida as a British Province, 1763-1784* (1943) ; and Rembert W. Patrick, *Florida Under Five Flags* (1945). Two younger scholars, Charles W. Arnade and John Jay DePaske, are now at work on the subject of Spanish Florida, and will add greatly to information about the period to 1763.

Distinguished accounts of Florida as a part of the international scene have been produced since Fuller's study. Some of them almost seem to have been written solely as supplements to Fuller's pioneer book; all of them are helpful in understanding the acquisition of Florida. From the Johns Hopkins University came forth *The West Florida Controversy, 1798-1813* (1918) by Isaac J. Cox. Herbert E. Bolton, the inspiring historian of the University of California, published his study of *The Spanish Borderlands; A Chronicle of Old Florida and the Southwest* (1921). Next there was Julius W. Pratt, *Expansionists of 1812* (1925), one of the most provocative books ever done in American historiography, and he did not neglect Florida. Another modern study of special import was *Pinckney's Treaty: A Study of America's Advantages from Europe's Distress, 1783-1800* (1926) by the leading authority on American diplomatic history, Samuel Flagg Bemis. Of special significance, too, were Arthur P. Whitaker, *The Spanish-American Frontier, 1783-1795* (1927), and his *The Mississippi Question, 1795-1803* (1934), as well as Marquis James, *Andrew Jackson, the Border Captain* (1933).

From California, brought on by Bolton's leadership, there poured forth three books which added to the Florida story. E. H. Tatum, *The United States and Europe, 1815-1823* (1936), led the way, to be followed by the *United States and the Disruption of the Spanish Empire, 1810-1822* (1937) by Charles C. Griffin. The climax arrived with Philip C. Brooks, *Diplomacy of the Borderlands: The Adams-Onís Treaty of 1819* (1939), based upon an examination of historical materials in Spain, France, England, and the United States. Brooks showed, among other things, that claims were not tied to the cession of territory. Bemis summarized much of what had been written in his monumental account of *John Quincy Adams and the Foundations of American Foreign Diplomacy* (1949). Bemis dubbed the Florida treaty "the Transcontinental Treaty with Spain." Rembert W. Patrick, with *Florida Fiasco; Rampant Rebels on the Georgia-Florida Border, 1810-1815* (1954), filled in a neglected aspect of his state's history.

Each of these historians was a revisionist. Each of them represented progress in historical research and writing, for such progress is inevitable. Fuller wrote history as it was being written during his time, and was honored for his efforts with a degree from Yale University, the first American university to award a doctoral degree based on research. He did not receive a doctoral degree, of course, but his alma mater thought he deserved a reward for his endeavors. The other historians have written from the more scholarly perspective of their times. This essay is a case in point. We write as we do today because we have learned to do so from our predecessors including the author of *The Purchase of Florida*. We can still learn something from Hubert Bruce Fuller.

WEYMOUTH T. JORDAN

The Florida State University

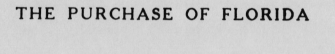

THE PURCHASE OF FLORIDA

THE PURCHASE
OF FLORIDA

ITS HISTORY AND DIPLOMACY

BY

HUBERT BRUCE FULLER, A. M., LL. M.

WITH MAPS

CLEVELAND
THE BURROWS BROTHERS COMPANY
1906

REPUBLICAN PRINTING COMPANY
CEDAR RAPIDS, IOWA

TO THE MEMORY
OF
MY BELOVED FATHER

ROBERT B. FULLER

CONTENTS.

PREFACE.

THE acquisition of Florida, our early relations with Spain, and the struggle to secure New Orleans and the Mississippi, are critical and interesting chapters in American history. Their importance and magnitude are but slightly considered by many of wide culture, and are but vaguely appreciated even by those who have made a special study of the history of the nation.

In connection with post-graduate work at Yale University, where this essay was awarded the George Washington Eggleston Prize in American History, in 1904, the author became aware of the poverty of historical writing devoted to these significant matters in the diplomatic history of the United States, and was impressed with the advantages which might accrue to students of American history, from an unprejudiced and accurate account of the acquisition of Florida and our early entanglements with the Spanish nation. Through the courtesy of the late Hon. John Hay, then Secretary of State, and of Assistant Secretary Adee, the diplomatic correspondence of the period in question was placed at the disposal of the writer.

Some idea of the importance of the questions involved and the attention they received from our national officials may be inferred from the fact that the author was obliged to examine some fifty volumes of official manuscript in order to secure the necessary data for a proper treatment of the subject. The original correspondence, all carefully examined and compared, included Instructions to United States

Ministers in Europe, Domestic Letters, Notes to Foreign
Legations, Letters of Foreign Ministers in the United States
to the State Department, Letters from our Ministers Abroad
to the State Department, and the Personal Letters of the
various Ministers of the United States to Spain, France and
England. Vols. XII and XIII of the Domestic Letters,
and Vol. I of Notes to Foreign Legations were lost at the
time of the British occupation of Washington in 1814, and
have never been recovered.

The letters now extant in the State Department, many
in French and Spanish, and not heretofore translated, reveal
much of the inside history of our early national life. This
mass of correspondence and notes, for the most part,
furnishes the authority for the statements of fact made
in the following pages. The conclusions derived have been
drawn in an earnest effort to be fair and to avoid prejudice;
national vanity and a mistaken patriotism have misled many
authors.

The province of the historian is to present facts; to be
correct rather than pleasing; to criticise, if occasion require,
yet always justly. Fortified by the results of fullest research,
he should state truly what has happened, and be guided in
conclusions by the laws of evidence. He should seek to
accomplish the complete subjection of personal, political and
patriotic prejudices. The narrative should be based prim-
arily upon an examination and appreciation of original
documents. Personal memoirs, contemporary chronicles,
and biased biographies and diaries are not to be ignored,
but they must be subordinated to documents of acknowledged validity — such as authentic dispatches, original instructions, executive decrees and legislative enactments.
Such gaps in history as cannot be filled should be bridged
with great care.

If the author has criticised government officials and

officers of the army, or their conduct of affairs, it has been done solely to subserve the ends of historical accuracy.

Acknowledgment must be made to Mr. Andrew H. Allen, the Librarian of the Department of State, and to Mr. Pendleton King, Chief of the Bureau of Indexes and Archives of that department, and to Mr. P. Lee Phillips of the Congressional Library, for their uniform courtesy and valuable assistance; to Professor Arthur M. Wheeler of Yale University, for his kindly criticisms, valuable suggestions and friendly encouragement; and also to Professor Theodore S. Woolsey and Professor Edward G. Bourne of Yale University; the Hon. Hannis Taylor, of the Spanish Claims Commission and one time Minister to Spain; Professor Charles C. Swisher of George Washington University; Justice David J. Brewer of the United States Supreme Court; and Mr. T. Fletcher Dennis of Washington, D. C., for assistance and advice always graciously afforded, and most gratefully received.

HUBERT BRUCE FULLER.

Cleveland, Ohio,
    February, 1906.

DIPLOMATIC HISTORY OF THE PURCHASE OF FLORIDA

CHAPTER I.

EARLY RELATIONS WITH SPAIN.

FLORIDA — the land of the fountain of youth, of fabled riches, of unrivaled beauty, was the central figure of the romance and tradition of the sixteenth century. But her history was more a tragedy than a song. Here explorers, brave knights, soldiers of fortune, lured by the siren songs of wealth and the hope of glory, suffered and died and the world knew them no more. Here were armies sacrificed to satiate the vengeance of European monarchs — massacred by savage redskins or other vengeful enemies, with every refinement of cruelty that an ingenious mind could conceive or an experienced hand execute. Here Spanish and French and English all contributed something to the horror-laden history of colonial conquest, each in turn learning the awful penalties of the law of retribution.

Army after army buried itself in these swamps and forests — their bones left to bleach in the woods after being torn asunder by wild beasts or cruel natives to whom the whites had brought only the gospel of hate. And in these primeval forests, in a fruitless endeavor to explore the world of fabled romance, many a brave cavalier found the grave of· his ambition. Bound by the thraldom of stupid traditions, they pursued the fateful errand of death and failure; no city of gold was their reward, no treasure-mine offered remuneration; only misery and death and the immunities of a forgotten grave.

But these expeditions were not of exploration and avarice alone; they were also of holy mission; for the adventurer and priest were companions, the one seeking the reward of gold, the other the nobler reward of souls won to Christianity. But their methods were much the same; fire and sword served them in place of argument and conviction. The beautiful picture of self-sacrificing priests gone into a wild country to carry salvation to an unfortunate race, was not without its darker shadows. For they brought the inquisition with its horrors, and the fagot showed to a lurid heaven that even untutored savages can die for their convictions and for principle.

After the early period of discovery and settlement had passed, the American colonies became entangled in the wars of the continent. In 1666, again in 1719, and in 1725 various attacks on Florida had been made by the southern colonists entailing a bitterness of feeling between these provinces, which was destined to endure and bear fruit for more than a century. Fire and sword, famine and disease visited the colony in rapid and ruinous succession.

By the treaty of Paris in 1763, Florida was ceded to Great Britain in return for Cuba, and a new life was opened to this province — the fairest, yet the bloodiest of our domain. For Spain has ever viewed her colonists as slaves whose blood and tears might well be shed to advance her own proud ease and splendor.

With the change of title the Spanish people quite generally emigrated from the country which had been under the Castilian flag for two centuries. Two hundred years of disappointment and sorrow they had been. Outside the garrisoned walls little had been accomplished, for the Spanish were soldiers not civilians, gentlemen not agriculturists.

Under the English the province increased in population

and wealth; commerce flourished and friendly relations were established with the southern colonies. But when in 1775 the first guns of freedom were fired, they awakened no response in the hearts of the people of Florida. The other southern colonists might cheer the heroes of Lexington and Bunker Hill and call the minute-men patriots, but to Florida they were traitors, for Florida alone remained loyal. It was too new a possession and the people too well governed to feel the keen dissatisfaction and unrest which breed revolution. For to them English misgovernment seemed a blessing after the wrongs they had endured from the Spanish. And further, many colonists were the recent beneficiaries of the generous land-grants of the English king. No bells and bonfires in Florida proclaimed the Declaration of Independence; no liberty poles arose in her public squares. On the other hand when news of the events of July 4, 1776, reached St. Augustine, John Hancock and Samuel Adams were hanged and burned in effigy by a cheering crowd of loyalists.

Naturally this proud city, which had been called by her former monarchs "the faithful city of St. Augustine," became, during the war, a depot and *point d'appui* for the British in their operations against the southern states and large forces at times were stationed there. Incursions were made from time to time into Georgia to be followed by counter-incursions into Florida. In the summer of 1778 two bodies of armed men marched from St. Augustine into Georgia, where after laying waste a part of the country about Sunbury and the Ogechee River they were forced to retreat. The Americans numbering some two thousand, under General Robert Howe, this same year of 1778 attempted to reduce St. Augustine. The British abandoned Fort Tonyn at the mouth of St. Mary's River, where so many privateers had been fitted out, and withdrew into the walls of St. Augustine which must have soon fallen had not the deadly insects and a wasting sickness attacked the colonists.

In that year alone nearly seven thousand loyalists from the southern colonies emigrated to Florida. For the Georgia legislature had attainted with treason the refugees, and their property was declared forfeited to the state and ordered to be sold. Georgia's position was a most difficult one; for close to her was not only a loyal colony whose bitterness and effective strength had been increased by these Tory fugitives, but also the most powerful tribe of aborigines on the continent, hostile and revengeful.

In short, Florida had become a haven of refuge for the king's troops and Tories, and these marauding expeditions, citizens, Tories, Scopholites, Minorcans and Indians, were banded together under the name of Florida Rangers. With all the withering desolation of civil war the struggle went on; Ranger and Liberty Boy, Florida and Georgia, perchance brother and brother, or father and son — such is the sad tale the historian must record. To old St. Augustine, particularly after the fall of Charleston, the cartel ships brought their loads of prisoners and here were confined many Americans of prominence in the Revolutionary struggle.

When the war was ended the planters returned to their fields, the artisans to their trades. Many loyalists who had refused allegiance to the new government came to Florida to live again under English colors or await the time when bitterness and prejudice might disappear from their former homes. The province, under the impetus of British government, took on new life and added prosperity. But one day, in 1783, a ship arrived in the harbor of St. Augustine and all was changed; the darkness and despair of ruin settled upon the province. For the king of England and the king of

Spain had indulged in a game of chess: they had traded
pawns; Spain took the Floridas and Jamaica went to England.   Florida was well nigh deserted; for the English
subjects, bidding farewell to their old homes, with tears
and lamentations, parted from brother and sister, mother
and father.   It was the scene of Grand Pré repeated; many
found ruin and want on the shores of Jamaica while others
returned to the now United States, there to experience the
injustice of successful foes.

The cross of St. George was superseded by the Spanish
flag, Spanish troops manned the forts and Spanish grandees
dispensed the laws.   And with their return industry and
agriculture were suspended and commerce blotted out, while
poverty and desolation took their place.   The revolted colonies were a nation, loyal Florida a Castilian province.

The Declaration of Independence had hurled defiance
at Great Britain and announced to the world the birth of a
new nation, which was viewed with ridicule and contempt
by many of the European countries, while others watched
the scene in wonder, speculating whether here, at last,
might be the weapon with which to humble an ancient
enemy.

Those early years were fraught with perils that made
our national existence precarious.   The sinews of war were
wanting and success was possible only with the alliance and
aid of the ancient monarchies of Europe.   Ambassadors —
among the grandest men of the infant nation — were sent
abroad, there on suppliant knee to seek the material and
not alone the moral support without which the new-born
must perish.   To Madrid was dispatched the diplomatic
and well-born Jay, to seek some aid for the new republic
from the old Castilian rulers whose name had ever been
synonymous with all things anti-Republican, who above all
stood for the divine right of kings.   Spain was not for-

getful of the lost Armada, nor was she unmindful of the numerous scores against England, and while she might view with intense satisfaction the loss to that country of her fairest possessions, yet that alone would not move her to action.

At first she viewed with alarm the prospect of a new nation in North America so near her own. It was not America free that Spain desired; it was America dependent, but disaffected. For thus both the colonies and Great Britain would be unable to pillage Spanish America. At first then Spain gladly contributed, so far as she could — without exhausting her already embarrassed treasury or causing a public rupture — to maintain the colonies in this state of permanent disaffection.

But the Revolution progressed. The American arms held their own and the issue looked toward actual independence. Would Spain actively assist in a movement which might prove so seductive to her own colonies: would she thus help build up a power founded upon political principles in hostility to her own theories and traditions?

Montmorin, the French minister of Madrid, wrote to Vergennes: "I have no need to tell you, sir, how much the forming a republic in these regions would displease Spain, and in fact, I believe that would neither suit her interests nor ours."

Mirales, who came to Philadelphia from Spain in 1780 on a mission of inquiry, was so far imbued with the prejudices of his principals as to be incapable of giving in return a fair account of American affairs. The more he saw, the more he was appalled at the spectacle of the United States, not merely wresting the Mississippi Valley from Spain, but inciting Spanish South America to revolt.[1]

With prophetic foresight Vergennes declared that if

1. Wharton's International Law, Vol. I, p. 442; Bancroft's Hist. of the U. S., Vol. V, p. 301.

the United States won a place among the independent nations, having fought to defend its hearth fires, it would next desire to extend itself over Louisiana, Florida and Mexico, in order to secure all the approaches to the sea.

Actuated by these ideas and with elusive and adroit Castilian diplomacy, the Spanish met the American representatives with mingled feelings of annoyance, displeasure and alarm. This was the second stage of the Spanish attitude toward the American Revolution.

By force of circumstances she was hurried on to the third stage. Unconsciously and irresistibly drawn by the logic of events into the whirlpool of that war which France, in the name of the colonies, was waging against Great Britain, Spain found solace and encouragement in the thought that at last was come the opportunity to avenge her wrongs; to wrest Gibraltar from the hands of the hated intruder, and on the successful issue of the war to rise again to the position of a first-class power.

The possibility of a Spanish alliance had long been a pleasing and fruitful topic of debate in the continental congress, and in 1778 suggestions were repeatedly made in that body as to what might be offered as an inducement to this coveted arrangement. Finally the different ideas were crystallized in the form of a motion offered September 10, 1779, by Mr. Dickinson: "That if his Catholic Majesty shall determine to take part with France and the United States of America, in such case the minister plenipotentiary of the United States be empowered in their name to conclude with the most Christian and Catholic Kings, a treaty or treaties, thereby assuring to these States Canada, Nova Scotia, Bermudas and the Floridas, when conquered, and the free and full exercise of the common right of these States to the fisheries on the banks of Newfoundland and the other fishing banks and seas of North America, and also the free navigation of the Mississippi into the sea."[1] But in this grant of the territory of the Floridas it was always provided, "that his Catholic Majesty shall grant to the United States the free navigation of the Mississippi into the sea and establish on the said river at or somewhere southward of 31° north latitude, a free port or ports," for all merchant vessels, goods, wares and merchandise belonging to the inhabitants of the States. The United States might well be thus generous in her terms, for her enemy and not herself was being despoiled. With these terms as a basis, Jay was directed to conclude a treaty of comity and alliance at the court of Madrid. These offers, however, did not coincide with Spanish ideas, and counter-propositions were made: these are shown in a communication of the French minister to congress, February 2, 1780, on the "Terms of Alliance proposed by his Catholic Majesty," setting forth, "certain articles which his Catholic Majesty deems of great importance to the interests of his crown, and on which it is highly necessary that the United States explain themselves with precision and with such moderation as may consist with their essential rights. That the articles are:

"(1)   A precise and invariable western boundary of the United States.

"(2)   The exclusive navigation of the River Mississippi.

"(3)   The possession of the Floridas; and

"(4)   The lands on the left or eastern side of the River Mississippi.

"That on the first article it is the idea of the cabinet of Madrid that the United States extend to the westward no farther than settlements were permitted by the royal proclamation of 1763. On the second that the United States

---

1. Wharton, Vol. III, p. 311.

do not consider themselves as having any right to navigate the River Mississippi, no territory belonging to them being situated thereon. On the third that it is probable that the king of Spain will conquer the Floridas during the course of the present war. On the fourth that the lands lying on the east side of the Mississippi are possessions of the crown of Great Britain and proper objects against which the arms of Spain may be employed for the purpose of making a permanent conquest for the Spanish crown." [1]

A certain faction were willing to barter away our right to the navigation of the Mississippi, if thereby they might secure so promising an alliance, but the statesmen for the most part insisted that this must never be the price of any treaty, no matter how beneficial.

In a letter to Jay, Benjamin Franklin wrote, "Poor as we are, yet, as I know we shall be rich, I would rather agree with them to buy at a great price the whole of their [Spanish] right on the Mississippi than to sell a drop of its waters. A neighbor might as well ask me to sell my street door." [2] But Spain, insistent on exclusive right to the navigation of the river from its source to the gulf, would listen to no propositions which did not guarantee her this. In 1780 we find her demanding the Mississippi as the consideration for the loan of one hundred thousand pounds sterling. The Spanish asserted with warmth that the king would never relinquish the navigation of the Mississippi, and that its exclusive ownership was the sole advantage they would obtain from the war. [3]

The colonies insisted that there need be no fear of future complications over this waterway, for it was the boundary of several states in the Union, and that the cit-

---

1. Wharton, Vol. III, p. 489. MSS. State Department.
2. Dated Passy, Oct. 2, 1780. Wharton, Vol. IV, p. 75.
3. Conference between Jay and Count de Florida Blanca Sept. 25, 1780.

izens of these states, while connected with Great Britain, and since the Revolution, had been accustomed to the free use of the stream in common with the Spanish subjects and that there had been no trouble. Spain by the treaty of Paris had ceded to Great Britain all the country to the northeastward of the Mississippi; the people inhabiting these states while subject to Great Britain and even since the Revolution, had settled at various places near the Mississippi, were friendly to the Revolution, and, being citizens, the United States could not consider the proposition of assigning them over as subjects of another power. [1]

So far from granting the navigation of the Mississippi, Jay was directed to seek an arrangement by which, if Spain should capture the Floridas, the United States could share the free navigation of the rivers which traversed these provinces and emptied into the Gulf of Mexico. Americans believed that the Mississippi had been planned by the Creator as a natural highway for the people of that upper country whose extent and fertility had already attracted the eye of the frontiersmen. They believed that this country would be quickly settled, that there was neither equity nor reason in compelling the inhabitants to live without foreign commodities and lose the surplus of their productions, or be compelled to transport them over forbidding mountains and through an immense wilderness to the sea, particularly when at their very door was the most magnificent highway of the continent. [2] Spain maintained that the present generation would not want this right of navigation and that future generations could well dispose of the question when it should become a live one. The king of Spain considered the ownership of the Mississippi River far more important to his dynasty than the recovery of Gibraltar, and the maxims of policy adopted in the management of the Spanish col-

1. Instructions to Jay in Congress, Oct. 4, 1780. Wharton, Vol. IV, pp. 78, 79.
2. Jay to President of Congress, Nov. 6, 1780. *Ibid.*, p. 167.

onies required that only the Castilian banner should appear on the Gulf Waters.[1] But the colonies insisted upon their moral and legal right to this outlet. True, it was a question which belonged largely to the future, but they were unwilling to thus hypothecate that future and retard their own development. Further, the treaty of alliance of 1778 with France, had guaranteed to that country the free navigation of the river. European complications, however, forced Spain into the contest, not as an ally of the colonies, but of France.[2]

Yet for the accomplishment of the general purposes of the war, America became an essential ally. A large part of the British naval force was located in American waters, engaged in blockading as well as in more active service, and the situation demanded all the land force which England could command. Spain, however, did not yield to the persistent representations of France and America until an offer of mediation on her part had been curtly rebuffed by the British minister.

Still she constantly refused an alliance with America except upon what were felt to be the preposterous terms she had already offered, and a small wonder is it that congress felt that, as the price of a treaty, she was seeking to despoil an ally. Now that she was actually a party to the war, the necessity for a treaty became less urgent, for was she not at war with England as effectively for her own objects as she would be for ours, and why donate to her the valuable Mississippi? Doubtless the effect of a Spanish-American alliance on England and other nations would be favorable to the United States, but the price was exorbitant. Jay remarked: "The cession of this navigation will, in my opinion, render a future war with Spain unavoidable and I shall

1. Carmichael to Committee on Foreign Affairs, Nov. 28, 1780. Wharton, Vol. IV, p. 167.
2. By secret convention of April 12, 1779, with France.

look upon my subscribing to the one as fixing the certainty of the other."[1] But Spain proceeded to accomplish by force of arms that which she had been unable to secure by diplomatic arrangement with the struggling colonists. Declining to recognize any right of the colonies to the Mississippi or any land bordering thereon, either to the east or west, she found thus a fruitful field for her arms and her valor. In January, 1781, an allied Spanish and Indian force set out from the town of St. Louis of the Illinois and captured the post of St. Joseph. In the name of his Catholic Majesty they took possession of the town and surrounding country with impressive formality. Thus had the American struggle for liberation become also a Spanish war of conquest. The capture of St. Joseph caused ill-concealed alarm among the American leaders. Speaking of this conquest, Franklin, in a letter to Livingston, said: "While they decline our offered friendship, are they to be suffered to encroach on our bounds and shut us up within the Appalachian Mountains? I begin to fear they have some such project."[2]

Montmorin, writing to Vergennes of a conversation with Count de Florida Blanca in 1782, says:

"I thought right, Monsieur, to report these incidents to you, in making you observe the condition of things and understand the absolute carelessness, or even repugnance of Spain to the establishing the independence of America. If it is so marked now, what will it be when Spain succeeds in taking Gibraltar? Then the war will have no other object than that same independence which she now regards with so much indifference, and perhaps fear.

"I confess, Monsieur, that this idea torments me. Remember, Monsieur, that the system of M. de Florida Blanca has always been to make Spain mediator between England

---

1. Jay to Congress, Oct. 3, 1781. Wharton, Vol. IV, p. 743.
2. Dated Passy, April 12, 1782. Wharton, Vol. V, p. 300.

and her colonies. He has followed that system with pertinacity. He has never wished to declare himself openly for the United States, and even now he seems to draw himself away from them still more. This conduct seems to me to announce very evidently the desire that England should address herself to Spain to obtain a modification to the independence of America, that will make the sacrifice less hard." [1]

In 1781 when negotiations for peace between Great Britain and the United States were seriously considered, the question of the western boundary of the new nation became of paramount importance. Should England retain that portion of the United States bordering on the Mississippi, as it seemed likely that she might, the neighborhood of her possessions would be immediately dangerous to our peace. Should she also retain Canada and West Florida or even Canada alone, by applying herself to the settlement of that country and pushing her trade with vigor, a new nursery for her marine would be speedily established.

From the confidence that the western territory lay within the United States, the British posts were reduced and the American government exercised in that section. Large bounties of land had been promised to the already discontented and mutinous army, and the country was furthermore relied on as an important source for discharging the debts piled up in eight years of war. By the surrender of this tract to Great Britain a large number of people, men, too, not behind their eastern brothers in zeal and suffering for the cause of liberty, would be thrown back within her power.

To the absurd and dangerous Spanish proposition that the western boundary be a line one mile east of the Mississippi, the objection was made that the only principle which

---

1. Madrid, March 30, 1782. Wharton, Vol. V, p. 287.

could justify such a limitation, would also justify mutilations of an immense extent.[1] Deserted by their allies and opposed by their enemies, the colonies had much to fear from the peace negotiations. England was reluctant to acknowledge the independence of her "rebellious subjects." Spain, at length, reconciled to their freedom, sought to circumscribe and weaken them. France, though seeking their freedom, feared the reconciliation and possible future alliance of the old Anglo-Saxon nation with the new, and so sought to place the late colonies in a position of tutelage to her. Friend and foe alike feared their strength. Nor did the subsequent history prove the French and Spanish fears to have been without reason. For the American example in a few short years inspired the French Revolution, and pointed out the way to struggling South American colonies to emerge from their cruel tyrannies. Count de Florida Blanca's fears were not unfounded; for the United States has turned its guns on both the allies of its early days.

As the final date of the peace convention approached it became more evident that a determined effort was to be made to shut in the new nation by the Appalachian Mountain Ranges, and congress adopted a series of instructions to guide the American commissioners in their task.

It was not to the interest of our French allies that an amicable treaty, such as would inspire mutual confidence and friendship, should be consummated between England and the colonists. Their purpose was to plant such seeds of jealousy and discord in the pact as would compel our subservience to them. They sought to keep some point in contest between America and England, to the end of the war, to preclude the possibility of our sooner reaching an agreement, to keep us employed in the war, to make us

---

1. Secret Journal of Foreign Affairs, p. 153. August, 1782.

dependent on them for supplies, and, even after the treaty, to compel us to look to them for protection and support. These considerations inspired France in her purpose to make England formidable in our neighborhood, and to leave us as few resources of wealth and power as might be consistent with our national integrity and independence. [1]

In a conference between Jay and the Count d'Aranda, the Spanish diplomat insisted on two principal objections to our right to the Mississippi River. First, that the western country had never been claimed as belonging to the ancient colonies. That previous to the last war (1763) it belonged to France and after its cession to England remained a distinct part of her dominions until by the conquest of West Florida and certain posts on the Mississippi and the Illinois rivers, it became vested in Spain by right of conquest. Secondly, that, supposing the Spanish right of conquest did not extend over all that country, still it was possessed by free and independent nations of Indians whose lands we could not consider as belonging to us. In accordance with his views thus expressed, Count d'Aranda sent Jay a map with the proposed western boundary line marked in red ink. It ran from a lake near the confines of Georgia, but east of the Flint River, to the confluence of the Kanawha with the Ohio, thence round the western shores of lakes Erie and Huron, and thence round Lake Michigan to Lake Superior. [2]

Jay seems to have been thoroughly convinced from the conferences with Count de Vergennes, the French minister of foreign affairs, and his private secretary, M. de Rayneval, that France would oppose our boundary pretensions, that they would oppose our extension to the Mississippi, and our claim to the free navigation of that river. They would probably support the English claims to all the country above

1. Letter from Jay, Nov. 17, 1782. Wharton, Vol. IV, p. 48.
2. Jay to Livingston, Nov. 17, 1782. Wharton, Vol. VI, pp. 22-23.

31° and certainly to all the country north of the Ohio. And that in case we refused to divide with Spain in the manner proposed, she would aid that country in negotiating for the territory she wanted east of the Mississippi and would agree that the residue should remain to England. [1]

The good faith of France in the preliminary negotiations of 1782 has been a fruitful source of discussion among historians, and while the Bourbon dynasty was without doubt guilty of treachery to America, there is not sufficient proof to sustain all the suspicions of Jay at this juncture. La Fayette, while passionately disclaiming any love or partiality for Spain, still insisted that she was earnestly desirous of maintaining harmony and living in friendship and neighborly union with the United States. [2]

In the final peace provisions Florida was allotted to Spain without any remonstrance by the United States. The conviction, prevailing as far back as 1777, that the independent sovereignty of the new nation would necessitate sooner or later the absorption of Florida and the Mississippi valley, may consistently explain why the United States made no objection to Florida's going to Spain from whom it could be more readily obtained than from England. Time, without treaty, so argued Luzerne in a dispatch to Vergennes, will in forty years fill the valley of the Mississippi with the population of the United States and if so there is no use in hazarding peace for a stipulation which without being expressed is one of the necessities of the future. [3]

By the final treaty of 1783 the free navigation of the Mississippi was given to the United States. The Spanish ministry vigorously protested that the navigation of the river could not be ceded by the king of England, and that

1. Letters of Jay to Livingston, Paris, Nov. 17, 1782.
2. La Fayette to Livingston, Bordeaux, March 2, 1783. Wharton, Vol. IV, p. 269.
3. Wharton, Vol. I, p. 358.

his cession could have no real force unless the Catholic king should think proper to ratify it. This question caused an acrimonious discussion, which, not settled until 1795, threatened at various times to plunge the two countries into war. The Spanish arms, they insisted, had conquered and possessed two harbors of the river on the day the treaty between Great Britain and the United States was concluded — the 30th day of November, 1782 — hence England could not dispose of it. [1]

In the final treaty the southern boundary of the United States and the northern boundary of the Floridas was fixed at 31° north latitude. Here were the germs of another controversy with Spain. During the British occupation of the Floridas the boundary had been 32° 28′. The boundary of 31° was based on the charter of Georgia given by George II, which he had no right to grant since it embraced territory that then belonged to Spain. She refused to evacuate that portion of West Florida which lay between 31° and 32° 28′, basing her refusal on the ground that she had driven the English out of this province before the treaty of Paris, and England had no right to cede lands which belonged to Spain by the unquestionable title of conquest. This question, like that of the Mississippi navigation, remained a subject of contention for twelve years.

The American envoys contended that England had the undoubted right to fix the line wherever she pleased, the provisional articles of her peace with the United States having been signed and also ratified before the signature of the Spanish preliminaries in 1783.

In the treaty with the United States there was a separate article as follows:

"It is hereby understood and agreed that in case Great Britain at the conclusion of the present war, shall recover,

---

1. Secret Journal of Foreign Affairs, Vol. III, p. 517.

or be put in possession of West Florida, the line of north boundary between the said province and the United States, shall be a line drawn from the mouth of the river Yassous where it unites with the Mississippi due east, to the river Apalachicola."

Does not this clause raise some question as to the integrity and sincerity of the two contracting parties? By the cession of Florida to Spain, and the independence of the United States, the concern of Great Britain with the Florida boundaries terminated, and it now becomes a Spanish-American issue.

CHAPTER II.

THE boundaries established by the Proclamation of 1763, irregular and manifestly unsatisfactory, were adopted by the treaty of Paris which gave us a place in the brotherhood of nations.

The southern boundary, particularly, seemed likely to cause grave complications, partly from its irregularity and partly from its arbitrariness, for the barrier of an unseen and imaginary line is unable to withstand the resistless logic of national and racial history. From the Mississippi River it followed the 31st degree of latitude to the Chattahoochee River, then down that stream to the junction with the Flint; thence in a straight line to the source of the St. Mary's River and, following that stream, to the Atlantic Ocean. It seemed but natural that with the unity, growth and expansion of the young republic, new boundaries would become essential. Spain and England maintained their hostile positions on our different sides, vultures poised in the air ready to swoop down and devour the carcass of the nation whose dissolution seemed imminent. Nor did France seem likely to hold back at such a crucial moment. Our representations to those countries were met with contempt, our protests with mirth, our threats with ridicule. Anarchy raised high its head throughout the land. War and a common danger had brought union and friendship; peace and tranquillity proved but the forerunners of a disunion and jeal-

3

ousy whose ravages were scarcely less devastating than those of fire and sword. Cold type fails adequately to describe the conditions existing in those states which had driven from their confines the proud armies of the haughty Briton, but could not now cope with the insignificant and contemptible rebellions of demagogues, fanatics and whisky distillers — the aristocracy of the disreputable. On all sides the European countries proceeded to acquire by fraud and cunning what they had failed to secure by treaty. The British still retained the northern line of forts which they were pledged to evacuate and even pushed them farther south until they were in the region of the present city of Cincinnati.

Spain imitated the example of our northern neighbor. Nor were the Spanish claims entirely without merit. She had a measure of right to the boundary of 32° 28′, for she had conquered that, and, even more, had carried her flag to the Great Lakes. She occupied and garrisoned the posts of Natchez and Walnut Hills. The boundary of 31° had its origin in the grant of Carolina by Charles I, but this was then understood to be the latitude of the St. John's River. When Oglethorpe planted his colony of Georgia he attempted to acquire possession of the land down to the St. John's River. In 1763 the line between Georgia and Florida was fixed at St. Mary's River, and the northern boundary of West Florida at 31°. In 1765 a commission to the governor of Georgia extended that province to the Mississippi. This jurisdiction was revoked two years later by the terms of the commission given to Governor Elliott in which West Florida was extended northward to 32° 28′. The region north of this was reserved during the period of most extensive British control for the Muskogee Indians. Thus Spain had repudiated the right of England to fix the southern boundary of the United States at 31° and proceeded to fortify the Mississippi as far north as the post of New Madrid. Chickasaw Bluff (now Memphis) and Walnut Hills (now Vicksburg) were included in the zone of Spanish fortifications. In June, 1784, at Pensacola, the capital of West Florida, a treaty of amity and commerce was concluded between the representatives of the Seminole Indians and the officers of the Spanish government, whereby the subscribing savages bound themselves and their peoples to obey the orders to be communicated from Louisiana and Florida and to "expose for the royal service of his Catholic Majesty our lives and fortunes," and to give special trade and commercial rights to the Spanish traders. These Indians were mostly domiciled in the territory claimed by both Spain and the United States.

Meanwhile the course of society was moving irresistibly onward, pushing back the virgin forests and the untamed savages; the frontiersman and the pioneer, the fearless scouts of civilization, had crossed the mountains, and were beginning to form settlements along the Ohio and its tributaries. Though the Alleghenies had not served to discourage their migration, they presented a formidable barrier to any extensive traffic or intercourse between the new country and the old, the West and the East, the transmountain and the seaboard peoples. Their natural outlet was in another direction. The Ohio, the Mississippi, and the Gulf of Mexico were the successive links in the waterway which could furnish them an easy and natural communication with the outer world. The free navigation of the Mississippi they felt to be theirs by moral right, by legal right, and by treaty right. Thoroughly inured to the dangers and hardships of the forests — natural difficulties they could tolerate. But of artificial restraint, the dictates of treaty, or of law, they were intolerant. Soon restive and rebellious under the treatment accorded them by the "down-

river Spanish" they began to show them that ill-concealed
hatred and contempt which had been their heritage from
the days of Drake and the Armada.

These Westerners whose life was a constant, bitter and
terrible struggle with the very elements of nature, were
in poor frame of mind to respect the dictates of laws and
treaties which meant only added hardship.   Patriotism,
maintained at the cost of terrible suffering, and stunted by
injustice and oppression, can never attain the luxurious
growth of unwavering devotion.   And Spain was not slow
to take advantage of this unrest in our Western country.
In 1786 and 1787, she was insidiously laboring on our southwestern border to divert the allegiance of the trans-Alle-
gheny settlers who had become particularly inflamed over
a project lately pending before congress, to barter our Mississippi rights for certain commercial privileges mainly advantageous to the North and East.

In the spring of 1786, Gardoqui, the Spanish minister,
wrote to Jay requesting him to lay before the continental
congress the question of a treaty with Spain which should
settle the boundary dispute and the claim to the navigation
of the Mississippi. Jay was informed that his Catholic
Majesty "will not permit any nation to navigate between the
two banks belonging to his Majesty."   Further, that Spain
refused to be in any way bound by the western and southern boundary lines fixed by the treaty of peace between
England and America.   The Spanish minister also requested
the immediate payment of the principal of the debt contracted by the United States in Spain during the Revolution,
warned them of the danger of losing the Spanish trade in
case no treaty were concluded, and, by way of inducement,
reminded Jay of the influence of the king of Spain with
the Barbary powers, which the king might use in the inter-

ests of America, if a satisfactory treaty were secured.[1]
There were many in congress at this time willing to make
a treaty with the Castilian king, fixing the Florida line at
32° 28′ and these same legislators consented to give Spain
the full control and navigation of the Mississippi River for
a period of twenty or thirty years. But the Spanish proposition of a western boundary line was nowhere viewed
seriously in this country and we are inclined to doubt if it
were even in the palaces where it originated.

But Gardoqui refused in any event to consent to any
article declaring our right to the Mississippi in express terms
and stipulating to forbear the use of it for a given time. [2]
Gardoqui, now cognizant of the secret article of the treaty
of 1783, although soon willing to drop the contention for
a cis-Mississippi boundary, insisted upon a treaty giving to
Spain the line of 32° 28′ and the exclusive navigation of the
Mississippi. Stronger counsels prevailed in congress
and no agreement was reached. The feeling that a new
form of government would soon displace the confederation
caused a suspension of negotiations until the new régime
had been established. [3]

Soon after the close of the Revolutionary War, Spain
began to forward to the United States complaints of the conduct of those Americans who had settled within the Spanish
lines, or along their borders. There was a suspicion and
dread of American "conquest by colonization;" nor do the
fears of the Spanish seem to have been entirely groundless. With a surprising lack of ordinary foresight, Spain
had issued an invitation to emigrants to settle in her country — both in the Floridas and in Louisiana. Further,

1. Gardoqui to Jay, May 25, 1786. MSS. State Dept., letter No.
126, Negotiation Book, pp. 26-31.
2. Jay to Congress, April 11, 1787, letter No. 124, Negotiation
Book, p. 127.
3. Congressional Resolution, Sept. 16, 1788, letter No. 125, Negotiation Book, p. 170.

this invitation was a few years later made more attractive; one thousand acres of land gratis to every American who would remove to West Florida — and four hundred dollars for every hundredweight of tobacco which he might raise and deliver at New Orleans, exemption from all taxes and military service, and extravagant prices for all provisions and farm products. These same terms were offered settlers upon the western banks of the upper Mississippi. General John H. McIntosh, an officer in the Revolutionary army and a defender of Sunbury, accepted the invitation and occupied land near Jacksonville, and for two years held office under the Spanish régime. Then, detected in plots to overthrow the Spanish authority, he was sent to Havana and imprisoned in Moro Castle.

Georgia proceeded to enter into treaties with the Creek Indians for the establishment of a boundary and the purchase of certain of their lands, without regard either for the rights of Spain or the United States. It seems inaccurate to dignify by the name of a treaty an agreement made between Americans and helpless Indians, amid a scene of drunkenness, debauchery and fraud, disgraceful alike to the commissioners who were concerned in it, and the state which sought to enforce it. The treaty of Galpinton (1785) between Georgia and the Creeks was one of this character: The Creeks claimed, with justice, that in this and other agreements the contracting Indians were either drunk, or without power, or induced by fear or fraud. In private sales similar methods were pursued. The trader or settler meeting a stray Indian indulged with him in a bottle of "fire water" and the victim the next day found to his surprise and indignation that his pale-faced host possessed a deed to all his property. Small wonder that the Indians complained of all this "pen-and-ink work." Nor did the settlers pretend to respect the treaty limits secured even in this disreputable manner. General Henderson called back-woodsmen in general "a set of scoundrels who scarcely believed in God or feared the devil." The tribes, gradually yielding to superior force, retreated, followed, or rather attended, by those inseparable parasites, Indian traders, a species of the white race that has never found a panegyrist or deserved one; a crew of whom nothing good has ever been said, though a few probably do not deserve the stigma which has blackened the name. This swarm of traders with its long train of pack-horses and apprentices thus kept pace with the slow and uncertain movement of the redskins. This constituted the primary stratum of civilization or society in that, as in most, sections; but "civilization" is a term which can hardly belong to such a mongrel horde.

Under the leadership of the astute and diplomatic half-breed, McGillivray, the Creeks were disposed to peace, difficult as it was to secure. Skillfully arraying interest against interest, he sought to husband the strength and resources of his peoples, by a strict neutrality without giving cause for offense to either neighbor. But the Georgians continued their incursions and even the authority of McGillivray was barely sufficient to repress the hostile passions of his followers. In 1785, we find that the Georgians had made incursions into Florida which congress, by a resolution of October 13, 1785, felt called upon to expressly disavow. Again on the eleventh of September, 1786, a resolution of congress was passed deprecating "the conduct of some people in that state towards the Spaniards," with the' warning that "such measures will be taken as may prevent the like in the future."

In 1785 the Georgia legislature organized the territory lying between their western boundary and the Mississippi River, opened the lands for general sale (thus precipitating the infamous Yazoo land frauds), and appointed as gov-

ernor one Thomas Green. Some of the points comprised
within these demarcations were fortified and garrisoned by
Spanish troops and the greater portion was included within
the area claimed by the Spanish as conquered by their arms.
Thomas Green had settled within this disputed territory near
the fort of the Natchez, in 1782, as a subject of the Spanish king, but he seems to have been clandestinely plotting for
the subversion of the Spanish rule — another example of
the familiar "conquest by colonization." Congress replied
to the representations of Gardoqui by asserting that, though
they claimed and insisted on their title to this territory in
question, yet they disavowed the act of the state.[1]   Georgia
and the Carolinas, together with their western territories,
were undoubtedly full of adventurers constantly conspiring
against Florida and neighboring Spanish possessions.

Secretary Knox, in his letters and reports to congress,
is repeatedly led to speak of "the most unprovoked and
direct outrages" against the Indians of the South "dictated
by the avaricious desire of obtaining the fertile lands possessed by the said Indians." Colonel Sevier figures as the leader
of many expeditions against the Spanish and Indians whom
he slaughtered without discrimination of age or sex. A
bloody page of our history, these avaricious and unprincipled
men were writing. Whole villages were put to the torch
and their inhabitants either forced to flee to the forests, there
to experience the horrors of starvation and exposure, or to
be more mercifully offered up as sacrifices to the white man's
cruelty and greed. Yet the Indians seem to have honestly
sought a treaty of peace with the United States, full well
realizing that any armed resistance on their part must mean
national or tribal extermination.[2]   The patriotic American
must feel the flush of shame as he reads of the most

---

1. Gardoqui to Congress, Sept. 23, 1785, letter No. 125, Negotiation Book, pp. 23-25.
2. Letter No. 150, MSS. State Dept. 3, pp. 405-407.

cruel, unwarranted and blood-thirsty manner in which peaceable Indians were murdered in their fields and robbed of their lands. [1]

The settlers robbed the Indians, avoided war with them by a treaty, and then, directly violating the treaty, seized more lands. At times they sought to provoke the Indians to a general war that they might thus deprive them of all their lands. In such a condition of affairs it is not surprising that many innocent settlers on both sides of the Florida line were pillaged by the lawless element of both Indians and whites, nor is it surprising that many negro slaves took advantage of the opportunity to escape to the Spanish territories and thereby add another element of ill feeling and hostility to that already engendered.

The Articles of Confederation did not grant power to congress to control Indian tribes in the limits of any state. Therefore the United States was unable to interfere in the dispute between Georgia and the Indians, for though the Creeks were an independent nation, they were within the boundaries over which the state of Georgia exercised legislative control. Secretary Knox recommended that congress persuade Georgia and North Carolina to cede their western lands to the United States, for thus the affair with the Creeks, Choctaws, Chickasaws, and Cherokees would become national and the United States could enforce the treaties which the Indians claimed had been violated.[2] Small wonder is it that these Indians thus harried and pillaged should turn to the Spanish for counsel and assistance. The settlers could scarcely have been unaware that the certain consequence of their lawless outrages would be a terrible carnage on their frontier. To them, Indians were without rights and might be killed as indifferently as venomous snakes.

1. Letter No. 150, MSS. State Dept. 3, pp. 349, 362 and 373.
2. MSS. State Dept., letter No. 151, pp. 275-282.

Constant rumors reached the sensitive ear of the ready Gardoqui, that plots and counterplots were being hatched against the Spanish territories to the south and west. In 1787 a letter from one John Sullivan, a deserter from the American Revolution, and an ordinary example of crank and soldier of fortune, aroused the fears of the Spanish minister who brought the matter to the attention of congress. The letter was an open one, published in a southern paper of that year, and was written in the bombastic style which easily betrayed the character of the author. He had doubtless heard something of an anti-Spanish expedition and, with the self-conceit and importance of the harmlessly insane, had made himself a constituted organizer and leader of "this host of Myrmidons" who, as an "overwhelming inundation," were preparing "to pour down along the waters of the Mississippi into the Bay of Mexico."[1] Further complaints were made of sinister meetings at North Fort in North Carolina, for the purpose of conspiring against New Orleans and the Mississippi.[2] While Gardoqui was often misled by vague rumors, the spirit of the Western settlers was such that hostile expeditions were without doubt secretly planned and openly threatened.

The reports that congress intended to barter away the rights of the United States to the Mississippi tended to increase the hostility of the Westerners and incite them to seek their own salvation by the strong arm. In 1787 and 1788, Kentucky openly proposed to declare her independence not alone of Virginia but also of the United States, which had shown such an utter contempt for her rights and interests. Spanish agents were at work sowing seeds of discontent but at no time did the Kentuckians turn a willing ear to the Castilian blandishments. Unfettered by diplomatic and treaty restraints, Kentucky felt that, inde-

---

1. Letter No. 125, Negotiation Book, pp. 146, 148, 154.
2. *Ibid.*, p. 171.

pendent, she could more easily accomplish her purpose of securing New Orleans and the Mississippi River, and so the Spanish appeals and manifestos fell upon barren soil. The vicious public-land system then in vogue did much to render intolerable the position of the Western settlers. The method of selling those domains to land and settlement companies had little to recommend it, for the lands were held at a forbidding figure. They should have been given to settlers for homestead claims after the manner of later years. This would have encouraged emigrants to settle between the Mississippi and the Wabash and by increasing their numbers would have made more difficult the machinations of the Spanish on the south and west, and the English on the north. [1]

Couriers from the Western settlements brought such disquieting reports that in the fall of 1787 the secretary of war addressed instructions to General Harmar, commandant on the frontiers, directing him to ascertain what plots, if any, were being formed, the number, names and character of the participants, their equipment and armament, their object, and, if necessary, to employ force to repress any hostilities. After an investigation General Harmar reported that no plot hostile to any foreign nation had been discovered. [2]

Jay, the secretary of foreign affairs, seems to have more thoroughly grasped the true situation and appreciated the necessity for a treaty with Spain which would remove all points of dispute. He sought to impress upon his fellow officials the fact that Spain would be our best country for trade and that the United States had much to hope for from that country in a commercial treaty. Further, he appreciated the fact that France and Spain were on friendly terms through marriage alliances, that in case of a Spanish-

1. Letter No. 150, MSS. State Dept. 3, p. 519.
2. Letter No. 125, Negotiation Book, pp. 163-168.

American rupture France would assist her Bourbon neighbor and not us; and that the Spanish influence with the Barbary powers was of no small moment. In an address to congress, August 3, 1786, he declared, "We shall, I think, either find her in America a very convenient neighbor or a very troublesome one." To all of Jay's representations Gardoqui's concluding answer was that his king would never consent to any compromise on the question of the Mississippi River: that it was a maxim of Spanish policy to exclude all mankind from their American shores. Jay insisted that the adjacent country was fast filling with people and that the time must surely come when they would not peaceably submit to being denied the use of the natural highway to the sea. Gardoqui replied that that question could be diplomatically adjusted at such future time as it might arise, for, at most, it was a remote and highly improbable contingency, as, in his mind, the rapid settlement of that country would be so injurious to the older states that they would find it necessary to check it.

Appreciating the advantages to be gained by a treaty, and, feeling that the Mississippi navigation was not of present importance, a forbearance to use it, while we did not desire or need it, could be no great sacrifice, Jay advocated a treaty limited to twenty-five or thirty years, the United States giving up the river for that period. Spain excluded the subjects of the United States from the river and held it with a strong hand; she refused to yield it peaceably and therefore it could be secured only by an appeal to the arbitrament of war. But the United States were unprepared for war with any power and many of the eastern and northern states would have refused to supply troops at that time for the purpose of securing a right which they felt in no way concerned them. Thus Spain would continue to exclude us from the river. Would it not then be best to consent, and for a valuable consideration, to forbear to use what it was not in our power to use, at any rate? From the temper manifested in many of the papers published in the Western country it was apparent that the United States must shortly decide either to wage war with Spain or settle all differences with her by a treaty on the best terms in their power.

To quote Jay in his able presentation of the case:

"If Spain and the United States should part on this point, what are the latter to do? Will it, after that, be consistent with their dignity to permit Spain forcibly to exclude them from a right which at the expense of a beneficial treaty they have asserted? They will find themselves obliged either to do this and be humiliated or they must attack Spain. Are they ripe and prepared for this? I wish I could say they are..... Not being prepared for war I think it to our interest to avoid placing ourselves in such a situation as that our forbearing hostilities may expose us to indignities. It is much to be wished that all these matters had lain dormant for years yet to come, but such wishes are vain — these disputes are agitating — they press themselves upon us, and must terminate in accommodation, or war, or disgrace. The last is the worst that can happen, the second, we are unprepared for, and therefore our attention and endeavors should be bent to the first."

If we should not secure the treaty,

"The Mississippi would continue shut — France would tell us our claim to it was ill-founded. The Spanish posts on its banks and even those out in Florida, in our country, would be strengthened, and that nation would bid us defiance with impunity, at least until the American nation shall become more really and truly a nation, than it at present is, for, unblessed with an efficient government, destitute of funds and without public credit either at home or abroad, we should be obliged to wait in patience for better times or plunge into an unpopular and dangerous war with very little prospect of terminating it by a peace either advantageous or glorious."[1]

In Jay's report to congress the following year the same subject is discussed at length.[2] He says:

"Your secretary is convinced that the United States have good right to navigate the river from its source to and through its mouth and, unless an accommodation should take place, that the dignity of the United States and their duty to assert and maintain their rights, will render it proper for them to present a memorial and remonstrance to his Catholic Majesty insisting on their right, complaining of its being violated and demanding in a temperate, inoffensive, but at the same time in a firm and decided manner, that his Majesty do cease in future to hinder their citizens from freely navigating that river through the part of its course in question. Your secretary is further of opinion that in case of refusal it will be proper for the United States then to declare war against Spain. There being no respectable middle way but peace and war, it will be expedient to prepare without delay for one or the other: for circumstances which call for decision seem daily to accumulate.

"With respect to prescribing a line of conduct to our citizens on the banks of the river our secretary is embarrassed. If war is in expectation then their ardor should not be discouraged, nor their indignation diminished, but if a treaty is wished and contemplated, then those people should be so advised and so restrained as that their sentiments and conduct may as much as possible be made to quadrate with the terms and articles of it. . . . . He (your secretary)

1. Jay in a speech to congress, Aug. 12, 1787, Letter No. 125, Negotiation Book, pp. 40-56.
2. April 12, 1787.

also takes the liberty of observing that a treaty disagreeable to one-half of the nation had better not be made, for it would be violated — and that a war disliked by the other half would promise but little success, especially under a government so greatly influenced and affected by popular opinion."

Spain absolutely declined to make a treaty for a limited period or one which in any manner recognized any right or claim of the United States to the Mississippi River. Thus the question remained no nearer a solution — though demanding immediate arrangement — at the installation of the federal government and inauguration of Washington.

In the meantime Spanish authorities were actively engaged in stirring up the spirit of unrest in the West. They promised the free navigation of the Mississippi in return for the acceptance of Spanish sovereignty by Kentucky and the Tennessee and the Cumberland settlements.

The Westerners were gravely impressed with the effectiveness of the mountain barrier dividing them from the coast states. Scarcely were they to be blamed if loyalty to the Union rested lightly with them, and even if a strong separatist feeling prevailed. The value of the Union to them was measured only by the scale of its efficiency in protecting them from the Indians and securing them the Mississippi. A rope of sand, what protection could the confederation offer, to win support or inspire respect? For the type of life displayed on the seaboard the frontiersman had little sympathy and less regard. To the "fierce inhabitants of the West" there was little love for a government that levied taxes without giving return, whose seat of power was an impossible two months' journey, and whose posts of honor and influence were monopolized by the self-seeking politicians of the effeminate East.

The thirteen states as independent bodies were considering the question of ratifying the constitution. The Western settlements quite naturally were inclined to decide their own allegiance at the same time and by the same manner. Some favored complete independence, some would have willingly returned to England. Some were desirous of connecting themselves with Spain — for that meant New Orleans and the world beyond. With true human instinct they balanced rewards and penalties. Yet as a whole they preferred the Union.

General Wilkinson, Judge Sebastian, Colonel Sevier, the redoubtable George Rogers Clark, and even the honored Robertson showed distinct Spanish proclivities, and went so far as to accept pensions, or douceurs, from Spain for their support. Daniel Boone, still the forerunner of civilization, growing restless under the approaching tide of humanity, pushed across the upper Mississippi, and in a newer and wilder region became a Spanish official. New Madrid was settled by Americans, colonists accepting the sovereignty of Spain.

The defeat of the Spanish intrigues in the West was really compassed — though Spain did not and could not realize it until later years — when the new constitution was ratified, and a strong power was substituted for what out of generous charity we may call the government of the confederation. As the United States grew stronger, Spain, weakened by the French Revolution and the Napoleonic wars, gradually lost her former prestige and could hope to gain only through intrigue that which had been denied her arms. Instead of Spain annexing portions of the United States, this country took advantage of Spain's weakness and forced from her one after another of her fairest provinces.

Foreign emissaries in this country were firmly convinced that the politics of the Western communities were rapidly approaching a crisis, and could terminate only in an appeal either to Spain or England, who were playing their analogous parts on our unstable frontiers. It seemed probable that an independent confederacy under the protection of some European power might be the outcome of the needs of the West and the impotency of the East. Jefferson grasped the true inwardness of the situation when he insisted that we must either reconcile ourselves to the loss of the West or wrest what we needed from Spain.

Troubles along the southern border between the Creeks and white settlers increased and war seemed the probable outcome. Washington, soon after assuming office, appointed commissioners to treat with the Indians and fix a satisfactory boundary line — one that might insure peace and tranquillity in that section. But the mission was a failure, as had been the previous one constituted during the period of confederation. As a last resort Washington determined upon a personal interview with McGillivray the Creek chief, who in June, 1790, set out for New York City, at the head of thirty Indian chiefs. On the road these aborigines were greeted with continuous and enthusiastic ovations and their reception at the temporary capital partook of the homage generally paid those of distinguished rank and birth. New York City on the day of their arrival presented a gala appearance. Tammany Hall, even then a powerful and historic institution, turned out in full regalia, and the national congress in a body waited on the visitors, by this time thoroughly impressed with the warmth and sincerity of their reception. A treaty was negotiated by which the Oconee lands — which had been the principal ground of dispute — were ceded for an annual payment of $1,500 and a distribution of merchandise. The question of boundary was settled, at least until the whites should desire more — the Indians had not then learned the futility and

4

faithlessness of treaties — the Indian territory was guaranteed against further encroachment — a hollow mockery. A permanent peace was provided for.   The Creeks and Seminoles placed themselves under the jurisdiction of the United States and renounced their right to make treaties with any other nation.   Such was the open treaty.

Then a secret treaty was negotiated between McGillivray and the United States which stipulated that after two years the Indian trade should be turned to points in the United States—clearly a violation of certain articles in the Spanish-Indian treaty of a few years before.   McGillivray was appointed Indian agent of the United States and, in imitation of continental methods, was given the rank of brigadier general, with annual pay of $1,200.   The treaty was bitterly criticised and the Indian chief was much maligned for his part in it.   The Indians claimed that their choicest lands had been surrendered for an inadequate consideration; yet the only alternative was a war in which the Creeks must have been crushed.   Further the United States was pledged to keep the Indian territory inviolate — history had not then shown how little that meant.   The treaty was manifestly unfavorable to the Spanish, and in violation of rights which they had secured in 1784.   Nor would they quietly submit to the loss of the Indian trade and consequent bankruptcy of the trading house of Panton and Company, the chief proprietors of Spanish sovereignty in those parts.   Spanish emissaries increased the dissatisfaction of the Indians who sullenly determined to oppose the running of this new boundary against which even McGillivray had protested at New York, insisting that he could not guarantee it.   This Indian chief has been greatly berated for his trickery and double dealing but his course seems to have been the only one possible, for by thus balancing America against Spain and avoiding war with either nation he prevented the extinction of his tribe. His was a hard task and that his tribe continued to exist from year to year was his vindication.

General William Augustus Bowles, an American deserter of the Revolutionary army, with the aid of a band of adventurous settlers and disaffected Indians, whom he had won by fair promises of unlimited booty, in 1789 made an abortive attempt to capture Florida from the Spanish. Such incursions across the borders — at this time quite the order of the day — served only to increase the general disorder and bitterness of feeling already existing in that section. Settler pitted against Spaniard in an effort to win the Indian favor; mercenary speculators grasping after Indian territory; and Spanish intrigue — the only substitute for the force of the Americans — stimulating savage passions. Small wonder that shocking atrocities were committed. The federal government was doubtless sincere in its wish to secure the establishment of well-defined boundaries, the protection of the frontier, and peace among the southern tribes.

The treaty of 1790 in New York ignored the Georgian treaties and thus bitterly incensed the Georgia settlers. Owing to the "double dealing" of the chief, McGillivray, the freebooting settlement of General Elijah Clarke, seeking every opportunity to overthrow the Florida government, the intrigues of the trading house of Panton and the Spanish emissaries, and the indignation of the Georgians at the manner in which their wishes had been disregarded and overruled, the stipulations of the New York treaty were never carried out; and the horrors of a border warfare loomed darkly over the southern horizon. Secretary Knox in a report to Congress had insisted that an expedition against the Creeks would require a force of twenty-eight thousand men and the cost of such an expedition would be at least $450,000. He had a profound respect for the fighting qualities of the Creeks and in comparing them with the Wabash tribe, said they "are not only greatly superior in numbers but are more united, better regulated and headed by a man whose talents appear to have fixed him in their confidence." [1]

Immediately after the inauguration of the new government the question of a Spanish treaty was taken up by the department of state with the determination to push it to a successful issue. Realizing the intimate relations between the courts of France and Spain, Jefferson sought to secure the French support. Accordingly Jefferson instructed William Short, our minister to France, to secure the assistance of La Fayette and M. de Montmorin at the court of Spain, and impress upon them "the necessity, not only of our having a port near the mouth of the Mississippi River (without which we could make no use of the navigation at all) but of its being so well separated from the territories of Spain and her jurisdiction as not to engender daily disputes and broils between us." For, continues Jefferson,

"It is certain that if Spain were to retain any jurisdiction over our entrepot, her officers would abuse that jurisdiction and our people would abuse their privileges in it: both parties must foresee this and that it will end in war: hence the separation. Nature has decided what shall be the geography of that in the end, whatever it might be in the beginning, by cutting off from the adjacent countries of Florida and Louisiana, and enclosing between two of its channels a long and narrow slip of land called the Island of New Orleans. The idea of ceding this could not be hazarded to Spain in the first step: it would be too disagreeable at first view, because this island with its town constitutes at present their principal settlement in that part of their dominions, containing about ten thousand white inhabitants of every age, and sex: reason and events however, may by

1. Letter No. 151, MSS. State Dept., p. 359.

little and little, familiarize them to it. That we have a right to some spot as an entrepot, for our commerce may be at once affirmed — the expediency too may be expressed of so locating it as to cut off the source of future quarrels and wars. A disinterested eye looking on a map will remark how conveniently this tongue of land is formed for the purpose: the Iberville and Amit channel offering a good boundary and convenient outlet on the side for Florida and the main channel an equally good boundary and outlet on the other side for Louisiana: while the slip of land between is almost entirely morass or sand bank: the whole of it lower than the water of the river in its highest floods: and only its western margin (which is the highest ground) secured by banks and inhabited: I suppose this idea is too much even for the Count de Montmorin at first, and that therefore you will find it only in general terms a port near the mouth of the river with a circumjacent territory sufficient for its support, well defined, and extraterritorial to Spain, leaving the idea to future growth."

In 1790 the probability of a war between England and Spain presented a favorable opportunity for pressing our claims at the Castilian court. In a special set of instructions, Mr. Carmichael, our minister to Spain, was directed in meeting the Spanish secretary to

"Impress him thoroughly with the necessity of an immediate settlement of this matter and of a return to the field of negotiation for this purpose: and though it must be done delicately yet he must be made to understand unequivocally that a resumption of the negotiation is not desired on our part, unless he can determine in the first opening of it to yield the immediate and full enjoyment of that navigation. . . . There is danger indeed that even the unavoidable delay of sending a negotiator here may render the mission too late for the preservation of peace: it is impossible to answer for the forbearance of our Western citizens. We endeavor to quiet them with the expectation of an attainment of their rights by peaceable means, but should they in a moment of impatience, hazard others, there is no saying how far we may be led: for neither themselves nor their rights will ever be abandoned by us. But should an accommodation take place, we retain indeed the same object and the same resolutions unalterably: but your discretion will suggest that, in that event, they must be pressed more softly and that patience and persuasion must temper your conferences till either these may prevail, or some other circumstance turn up which may enable us to use other means for the attainment of an object which we are determined in the end to obtain at every risk." [1]

Owing to the prospect of an English-Spanish war it seemed likely that Great Britain would seize New Orleans. To England, Jefferson directed John Adams to intimate that we could not look with indifference upon the acquisition by that nation of Louisiana and Florida, for, he declared, "a due balance on our borders is not less desirous to us than a balance of power in Europe has always appeared to them." He insisted to Washington that rather than see Louisiana and Florida added to the British Empire, the United States should join actively in the general war then supposed to be pending. Circumstances, however, did not take the favorable turn hoped for and nothing came of this attempt at arbitration. But at home matters rapidly assumed serious proportions. The Western settlers became more and more restive and inclined to replace the rules of international law with the judgment of force, while in the South the lawless element held high carnival: and complaints were constantly made by Spanish and American officials of frequent and wanton violations of territory. [2]   War seemed imminent.   In

---

1. Letter No. 121, Foreign Letters, p. 376. Jefferson to Carmichsel, Aug. 2, 1790. Trescott's Diplomacy of Washington and Adams's Terms, p. 226.
2. Carondolet, writing of the settlements beyond the Alleghenies

1791 statements persistently appeared in the newspapers that hostilities between the United States and Spain were inevitable, and that preparations for a resort to force were being made by both nations. These reports were given full credit abroad. [1]

Spanish officials continued to guard the Mississippi River, imprison all Americans captured thereon, and confiscate their goods. Each seizure added another element of danger to the situation already felt to be most critical. Jefferson fully appreciated the acuteness of the situation, and directed Carmichael to push negotiations to a determination. "An accident at this day," he wrote, "would put further parley beyond our power: yet to such accidents we are every day exposed by the irregularities of their officers and the impatience of our citizens. Should any spark kindle these dispositions of our borders into a flame, we are involved beyond recall by the eternal principles of justice to our citizens, whom we will never abandon. In

declared: "This vast restless population, progressively driving the Indian tribes before them and upon us, seek to possess themselves of all the extensive regions which the Indians occupy — at the same time that they menacingly ask for the free navigation of the Mississippi. If they achieve their object, their ambitions would not be confined to this side of the Mississippi. Their writings, public papers, and speeches all turn on this point, the free navigation of the Gulf by the rivers . . . . which empty into it, the rich fur trade of the Missouri, and in time the possession of the rich mines of the interior provinces of the very kingdom of Mexico. Their modes of growth, and their policy are as formidable for Spain as their armies. . . . . Their roving spirit and the readiness with which they procure sustenance and shelter facilitate rapid settlement. A rifle and a little corn meal in a bag are enough for an American wandering alone in the woods for a month. . . . . With logs crossed upon each other he makes a house and even an impregnable fort against the Indians. . . . . Cold does not terrify him and when a family wearies of one place, it moves to another and settles there with the same ease. If such men come to occupy the banks of the Mississippi and Missouri, or secure their navigation, doubtless nothing will prevent them from crossing and penetrating into our provinces on the other side, which being to a great extent unoccupied, can oppose no resistance."

1. Short to Jefferson, July 24, 1791. Vol. I, Instructions, MSS. State Dept., p. 101.

such an event Spain cannot possibly gain, and what may she not lose?" [1]

M. Gardoqui, the Spanish envoy, was impressed with what he felt to be the local aspect of the Mississippi question and so reported to the court of Madrid. The navigation of the Mississippi, he felt, was only demanded to pacify the Western settlers and that the eastern or maritime states were not only indifferent but probably even hostile to the idea. While to a limited extent this had been the feeling, it had given way to a strong sentiment in favor of securing our demands in that quarter even at the cost of war. The Spanish court was more likely to trust the reports of Gardoqui, who had now returned home, than the representations of the American minister, whose interests demanded that this belief be completely eradicated. "The very persons to whom M. Gardoqui alluded are now come over to the opinion heartily that the navigation of the Mississippi in full and unrestrained freedom is indispensably necessary and must be obtained by any means it may call for."

In the light of a hundred years Jefferson's argument for persuading Spain to cede New Orleans and Florida and grant us the navigation of the Mississippi shades on the humorous. As a neighbor, he declared, the United States would be safer for Spain than would England, for conquest was inconsistent with our principles of government and our theories of right. Further it would not be to our interest for ages to come, to cross the Mississippi or maintain a connection with those who should.

But nothing more, worthy of record, was done until the administration received an intimation from the Spanish government that it would resume negotiations at Madrid. War clouds were lowering over Europe. The wild excesses of revolution and anarchy had awakened the continent.

---

1. Vol. I, Instructions, p. 26. Jefferson to Carmichael, April 11, 1791.

Peace abroad was necessary that the nations might suppress resistance at home. Washington in December, 1791, nominated Carmichael, then chargé d'affaires in Spain, and Mr. Short, then chargé in France, commissioners plenipotentiary to negotiate and conclude a treaty with Spain. The question of the Florida boundary and the navigation of the Mississippi were to be settled. In addition the treaty should provide for certain commercial advantages in the Spanish-American possessions. The commissioners were instructed along the lines already developed, but were cautioned that the treaty should neither expressly nor by implication concede any claim of Spain to the Mississippi: that this should be taken as a right and not as a grant from Spain: neither should any compensation be given for the navigation. If this was insisted on, it should be set off by the duties already paid at New Orleans and the claims for the detention of American shipping at that port. The commissioners did not meet at Madrid for a full year after their appointment.

At that time history was being made with incredible rapidity. The French, mad with the enthusiasm of liberty and license, and particularly hostile to the reigning houses of Europe, had started on their mission of carrying freedom to the oppressed and founding republics in all lands. As a likely field for this work the Spanish-American possessions did not long escape their attention and, further, had not Spain invited their loss by uniting with legitimate Europe to overthrow republican France? It came to the ears of Jefferson that France proposed to send a strong force early in the spring of 1793 to offer independence to the Spanish-American colonies beginning with those bordering on the Mississippi. To prevent any hostile feeling or demonstration on the part of the United States, she did not object to an arrangement by which the Spanish holdings on the east side of that river should be received into our confederation.

"Interesting considerations," writes Jefferson to Carmichael and Short, "require that we should keep ourselves free to act in this case according to circumstances, and consequently that you should not by any clause of treaty bind us to guarantee any of the Spanish colonies against their own independence nor indeed against any other nation. For when we thought we might guarantee Louisiana on their ceding Florida to us, we apprehended it would be seized by Great Britain, who would thus completely encircle us with her colonies and fleets. This danger is now removed by the concert between Great Britain and Spain and the times will soon enough give independence and consequent free commerce to our neighbors, without our risking the involving ourselves in a war for them." [1] For Louisiana or the Floridas to fall into the possession of hostile England, it had been felt, would be ample ground for actual intervention on the part of the United States. In the hands of decadent and paralytic Spain it was thought that in time they would certainly gravitate into American possessions.

The commissioners met at Madrid about the first of February, 1793, but in the kaleidoscopic change of events circumstances were now vastly different from those which had induced their appointment. The ministerial power of Spain which had been transferred from Count d'Aranda, had again been shifted, and was now held by Godoy, the notorious libertine and paramour of the Spanish queen. The difficulty between England and Spain was settled and had been superseded by most friendly relations. The conciliatory attitude which Godoy had adopted towards France in the hope of saving the unfortunate King Louis was rudely destroyed by his decapitation. This change was soon followed by a French declaration of war against Spain, and

_____

1. Vol. I, Instructions, p. 260. Jefferson to Carmichael and Short, March 23, 1793.

the American commissioners were thus deprived of the
support upon which they had fondly relied from the only
power in Europe able and willing to facilitate the negotiations. Even worse, the inevitable tendency of events led to
an alliance between Spain and the combined enemies of
France at whose head stood, hated and hating, England.
The relations between England and the United States were
most unfriendly and, at this very period, war between these
two countries was considered imminent. Spain quickly concluded an alliance offensive and defensive with England,
whose terms fully covered any contingency of hostilities with
the United States. The commissioners realizing the unfortunate state of affairs wrote to Jefferson: "We cannot help
considering it unfortunate that an express commission
should have been sent to treat here." Surely circumstances
had not conspired to give any hope of success.

Gardoqui, late Spanish minister to the United States,
was appointed to conduct the negotiations. While here he had
been thoroughly impressed with our weakness and the divided feeling on the Mississippi question, and was impervious to
all arguments. The commissioners wisely determined not
to press their case, and found this course quite agreeable to
the ever dilatory and procrastinating policy of Spain. Instructions from Philadelphia directed them to proceed. They
managed to reach Godoy but were unable to make any
headway on the main points of their mission. They laid
before him, however, certain complaints on the Spanish
interference with the Indians along the southern border,
and secured his promise, of whatever value they might
have considered this, that Spain would not interfere in case
the United States should declare war against the refractory
redskins. Continued failure induced the dissolution of the
commission, and Carmichael took his departure leaving
Short at Madrid credited as chargé. He found much

difficulty in being either received or acknowledged, even in that capacity.

In the meantime the troublesome and autocratic Genet had landed in America and was proceeding in that autocratic and insulting course which ended in the demand for his recall. Taking every advantage of the popular enthusiasm then existing in favor of the French cause, he proceeded in defiance of international law and American sovereignty to fit out privateers and enlist volunteers for the French service. The French government had imposed upon him the double character of accredited diplomat and revolutionary propagandist. Intrigue in Kentucky and the South, and the conquest of Louisiana were the prime objects of his mission — a point generally ignored in the treatment of this interesting character and his turbulent career in the United States. Arriving at Charleston in April, 1793, he energetically set about his prescribed tasks.

Ignoring Washington's proclamation of neutrality, Genet carried things with a high hand, confident of his success in an appeal to the people, if that became necessary. He approached Jefferson who, forbidding any attempt to involve American citizens, expressed indifference as to what insurrections might be excited in Louisiana, and even declared that a little spontaneous invasion would promote the interests of the United States. Expecting that America would soon be at war with Spain, our secretary of state may have deemed it wise not to cut himself off from an acquaintance with Genet's designs against the Spanish colonies, particularly since the movement was represented as nothing more than a plan to give independence to Louisiana.

Genet had two anti-Spanish projects on foot, one for a military expedition, to be organized in South Carolina and to rendezvous in Georgia, for the invasion of Florida, the other for a like expedition against New Orleans and Louisiana, to be set on foot in Kentucky. French emissaries were freely employed, and for the Florida enterprise Governor Moultrie of South Carolina, General Elijah Clarke of Georgia, Samuel Hammond, and William Tate, all men of honor and standing in the South were speedily enlisted. The expedition under the command of General Clarke, according to the prospectus, was to be supported by the French fleet.

Plans for the conquest of Louisiana had been presented to the French authorities when the relations between France and Spain became strained, after the outbreak of the French Revolution, but the plan of expedition here attempted seems to have been proposed by George Rogers Clark, who had distinguished himself during our Revolutionary war by the conquest of the Illinois country, but who was now reduced to an equivocal position from the combined influence of intemperance and pecuniary embarrassment. In 1788, he had offered his services to Spain, for a land-grant, and was now even more ready to expatriate himself for France. Genet's agents and Clark, in Kentucky, actually undertook the procuring of supplies and boats and sought to interest the discontented Kentuckians in the scheme for securing the freedom of the Mississippi by replacing Spain at its mouth by the French Republic.

Unquestionably there existed in Kentucky highly inflammable materials. Her allegiance and patriotism had already been severely tested, and the refusal by Spain of the free navigation of the Mississippi was regarded as a great grievance and suspicions were generally entertained that no proper efforts had been made to secure it. George Rogers Clark declared that he could raise fifteen hundred men and the French at St. Louis, with the Americans at the Natchez would eagerly join his command. With the first fifteen hundred all Louisiana, beginning at St. Louis, could be won for France, and with the aid of two or three frigates at the mouth of the Mississippi, he would agree to capture New Orleans and the rest of Louisiana. And only a little further assistance would be needed to secure Pensacola and even Santa Fé and the rest of New Mexico. By July, Genet wrote home that he was arming Kentucky and preparing a general insurrection in the provinces adjoining the United States.

But Genet's disregard for our national authorities served as a boomerang; he lost his most powerful friends and popular sentiment proved fickle. His plottings, however, aroused the Spanish governor Carondolet, whose force of sixteen hundred men was strung along six hundred leagues of river navigation. Urgently demanding reinforcements from home, in the anxious moments of despair he wrote to the English in Canada for assistance.

At the moment when success seemed assured Genet's career was terminated by the fall of the Girondist party in France. Genet was recalled and a new minister, Fauchet by name, arrived with instructions to terminate an expedition, which, had not Washington refused his connivance, must have been a success. An advance by the United States on the debt due to France, on which Genet relied, would have enabled him to proceed with these plans as well as the maritime war against England on the American coast. But he failed to support the project with efficient organization and financial resources and it collapsed under the hostility of the federal authorities. Only about two hundred men had been under arms, but many others awaited the call to war.

In one of its aspects the movement was a continuation of the efforts of the Westerners to expel the Spanish from the Gulf of Mexico — efforts which found later expression in Jackson's expedition, and in the Mexican and Cuban wars. In another of its aspects it was a phase of the repeated designs of France to recover her control of Louis-

iana, for it is a mistake to suppose that this design dates
from the efforts of Napoleon and Talleyrand in 1799 and
1800.

If the Clark expedition had been more efficiently managed it was not so chimerical as it now appears. Its ultimate design was the conquest of New Orleans, Louisiana,
and New Mexico. Considering the weakness of Spanish
rule in Louisiana, the attitude of leading Westerners, the
excited feeling in the West against Spain and the Federal
authorities, the expectation of statesmen like Jefferson that
a war with Spain was inevitable, and the widespread sympathy for France in the United States, such a proposal as
Clark's was not without hope of success. The details of
its inception and progress reveal the inchoate condition of
national feeling in the West and the many hazards which
beset our control of the Mississippi Valley.

Genet had found an active lieutenant in General Elijah
Clarke, an officer of prominence in the Revolution, who had
for some time been an active disturber of the peace on the
Florida border. [1] First a leader in unwarranted violations
of the McGillivray Indian treaty of 1790, he had made war
on the Indians and the Florida Spanish. Under Genet's
advice and assistance he formed a party in Georgia, called
the Sans Culottes, based on hatred of the Spanish, and
sympathy for the French control of the Spanish-American
possessions. He was guilty of the grossest violations of
neutrality and repeatedly attacked the Spanish posts. At
the head of a band of adventurers with whom Georgia
abounded, he invaded Florida and established a post on the
St. Mary's River. This enterprise he was soon compelled
to abandon. And with some measure of justice the Spanish
minister complained that the American officials in that

---

1. For the Genet-Clarke correspondence see the Annual Report of
the American Historical Association of 1896, Vol. I, page 930.

quarter were in sympathy with these marauders, if they
did not actively countenance and assist their plans. Clark
had set an example which others of his ilk were not slow to
follow, to the consternation of the Spanish authorities of
that section. As an inducement and reward for his work
he, together with George Rogers Clark, was commissioned
a major general in the French service.[1] The bold and
unblushing manner in which Genet conducted his operations
induced many to believe that he had at least the secret if not
the open connivance of the federal government.[2] The
French designs against Louisiana continued unabated even
after Genet's recall. His work was not without its results,
and, under his encouragement and advice, there were numerous violations of Spanish sovereignty by American citizens. The Spanish representative, M. Jaudenes, repeatedly
called the attention of this government to these matters in
his correspondence in 1793 and 1794.

At the close of 1793 the bitter warfare between
Hamilton and Jefferson had reached a climax and upon the
resignation of the latter, Edmund Randolph, the attorney
general, was transferred to the state portfolio and to him
fell the task of directing the Spanish negotiations.   By
midsummer of 1794 it had become clear to the administration
that Spain was tired of the English treaty and sought an
arrangement with France. It was felt that this might offer
a good opportunity to win Spanish gratitude and a Spanish
treaty by a friendly mediation in the quarrels from which
Spain wished herself extricated. Apparently the time was
not yet come for that. The danger of a Spanish-American
war became more threatening. The spirit of Kentucky was
growing daily more bitter and defiant, and the acts of the

1. See Boston Sentinel, Nov., 1793, Jan., 1794. Congressional Documents, and Vol. V, Domestic Letters, pp. 319-321, Jefferson to the Governor of Kentucky.
2. Vol. II, Instructions, p. 63, Randolph to Short, March 16, 1794.

settlers more bold and warlike. The government dreaded each stage from the West, lest it bring news of some fresh overt act which would precipitate hostilities. For it was felt that at this time a declaration of war would mean a conflict, not alone with Spain, but also with her ally Great Britain. Writing in cipher to Short in August, 1794, Randolph directed him to "counteract the impressions which the unlicensed violence of our Western citizens may make upon the Spanish court." Short was further directed

"To ascertain as soon and as certainly as possible—

"1. Whether Spain counts upon the Union of Great Britain in maintaing the exclusive right to the Mississippi?

"2. What overtures have passed between them on this subject?

"3. Supposing the war with France to be settled, and the French Republic established, what douceur could Spain afford to England for entering into a war with the United States?

"4. Do the progress of the ardor for liberty and arming of the Spanish peasantry develop no reason to apprehend a convulsion in Spain?

"5. Will not the distress of the Spanish government for money compel them to such a resort to the people as will awaken the sense of their real efficacy in all governments and enable them to urge demands of reform, to which an indigent prince dependent upon his subjects for supplies, will always be exposed?

"6. Is there any mode in which our influence with France could be used that would accomplish for us the navigation of the Mississippi?

"7. In what parts and through what means is Spain most vulnerable in South America — and to what part are her suspicions directed?

5

"8. What force by land or sea could she send to any foreign country in case of war?

"9. In what particular is it supposed in Spain that the United States if at war with her could be the most injurious to her? In short you perceive from these questions, that the mind is driven into an anticipation of a painful possibility and therefore whatever else belongs to this subject, although not comprehended in the above questions, you will be so good as to communicate. But notwithstanding these inquiries you may never hesitate to give the most unqualified assurances, that we deprecate the most distant interruption of our harmony."[1]

Spain now thoroughly weary of the unnatural alliance into which Godoy had been forced by popular clamor, sought a way to withdraw from a war more honorable to the bravery and patriotism of her troops than it had been successful. It was supposed that the relations between England and the United States were growing more hostile, and with France were improving under the able hand of Madison. In view of these circumstances the Spanish government made advances to France through the American minister at Paris and took the necessary steps to resume direct negotiations with the United States, broken off by Carmichael's departure and the Spanish refusal to receive or recognize Short.

On August 16, 1794, Jaudenes, in a communication to the secretary of state, expressed his regrets that so little progress had been made in the negotiations between the two countries and stated that His Majesty desired to renew the negotiations, provided commissioners be sent who should have unrestricted powers for a general treaty and not be bound by secret instructions which would defeat it. The powers which had been given to Carmichael and Short

---

1. Edmund Randolph to Short, Aug. 18, 1794.

were not ample, he complained; nor were those two commissioners personally satisfactory. "The lack of decorum" and "well known misconceptions" of Carmichael were commented upon; and the "want of circumspection in conduct" of Short had made him personally undesirable. A man of "character, conduct and splendor" was desired by the Spanish government. By "character" was meant a "diplomatic grade invested with full powers for all objects;" by "conduct," a "proper attention to the court and a proper behavior in the management of the negotiation;" by "splendor" a "personal dignity and self-respect." In short the rank of Carmichael and Short, both chargés had not flattered the Spaniards. Nor was the idea of returning the same commissioners wholly pleasing to them. In consequence of these intimations the president, in November, 1794, appointed General Thomas Pinckney, then minister at the court of St. James, minister plenipotentiary with full powers to conclude a treaty with Spain. Thomas Jefferson having been offered this special mission had declined. Pinckney did not however reach Madrid until the summer of the following year.

The instructions to Pinckney sought to impress upon him the impatience and hostility of the Kentuckians and the necessity for a prompt determination of the Mississippi question. If Spain should refuse this, the United States, it was felt, ought to be immediately apprised of the fact, that they might prepare for the alternative of war. Yet Pinckney was warned not to give the Spanish minister any reason for supposing that we had determined upon hostilities, for, writes Randolph in a cipher dispatch, "if we break off in ill humor, we in some degree lose the choice of peace or war. If we show no symptom of ill temper we are not debarred from resorting to any expedient which we approve. It is not impossible too that in the settlement of peace with

France some opportunity may be presented if we should be disappointed now. If any hint of this sort should be capable of improvement you will doubtless communicate your ideas to our minister at Paris. Our reputation with the French government is on a strong footing. It is of immense importance for us to know, if it can be ascertained, whether Great Britain is under no engagement to Spain, to support her in the retention of the Mississippi." [1]

By this time a new question of dispute had arisen for diplomatic adjustment, or if that should fail, for the decision of the sword. The vessels of the United States were being constantly seized by Spain, as well as by others of the allied powers of Europe, upon the most frivolous and unwarrantable pretexts. The seizure of one vessel in particular, the Dover cutter, had been the subject of continual diplomatic representations by this government to the Spanish officials. Built in Havre de Grace, it had been seized by a Spanish governor in the Western Islands for the use of the Spanish government, nor had any compensation been made for it. The complaint for this outrage had been forwarded to Madrid by Jay in the spring of 1786. Of late, more seizures had aroused the United States and to Pinckney was committed the further question of the spoliation and vexation of our commerce and a full power given him to treat upon this as well as the other subjects. [2] These encroachments upon our commerce had been accompanied by further encroachments by the Spanish posts on the Mississippi River. Governor Guioso, the Spanish intendant, had recently established a fort at what was called Chickasaw Bluff — above the 35° of latitude.

At this time, owing to the European complications, Spain feared a break with the United States, partly because

---

1. Vol. II, Instructions, p. 245, Randolph to Pinckney, Nov. 18, 1794.

2. *Ibid.*, p. 294, Randolph to Thomas Pinckney, Dec. 25, 1794.

of the entente cordiale existing between this country and
France, and partly from fear of another war which, she
felt, must multiply the misfortunes which she had suffered
in her alliance with England, when the French armies had
overrun her mountain districts and established themselves
upon her soil. In fact Spain was desirous of an alliance
with this country.[1] The three campaigns against France,
after the English-Spanish alliance — more creditable to the
valor of the Spanish troops than to their military ability —
had been most unfortunate. The combination between the
Castilian and the Saxon had been a forced one — of the
head rather than the heart — without that sympathy and
unity from which alone can come success. Randolph had
said, "My conviction is firm that the courts of Madrid and
London are cordial in nothing but a hatred of the United
States and a determination to harass them through the
Indians."[2] But he might have added that they were no less
cordial in their hatred of revolutions, especially of the
French variety, for this it was that had induced the alliance.
But, constantly humiliated on the field of battle, the Castilian soon tired of an alliance with those for whom, with
their mother's milk, they had imbibed a bitter hatred. They
looked with fond eye toward the triumphant militarism of
a people with whom they had always had much in common
and to whom they were bound by the ties of gratitude and
of blood.

The internal changes in French politics opened the
prospect of a more stable and conservative government
for that country, and the peace of Basle (April 5, 1795)
proclaimed the defection of Prussia, the keystone of the
continental combination. In the meantime Spain, having
deserted England, grew suspicious of her. She feared and
suspected an Anglo-American arrangement. England, she

1. Vol. II, Instructions, p. 32, Pickering to Short, Aug. 31, 1795.
2. *Ibid.*, p. 185, Randolph to Monroe, Sept. 25,. 1794.

thought, was endeavoring to excite the United States against her, and she anticipated a concert of measures between these two powers against her American possessions. This suspicion was founded upon the Jay treaty with England — the extent of which was not yet fully understood at Madrid — and was confirmed by letters from the Spanish chargé d'affaires at Philadelphia.[1] This danger must be met by a Spanish-American treaty. Writing in March to our secretary of state Mr. Short said: "The rapid successes of the French armies in Holland — the desire of this court to find out some means of pacification — the close friendship between the United States and France combine to show the importance of the present moment. The minister would willingly make use of me as the means of sounding the French government and ascertaining their dispositions as to peace — but the stumbling block of the unsettled state of our affairs with Spain constantly presents itself."[2]

After Jay's treaty with England the whole diplomatic situation in respect to the Mississippi Valley was changed. The United States bought a peace with England by sacrificing the friendship of France. The possession of Louisiana offered to France the opportunity to injure England and render the United States more subservient to her policy. Fauchet was convinced that Louisiana would furnish France the best entrepot in North America for her commerce and raw material, and a market for her manufactures, a monopoly of the products of the Mississippi territories, and a means of pressure on the United States. He declared that unless a revolution occurred in Spanish policy the force of events would give Louisiana to the United States. It now became more than ever a cardinal point of French policy to secure this province from Spain.

An active alliance with the United States was what

1. Letters of Wm. Short No. 193, Vol. IV.
2. Wm. Short to Jefferson, March 3, 1795.

Spain earnestly desired at this time, and she expected the new American envoy to be provided with powers and instructions to conclude an alliance as well as terminate the troublesome questions then pending. To secure this alliance, Spain was willing to pay a high price on other points. But the United States wisely declined to entangle themselves in the mad delirium of war by any such connection. [1] On the 22nd of July, 1795, a treaty was concluded between Spain and France. In return for this peace Spain ceded to the revolutionary republic the Spanish half of San Domingo. Humiliated and infuriated at this defection, England declared war upon her late friend. It was now rumored in Spain that England intended to take possession of a Spanish harbor, land an effective army, compel Spain to fight against France and to further attack the Spanish possessions in America. Ignorant of the Jay treaty, France earlier in the year sought to aid a Spanish-American conciliation, but nothing had come of this attempt.

In midsummer, Thomas Pinckney at length reached Madrid, where, sent as he had been at the instance and invitation of the Spanish minister, he expected rapidly to conclude a treaty. The differences to be settled by the commissioners shaped themselves into three groups. First was the subject of commerce, but Spain refused to discuss this point despite Pinckney's protest that the mission was of Spanish origin. The Spanish chargé at Philadelphia had expressly stated that Spain was "ready to treat upon the points of limits, Indians, commerce and whatever may conduce to the best friendship between the two countries." Pinckney therefore intimated that he had a right to expect an arrangement of the commercial interests of the two countries. But as the United States were not willing to force themselves into

---

1. Wm. Short to Jefferson, March 3, 1795.

connection with a reluctant people, he would not press what he could not but consider his right.

The second point concerned the navigation of the Mississippi. Spain, while admitting that its navigation should be free to both nations, objected to the arrangement suggested by the United States for a commercial depot at New Orleans. Spain further insisted that the language of the article conveying the right should be of a strictly exclusive character, restricting the navigation to the subjects of Spain and to the citizens of the United States. This, of course, . could not be considered, as it would violate our treaty obligations to England, if not to France.

As to the third point, that of reclamations, Spain insisted that all captures should be divided into two periods — the one preceding April 6, 1795, in which the rule of decision should be the maritime regulations of Spain then at war with France; and the other, following that date, in which the decisions should be upon the usual grounds of international law. To such a division Pinckney positively and unequivocally refused his assent. Conformably with the traditional quibbling and procrastination of Castilian diplomacy, the negotiations dragged their weary course, varying only with the fluctuation of European and Spanish politics. Wearied and indignant at the apparent lack of faith and their persistence in maintaining their position, Pinckney at length demanded his passports on the 24th day of October.

This show of spirit and determination on the part of the American envoy aroused the Spanish minister to the necessity of action. Having thrown herself into the arms of England she had been despoiled of her territories by the French armies. Now deserting her former mistress and cultivating a French amour, Britain had turned upon her and was driving her fleets off the sea. Dreading an Anglo-

American alliance, or a separate declaration of war by the United States, badgered at all points and fearing greater humiliations, Spain consented to a compromise of the difficulties and at San Lorenzo el Real, October 27, 1795, a treaty of friendship, limits, and navigation was signed in behalf of Spain by Godoy.

This treaty was decidedly favorable to the United States. It established as boundaries East and West Florida on the south and, above latitude 31°, the middle of the Mississippi River. Illegal captures made by Spain during her late war with France were compensated for, favorable rules were prescribed for neutral commerce, and Indian aggressions on either side, together with the arming of privateers, were discountenanced. But the chief diplomatic exploit was in gaining Spanish recognition of the right, so long and so strenuously asserted by the United States, to the free navigation of the Mississippi River; to which was added a three years' privilege of deposit at the port of New Orleans, free of duty. Thus was paved the way for that magnificent internal commerce so soon to become fabulous in its value, which has made that river the most crowded highway of domestic trade in the world. The claims commission provided for in the treaty met in Philadelphia, terminating their duties December 31, 1799, after having made awards to the amount of $325,440 on account of the Spanish spoliations. It is not unlikely that the conclusion of the Jay treaty with England strongly influenced Spain to agree to a treaty at this time. For our arrangement with Great Britain destroyed all hopes of a concerted action between Spain and that nation against our Western country. Since the treaty of 1783 Spanish agents in North America had made frequent advances to the Canadian authorities for a joint English and Spanish policy against the Americans, all of which found expression in the tortuous Indian relations they had pursued.

The treaty of 1795 marked the first step in our territorial expansion. Jefferson wrote as early as 1786, from Paris: "Our confederacy must be viewed as the nest from which all America, North and South, is to be peopled. We should take care, too, not . . . . to press too soon on the Spaniards. Those countries cannot be in better hands. My fear is that they are too feeble to hold them till our population can be sufficiently advanced to gain it from them piece by piece. The navigation of the Mississippi we must have. This is all we are as yet ready to receive." Voyageurs, like Brissot, had prophesied the secession of the West; Washington had dreaded it; Western leaders, Wilkinson, Sevier, Robertson, Clark, Butler, had sold their services to secure it; and Spain and England had negotiated to that end. Had the United States failed to secure free navigation it would have withdrawn, and for the want of sea power to protect its commerce passing from the mouth of the Mississippi through the Gulf, it must have allied itself with a foreign power.

Firmness rather than skill, determination rather than finesse, were required for the negotiation of the instrument. Political circumstances had compelled Spain to yield to the demands of the United States. She had made concessions which except for extraneous forces might have been postponed for years. The treaty and the ministers who negotiated it were similarly applauded in both countries. As a recognition of his diplomatic success, Thomas Pinckney, on his return home, was named by the Federalists as the associate of Adams on the presidential ticket. The treaty of Basle and that with the United States were hailed by the corrupt court of Spain — one of the worst in her national history—as great triumphs, and Godoy as a reward received the title of Prince of Peace.[1]

The country of Charles V. was at this time under the absolute rule of Godoy who, as a young lieutenant in the army, had become the paramour of the faithless queen and through her favor had been named prime minister. Under his régime the price of office had been such as to exclude men of any nobility either of mind or character — they were the rewards of those willing to submit their wives and daughters to the embraces of this libertine. Miserable Spain, dishonored in the shame of her queen, and ruled by men the most contemptible, willing for paltry office thus to sell their own honor!

---

1. In his memoirs Godoy felicitates himself on the American treaty and claims that he secured "unexpected advantages" though of what nature we cannot conjecture, for he virtually yielded all the demands of his adversary.

CHAPTER III.

THE PURCHASE OF LOUISIANA.

THE treaty of 1795 provided that the contracting parties should name commissioners to run the boundary line between Florida and the United States. As the American linesman was sent one Andrew Ellicott, who immediately repaired to the post of Natchez on the Mississippi. A vain man whose pretensions and bombastic manner made him an object of ridicule, he reached the Spanish post with an idea that he was a sort of ambassador or envoy extraordinary rather than a mere astronomer or surveyor. Naturally irascible, his frequent toasts to the health of his country and himself scarcely tended to sweeten his disposition.

In his imaginary capacity of a diplomat accredited, or commanding general on the field, he sent daily and often hourly letters and remonstrances to the Spanish governor, Gayoso. He proceeded to stir up trouble among the settlers of this region, though they are represented to have been thoroughly contented under the mild rule of the Spanish. For nominal fees they had received liberal grants of land. They had paid no taxes, had been exempt from military service, had been allowed free access to the market at New Orleans, and had been paid a liberal price for their tobacco. Prior to the advent of the meddlesome Ellicott and his tempest in a teapot, no discontent seems to have existed. [1]

---

1. Lowry's History of Mississippi, p. 148.

By the second article of the treaty it was stipulated that the garrisons found to be above the line of demarcation — that of 31° latitude — should be withdrawn. The line had neither been run nor had the garrisons been withdrawn. Some of the Spanish posts were undoubtedly above this line — but their garrisons were not removed. In response to the American representations on this matter, the Spanish minister, D'Yrujo, replied:

"It appears that the first operation ought to be to draw this line in order to know which were the garrisons which were to be withdrawn according to the article cited and although the Natchez and some other Spanish posts are probably situated above the said line of demarcation the formality and delicacy which one government owes to another required that Mr. Ellicott should not pretend to take possession of the territory until the said demarcation should be made: and the more so as he had been informed officially that the Spanish engineer M. Guillemard was already on his way to fulfil this part of his commission. Mr. Elliott not attending to these just observations immediately, began to wound the feelings of the Spanish commander by hoisting the American flag on a territory before having jointly made the astronomical observation for ascertaining the course of the line. Not content with this he began to exercise an authority which was unlawful for the same reasons: to-wit, that of recruiting for the United States in a place which was then under the jurisdiction of the Spanish government. These imprudences which can admit of no excuse gave rise to a personal resentment from which there is little to hope with respect to harmony between the commissioners in the future."

In a proclamation issued in 1797 by Carondolet, the governor of Louisiana, the delay in transferring the posts was excused because of an apprehended expedition by the

British from Canada: a belief that the advance of the American troops was with a hostile design of surprise, and in the expectation of an immediate rupture between France — the intimate ally of Spain — and the United States. The United States should either leave the posts in the hands of Spain, the proclamation declared, or secure her against an article of the British treaty which exposed them to be pillaged.

Probably the real reason for this delay was the expectation of a breach between France and the United States which might furnish an excuse for the non-fulfillment of the treaty. There is little doubt that Spain, then under the influence of France, either to protect her own possessions or with a view of ceding them to that nation, had determined to defeat the execution of the treaty.

At New Orleans it was confidently believed that the French would soon own Louisiana and the Floridas. But Spain was not yet ready to cede them; her present purpose was to alienate the Western country from the Union and establish over it a government under her own influence. Considerable trouble in regard to the delivery of the posts was occasioned by the uncertainty as to the meaning of the treaty provisions therefor. The United States contended that they should be delivered in the condition in which they then stood while Carondelet insisted that it could never have been the intention of his Catholic Majesty to deliver up any fortifications on which he had expended great sums of money and which through political vicissitudes might perhaps be one day prejudicial to his subjects.[1] Ellicott felt called upon to secure them by force or strategy. Governor Gayoso having discovered these hostile intentions of the engineer, minister plenipotentiary and ambassador extraordi-

---

1. Letters to Secretary of State, Vol. I, p. 1. D'Yrujo to Secretary of State, Jan., 1797.

nary, took such measures for the defense of the fort at Natchez as to foil any attempt to capture it by surprise.

However much the treaty of 1795 may have been applauded by both parties as a diplomatic victory, the correspondence of the ensuing years shows how utterly it had failed to smooth the ruffled waters. The Chevalier d'Yrujo repeatedly complained to Pickering of the violation of Spanish territory by the inhabitants of Georgia. Slaves had escaped from their masters and, reaching the border, had found safety in the wilds of Spanish Florida. Failing to secure their return by peaceable methods the Georgia settlers had taken the matter in their own hands and recaptured the fugitives in joyful contempt of all restraints of international law. [1]

In the meantime England and Spain, recent allies, had become embroiled in a war whose echoes were heard on this continent. With a view to attacking the Spanish possessions in the Floridas, overtures were made by the English to General Elijah Clarke of Georgia, whose intrigues against these same regions we have already noted. The Spanish minister further took occasion to complain to our secretary of state of aid given by officials in those regions to some measures set on foot by the British to attack Amelia Island. [2]

In June of this year (1797), President Adams sent a communication to the senate complaining that the Spanish in Louisiana were interfering with the demarcation of the boundary line. Feeling had become so strong on this question that war was feared. As a justification or an excuse for not giving up the posts on the Mississippi, D'Yrujo advanced the clause in the Jay treaty with England giving that power certain rights and privileges on this waterway

---

1. Domestic Letters, Vol. X, p. 13.
2. *Ibid*, pp. 35-57.

inconsistent with and even in violation of the provisions of the Spanish treaty which undertook to confine the navigation to the United States and to Spain. [1]

It was evident that the Spanish would use force, if necessary, to prevent our making an establishment at Natchez — one of the posts in dispute about forty miles north of 31° latitude. Added to these difficulties were the still troublesome Indian questions. In answer to the American claims that the Spanish officials were inciting the Indians in the southwest, D'Yrujo made the counter-claim that the Americans were really inciting the redskins in the hope that under the cover of an Indian war they could seize more land and possibly capture some of the Spanish territory. The correspondence, diplomatic more in name than in fact, rapidly grew bitter and acrimonious, each party to it insinuating that the other was guilty of misrepresentation. [2] Pickering, whose manner of conducting such a correspondence partook more of the nature of the cross sword with its heavy swinging blow than the rapier with its keen, graceful thrust, was scarcely the equal of the skillful and diplomatic D'Yrujo, who was particularly fitted for such contest though later guilty of grave indiscretions.

Among the papers transmitted to congress by the president was a letter connecting Colonel William Blount, a senator from Tennessee, with an attempt to incite the Indians of that section for the purpose of forwarding a scheme for invading the Spanish territories with the connivance and assistance of the British. Upon the basis of this letter, the house of representatives presented articles of impeachment.

In brief, Blount's scheme was to transfer New Orleans and the neighboring districts to the British by means of a joint expedition, England to furnish a naval force, and a

1. Domestic Letters, Vol. X, pp. 58, 77, 85.
2. *Ibid.*, pp. 111-134.

co-operating force of backwoodsmen and Indians to be raised on the western frontier of the United States. Heavily involved in land speculations in Tennessee and wishing to organize an English company for the purchase of his property, Blount dreaded the consequences of a transfer to the French, a military and not a commercial nation, of the outlet of the Mississippi. He believed that it would be for the best interests of the Western people, as well as for his own personal benefit as a land speculator, that Louisiana should pass into the possession of the English.

As it was too late for a trial at that session, the senator was meanwhile sequestered from his seat. In December, 1798, when Congress assembled for the third and final session, the senate, after this long delay, resolved itself into a high court of impeachment to try the alleged conspirator for high treason. Meanwhile, having been elected to the state senate of Tennessee and chosen its president, Blount declined to appear in person before the United States senate to answer the charges in the articles of impeachment. His counsel, for he had taken the precaution of being represented, pleaded to the jurisdiction of the senate court on two grounds:

(1) That senators are not "officers," who, in the meaning of the constitution of the United States, were liable to impeachment.

(2) That, having been expelled from that body, Colonel Blount was not now subject to trial even as a senator.

This plea to the jurisdiction was sustained by the senate, though it is difficult to state whether on one or both of the grounds alleged. Suffice it to say that, unfortunately, the case was never reviewed and decided on its merits and thus by a legal technicality ended the first as did most of the later federal impeachment trials. The historian must la-

6

ment this termination of a proceeding which, had it been carried through, would have resolved the questions then in dispute with Spain and left to future generations some light on the murky intrigues which were so frequent at that time and in that section.   To the layman an acquittal on a technicality, then as now, was an added proof of the defendant's guilt.   Else why should he not rather court than flee from an investigation which would exonerate and remove all stain or doubt?   Colonel Blount, notwithstanding this somewhat undignified termination of his senatorial career, became a popular leader in his own state where what was looked upon as a martyrdom for a popular cause endeared him to the hearts of his fellow people.

D'Yrujo sought to justify the action of the Spanish officials in Louisiana in refusing to deliver up the posts along the Mississippi and in resisting a present survey of the boundary line upon the very basis which had been disclosed in Senator Blount's letter — that of hostile intrigues against Florida and Louisiana aided by Great Britain.   Spain sincerely apprehended that if the Natchez and other Mississippi posts were evacuated a clear road would be opened for the British into Louisiana.   This representation upon the part of D'Yrujo seemed to Pickering but a miserable subterfuge of Spanish policy.   We were not likely to submit patiently at the hands of that country to the indignities we had suffered from England when she, pursuing what appeared to be a similar policy in defiance of treaty obligations, had maintained for four years a series of forts upon our northern frontier.   But the revelations of Blount's letter bearing out the accusations of a British intrigue against Florida justified Spain not only in her refusal to surrender these posts but in actually strengthening her fortifications in that territory as well as in Louisiana and along the Mississippi — as a measure of defense in short.

With more of childlike simplicity than diplomatic skill Pickering immediately turned the Spanish ambassador's letter over to Liston, the British minister, demanding an explanation with something of an intimation at the same time that D'Yrujo's accusations were not taken seriously by the United States. Liston admitted that certain individuals had proposed such a plan of action to him — that the English should invade Florida and the neighboring Spanish territory by sea and then rely upon the assistance and co-operation of American citizens — but that he and his government had refused to countenance the scheme for the reason that it would arouse the Indians and violate the neutrality of the United States. In view of the English record in inciting our northern Indians at this and later periods and her notorious contempt for that American neutrality, for which she here professed such a respect, we are inclined to doubt the merit and veracity of England's reply, especially since Liston abruptly declined to furnish further particulars. But his denial suited our desires and so it was accepted. The Spanish minister, however, insisted upon his original accusations and rightfully took exception to Pickering's undiplomatic method of approaching the English representative.

D'Yrujo here foolishly resorted to a newspaper statement. Pickering retorted likewise through the agency of the press and sent copies of this letter to his political friends that they might rejoice with him in his undignified course. Fisher Ames, in a letter congratulating the secretary of state upon the merits of his published reply to "the little Don," wrote, "You have not left a whole bone in his skin." Pickering more than once expressed his contempt for "the Spanish puppy" to whom he constantly imputed dishonorable motives. Without in any sense meaning to defend all of the actions of D'Yrujo, Pickering's attitude toward him, based mostly on prejudice and preconceived ideas, was unfair

and conspicuously out of place, in one holding the office of
secretary of state.   While there exists no real opposing evidence to the truth of Liston's disclaimer, one of the letters
in the published correspondence signed "Robert Liston,"
seems inconsistent with that minister's representations.   The
contrast between Pickering's contemptuous attitude toward
D'Yrujo and his deferential manner toward Liston was
most marked.

D'Yrujo in the meantime received further information
which confirmed him in his suspicions of an English attack.
This plan was to attack upper Louisiana and surprise the
posts of St. Louis and New Madrid, by a descent of the
Mississippi, through either the Fox or Ouisconsin or Illinois rivers or other parts of the territory of the United
States, which the Americans were not in a position to defend. [1]   Senator Blount's letter, the Spanish minister felt,
vindicated him in his accusations and he hastened in the
name of his Catholic Majesty to request for the suspended
senator a satisfaction proportioned to so scandalous a crime
and all the pains and punishments which the laws of the
country dictate for such offenses.[2] Nor was D'Yrujo's indignation soothed by Blount's acquittal upon the mere legal
technicalities which his counsel were able to raise.

At the same time the troublesome Ellicott and the
American commander in that section, Percy Smith Pope,
were engaged in an abortive attempt to stir up hostility to
the Spanish about Natchez and the Nogales. [3]   During this
year D'Yrujo addressed a complaint to Pickering on the violation of Spanish territory and a request for due reparation
and punishment for the participants in what appeared to be
a slave raid into Florida.   As was natural along this na-

1. Vol. I, Foreign Ministers to Secretary of State.   D'Yrujo to Secretary Pickering, March 2, 1797.

2. *Ibid.*, D'Yrujo to Pickering, July 6, 1797.

3. Vol. I, Domestic Letters.   Gayoso to Pope, June 13, 1797.

tional boundary line, slaves constantly escaping from their masters on either the one side or the other made their way into Florida or Georgia; these slaves had formerly been reciprocally delivered up to their rightful owners by the Georgia or Spanish officials and serious trouble thereby averted. On one occasion some five slaves escaping from their Spanish owners in Florida made their way into Georgia where the officials declined to surrender them and met with the reply that the governor of Florida would in the future decline to return any more escaping from the United States. This bit of reciprocity inspired by Georgia herself aroused much feeling and the settlers determined to take matters into their own hands. William Jones and John Knoll were the leaders in a particularly offensive raid to recapture fugitive slaves. These repeated and contemptuous violations of her territory, arousing Spain to the real humiliation and helplessness of her situation, brought energetic protests from D'Yrujo. There is abundant proof that the preparations for this expedition were known and connived at by the people of Georgia and even by the American commandant of that region.

Nor were Pickering's attacks the only onslaughts against which the Castilian minister was forced to contend. The year 1797 was for D'Yrujo full of untoward incidents and he must have fully realized what a thankless task it is to serve a master unpopular in the country to which he is accredited. The American press, especially at Philadelphia, subsidized by the different parties, had of late increased in malignity and bitterness. The Federalists largely patronized a paper known as Porcupine's Gazette, published by William Cobbett, an able but scurrilous writer who, in his effusions, frequently went under the euphonious name of "Peter Porcupine."[1] Ostensibly the mouthpiece of the ultra-

1. William Cobbett, a British journalist born in 1762, had in his younger days a strange career of romance and adventure, first in the

Federalists, of whom Pickering was an excellent example, the paper served as a means of propagating British opinions of a deeper design.

D'Yrujo having protested to the United States against the Jay treaty as hostile to his Catholic Majesty, Porcupine's Gazette proceeded to abuse him and his master in terms the most bitter and disgusting. In at least three different editions of his paper during the month of July, in letters signed "Philip Fatio," D'Yrujo had been thus addressed. A few examples of the phrases found therein serve to show their general tenor and justify D'Yrujo's protests to our government. "Don de Yrujo was another Quixote." "It gives his story the lie." "The posts are never to be given up, the line is never to be run. No such things are intended." "But indeed what notions of honor can reasonably be expected from the representative of a power who, for the sake of imaginary security, has deserted and treacherously turned his arms against his ally." [1] "From a tawny pelted nation which Americans have ever been taught to despise." "You are the only nation on earth who can vie with the French in perfidy and cruelty." [2] "But because I know it

army and later in Paris. The anarchy and excesses of the Revolution drove him from France and he emigrated to Philadelphia. Here he advocated the Federalist cause in a newspaper which he set up. He also attacked Dr. Benjamin Rush for his system of treating yellow fever and other dangerous maladies by wholesale bleeding. Although Dr. Rush secured a verdict for $5,000, Cobbett succeeded in overthrowing this barbarous theory. In 1800 Cobbett returned to London and published the "Works of Peter Porcupine" which had an immense sale. He soon became obnoxious to the government and was often prosecuted for libel. In one case he was fined £1000 and sentenced to Newgate for two years. In 1816 he established the "Twopenny Trash," which had so large a sale and so aroused the workingmen as to inspire the active hostility of the government. After being forced to leave England for two years, he was elected to Parliament in 1832. He was the author of many books and with an extraordinary command of English he established a reputation as a satirist second only to that of Swift and Junius. The inveterate foe of humbug and tyranny he nevertheless wrote with much justice and good sense.

1. Gazette of July 14, 1797.
2. *Ibid.,* July 15.

is your office to dress up the sweepings of Don Carlos' brains and render them less disgusting to public view." "Instead of a stupid, vain, insolent, half Carmagnole, half donlike composition." "Your dear, natural, atheistical, cutthroat allies have sunk us almost to a level with yourselves: under their bare influence Americans are fast descending to that last degree of degeneration at which the Knights of Castile have already arrived."[1]

With righteous indignation at this abused and abusive liberty of the press D'Yrujo requested that the author be properly punished. The attorney general laid the matter before the grand jury of the federal circuit court and Cobbett was bound over. McKean, the able chief justice of Pennsylvania, whose daughter D'Yrujo shortly afterwards married, issued a warrant charging the editor with having published "certain infamous libels on the king of Spain, the Spanish nation and the Spanish minister." But such was the political condition of that time that no indictment was returned against the malefactor either in the federal or state courts, despite an able and effective charge by McKean upon the law of libel as applicable to the case at hand. As Cobbett was already under bond to keep the peace, for having too freely indulged his desire for vituperation in former cases, his recognizance was declared forfeited. The incident scarcely served to expedite the settlement of the questions at issue and the memory of these insults long rankled in the mind of D'Yrujo. Surely a nation, even though the freedom of the press be one of its vital principles, owes to foreign representatives full protection against such base and unwarranted insults.

By this time the United States was actively engaged in preparation for war with France. By a treaty of 1796 France and Spain had mutually guaranteed each other's

---

1. Gazette of July 19, 1797.

territory in the Old and New World. With this as a basis, or more likely as an excuse, designs similar to those betrayed by Blount's letter were being secretly considered by a group of ultra-Federalists of whom the secretary of state was at the head, though King and Hamilton were high in the councils. Our minister at London was to approach the English government with the design as a mutual undertaking against the common enemies. In furtherance of this plan we find Pickering conducting the Spanish correspondence in such a manner as to invite or force a quarrel, while he sought to promote an alliance with England.

The complete project of these conspirators has never been understood by posterity, if indeed it ever reached the point where even its promoters were clear as to its provisions. But as a factor in the general scheme a joint expedition under the surveillance of England and the United States was to be undertaken against the Spanish-American colonies to incite or enable them to throw off Spanish rule. Pitt had planned some such undertaking in the Anglo-Spanish crisis of 1790 and the present Spanish alliance with France now offered the opportunity for its trial. Miranda, a South American by birth, one of those soldiers of fortune of whom in that day there was a superabundance and who today are not unknown, secretly sought the ear of the English ministry, using the well-known disaffection in the Spanish colonies as an inducement. As was eminently fitting the English were to furnish the navy, the United States the army.

Following the traditional lines of such plots, a division of the spoils was agreed upon ere the scheme was hardly under way. The West Indies as a South American market for her manufactures, together with rights across the Isthmus, was to be England's share, while to the United States was set apart the Floridas and all Spanish territory east of the Mississippi. It is impossible to state just how many of the Federalist leaders were in on the ground floor, so to speak, of this vast international bubble. Washington, we may be sure, was not. Adams had been approached by Miranda himself, but gave little encouragement to the scheme, partly from his dislike for Hamilton, who was a leading figure. Robert G. Harper, of South Carolina, the administration leader in the house, was naturally in favor of the plan, for any anti-Spanish project readily found favor with the South at that time. In fact, in 1797, Harper had suggested both to congress and his constituents the idea that a conquest of the Mexicos and the Floridas ought to furnish a sufficient consideration for an Anglo-American league against the two Latin nations. But Harper, with his inability carefully to guard a secret, was not received into the innermost chambers of the high temple of the plotters.

Pickering and King were engaged in conferences on the subject before the departure of Pinckney and Marshall for France. Great Britain, realizing the dangers of her own isolation and the prospect of a French invasion, had given Liston sufficient powers to arrange such agreements with the United States. The "X. Y. Z." correspondence having been displayed to the anxious public, Pickering approached Hamilton with a project for capturing Louisiana. [1] Having already, between April and August, received several letters from the leader, Miranda, Hamilton, carefully concealing their contents from his patron, Washington, forwarded a reply to our minister at London to be delivered or de-

---

1. The French government, enraged with the United States because of the Jay treaty and the election of the Federalist John Adams, resorted to depredations on American commerce, and ordered our minister to leave Paris. In an effort to arrange matters amicably, Adams sent to France a commission consisting of Charles Pinckney, John Marshall, and Elbridge Gerry, but the notably corrupt government refused to receive them. However emissaries from Talleyrand approached them secretly with the suggestion that if the United States should bribe certain members of the French government with liberal sums of money, the attacks upon American shipping would be stopped. These letters, signed "X. Y. Z." have always been known as the "X. Y. Z. dispatches."

stroyed at his discretion. The scheme was such as might cap-
tivate and dazzle the brilliant Hamilton with his all-consum-
ing thirst for military glory. The seducing panorama before
his hungry eyes was the battlefield of South America where
he might win an immortal halo, as the liberator of the
Spanish colonies, the Washington of the South. Hamilton's answer approved the scheme, provided the United
States should have the principal agency and furnish the entire land force in which event he, of course, would play the
leading rôle. Hamilton declared, as early as 1793, that we
must have the Floridas and Louisiana as soon as possible.
Spain he considered a constant source of annoyance and
he insisted that the sooner we drove her off the continent
the better — and before Great Britain should expel her. To
unite the American hemisphere in one great society of common interests and common principles was his aim.

Preparations were speedily completed across the water
and in October Miranda wrote to Hamilton, "All is ready
for your president to say the word." But the word was
never said and one of the greatest men of whom we have
either the memory or the tradition, sorrowfully but unwill-
ingly saw slip from his hands what he felt to be the grand
opportunity of his life. In fact Adams had not been initiated
into the real secrets. He, like Washington, was to be gradually drawn into the net. In the last efforts of despair we
find Hamilton later approaching Gunn and Otis on the subject, loathe to be deprived of this opportunity for fame and
glory. "Tempting objects are within our power," he writes
to Otis, and even in June of the following year we see him
urging upon the reluctant members of Adams's official family the completion of our provisional land forces in the hope
that some chance might yet secure these "tempting objects"
to him. "Besides the eventual security against invasion,"
he argued as a reason for his contention, "we ought cer-

tainly to look to the possession of the Floridas and Louisiana, and we ought to squint at South America." Thus passes into oblivion a scheme at first apparently so pregnant with glory, but now so full of mystery and uncertainty. The whole matter seems to have been successfully hidden from Spain. [1]

But new troubles were preparing for the unhappy D'Yrujo. Having been persuaded of the absolute liberty, or, more properly, license of the press in this country, the Spanish minister proceeded to contribute to its columns and in one of the Philadelphia gazettes appeared D'Yrujo's last letter to the secretary of state, together with additional "defamatory strictures" of the official in question.

This indiscretion on the part of D'Yrujo, for such the Spanish secretary of state admitted it to be, resulted in a request to the Spanish government for his recall. Moreover, the secretary of state complained that D'Yrujo's letters to him were "insulting and indiscreet." A letter was dispatched to D'Yrujo from Spain informing him that his conduct in the matter had been improper and was not approved at home. But that nation showed no desire to comply with our request for the recall of its faithful but possibly too ardent official. Various specious reasons were alleged for delay in the matter. The desire for a special letter from the president of the United States requesting D'Yrujo's recall, the impossibility or difficulty of finding a suitable person for the place, and stress of business preventing due consideration of the matter, were among the reasons cited for postponing his recall. Humphreys, our minister to Spain, in a letter to the secretary of state, stated the real reason to be D'Yrujo's connection with certain leading men in Spain in the profits of an exclusive flour trade between the United States and the Spanish colonies and that his presence in

1. Schouler's History of the United States, Vol. I, pp. 422-424, 438, 450.

America was necessary to conduct that business. [1] The demand for D'Yrujo's recall seems to have been a part of Pickering's bellicose attitude toward that official in seeking to force a breach with Spain and promote an English alliance. But D'Yrujo remained and continued to represent his country's interests and conduct the flour trade.

In the summer of 1798 D'Yrujo addressed a note to Pickering complaining that an armed force of Americans consisting of about one thousand men with considerable artillery and a few armed boats were gathering in the district of Natchez. "I cannot avoid inquiring from you," he writes, "in what light is Spain to view this considerable collection of forces upon her frontiers." Pickering, with mock indignation, denied the existence of any such armaments and branded D'Yrujo's complaint as an excuse for delay in delivering up the posts. In fact, however, the posts had already been evacuated, the Spanish moving from Natchez March 30, 1798, and from the Walnut Hills (now Vicksburg), a few days later.

During the winter of 1799 and 1800 D'Yrujo repeatedly complained of the preparations of an American adventurer, by the name of William Bowles, to commit hostilities against the Floridas by inciting the Indians within the limits of the United States — and requested the United States either to help capture him or expel him from their territories. In March, 1801, D'Yrujo wrote to Levi Lincoln, Pickering's successor, that certain letters of Bowles had been secured incriminating several prominent citizens of Georgia in an attempt to incite the Indians and settlers to war and under this cover attack the Spanish possessions. "It is now time," said D'Yrujo, "to restrain these unquiet spirits who, since the discovery of Blount's project, have been continually

---

1. Letters of David Humphreys, 1790-1801. MSS. State Dept., Aug. 6, 1799.

projecting plans of this nature," — apparently utterly uncon-
scious of the fact that the late secretary of state and many
Federalists high in the councils of the nation were among
those of whom he wished made "an example of severity"
that would perhaps "quell the turbulent spirit."

In 1802 the Western country was thrown into a tur-
moil of excitement by the news that the port of New Orleans had been shut against the commerce of the United
States from the ocean into the Mississippi and that the
right of deposit had been prohibited, in direct and gross
violation of the terms, as well as the spirit, of the treaty
of 1795. James Madison, Jefferson's secretary of state,
addressed a severe remonstrance upon the subject to
D'Yrujo, requesting him to use his influence to have the
order rescinded and notifying him that "the United States
will claim indemnification for all losses occasioned to American citizens through this matter."[1] At the same time our
minister at Madrid was directed to present a strong protest
to the Spanish ministry upon the subject.

The port not having been opened in the spring of the
following year, Madison addressed an even stronger communication to the Spanish minister. It was found that not
only had the right of deposit been rescinded but that this
had been followed by a "vigorous prohibition of the ordinary
hospitalities between the citizens of the United States and
the Spanish inhabitants." The season of the year having arrived when this outlet for the produce of the Western
citizens became essential, D'Yrujo was requested to employ
every expedient to hasten an adjustment of the wrong that
had been done. That in this critical posture of things, a
regard for the good faith of the Spanish sovereign and a
prudent attention to the heavy indemnifications with which

---

1. Vol. XIV, Domestic Relations, p. 112. Madison to the Chevalier
D'Yrujo, Nov. 25, 1802.

the responsibility was threatened, demanded that D'Yrujo instantly "resort to such peremptory injunctions as may re-
claim the intendant from his errors and by giving to the
violated treaty its due effect, rescue from immediate danger
the confidence and good neighborhood, which it is the interest of both nations to maintain." [1] The reason for this
action upon the part of the intendant seems never to have
been fully explained. At any rate D'Yrujo made no attempt
to justify it, and the whole matter seems to have embarrassed the Spanish minister who, however, sought to mollify
the American wrath while waiting to see whether the order
emanated from Madrid. The losses suffered by thus closing
the port of New Orleans became a troublesome point of
controversy in the ensuing Spanish negotiations. The
Westerners were determined to regain the port even at the
point of the sword and war must surely have followed had
not the Spanish intendant soon opened the river, now choked
with waiting vessels.

It seems certain that the closing of the Mississippi and
the port of New Orleans was the act of the intendant — that
the governor of that province did not concur in it. In February of 1803, D'Yrujo, in a letter to the secretary of state,
expressly disclaimed the act of that official both for himself and the Spanish government. [2] Charles Pinckney, now
minister at Madrid, was requested to present the matter
strongly to the Spanish ministry and acquaint them with the
feeling aroused among our Western citizens.

"The Mississippi is to them everything," writes Madison. "It is the Hudson, the Delaware, the Potomac and
all the navigable rivers of the Atlantic states, formed into
one stream. The produce exported through that channel
last year (1801) amounted to $1,622,672 from the districts
of Kentucky and Mississippi only, and will probably be

1. Vol. XIV, Domestic Letters, Madison to D'Yrujo, March 10, 1803.
2. D'Yrujo to Secretary of State, Vol. I, Feb., 1803.

fifty per cent more this year, from the whole Western country. Kentucky alone has exported for the first half of this year (1802) $591,432 in value, a great part of which is now, or shortly will be, afloat for New Orleans and consequently exposed to the effects of this extraordinary exercise of power — should he (the intendant) prove as obstinate as he has been ignorant or wicked, nothing can temper the irritation and indignation of the Western country but a persuasion that the energy of their own government will obtain the most ample redress." [1]

In 1800 John Marshall, then secretary of state under President Adams, had requested Humphreys to lay before the court of Spain the protests of the United States for the spoliation of our commerce.

"1. The capture of our merchant vessels by privateers manned in whole or in part by Spaniards and fitted out in Spanish ports.

"2. The merchant vessels of the United States prosecuting a peaceful and lawful commerce have been, when captured and carried into the ports of Spain, condemned with their cargoes, as good prizes to the captors." [2]

France, in her war against the United States, taking advantage of her domination of the peninsula, had fitted out privateers against American commerce in Spanish ports, and had there established courts for adjudging prizes. Humphreys was directed to make such representations to the court of Madrid as would put a stop to these irregular methods, and to insist on payment for all seizures in the past, as well as a convention for the adjustment and payment of these claims. The secretary further complained that Spain had not promptly and fairly met the awards under

---

1. Vol. VI, Instructions, MSS. State Dept., p. 62. Madison to Charles Pinckney, Nov. 27, 1802.

2. *Ibid.*, Vol. V, p. 358. John Marshall to David Humphreys, Sept. 8, 1800.

the indemnity clause of the treaty of 1795. The illegal seizure of American vessels was continued "under pretext that Gibraltar is being blockaded."[1]

Poor Spain, harassed on all sides in Europe and America, bankrupt and bleeding, became, year by year, more deeply enmeshed in the toils by her ally, who did not hesitate to despoil friend and foe alike. A pretty question of international law is presented when we come to consider the liability of a country whose forms of law and instruments of government are made the tools of another country in prosecuting wars against enemies toward whom the first nation is neutral. Though Spain might be liable, the pen must note a sigh of regret as it sums up her unwilling crimes and records the judgment of impartial law against her.

In the spring of 1802 Pinckney was requested to arrange with Spain a convention for the payment of the claims of the United States, falling into several groups, viz:—

1. Those by capture of vessels.

2. Attachment of property of citizens of the United States by Spain for supposed breaches of her fiscal regulations.

3. Unjust and ruinous prosecutions against our citizens upon criminal allegations.

4. By the tender laws, whereby our citizens have been paid in a depreciated medium for specie contracts.[2]

Pinckney was further directed to sound Spain upon a cession of New Orleans and the Floridas and, if that proposition did not meet with favor, to treat for the navigation of the Mobile, Chatahoochee and other rivers running through Florida, for the citizens of the United States, supporting our

---

1. Vol. IV, Instructions, MSS. State Dept. Madison to Pinckney, Oct. 25, 1801.

2. *Ibid.*, p. 21. Madison to Pinckney, Feb. 5, 1802.

claim to that right by the same arguments put forward to secure the navigation of the Mississippi.[1] While unsuccessful in his diligent attempts to conclude an arrangement for the cession of the Floridas, Pinckney succeeded in securing a convention for the settlement of our various claims. This convention, concluded August 11, 1802, provided for the appointment of a board of five commissioners to adjust the claims "for indemnification of those who have sustained losses, damages, or injuries in consequence of the excesses of individuals of either nation during the late war contrary to the existing treaty or the laws of nations." Ratified by the president of the United States January 9, 1804, the Spanish persistently refused to exchange ratifications until December, 1818, and as the convention was annulled by Article 10 of the treaty of 1819 it never went into effect.[2]

With the delay in revoking the order of the intendant which closed the Mississippi, representations expressing the peculiar sensibility of the Western country poured into Washington. From every quarter of the nation came protestations that our rights of navigation and boundary must be maintained. The only difference related to the degree of patience which ought to be exercised during the appeal to friendly modes of address. The Western irritation daily increased and many advocated an immediate redress by force of arms. The house of representatives passed a resolution explicitly declaring that the stipulated rights of the Mississippi would be inviolably maintained. The disposition of many members was to give to the resolution a tone and complexion still stronger.[3] The dark clouds of war lowered, a storm seemed about to break. D'Yrujo,

---

1. Vol. VI, Instructions, p. 27.
2. Treaties and Conventions, 1819, p. 1015.
3. Vol. VI, Instructions, MSS. State Dept., p. 70, Madison to Charles Pinckney, Jan. 10, 1803.

still representing his government at Washington, called the
attention of Madison to the reports that a certain Wilson
with fellow conspirators was endeavoring to rouse the people of western Pennsylvania, and to arm a band of adventurers with the hope that they would be joined by others
of the western states in attacking Louisiana.   He requested
that these conspiracies be suppressed lest they lead to more
serious difficulties, "whilst from the prudent measures of
this government and the justice of the king, the most prompt
and complete satisfaction may be expected for the impru-
dent measure of the intendant of New Orleans."[1]

We now come to treat of the first steps actually taken
by the United States to secure a settlement of the troublesome questions arising in the west and southwest by a
cession of the territory in that section.   As early as February, 1797, rumors had reached the ear of Pickering, of
an agreement on the part of Spain and an earnest desire
on the part of France for a transfer of Louisiana.   In fact
one of the French ministers in this country, Mr. Adet, had
avowed to Mr. Randolph, the former secretary of state,
that such was the wish of his government and that the cession of Louisiana to France was a preliminary to be insisted
on in a negotiation with Spain.   France had sought in 1796
to secure Louisiana by offering to join Spain in the conquest of Portugal.[2]   There were obvious reasons why such
a cession would be an object of grave solicitude to this
country.   The border and mouth of the Mississippi in the
control of a virile, militant nation, strongly aggressive, was
a different proposition, from possession by a weak monarchy
out of whose palsied hand the rich prize must soon
fall.   Further, the French were at that period openly hostile to the United States and their power to work injury upon

---

1. Vol. I, Ministers to Secretary of State, D'Yrujo to Madison, Feb.,
1803.

2. Vol. IV, Instructions to United States Ministers, p. 1.   Pickering to David Humphreys, Feb. 1, 1797.

this country if stationed at the mouth of the Mississippi, was unlimited. Humphreys at that date was directed to use cautiously every means within his power to prevent the proposed cession, by impressing upon Spain the great value of Louisiana and the necessity for her to retain possession of that province for the security of her other American dependencies. "The Floridas are mentioned as comprehended in the cession to France," continued Pickering. "This is also highly interesting to the United States to prevent." [1] A year later Pickering wrote to Humphreys in a cipher dispatch that on very reliable information he understood "that the French government have been pressing that of Spain to cede Louisiana to France and that the pressure is so urgent as hardly to admit of longer resistance — and that if the former peremptorily demands the cession the latter will not risk the consequences of a refusal." [2]

It became a matter of much importance to know the terms of any such cession and to learn just what was comprehended by it and whether New Orleans and the Floridas as well, had changed hands. Charles Pinckney, at Madrid, had been instructed to open negotiations for the transfer to this country of New Orleans and East and West Florida — in short, all the Spanish dominions to the east of the Mississippi River. Writing to the secretary of state in 1801 Pinckney said, "I believe it will be found that the Floridas are not included in the cession of Louisiana or considered so by Spain: New Orleans is, and it will remain for you to have the goodness to say whether I am to move further in this business or whether the Floridas will still be considered as a desirable acquisition." [3]

"I am moving with great caution," writes Pinckney, a

1. *Ibid.*
2. Vol. IV, Instructions, p. 277, Pickering to Humphreys, April 19, 1798.
3. Vol. VI, United States Ministers to Secretary of State, Pinckney to Secretary of State, Nov. 19, 1801.

few months later, "and preparing the best and most probable means of obtaining, if possible, the Floridas."[1]   Signs
were not wanting to show that Spain soon repented of the
treaty by which she had thus parted with so vast a part of
her colonial possessions. Uriquijo, the minister who had
negotiated the treaty, had been retired in disgrace and the
new minister sought to conclude an arrangement with
France for its repurchase.

But there were many reasons which united to make
it doubtful whether we could push our negotiations to
a successful issue.   If the object of France was to
obtain Louisiana in order to bridle the conduct of our
Western country and hold a check over their commerce
they would oppose any cession of Florida to us, for that cession would defeat her real purpose.   Further, France was
herself most anxious to secure the Floridas, and the Spanish ministry viewed with alarm a cession which would give
to this country ports on the Gulf of Mexico so near Cuba
and their American possessions.   France had persuaded
Spain of the desirability of having that nation as a barrier
between the United States and the Spanish colonies.
The proposition for the cession of the Floridas tended to
verify the French predictions.   But there remained one
hope — the bankrupt condition of the Spanish treasury — a
purchase and sale held out some slight chance of success.[2]

On March 24, 1802, Charles Pinckney, in a long
and able letter formally addressed Don Pedro C:eval-
los, the Spanish minister of state, on the subject of such
a cession.   The able and diplomatic presentation of the matter is sufficient justification for a lengthy excerpt therefrom.

"The extent of territory and uncommon rise and progress of the United States within the last eighteen years can-

---

1.   Vol. VI, United States Ministers to Secretary of State, Pinckney
to Madison, Nov. 24, 1802.

2.   *Ibid.,* Pinckney to Madison, March 20, 1802.

not be unknown to your Excellency. In this time the increase
of her inhabitants, commerce, strength and revenue have
been such as are unequaled in the rise and settlement of any
nation. It has, as it were by magic, placed a country, a
short time since scarcely known, among the first in point of
commerce, I may perhaps be warranted in saying that she
is now the second or third commercial nation in the world.
Above one-half of her territory is situated on the Mississippi
and the rivers and waters running into it. This territory has
been some time since divided into new states, some of which
are already from their population become members of the
American Government, and others already organized only
await the short period of their attaining a certain number of inhabitants to be admitted to participate in our legislative councils. Your Excellency must at once perceive
that not only to the rights and interests but to the wants
and convenience of so considerable and growing a portion
of the American people, it is peculiarly the duty of their
government to attend. To this portion of our citizens the
first and greatest object is the free and secure navigation of
the Mississippi and waters running into it. In order, however, to secure still farther this right and to remove every
possible danger of inconvenience or difference in opinion
and to fix forever such a great natural boundary between
the dominions of their good friend his Catholic Majesty
and the United States as will leave no possible room for
differences hereafter with a nation for whom the United
States cherish so much affection: The undersigned is expressly charged by his government to open a negotiation
with his Majesty for the purchase and cession of East and
West Florida: and should the cession have finally taken
place as is reported of that part of Louisiana lying on the
east bank of the Mississippi, the undersigned in the name of
his government most earnestly entreats to be informed of

it officially in order that his government may be enabled to take the same friendly measures and make the same sincere and affectionate proposals to their good friends, the French Republic, for the small part of Louisiana on the east bank of the river as they now do to their good friend his Catholic Majesty for the Floridas.

"In wishing this small increase of territory the United States have no object but that of securing the navigation of the only outlet so great a body of their citizens have for the produce of their labors and enterprise and of fixing so valuable and great a natural boundary between them and their neighbors. Their politics being those of peace and their pursuits agriculture and commerce, they wish to remove forever all room or chance for differences on points so essential as the navigation of this river and its waters and their boundaries and good neighborhood with their present friends.

"The enlightened councils of his Majesty having a perfect knowledge of the situation of this country, must at once see that these are the *pressing* but the *only* reasons. Our government being without ambition never wishing to extend its territory except in so singular a case as this and never having the least idea or desire to possess colonies or more territory than they own, except in this singular instance, they trust that his Majesty will, on this occasion, consent to the sale and transfer upon such reasonable terms as may be agreed upon by the two governments. [1]

"They are emboldened to be hopeful of this, not only from the desire they believe his Majesty always possessed to oblige them, but also from the knowledge he has, that as colonies for production and advantage, the sterility of the soil of the Floridas and particularly the eastern, make

---

1. In the light of a century this is a naive and remarkable statement.

them a yearly loss to the Spanish government and if, as
appears by the treaty lately published at Paris between
France and Spain, Louisiana is finally ceded to the former,
then certainly the retaining of the Floridas cannot be of
much value to the latter. . . . . In this proposition respecting the sale of the two Floridas the undersigned is
hopeful his Majesty will see nothing but the most earnest
desire on the part of the United States to prevent forever
any misunderstanding between them and their neighbors,
on the subject of the right to navigate the Mississippi, a
right so essential to the great and growing territory of the
United States, situated on its waters that its future commerce, navigation and prosperity must entirely depend on
its undisturbed exercise. A situation unequaled in any
other part of the world where, perhaps, it will be difficult
to find so vast a country altogether depending on the outlet of a single river. The United States fear that if at
any future period the government or governments which
may possess the banks on both sides of its mouth should
unhappily, from mistaken views, become disposed to dis-
turb their right that it may be the means of kindling flames
the extent and consequences of which cannot at present be
foreseen, or the manner in which they may affect the powers
having the most important possessions in that quarter of
the world.

"It is for this reason and to preserve to all the blessing
of tranquillity and undisturbed commerce that the United
States, the sincere and firmly attached friends of his Majesty,
wish to obtain from him a fair and friendly cession of the
Floridas, or at least of West Florida, through which several
of our rivers, particularly the important River Mobile, empty
themselves into the sea, and from their good friends, the
French, such portion of Louisiana (if deeded to them) as
will answer the important end the United States have in
view on this subject, namely: the securing the navigation of

a river with which and the streams running into it, more than five-eighths of the whole territory of the United States are watered, and on those terms of friendship and sound and liberal policy which will be likely to ensure forever the attachment and tranquillity of the respective governments." [1]

It became rumored in this country that Spain was about to disown the French treaty of cession. Should the cession fail for this or any other cause and Spain retain the title to New Orleans and the Floridas, Pinckney was directed to employ every effort to obtain an arrangement by which "the territory on the east side of the Mississippi including New Orleans may be ceded to the United States and the Mississippi made common boundary with a common use of its navigation for them and Spain." [2] For the sake of securing such a "precious acquisition to the United States as well as a natural and quiet boundary with Spain," Pinckney was directed besides the inducements suggested in his original instructions, to transmit a proposition of "guaranty of her territory beyond the Mississippi as a condition of her ceding . . . . the territory including New Orleans on this side." [3]

Meanwhile instructions were dispatched to Robert Livingston, our minister at Paris, to undertake to dissuade France from her purpose of securing Louisiana, not knowing whether the treaty of cession had definitely been concluded. But if the cession had already been made, Livingston was directed to ascertain whether it included the Floridas as well as New Orleans, and if so, to learn the price at which these would be transferred to the United States. [4]

---

1. Vol. VI, Letters from Charles Pinckney to Don Pedro Cevallos, March 24, 1802.

2. Vol. VI, Instructions, MSS. State Dept., p. 40, Madison to Charles Pinckney, May 11, 1802.

3. *Ibid.*

4. *Ibid.*, p. 35, Madison to Robert R. Livingston, May 1, 1802.

If it is possible "to obtain for the United States on convenient terms," writes Madison, "New Orleans and Florida, the happiest of issues will be given to one of the most perplexing of occurrences."[1] The United States government seems to have definitely concluded that the Floridas were a part of the French cession but yet directed our minister at Madrid that, although at present the cession wished by this country must be an object of negotiation with the French government, the good disposition of Spain in relation to it, must be cultivated, both as they may not be entirely disregarded by France, and as in the turn of events Spain might possibly be extricated from her engagements to France and again have the disposal of the territories in question.[2] While still pressing the subject of a cession to the United States, Pinckney was unable to secure an answer as to the sale from Cevallos, who employed the traditionally Spanish method of diplomacy, delay and procrastination.[3] At any rate, Pinckney was convinced that much more depended upon France than Spain, even if the Floridas had not been ceded to that nation. Priding themselves as they did upon the extent of their empire, Pinckney expected his proposition to fall upon deaf ears and, although not hopeful of success, felt greatly encouraged that the Spanish ministry was willing to even receive the proposition.

Livingston meanwhile, obedient to his instructions, had been pressing the matter with Talleyrand at Paris. "Florida is not . . . . included in the cession," he reported to Madison.[4] And in November he writes, "I have obtained accurate information of the offer to Spain: it is either to sell them Parma for forty-eight million livres or to exchange it for Florida. You see by this the value they put on Florida.

1. Vol. VI, Instructions, p. 56, Madison to Livingston, Oct. 15, 1802.
2. *Ibid.,* p. 52, Madison to Pinckney, July 26, 1802.
3. Pinckney's Letters, Pinckney to Madison, Aug. 30, 1802.
4. Letters of Robert Livingston to United States, Nov. 2, 1802.

I fear Spain will accede to their proposition." [1]   In all his letters to Talleyrand, Livingston speaks of the Floridas as entirely apart from Louisiana and containing the Mobile and Pensacola rivers.

Jefferson now determined upon a special mission to secure a settlement of the difficulty and selected Monroe to be joined with Livingston in a commission extraordinary to treat at Paris and with Pinckney at Madrid. "The object of Monroe's instructions," writes Madison, "will be to procure a cession of New Orleans and the Floridas to the United States and consequently the establishment of the Mississippi as the boundary between the United States and Louisiana." [2]   In order to draw the French government into the agreement, a sum of money was to constitute a part of the proposition, to which should be added such regulations of the commerce of that river, and the others emptying into the Gulf of Mexico, as ought to be satisfactory to France.

From news recently received by Jefferson it was inferred that the French government was not averse to negotiating on the grounds suggested. And Livingston was cautioned to use the utmost care in repressing extravagant anticipations of the terms to be offered by the United States, particularly of the sum of money as a bonus.

Speaking broadly it may be said that two considerations moved Napoleon in his purpose to sell Louisiana to the United States. First, the increasing jealousy between Great Britain and France and the known aversion of the former to seeing the mouth of the Mississippi in the hands of the latter and the imminence of a Franco-English war wherein England, with her superior navy, would promptly seize the province. In the second place the First Consul desired to build up a power on the western continent, which should

---

1. Letters of Robert Livingston to United States, Nov. 14, 1802.
2. Vol. VI, Instructions, p. 71, Madison to Pinckney, Jan. 18, 1803.
Ibid., p. 73, Madison to Livingston, Jan. 18, 1803.

balance England and hold that nation in check.[1] Of lesser
note but largely included in the considerations already
named, was the state of things produced by the breach of
our deposit at New Orleans; the situation of the French
islands, particularly the important island of San Domingo,
and the unsettled posture of Europe.

An order from the board of health of Spain for the
exclusion of all vessels from the United States, at this
juncture inspired a strong protest from the United States.
This unreasonable order together with the closing of the
port of New Orleans tended to bitterly increase the hostile
feeling toward that nation.

Again in February Pinckney addressed the Spanish
secretary of state in a strong plea for a cession of the
Floridas and New Orleans because,

"The government of the United States from many circumstances as well as from the conduct of the intendant feel
themselves every day more convinced of the necessity of
their having a permanent establishment on the Mississippi,
convenient for the purposes of navigation and belonging
solely to them. To obtain this they have authorized me to
say that, should his Majesty be now inclined to sell to the
United States his possessions on the east side of the River
Mobile agreeably to the propositions inclosed, the United
States will make to his Majesty, and I do now in their name,
make the important offer of guaranteeing to him and his
successors his Dominions beyond the Mississippi." His

---

1. It is commonly supposed that Bonaparte sold Louisiana for the
purpose of raising money from the necessity of replenishing a depleted
treasury. This is a mistake. It was a cardinal principle of Napoleon
to make war support war. Pursuing this theory he resolved war into
a game of loot, and he played the game well, robbing, pillaging,
and practicing the most outrageous and extravagant extortions upon
his fallen enemies. He virtually lived on plunder. It is true that at
this time he was anticipating an extensive war and that money
would be useful — yet that cannot be accurately considered as one of
the principal motives that induced him to part with Louisiana.

Majesty should consider well "the immense importance of this offer to the Spanish crown and to reflect how far it may be in the power of any other nation to make an offer so truly valuable and precious as this is to Spain. One that the United States would never have made but from a conviction of the indispensable necessity of their possessing a suitable establishment on this River and which this territory can alone furnish." [1]

In a conference between these two officials held at the end of March the Spanish minister informed Pinckney "that Louisiana had been ceded to the French including the town of New Orleans," a statement which by the ordinary rules of construction can only mean that Louisiana as ceded to France comprised the territory to the west of the Mississippi besides the city of New Orleans. This question became the subject of bitter dispute in later years.

Spain realizing the danger of breaking with the United States and thus driving us to join England, the time for securing such a cession seemed most propitious. While our representatives were too late to prevent the cession of Louisiana they were largely instrumental in saving the Floridas from going the same way. [2] The Chevalier d'Yrujo, in a letter to the secretary of state in the summer of 1803, definitely stated that Spain must decline to cede the Floridas because to do so would excite complaints from European maritime powers, that it would injure the reputation of his Catholic Majesty thus to dismember his states and because "this compliance would be offensive to France who was desirous of having the cession of the Floridas, offering advantageous terms: and nevertheless his Majesty did not accede to it notwithstanding the ties and considerations which unite us with that power." [3]

---

1. Vol. VI, Pinckney to Spanish Secretary of State, Feb. 4, 1803.
2. Vol. VI, Letters of Charles Pinckney, April 12, 1803.
3. D'Yrujo to Madison, July 2, 1803.

Cevallos, the Spanish minister, in a letter to Pinckney, similarly demurred to the proposition. "The system adopted by his Majesty," he writes, "not to dispossess himself of any portion of his states deprives him of the pleasure of assenting to the cessions which the United States wish to obtain by purchase, as I have intimated for their information to the Marquis de Casa Yrujo. By the retrocession made to France of Louisiana, that power regains the said province with the limits it had saving the rights acquired by other powers. The United States can address themselves to the French government to negotiate the acquisition of territories which may suit their interest." [1]

An analysis of the instructions to Livingston and Monroe discloses the views held by our government with regard to the desired cession and the French control of New Orleans and Louisiana proper. Jefferson felt that there was "on the globe one single spot, the possessor of which is our natural and habitual enemy. It is New Orleans. . . . . France placing herself in that door, assumes to us an attitude of defiance."

The new master of the mouth of the Mississippi was not a person whom an eloquent dispatch could intimidate. Spain held Louisiana merely on sufferance and it could be obtained from her at any time we might care to force the issue. But Napoleon would not be content with a couple of trading posts in a territory which could easily be transformed into an empire. The object was to procure a ces-

---

1. Cevallos to Pinckney, May 4, 1803.
"El sistema adoptado por S. M. de no desprenderse de porcion alguna de sus estados le priva del gusto de condescender à las cesiones que por compra quieren obtener los Estados Unidos segun tengo manifestado para inteligencia de estos al Marques de Casa Yrujo. Por la retrocession hecha à la Francia de la Luisiana recobro esta Potentia decha Provincia con los limites con que la tubo y salvos los derechos adquiridos por otras potencias. La de los Estados Unidos podra derigirse al Gubierno Francese para negociar la adquisicion de Territorias que convengas à su interés."

sion to the United States of "New Orleans and of West
and East Florida or as much thereof as the actual proprietor
can be prevailed on to part with." It was not clear just
what France had acquired. It was understood that she
had secured New Orleans, as part of Louisiana, and if the
Floridas had not been included in the cession it was considered not improbable that they had since been added
to it.

The danger of war with France was alluded to. If
she held New Orleans, continued conflicts and hostilities
were certain; and in such an event the United States would
ally herself with Great Britain. The low ebb of French
finances might persuade that country of the desirability of
making a sale. The motives of France in securing Louisiana were then discussed.

1. The eastern states favoring Great Britain, by holding Louisiana and the key to the commerce of the Mississippi River, France might be able to command the interests
and attachments of the western states and thus either also
control the Atlantic or seduce the western states into a
separate government and a close alliance with herself.

2. The advancement of the commerce of France by an
establishment on the Mississippi.

3. A further object with France might be the formation of a colonial establishment having a convenient relation
to her West India Islands and forming an independent
source of supplies for them. The cession of the Floridas
was particularly to be desired as obviating serious controversies that would otherwise grow out of the regulations,
however liberal, which she might establish at the mouths
of those rivers. The right of navigation to those rivers
was indispensable to procure the proper outlets to foreign
markets; this was a claim so natural, so reasonable, and so
essential that it must take place and in prudence ought to

be amicably and effectually adjusted without further delay.

In a plan of treaty embodied in the instructions the first article read:

"France cedes to the United States forever the territory east of the River Mississippi, comprehending the two Floridas, the Island of New Orleans, and the islands lying to the north and east of that channel of the said river which is commonly called the South Pass, together with all such other islands as appertain to either East or West Florida, France reserving to herself all her territory on the west side of the Mississippi." The commissioners were authorized as the highest price to offer fifty million livres tournois, about $9,250,000, this sum to be applied to the claims of the citizens of the United States and the remainder to be paid to France. This price was to be the consideration for the cession of "the Island of New Orleans and both the Floridas." But should France be willing to dispose of only some parts of those territories the commissioners were instructed that "the Floridas together are estimated at one-fourth the value of the whole Island of New Orleans, and East Florida, at one-half that of West Florida." If France refused to cede the whole Island of New Orleans, the commissioners were instructed to buy a place sufficient for a commercial town on the bank of the Mississippi and to secure suitable deposits at the mouths of the rivers passing from the United States through the Floridas, as well as the free navigation of those rivers by citizens of the United States. [1]

By supplementary instructions the commissioners were authorized to treat with Great Britain for an alliance against France, if France should decline to treat with the United States. War seemed not unlikely. For, if France denied

---

1. Vol. VI, Instructions, pp. 81-95. Madison to Livingston and Monroe, March 2, 1803.

to this country the free navigation of the Mississippi, hostilities could not be avoided. [1]

Our minister to Great Britain, Mr. King, had been informed by the British minister, Addington, that in the event of war between Great Britain and France, England would in all likelihood seize New Orleans. The commissioners were therefore directed in no event to guarantee to France the territory west of the Mississippi, as, should Great Britain conquer it, the United States would be placed in a most embarrassing position. [2]

At the time the negotiations for the purchase of Louisiana were closed, Barbé-Marbois, the French minister, orally stipulated that France would never possess the Floridas, that she would relinquish all her rights and would aid us to procure them. [3]   Cevallos in an interview with Pinckney expressed the greatest surprise at the cession of Louisiana to this country, since France, in receiving it from Spain, had promised never to part with it. The entire Spanish ministry shared this feeling of chagrin and disappointment, realizing how much better it would have been had Spain kept the colony and sold it directly to the United States. [4]

The Duke of Parma, son-in-law of the king of Spain, was desirous of securing for himself the succession to the Grand Duchy of Tuscany that he might be raised to the dignity of king and have his dominions enlarged by the addition of Tuscany. France having promised these distinctions and enlarged territory in Italy, Spain, by the treaty of San Ildefonso, October 1, 1800, agreed to cede Louisiana which she had held for thirty-eight years. These terms of the treaty had not been carried out by France.

---

1.   Vol. VI, Instructions, p. 113.   Madison to Livingston and Monroe, April 18, 1803.
2.   Vol. VI, Instructions, p. 131, Madison to Livingston and Monroe, May 28, 1803.
3.   Livingston to Secretary of State, No. 74, April 13, 1803.
4.   Vol. VI, Pinckney to Secretary of State, June 12, 1803.

She had also agreed to secure the recognition of Russia and Great Britain for the king of Tuscany. This she had not accomplished. Furthermore she had agreed never to alienate the province to any nation except Spain.

On the fourth of September, 1803, and again on September 27th and October 12th of the same year, D'Yrujo protested against the cession to this country on the ground that France could not, in consonance with the treaty, dispose of the province and, further, that the consideration for the cession between Spain and France had failed.

There can and should be no other way to judge of the acts of a nation than by applying to them the same rules that we consult in passing judgment upon the acts of men. Let us frame a case in municipal law, fitting the conditions as nearly as possible to those which existed in the relations between Spain, France and the United States with regard to the Louisiana purchase.

A enters into a contract to transfer to B a piece of property, in consideration of B's securing to him certain rights. B, however, does not perform his part and the consideration of the contract thus fails. The contract is thereby rendered void. B takes steps to transfer the property to C. A, learning of this, notifies C that B does not possess and cannot pass a good title. Even if C be a purchaser for value from B his title will not stand as against A. It is a rule of universal application that if a person acquiring either a legal or equitable estate has, at the time of acquisition, notice of an existing interest or estate in the subject matter possessed by a third party, he will be held to have acquired only such an interest or estate as the owner could honestly transfer. A court of competent jurisdiction would, in the case supposed, not hesitate to restore full title and possession to A. Further let us suppose that B expressly contracts never to alienate the property except to retransfer it to A. Ignoring any irrelevant question,

8

which might arise as to whether such a contract violated the rule against perpetuities or was in restraint of trade, A's rights would be enforced by the courts, and title and possession restored to him were B to alienate the property to a purchaser with notice.

These were practically the conditions which existed in the history of the Louisiana acquisition. France had guaranteed to Spain, as consideration for the transfer of Louisiana to herself, to secure the recognition of the king of Tuscany by Great Britain and Russia. This France had not done, and the consideration having failed, the treaty was null and void. She had further agreed as part of the consideration never to alienate the province except to Spain. The United States was undoubtedly a purchaser with notice, for Spain on the fourth and twenty-seventh of September, and the twelfth of October, 1803, had served notice upon this country and protested against the sale. And fully as significant from the standpoint of municipal law is the fact that France, when she sold Louisiana to the United States, had not entered into possession, nor did she do so until December, 1803.

If we might suppose the dreams of the theorists realized and a court of international jurisdiction established, Spain as a litigant, applying the principles of municipal law, could have secured a decree compelling the United States to restore Louisiana to her; or had she so desired, she might have sued France for the original consideration and accompanying damages. The United States would have had recourse on France to secure the return of the purchase price. The author cannot believe that there are any two rules of right, one for nations and another for men. Nowhere does our religion teach two systems of ethics, but only one unalterable code, applicable alike to individuals and to nations. The only way to justify many of our national acts is to insist that there exists one code of morals by which we shall judge of men and another by which we shall judge of nations. The answer of course is that all nations do the same — which is true to a large extent and also very disgraceful. But custom does not make right or excuse wrong.

Many writers claim that Spain was estopped from protesting against the transfer of Louisiana to the United States, by the letter of Cevallos to Pinckney of May 4, 1803, wherein the following statement occurs: "The United States can address themselves to the French government to negotiate the acquisition of territories which may suit their interest." In the first place was the letter anything but an effort on the part of Cevallos to be rid of a persistently importuning minister, feeling as he did that Spain was protected by her treaty with France? Further the letter was undoubtedly written when Cevallos still expected Napoleon to carry out the stipulations of the treaty of San Ildefonso. Later it became clear that the treaty was null and void for want of mutuality, and then Spain served notice on the United States who could not be considered an innocent purchaser.

.A stronger nation, England for instance, would beyond doubt have appealed to the sword, but poor Spain, realizing her own helpless position and the futility of stronger representations, could only protest. She knew she could do no more, she knew that a resort to arms could only increase her humiliation and her losses — and the United States knew it too and treated her protests with silent contempt — and Louisiana became ours. When we realize the helplessness of Spain buffeted and kicked around by first England and then France, and our boot was in it too, we see in fact how little chance there was for her to secure any redress. Had she been a more virile power, and less hampered by misfortunes, she might have considered our acquisition of Louisiana, in spite of her representations, a *casus belli*.

The present time seemed most propitious for pushing

the Spanish government for a sale of the Floridas. War
had been declared between Russia and France and there
was every indication that by spring it would involve the
entire continent. General Bournonville, the French ambassador at Madrid, assured Pinckney that he had received
directions from his government to promote a disposition in
Spain to sell the Floridas to us. To French influence it
was believed was due our failure to secure the coveted
territory before. [1]

"The Floridas are not included in the treaty, being, it
appears, still held by Spain," wrote Madison to Pinckney.
Although it was true that Spain had refused to alienate any
part of her colonial possessions yet, "at the date of this
refusal," continued the secretary of state, "it was probably
unknown that the cession by France to the United States
had been or would be made. This consideration with the
kind of reasons given for the refusal and the situation of
Spain resulting from the war between Great Britain and
France lead to a calculation that at present there may be
less repugnance to our views. . . . But considering the
motives which Spain ought now to feel for making the
arrangement easy and satisfactory, the certainty that the
Floridas must at no distant period find a way into our hands,
and the tax on our finances resulting from the purchase of
Louisiana which makes a further purchase immediately less
convenient, it may be hoped as it is to be wished that the
bargain will be considerably cheapened." [2] Pinckney following instructions, continued to address overtures to Cevallos,
dwelling on the danger that Florida, from her position,
might cause a rupture between Spain and the United States;
that in reality the Floridas were a financial burden to Spain
costing far more than they returned; and that the United
States desired them from no spirit of aggrandizement or

---

1.   Vol. VI, Pinckney to Secretary of State, Aug. 30, 1803.
2.   Vol. VI, Instructions, p. 135, Madison to Pinckney, July 29, 1803.

dictate of ambition but merely to fill out the boundary and
insure against future disputes.

Monroe after the close of the negotiations for the purchase of Louisiana proceeded to London rather than to
Madrid, considering the time unfavorable for a Spanish
treaty. The strong protest and ill humor of Spain due to
the cession of Louisiana were the principal reasons against
attempting, at that time, to procure from the Spanish government the residuum of territory desired by the United
States. Indeed Spain presented so bold a front at this
juncture as to induce the belief that she had an understanding with some powerful quarter of Europe.

Writing to Pinckney, Madison discussed at some length
the Spanish motives in opposing the transfer and the folly
of such a course even if successful. In part he said:

"If it be her aim to prevent the execution of the treaty
between the United States and France in order to have for
her neighbor the latter instead of the United States, it is not
difficult to show that she mistakes the lesser for the greater
danger against which she wishes to provide.   Admitting,
as she may possibly suppose, that Louisiana as a French
colony would be less able as well as less disposed than the
United States to encroach on her southern possessions and
that it would be too much occupied with its own safety
against the United States, to turn its force on the other
side against her possessions, still it is obvious in the first
place that in proportion to the want of power in the French
compared with the power of the United States, the colony
would be insufficient as a barrier against the United States,
and in the next place, that the very security which she provides would still be a source of the greatest of all dangers
she has to apprehend. The collision between the United
States and the French would lead to a contest in which
Spain would of course be on the side of the latter; and
what becomes of Louisiana and the Spanish possessions beyond it, in a contest between powers, so marshaled? An
easy and certain victim to the fleets of Great Britain and the
land armies of this country. A combination of these forces

was always and justly dreaded by both Spain and France. It was the danger which led both into our Revolutionary war and as much inconsistency as weakness is chargeable on the projects of either which tend to reunite, for the purposes of war, the power which has been divided. France returning to her original policy has wisely, by her late treaty with the United States, obviated a danger which could not have been very remote. Spain will be equally wise in following the example and by acquiescing in an arrangement which guards against an early danger of controversy between the United States, first with France then with herself, and removes to a distant day the approximation of the American and Spanish settlements, provides in the best possible manner for the security of the latter and for a lasting harmony with the United States. What is it that Spain dreads? She dreads, it is presumed, the growing power of this country and the direction of it against her possessions within its reach. Can she annihilate this power? No. Can she sensibly retard its growth? No. Does not common prudence then advise her, to conciliate by every proof of friendship and confidence the good will of a nation whose power is formidable to her; instead of yielding to the impulses of jealousy and adopting obnoxious precautions, which can have no other effect than to bring on prematurely the whole weight of the calamity which she fears?" [1]

Louisiana then having become, by the ratification of the French treaty, a part of the United States, steps were immediately taken for the transfer of the province to its new owner. Claiborne, the governor of the Mississippi territory, was named as "governor of Louisiana and commissioner to receive the province from the French representative." Recent occurrences, particularly the protests of the Spanish minister against the cession, made it necessary to provide for such a contingency as the refusal by the Spanish authorities at New Orleans to give up the country according to her engagements with France. It must be borne in mind that although Spain had ceded Louisiana to France in October,

---

1. Vol. VI, Instructions, p. 149, Madison to Pinckney, Oct. 12, 1803.

1800, she had never actually delivered possession of the
province; Spanish troops still manned the garrisons at New
Orleans and Spanish grandees and nobles still dispensed
law and justice in that city. Jefferson determined to be,
prepared for all emergencies and to make good our title even
by employing force, an act of congress having duly authorized this course. General Wilkinson was named as commander of these troops. The first question was whether
our troops near New Orleans with the aid of well disposed
inhabitants could dispossess the Spanish authorities. Governor Claiborne was instructed to communicate with M.
Laussat, the French envoy, whose sanction and co-operation
were particularly desired. Should it be decided that a *coup
de main* was necessary, General Wilkinson should not hesitate. His forces were to consist of the regular troops near
at hand, as many of the militia as might be requisite, and
could be drawn from the Mississippi territory, and such
volunteers from any quarter as could be picked up. To
them would be added five hundred mounted militia from
Tennessee who had been already requisitioned. In order to
"add the effect of terror to the force of arms" word was
given out that measures were in train for sending on from
Kentucky and elsewhere a large force, sufficient to overwhelm all possible resistance. [1]

At a conference between the Spanish and French officials the method of transfer was agreed upon. With the
Spanish troops drawn up in solemn procession, in the
presence of a large concourse of people, the commissioners
representing France and Spain played their parts. The
French commissioner presented to the Spanish commissioner
the order of the king of Spain for the surrender of the
province, dated more than a year previous, and with this
the order of Napoleon to receive possession in the name of

---

1. Vol. XIV, Domestic Letters, Madison to Governor Claiborne,
Oct. 31, 1803.

France. The Spanish governor then surrendered the keys of the city and with the lowering of the Spanish and the raising of the French colors, amid the booming of artillery the authority of King Charles gave way to that of Napoleon. For the brief space of twenty days, the French administered the province; then the formal delivery was made to the United States as, with bands playing and colors flying, the American troops marched into the city. Again the cannon boomed and again Louisiana had changed hands.

For the crowd that witnessed the ceremonies on that twentieth day of December, 1803, Claiborne's promise that this transfer would be the last, fell on incredulous ears. Within a century, nay within the lifetime of men then living, Louisiana had six times changed rulers. Ninety-one years before when but a thousand white men had ventured within her limits, Louis XIV had farmed Louisiana to Antoine Crozat, the merchant monopolist of his day. Crozat in 1717 made it over to John Law, director general of the Mississippi Company who, in 1731, surrendered it to Louis XV. By treaty in 1762 it passed to the king of Spain; and Spain by the treaty of San Ildefonso had re-ceded it to France, who in 1803 sold it to the United States. The general impression prevailed among the American emigrants who crossed the Mississippi while Louisiana still belonged to Spain, and as early as 1793-95, that shortly the country would be annexed to the United States. It had been the policy of Spain to encourage American emigration into upper Louisiana. The distance to New Orleans was great and the intervening country was a vast wilderness penetrated only by a river difficult of navigation. The Spanish were in constant fear of a British and Indian invasion from Canada, and the Americans they knew to be naturally hostile to the British and thus ready to protect the country.

There was soon apparent in the city of New Orleans a strongly marked opposition to American sovereignty.

This antipathy, strong among the people, was still further increased by the emissaries of the old régime. By the terms of the treaty, the Spanish troops continued to hold the barracks, the magazines and the hospital and daily mount guard in New Orleans. Meanwhile American soldiers occupied redoubts about the city and in the tents along the marshes contracted poisonous fevers while their government at extravagant prices hired buildings for the storage of provisions, implements, tents, baggage and arms, powder and guns and hospital stores. Not until April, 1804, did the first detachment of three hundred Spanish troops depart for Pensacola.

For more than a year the principal commissioners, the commissary of war, the paymaster and treasurer of the army, the late intendant, the revenue and custom house officials, surgeons, chaplains, regimental officers of every rank lingered in New Orleans and openly boasted of the day not far distant when the trans-Mississippi territory would again be Spanish territory. Though the Americans might insist that the cession was a permanent one, yet why these Spanish officials? Was not their presence, so long after they should have departed or been ejected, proof that the recovery of the province was seriously contemplated? So prevalent was this belief that many feared even to show a decent respect for the territorial government lest, when the retrocession should come, they be made to suffer for their disloyalty. Much less could men be induced to accept office; and when October arrived and the government was about to organize five of the legislative council, appointed by Jefferson, refused to serve.

CHAPTER IV.

FOR $15,000,000 the United States had purchased a province and a quarrel.

In the early spring of 1804 congress passed an act, "For laying and collecting duties on Imports and Tonnage within the Territory ceded to the United States by Treaty of April 30, 1803, between the United States and the French Republic, and for other purposes." The eleventh section of this act read: "And be it further enacted that the president be, and hereby is, authorized, whenever he shall deem it expedient to erect the Shores, Waters and Inlets of the Bay and River Mobile and of the other Rivers, Creeks, Inlets and Bays emptying into the Gulf of Mexico, east of the said River Mobile and west thereof to the Pascagoula, inclusive, into a separate District and to establish such place within the same, as he shall deem expedient, to be the Port of Entry and Delivery for such District and to designate such other Places within the same District not exceeding two, to be Ports of Delivery, only. Whenever such separate District shall be erected, a collector shall be appointed to reside at each of the Ports of Delivery which may be established, etc." The indignant D'Yrujo, Gazette in hand, penned in burning words a letter to Madison on what he had at first believed to be an "atrocious libel against the government of this country," but which he now unhesitatingly declared as "one of the greatest insults which one power can be guilty of towards another" — words scarcely diplomatic but full of feeling withal. "How could I expect," he wrote, "that the American government which prides itself so much on its good faith, which is so zealous in the preservation and defense of its own rights would have violated with all the solemnity of a legislative act those of the king, my master, by usurping his sovereignty?[1] . . . What would have been the sensations of the people of America if, soon after the treaty made by Spain with the United States, in the year 1795, by which the boundary line between the territory of the two powers was fixed at the 31° of latitude, the king, my master, had authorized any of his chief officers in America to divide a part of Georgia into districts and to establish custom houses in various points of them, simply because it was imagined that the territory in which he chose to place them belonged to that portion which would remain to him according to the boundary line which had not then been drawn?

"The right which the United States arrogate of legislating in the territories mentioned in the said eleventh section is not better founded than would be that of his Catholic Majesty to have made laws in the former instance for a great part of Georgia. But even if the treaty of the thirtieth of April had given any ground or appearance of foundation for the establishment of such pretensions it was natural that the United States from a sentiment of justice, of delicacy and of that decorum and respect which nations owe to each other, should have proceeded by the ordinary way of negotiation to clear up their doubts and to establish their conduct upon a basis which would not be in contradiction to their principles.

"The congress however, so far from observing the established usages in cases of this nature, proceeds at once to a decision and not only authorizes the president to exe-

1. Vol. I, D'Yrujo to Secretary of State, March 7, 1804.

cute certain acts in West Florida which indisputably belongs to the king, my master, but expresses this in such vague and indefinite terms that the president may consider himself authorized by the said act to annex a part of East Florida to the district of which mention is made in the eleventh section and to place a collector of the customs in Apalache or Pensacola. . . . The authority given to the president is unlimited, east of the River Mobile, and comprehends indirectly the power of declaring or rather making war since it is not to be presumed that any nation will patiently permit another to make laws within its territories without its consent.

"If the act on the part of the United States of legislating in the possessions enumerated in the above mentioned section be a real insult towards the king, my master, even if there could exist any doubts as to the true limits of Louisiana acquired by the treaty of the thirtieth of April last, how much greater must that offense appear when there does not exist any well-founded reason by which the United States can establish any pretensions to West Florida."

The right to West Florida and the merits of the respective claims of the United States and Spain to that province have been an academic question for a century — even after its practical settlement by the treaty of 1819 — nor does the issue seem to have been satisfactorily determined, though one hundred years have rolled by since first it arose. It may be permissible then to take up and weigh the various arguments which have been presented, in an effort to reach the truth of the matter or rather to ascertain the merits of the case.

When, under Washington, the matter was first broached, the desideratum of this nation was the Floridas and New Orleans — the territory east of the Mississippi and south of our then southern boundary. And when Jefferson opened the negotiations with Napoleon for a purchase, it was not

the province of Louisiana but rather New Orleans and the
Floridas that he wished to secure. The fact that Spain had
not ceded the Floridas was only later known to the United
States. The correspondence of Jefferson clearly shows that
his idea was that by securing New Orleans and the Floridas
the United States would possess a well rounded national
domain east of the Mississippi. Therefore, we must conclude that Jefferson began the negotiation with the idea
that the territory of West Florida extended to the Mississippi with 31° latitude for its northern boundary, as settled
in the Spanish-American treaty of 1795. Had it been understood that West Florida extended only to the Perdido,
Jefferson should and would have given instructions to
negotiate for the purchase of both Floridas, New Orleans
and that part of Louisiana east of the Mississippi and between that river and the Perdido.

We will further recall that Napoleon made several
unsuccessful attempts to persuade Spain to cede the Floridas
to him after he had secured Louisiana by the treaty of San
Ildefonso and a minister, General Bournonville, was sent
to Madrid for that express purpose. Among other things
the duchy of Parma was offered in exchange, but to the
United States was attributed the failure of the negotiation.
From the extent of the seacoast, the number of good harbors and the situation of the Floridas, France, owning
Louisiana, was anxious also to possess those provinces. [1]

No definite limits had been stated in our treaty of purchase because they were not known. But the United States
construed the treaty in the manner most favorable to itself
— a disposition as natural among nations as among individuals. At the time of the delivery of the province of Louisiana at New Orleans, orders were obtained from the Spanish
authorities for the delivery of all the posts on the west side

---

1. Vol. VI, Instructions, p. 226, Madison to Livingston, March 31, 1804.

of the Mississippi as well as the island of New Orleans. With respect to the posts in West Florida orders for the delivery were neither offered to nor demanded by our commissioners. The defense of our side of the dispute together with a statement of our claims is clearly and succinctly given in a letter from Madison to Livingston. We can do no better than to quote therefrom at length.

"This silence on the part of the executive was deemed eligible — first because it was foreseen that the demand would not only be rejected by the Spanish authority at New Orleans which had in an official publication limited the cession eastwardly by the Mississippi and the island ot New Orleans, but it was apprehended, as has turned out, that the French commissioner might not be ready to support the demand and might even be disposed to second the Spanish opposition. Secondly because in the latter of these cases a serious check would be given to our title and in either of them a premature dilemma would result between an overt submission to the refusal and a resort to force. Thirdly because mere silence would be no bar to a plea at any time that a delivery of a part, particularly at the seat of government was a virtual delivery of the whole, whilst in the meantime, we could ascertain the views and claim the interposition of the French government and avail ourselves of that and any other favorable circumstances for effecting an amicable adjustment of Spain. . . .

"The territory ceded to the United States is described in the words following, 'the colony or province of Louisiana with the same extent that it now has in the hands of Spain, that it had when France possessed it and such as it ought to be according to the treaties subsequently passed between Spain and other states.'

"In expounding this threefold description, the different forms used must be so understood as to give a meaning to each description, and to make the meaning of each coincide with that of the others. The first form of description is a reference to the extent which Louisiana now has in the hands of Spain. What is that extent as determined by its eastern limits? It is not denied that the Perdido was once the east limit of Louisiana. It is not denied that the territory now possessed by Spain extends to the River Perdido. The River Perdido we say then is the limit to the east extent of the Louisiana ceded to the United States.

"This construction gives an obvious and pertinent meaning to the term 'now' and to the expression 'in the hands of Spain,' which can be found in no other construction. For a considerable time previous to the treaty of peace in 1783 between Great Britain and Spain, Louisiana as in the hands of Spain was limited eastwardly by the Mississippi, the Iberville, etc. The term 'now' fixes its extent as enlarged by that treaty in contradistinction to the more limited extent in which Spain held it prior to the treaty.

"Again the expression 'in the hands or in the possession of Spain' fixes the same extent, because the expression cannot relate to the extent which Spain by her internal regulations may have given to a particular district under the name of Louisiana, but evidently to the extent in which it was known to other nations, particularly to the nation in treaty with her, and in which it was, relatively to other nations, in her hands and not in the hands of any other nation. It would be absurd to consider the expression 'in the hands of Spain' as relating not to others but to herself and to her own regulations; for the territory of Louisiana in her hands must be equally so and be the same whether formed into one or twenty districts or by whatever name or names it may be called by herself.

"What may now be the extent of a provincial district under the name of Louisiana according to the municipal arrangements of the Spanish government is not perfectly known. It is at least questionable whether even these arrangements have not incorporated the portion of Louisiana acquired from Great Britain with the west portion before belonging to Spain, under the same provincial government. But whether such be the fact or not the construction of the treaty will be the same. The next form of description refers to the extent which Louisiana had when possessed by France. What is this extent? It will be admitted that for the whole period prior to the division of Louisiana between Spain and Great Britain in 1762-63 or at least from the adjustment of boundary between France and Spain in 1719 to that event, Louisiana extended in the possession of France to the River Perdido. Had the meaning then of the first description been less determinate and had France been in possession of Louisiana at any time with less extent than to the Perdido, a reference to this primitive and long continued extent would be more natural and probable than to any other. But it happens that France never possessed Louisiana with less extent than to the Perdido; because on the same day that she ceded a part to Spain the residue was ceded to Great Britain and consequently as long as she possessed Louisiana at all, she possessed it entire, that is in its extent to the Perdido. It is true that after the cession of West Louisiana to Spain in the year 1762-63, the actual delivery of the territory by France was delayed for several years, but it can never be supposed that a reference could be intended to this short period of delay during which France held that portion of Louisiana without the east portion, in the right of Spain only, not in her own right; when in other words she held it as the trustee of Spain; and that a reference to such a possession for such a period should be intended rather than a reference to the long possession of the whole territory in her own acknowledged right prior to that period.

"In the order of the French king in 1762 to Mons.

d'Abbadia for the delivery of West Louisiana to Spain it is stated that the cession by France was on the third of November and the acceptance by Spain on the thirteenth of that month, leaving an interval of ten days. An anxiety to find a period during which Louisiana, as limited by the Mississippi and the Iberville, was held by France in her own right may possibly lead the Spanish government to seize the pretext into which this momentary interval may be converted. But it will be a mere pretext. In the first place it is probable that the treaty of cession to Spain which is dated on the same day with that to Great Britain was like the latter a preliminary treaty, consummated and confirmed by a definitive treaty bearing the same date with the definitive treaty including the cession to Great Britain, in which case the time and effect of each cession would be the same whether recurrence be had to the date of the preliminary or definitive treaties. In the next place the cession by France to Spain was essentially made on the third of November, 1762, on which day, the same with that of the cession of Great Britain, the right passed from France. The acceptance by Spain ten days later, if necessary at all to perfect the deed, had relation to the date of the cession by France and must have the same effect and no other, as if Spain had signed the deed on the same day with France. This explanation which rests on the soundest principles, nullifies the interval of ten days so as to make the cessions to Great Britain and Spain simultaneous, on the supposition that recurrence be had to the preliminary treaty and not the definitive treaty, and consequently establishes the fact that France at no time possessed Louisiana with less extent than to the Perdido, the alienation and partition of the territory admitting no distinction of time. In the last place, conceding even that during an interval of ten days, the right of Spain was incomplete and was in transition only from France or in

9

another form of expression that the right remained in
France subject to the eventual acceptance of Spain; is it
possible to believe that a description which must be presumed to aim at clearness and certainty, should refer
for its purposes to so fugitive and equivocal a state of
things, in preference to a state of things where the right
and the possession of France were of long continuance
and susceptible of neither doubt nor controversy? It is
impossible. And consequently the only possible construction which can be put on the second form of description coincides with the only rational construction that can
be put on the first, making Louisiana of the same extent,
that is, to the River Perdido, both 'as in the hands of
Spain and as France possessed it.'

"The third and last description of Louisiana is in these
words 'such as it ought to be according to the treaties subsequently passed between Spain and other states.'

"This description may be considered as auxiliary to
the two others and is conclusive as an argument for comprehending within the cession of Spanish territory eastward
of the Mississippi and the Iberville, for extending the
cession to the River Perdido. The only treaties between
Spain and other nations that affect the extent of Louisiana
as being subsequent to the possession of it by France, are,
first, the treaty in 1783 between Spain and Great Britain and
secondly the treaty of 1795 between Spain and the United
States.

"The last of these treaties affects the extent of Louisiana as in the hands of Spain by defining the northern
boundary of that part of it which lies east of the Mississippi and the Iberville. And the first affects the extent
of Louisiana by including in the cession from Great Britain
to Spain the territory between that river and the Perdido;
and by giving to Louisiana in consequence of that reunion
and of the east and west part, the same extent eastwardly

in the hands of Spain as it had when France possessed it. Louisiana then as it ought to be according to treaties of Spain subsequently to the possession by France, is limited by the line of demarkation settled with the United States and forming a northern boundary and is extended to the River Perdido as its east boundary.

"This is not only the plain and necessary construction of the words but is the only construction that can give a meaning to them. For they are without meaning on the supposition that Louisiana as in the hands of Spain is limited by the Mississippi and the Iberville. Include this part therefore, as we contend, within the extent of Louisiana, and a meaning is given to both as pertinent as it is important. Exclude this part, as Spain contends, from Louisiana and no treaties exist to which the reference is applicable. This deduction cannot be evaded by pretending that the reference to subsequent treaties of Spain was meant to save the right of deposit and other rights stipulated to the commerce of the United States by the treaty of 1795—first because, although that may be an incidental object of the reference to that treaty, as was signified by his Catholic Majesty to the government of the United States, yet the principal object of the reference is evidently the territorial extent of Louisiana; secondly because the reference is to more than one treaty, to the treaty of 1783 as well as to that of 1795 and the treaty of 1783 can have no modifying effect whatever, rendering it applicable, but on the supposition that Louisiana was considered as extending east of the Mississippi and the Iberville, into the territory ceded by that treaty to Spain.

"In fine the construction which we maintain gives to every part of the description of the territory ceded to the United States, a meaning clear in itself and in harmony with every other part, and is no less conformable to facts, than it is founded on the ordinary use and analogy of the expressions. The construction urged by Spain gives on the contrary a meaning to the first description which is inconsistent with the very terms of it; it prefers in the second a meaning that is impossible or absurd, and it takes from the last all meaning whatever.

"In confirmation of the meaning which extends Louisiana to the River Perdido, it may be regarded as most consistent with the object of the first consul in the cession obtained by him from Spain. Every appearance, every circumstance pronounces this to have been to give lustre to his administration and to gratify a natural pride in his nation by reannexing to its domain possessions which had without any sufficient considerations been severed from it, and which, being in the hands of Spain, it was in the power of Spain to restore. Spain, on the other side, might be the less reluctant against the cession in this extent as she would be only replaced by it; within the original limits of her possessions, the territory east of the Perdido having been regained by her from Great Britain in the peace of 1783 and not included in the late cession.

"It only remains to take notice of the argument derived from a criticism on the term 'retrocede' by which the cession from Spain to France is expressed. The literal meaning of this term is said to be that Spain gives back to France what she received from France: and that, as she received from France no more than the territory west of the Mississippi and Iberville, that and no more could be given back by Spain.

"Without denying that such a meaning, if uncontrolled by other terms would have been properly expressed by the term 'retrocede,' it is sufficient, and more than sufficient, to observe first that with respect to France the literal meaning is satisfied: France receiving back what she had before alienated. Secondly, that with respect to Spain not only the greater part of Louisiana had been confessedly

received by her from France and consequently was literally
ceded back by Spain as well as ceded back to France.
But with respect to the part in question Spain might not
unfairly be considered as ceding back to France what
France had ceded to her; inasmuch as the cession of it
to Great Britain was made for the benefit of Spain to
whom on that account Cuba was restored. The effect was
precisely the same as if France had in form made the cession to Spain and Spain had assigned it over to Great
Britain; and the cession may the more aptly be considered
as passing through Spain, as Spain herself was a party
to the treaty by which it was conveyed to Great Britain.
In this point of view, not only France received back what
she had ceded, but Spain ceded back what she had received
and the etymology even of the term 'retrocede' is satisfied. This view of the case is more substantially just, as
the territory in question passed from France to Great Britain for the account of Spain but passed from Great Britain
into the hands of Spain in 1783, in consequence of a war
to which Spain had contributed but little compared with
France and in terminating which so favorably in this article
for Spain, France had doubtless a preponderating influence.
Thirdly, that if a course of proceeding might have existed
to which the term 'retrocede' would be more literally applicable it may be equally said that there is no other particular term which would be more applicable to the whole
proceeding as it did exist. Fourth, lastly that if this were
not the case a nice criticism on the etymology of a single
term can be allowed no weight against a conclusion drawn
from the clear meaning of every other term and from the
whole context." [1]

The United States appealed to France for her construction of the treaty. For her unfavorable answer she

---

1. Vol. VI, Instructions, p. 226, Madison to Livingston, March 31,
1804.

was promptly maligned by this country and her views discounted. "It may be observed," writes Madison to General Armstrong, "that nothing can be more preposterous than the joint attempt now made by the French and Spanish governments in discussing the boundaries of Louisiana to appeal from the text of the convention which describes them, to a secret understanding or explanations on that subject between those governments. France sold us Louisiana as described in the deed of conveyance which copies the description from the deed of Spain to France. If France sold more than she had a right to sell she would at least be bound to supply the deficiency by a further purchase from Spain or to remit *pro tanto* the price stipulated by us. But the case rests on a still better footing. France assigned to us Louisiana as described in the conveyance to her from Spain. Our title to the written description is therefore good against both, notwithstanding any separate explanation or covenant between them, unless it be shown that notice thereof was sent to the United States before their bona fide purchase was made. This is a principle of universal justice no less than of municipal law. With respect to France, it will scarcely be pretended that any such notice was given. On the contrary, she corroborated our title according to the text of the bargain by the language of M. Talleyrand to Mr. Livingston; she corroborated our particular construction of the text in relation to the eastern boundary of Louisiana by the language of M. Marbois; and she corroborated our construction in relation to both the eastern and western boundaries by her silence under the known extent to which that construction carried them. And with respect to Spain who is equally bound by the assignment of the ostensible title of France, unless she can prove a notice to the United States that the real title was different from the ostensible one, it is to be observed first that no such proof has ever been attempted, and next that

Spain cannot even pretend an ignorance of the necessity of such notice. This is evinced by her conduct in another instance where a secret stipulation with France contrary to the tenor of her treaty with France was alleged in opposition to the treaty of the United States with France. France it appears had promised to Spain through her minister at Madrid that she would in no event alienate the territory ceded to her by Spain. The Spanish government sensible as it was that this promise could not invalidate the meaning of the instrument which exhibited the title of France as absolute, and therefore alienable, no sooner heard of the purchase concluded at Paris by the minister of the United States, than she instructed her minister at Washington to communicate without delay to the government of the United States the alleged engagement of France not to alienate. This communication was made on the ninth of September, 1803; and so convinced was Spain of the necessity of the most formal notice on such occasions that the Spanish minister here repeated the same notice on the twenty-seventh of the same month with the addition of some other pretended defects in the title of France and urged on the government here an obligation to forbear under such circumstances to ratify the convention with France. Now, if it was necessary for Spain, in order to protect herself by a secret engagement of France not to alienate, against the overt transaction giving France a right to alienate, that she should give notice of that engagement to third parties, and Spain knew this to be necessary, the same course was equally necessary and equally obvious when the effect of the overt speculation as to the limits of the territory sold was to be arrested or restricted by any separate agreement between the original parties. Yet this course was not pursued. So far from it, Spain, in finally notifying through her minister here a relinquishment of her opposition to the assignment of Louisiana to the United States and consequently to the title of France as derived from the treaty itself, never gave the least intimation of any other secret articles or engagements whatever which were to qualify the descriptions of boundaries contained in the text of the treaty, fully acquiescing thereby in the meaning of the text according to the ordinary rules of expounding it." [1]

Spain insisted that she possessed West Florida not as Louisiana but as Florida; the notoriety of which derived confirmation from the titles of governors of Louisiana who were recognized as "governors of Louisiana and West Florida," thus distinguishing that part of the territory in question, "which from the circumstance of its situation was also placed under their command." This was evidenced by the title of the governors of the Havanna who in their character of captain generals have always governed under the title of "Captain generals of the two Floridas."

"Under a treaty of retrocession," argued D'Yrujo, "France could not hope that what we had never received from her should be returned to her: and the American government ought not to forget the epoch at which the king of Spain made the acquisition of this province at the expense of his treasures, of the blood of his subjects, and for the benefit of the American people.

"The expression which follows is less explicit but its meaning is evident from that of the passage which precedes it and from that improbability and even impossibility which would result from a vague and general sense. I allude to the following: 'Et qu'elle avait lorsque la France la possedait.' It is manifest that this indefinite expression can only refer to the period at which Spain delivered Louisiana to France because if a greater extent were sought to be given to it the other part of the third article could

---

1. Vol. VI, Instructions, p. 302, Madison to John Armstrong, June 6, 1805.

not take place which says that it be delivered 'avec la même étendue qu'elle a actuellement entre les mains de l'Espagne.' It is clear that if it were to be given with more 'étendue' it could not be 'la même qu'elle a actuellement entre les mains de l'Espagne.' Moreover any person who has any knowledge of the history of this country knows that France possessed formerly under the name of Louisiana a great part of the territories which now form the Western states. If, therefore, the sense of the said expression were to be admitted in its greatest latitude it would follow that Spain had obliged herself by the above mentioned third article to deliver to France a part of the states of Kentucky, Tennessee, the whole new state of Ohio, the Indiana Territory, etc., an absurd but necessary consequence if the interpretation were taken which some persons seem inclined to give to the expression 'lorsque la France la possedait.' "[1]

M. Laussat, the French envoy at New Orleans, who had delivered the province of Louisiana to Governor Claiborne and General Wilkinson, took no step while the province was in his hands, or at the time he transferred it to this country, calculated to dispossess Spain of any part of the territory east of the Mississippi. On the contrary in a private conference he stated positively that no part of the Floridas was included in the eastern boundary: France, having strenuously sought to have it extended to the Mobile, was peremptorily refused by Spain.[2]

In support of the claim of his government, D'Yrujo quoted to Madison from a journal published in the winter of 1803-04 by Ellicott, whom we recall as the perniciously patriotic representative of the United States on the boundary commission of the treaty of 1795, appointed by rea-

---

1. Vol. I, D'Yrujo to Secretary of State, March 7, 1804.
2. Vol. VI, Instructions, p. 188, Madison to Livingston, Jan. 31, 1804.

son of his reputation for knowledge of astronomy and geography. Speaking of the treaty of purchase of Louisiana in his journal, he said: "By the cession of Louisiana to the United States we gain but little on the Gulf of Mexico and are but little benefited as a maritime people. The important and safe harbors in both the Floridas still remain in the possession of his Catholic Majesty." [1]

In a letter to General Armstrong, Talleyrand states the French position: "Now it was stipulated in her treaty of the year 1801 that the acquisition of Louisiana by France was a retrocession, that is to say that Spain restored to France what she had received from her in 1762. At that period she had received the territory bounded on the east by the Mississippi, the river Iberville, the lakes Maurepas and Pontchartrain the same day France ceded to England by the preliminaries of peace all the territory to the eastward. Of this Spain had received no part and could therefore give back none to France. All the territory lying to the east of the Mississippi and Iberville and south of 32° north latitude bears the name of Florida. It has been constantly designated in that way during the time that Spain held it: it bears the same name in the treaty of limits between Spain and the United States: and in different notes of Mr. Livingston, of later dates than the retrocession, in which the name of Louisiana is given to the territory on the west side of the Mississippi, of Florida to that on the east side of it.

"According to this designation, thus consecrated by time, and even prior to the period when Spain began to possess the whole territory between the 31°, the Mississippi, and the sea, this country ought in good faith and justice to be distinguished from Louisiana.

"Your Excellency knows that before the preliminaries of 1762, confirmed by the treaty of 1763, the French pos-

1. D'Yrujo to Secretary of State, March 7, 1804.

sessions situated near the Mississippi extended as far from the east of this river, towards the Ohio and Illinois, as in the quarters of Mobile, and you must think it as unnatural after all the changes of sovereignty which that part of America has undergone, to give the name of Louisiana to the district of Mobile as the territory more to the north on the same bank of the river which formerly belonged to France.

"These observations, sir, will be sufficient to dispel every kind of doubt with regard to the extent of the retrocession made by Spain to France. It was under this impression that the French and Spanish plenipotentiaries negotiated and it was under this impression that I have since had occasion to give the necessary explanation, when a project was formed to take possession of it. I have laid before his Imperial Majesty the negotiations of Madrid which preceded the treaty of 1801 and his Majesty is convinced that during the whole course of these negotiations the Spanish government has constantly refused to cede any part of the Floridas even from the Mississippi to the Mobile.

"His Imperial Majesty has moreover authorized me to declare to you that at the beginning of the year XI General Bournonville was charged to open a new negotiation with Spain for the acquisition of the Floridas. This project which has not been followed by any treaty is an evident proof that France had not acquired by the treaty retroceding Louisiana the country east of the Mississippi. . . .

"He (Napoleon) saw with pain the United States commence their differences with Spain in an unusual manner, and conduct themselves towards the Floridas by acts of violence which, not being founded in right, could have no other effect but to injure its lawful owners. Such an aggression gave the more surprise to his Majesty because the United States seemed in this measure to avail themselves of their treaty with France as an authority for their proceeding, and because he could scarcely reconcile with the just opinion which he entertains of the wisdom and fidelity of the federal government a course of proceeding which nothing can authorize towards a power which has long occupied and still occupies one of the first ranks in Europe." [1]

In a letter to M. le Chevalier de Santivanes, 5 Germinal, XIII, Talleyrand said: "His Majesty having no pretensions but to the territory situated to the west of the Mississippi and of the River Iberville, (he) has not authorized his commissary at New Orleans to take possession of any other province and he did not cede any other to the United States." General Armstrong in a letter to Pinckney speaks of approaching Talleyrand, whose laconic and decisive answer was that "the more they considered the subject the more France was convinced Spain was right on every question of the controversy with us." This statement on the part of France called forth a vigorous and indignant letter from Monroe to Bournonville. "Like you, I have been a soldier," he writes, "have fought for my country, and am accustomed to speak with freedom. Permit me to ask on what principle can France say anything respecting the limits of Louisiana after refusing to do it in her treaty with us, and inserted the third article of the treaty of San Ildefonso as the only rule by which we were to ascertain them? She did not insert the limits then because she did not know them. If she knew them then why did she not tell us of them? Is it proper to come forward now and give definition of any part to our prejudice, which was then withheld, after we have executed the treaty with so much good faith?" [2]

1. Vol. VII, United States Ministers at Spain to the Secretary of State, p. 49, Talleyrand to Armstrong, Dec. 21, 1804.

2. Vol. VII, Ministers at Spain to Secretary of State, p. 263, Monroe to Gen. Bournonville, May 23, 1805.

The cession of Louisiana was limited by three conditions:

(1) The territory was ceded "with the same extent that it now has in the hands of Spain and (2) that it had when France possessed it; and (3) such as it should be after the treaties subsequently entered into between Spain and other states." In all instruments the first law of construction is consistency. These conditions then are to be interpreted consistently with each other.

"With the same extent that it now has in the hands of Spain." The two Floridas belonged to Spain but hers was a title secured in 1783 from England. This title extinguished all French claims, for by the treaty of 1763 France had ceded all east of the Mississippi to England. Following the language of the English proclamation of 1763 Spain maintained, after 1783, the divisions of East and West Florida. In the old maps, as of D'Anville, Florida is mentioned in the singular and Louisiana was commonly made at the same time to cover a large space of country to the east of the Mississippi. But in the later maps when the "Floridas" have been spoken of in the plural number, Louisiana is bounded on the east by the Mississippi. There is no need here to repeat the arguments already set forth to show that under Spain the Floridas extended to the Mississippi, and that the province west of that river was known as Louisiana.

By the Family Compact of the Bourbons, the treaty of August 15, 1761, it was agreed between France and Spain that whoever attacked one crown attacked the other. Spain thus joined France in her war against Great Britain, but, losing Havana and Cuba, the Bourbon allies were soon convinced that it was best for both to bring the war to a termination. Now by the Family Compact it had been agreed that when the war was concluded they should balance the advantages which one might have received against

the losses of the other. But so disastrous had been the
fortunes of war that, when the peace of 1762-63 was negotiated, France possessed no balance of advantages to offer
to England for the restoration of Havana and Cuba to
Spain. France therefore determined to give up one of
her own unconquered provinces in order to secure a fair
peace for her ally: this province was Louisiana which then
crossed the Mississippi to the east. This was to be transferred to Spain on condition of her joining with France in
making over to England everything to the east of the Mississippi, England having consented to receive the territory
thus bounded as the equivalent of her Spanish conquests.
It seems to have been arranged with the Spanish envoy
at Paris that the formal offer of Louisiana to his court
should take place on the very day (November 3, 1762)
when this territory was offered to England. France appears merely to have offered and not at that time to have
ceded Louisiana to Spain: further, the cession of Florida
to England was open to recall, the preliminaries not having
been ratified. But Louisiana with its new limits was accepted by Spain on the thirteenth of November, 1763, though
Spain did not receive possession until 1769, and also by
ratification of the preliminaries with England on the twenty-
second of November, 1763.

These then were not only contemporary but also connected transactions, all to be established together or all to
be rejected together. But all being established together,
the acceptance of Louisiana is to be considered as operating back to the date of the offer, while the ratification
of the preliminaries equally extends back to the date of
signing them.

It is true that the treaty reads "in the same extent that
it had when France possessed it." These words are followed by others creating a limitation upon them "such as
it should be after the treaties subsequently entered into

between Spain and other states." Let us observe the effect
of this clause upon the former. "Subsequently" must relate to any foreign state except France. 'Since France as
a monarchy held Louisiana, Spain had made at least two
treaties, the one of cession to England in 1762-63, and the
other of arrangement with the United States in 1795.
By the first treaty the boundaries of Louisiana and the two
Floridas were formed and by the second they were acknowledged — the Mississippi being the eastern limit of
the one and the western limit of the other. The province
of Louisiana to the west of the Mississippi had not been the
subject of any treaty by Spain. There seems to exist an
opposite design of each of the clauses. The first evidently meant that Napoleon was to receive Louisiana (that
is to the west of the Mississippi) as France held it during
the monarchy without regard to any alterations of its shape
produced by any colonial or governmental regulations on
the part of Spain.

The second clause was designed to secure to Spain the
boundaries which it had both given to and received back
from England as the western boundary of the Floridas.
It was further designed to establish those concessions which
had been made to the United States by the treaty of 1795.
This interpretation of the two clauses seems to be the only
one possible to secure even a measure of consistency. [1]

At the end of the French war or contest for colonial
possession, French power was gone. By the treaty of
peace France gave to England Nova Scotia, Acadia, Cape
Breton, Canada, all the islands and all the coasts of the
Gulf and River St. Lawrence, and divided her possessions
in what is now the United States into two grand divisions:
the line of partition was the Mississippi River to the Iberville, thence through the Iberville to Lake Maurepas and

---

1. Remarks on a Dangerous Mistake made as to the Eastern
Boundary of Louisiana, by Benjamin Vaughan, published 1814.

along the north shore of Lakes Maurepas and Pontchartrain to the Gulf of Mexico. All to the east she ceded to England, all to the west to Spain. England divided this cession which she had received: from the junction of the Yazoo and Mississippi rivers she drew a line due east along a parallel to the Appalachicola and down that river to the Gulf of Mexico and named that country West Florida. To what we know as the state of Florida, east of the Appalachicola, she gave the name of East Florida. For twenty years these boundaries remained untouched: in 1783 Great Britain made the northern boundary of West Florida the parallel of 31° from the Mississippi to the Appalachicola and gave the Floridas to Spain.

In all truth Spain received East and West Florida from England, not from France. By the treaty of San Ildefonso Spain agreed to return to France what she had received from that country in 1762 and not what England had given her in 1783.

But Jefferson and Madison read otherwise: they said that in 1800 West Florida belonged to Spain: West Florida was at one time a part of Louisiana: in 1800 Spain receded Louisiana to France: therefore she receded West Florida. That France had once owned West Florida, that Frenchmen had built Mobile and Biloxi, that French authority had once been recognized on the Perdido, sufficed for Jefferson and Madison — West Florida they were determined to have. If we apply to this treaty the rules which we apply to a real estate transaction of lesser magnitude in private life, the inconsistent, untenable claims of our government become apparent.

It is safe to say that had England or France or some equally virile power, capable of resisting and avenging all encroachments, been in possession of Florida, our course in this dispute would have been far less aggressive. But Spain, poverty stricken and oppressed at home, incapable of resisting pressure abroad — of her we had no fear, and having no fear we proceeded as our interests rather than our conscience dictated. And should Spain resist, should war follow, would it not be even more welcome than peaceable submission or ineffectual protest, for thereby we would acquire East Florida as well, and perchance more?

CHAPTER V.

WEST FLORIDA AND LATER NEGOTIATIONS.

ON EVERY side the officials of the United States were urged to present a bold front and insist upon our alleged rights to West Florida. "I think there can be no doubt of your right to go to the Mobile," writes Livingston, though admitting that the country between that and the Perdido had always been unsettled between France and Spain. [1] At any rate he advised Madison to take advantage of the ambiguity in the treaty by seizing West Florida as far as the Perdido. "The time is particularly favorable to enable you to do it without the slightest risk at home," said he. "With this in your hand East Florida will be of little moment and will be yours whenever you please. At all events proclaim your right and take possession."

In fact the dispute as to the eastern boundary of Louisiana was but a small portion of the difficulty. All of the boundaries of that province were uncertain. The southern boundary was the gulf, but whether it went to the Sabine or the Rio Bravo was not known. The mountains, wherever they were, constituted the western limit and the English possessions equally uncertain were understood to bound it on the north.

Monroe's advice was as belligerent as that of Livingston. "Take possession of both of the Floridas and the whole country west of the Mississippi to the Rio Bravo

---

1. R. R. Livingston to Secretary of State (Madison), May 3, 1804.

unless it be thought better to rest at the Colorado: though
we think the broader the ground the better. In this view
all Spanish posts should be broken up within those limits.
On that ground we might negotiate. The refusal to pay
for the suppression of the deposit and for Spanish spoliations would justify taking possession of East Florida. The
refusal to compromise the affair of the western limits, of
French spoliations, and of West Florida gives a fair right
at least to take what belongs to us." [1] This sounds bellicose, especially from the mild and diplomatic Monroe.
But he was firmly convinced that France was supporting
Spain in some ulterior scheme and that our course must
be a bold one: decisive action alone would preserve any
hope of securing Spanish spoliations due to the French
cruisers, the suppression of the deposit, and our claim to
West Florida.

In 1804 Monroe proceeded to Madrid to press negotiations with the Spanish ministry for the sale of Florida, the
settlement of spoliation claims, and determination of boundaries. He was instructed not to consent to the perpetual
relinquishment of any territory whatever eastward of the
Rio Bravo. The zone idea was suggested as a favorable
method of preventing encroachments by either Spanish or
American settlers. As the United States secured further information concerning Louisiana she became more averse to
the occlusion for any long period of a "very wide space of
territory" westward of the Mississippi. If the Rio Bravo
could be made the limit of the Spanish settlements and the
river Colorado the limit to which those of the United States
might be extended: and a line northwest or west from the
source of whatever river might be taken for the limit of
our settlements to the junction of the Osage with the Missouri, and thence northward parallel with the Mississippi,
with an interval to be unsettled for a term of years — such

1. Vol. VII, Monroe to Madison, May 25, 1805.

was our aim.[1] The question of a European war it was understood would determine the advisability of pressing these matters. The perpetual relinquishment of the territory between the Rio Bravo and Colorado was not to be made: no money was to be paid in consideration of the acknowledgment by Spain of our title to the territory between the Iberville and the Perdido. If neither the whole nor part of East Florida could be obtained it was deemed important that the United States should own the territory so far as the Appalachicola and have common if not exclusive right to navigate that stream. Great care was to be exercised that the relinquishment by Spain of the territory westward of the Perdido be so expressed as to give to the American title the date of the treaty of San Ildefonso.

In the summer of 1804 the report of a clash between Spain and the United States in the territory in dispute had reached Europe and, being published in the English gazettes, was given general credence. "Be assured the only way to deal with this government is to be firm and show them you are determined to support your rights and they will give way immediately," writes Pinckney from Madrid, who a short time later was given leave to return home after Monroe had been designated to take his place.[2]

In the meantime France had arrayed herself on the side of Spain in such manner that that nation was neither permitted nor disposed to grant our claims either with respect to West Florida or the French spoliations. The alternative to a successful issue of the negotiations was declared by Madison to be war, or a state of things guarding against war for the present and leaving our claims to be hereafter effectuated.

---

1. Vol. VI, Instructions, p. 244, to James Monroe and Charles Pinckney, July 8, 1804.

2. Vol. VI, Pinckney to Madison, Oct. 8, 1804.

"It may be fairly presumed," wrote Madison, "considering the daily increase of our faculties for a successful assertion of our rights by force that neither the nation nor its representatives would prefer an instant resort to arms, to a state of things which would avoid it without hazarding our rights or our reputation. The two articles essential in such a state of things are, first a forebearance on the part of Spain as well as of the United States to augment their settlements or strengthen in any manner their military establishments within the controverted limits, secondly not to obstruct the free communication from our territories through the Mobile and other rivers mouthing in the Gulf of Mexico, or through the Mobile at least. . . . .

"I forbear to repeat the grounds on which the right of the United States to the use of those rivers is to be placed. They are already in the archives at Madrid; more effect, however, is to be expected from the necessity which a refusal of the navigation will impose on the United States to enforce their claim than from any appeal to the principles which support it; and this necessity must be permitted to impress itself fully on the Spanish councils." [1]

In the meantime Pinckney and Monroe had made their final propositions for a treaty to M. Cevallos. If his Catholic Majesty would cede the territory eastward of the Mississippi and arbitrate the claims of the citizens and subjects of each power according to the convention of 1802, as yet unratified by Spain, the United States agreed to make the Colorado River the boundary between Louisiana and Spain, ceding all right to any territory westward of that line. Further they offered to establish a district of territories, of thirty leagues on each side of that line, or on the American side only, from the Gulf of Mexico to the northern boundary of Louisiana, to remain forever neutral and unsettled, and to relinquish the claim to spoliations which were committed by the French within the jurisdiction of Spain in the course of the last war — the United States to compensate the parties in a sum to be specified, and to re-

1. Vol. VI, Instructions, p. 295, Madison to Monroe, May 23, 1805.

linquish all claim for injuries growing out of the suppression of the deposit at New Orleans.[1]

The special mission ended the latter part of May, 1805, by the total rejection in the highest tone by Spain of every proposition made. She refused to pay a shilling or even to arbitrate the French spoliations: she refused to yield a single foot of West Florida: she insisted on a line between the Adaes and Natchitoches to cut the Red River as the western limit of Louisiana: and she refused to ratify the convention of 1802.[2]

We are inclined to wonder at and at the same time to applaud the firm stand taken by Spain at this time. Attacked by ravishing famine and devastating pestilence, drained of every farthing by her French ally and master, and buffeted about by France and England, an object of pitiable contempt to all Europe, her position was doubly grievous. Yet it was France rather than Spain that refused us, for French councils were predominant at the court of Madrid. Spain, naturally haughty and slow in her movements, was extremely jealous and fearful of the United States. She accused this country of all manner of ulterior designs to which, since the days of the Miranda plot, we had given little thought. She suspected that we looked with wistful eye to her rich but feeble dominions in our neighborhood, and this suspicion it had been the policy of other nations to excite and encourage. Pinckney was convinced that with the commencement of war our affairs at Madrid would take a more favorable turn: once persuaded that war was inevitable she would sell Florida to us rather than see it falling — as it must — without opposition into the hands of England. "Spain is saving Florida as a means

1. Vol. VII, Letters of Ministers to Secretary of State, p. 231. Pinckney and Monroe to Cevallos, May 12, 1805.
2. Vol. VI, Pinckney to Madison, May 28, 1805.

of settling our claims and riveting our affection and friendship." [1]

Jefferson and Madison, in their instructions to Livingston, seem to have lost sight entirely of the true character of the French government at that time. To talk of France being bound to us "no less by sound policy than by a regard to right" is but childish prattle and inane stupidity when we stop to consider for a moment the man then at the head of the French government. Does any one suppose that Napoleon stands out in history as the exponent of "sound policy" or "regard for right?" Well might Madison write these dawdling sentiments, but of what weight were they? He might dilate upon the necessity of France preserving our friendship, but what of it? For France it was Spain or the United States, and there could be no American friendship as long as there were grounds for dispute between Spain and this country.

It amounted to nothing if Madison did insist that a transfer from Spain to the United States of the territory claimed by us, or rather of the whole of both Floridas, was nothing more than a completion of the policy which led France to cede Louisiana. Two conditions alone could have induced Napoleon to favor such a transfer; the first to prevent the province from falling into the hands of her inveterate enemy England, the second that of financial considerations — the same causes which had induced the sale of Louisiana. We are forced to believe that Napoleon sought to convert the negotiations with Spain at this time into a pecuniary job for France and her agents. Cash was desired as a consideration for a transfer — not such intangible arrangements as a release of spoliation claims or of trading one country for another.

In a letter to Breckenridge, under date of August 12, 1803, Jefferson wrote: "Objections are raising to the east-

1. Pinckney to Madison, Jan. 24, 1804.

ward against the vast extent of our boundaries and propositions are made to exchange Louisiana or a part of it for the Floridas. But as I have said we shall get the Floridas without and I would not give one inch of waters of the Mississippi to any nation, because I see in a light very important to our peace the exclusive right to its navigation and the admission of no nation into it." [1]

Jefferson's decision was strongly upheld by his advisors and counsellors. "The United States," writes James Bowdoin from Paris, "should pursue that line of conduct which best comports with their present interest, regardless of the views or feelings of this or the Spanish government. I take it they are neither in a situation to bring their force to bear nor in a condition to go to war with the United States, and that our commerce is absolutely necessary to both, from which I infer that if they should be pressed to the alternative of an open rupture or to yield the points in controversy they will be obliged to give way. . . . . The United States can have nothing to fear from these governments, especially the Spanish, by a decisive line of conduct." [2]

General Armstrong and Monroe, after conferring on the situation, likewise advised a measure of decision and tone as necessary, as well to our safety as to our honor, adding however, a word of caution lest we compromise ourselves with France, for by her treaties that country was bound to assist Spain in any and all wars. They wrote:

"It has occurred to us that the following might probably have effect: to take possession of the whole country westward of the Mississippi to the Rio Bravo, removing the Spanish posts that are on this side of it. To say nothing at present about the eastern side, the law remaining of course in force: to have a force at command in Tennessee and Georgia ready to take the Floridas at pleasure, being

1. Jefferson's Works, Vol. IV, p. 499.
2. Vol. IX, James Bowdoin to Madison, Dec. 2, 1805.

resolved not to permit the force of Spain or France to be increased there: that a power should be given to the president to suspend all intercourse with the Spanish colonies to be exercised at his discretion and indeed an adequate power over the whole subject. . . . . The above is the mildest course which it would in my judgment be proper to take, and in taking it, it ought to be understood that if the terms we demanded were not peremptorily accepted it was only a commencement of a system of others more decisive and important. . . . . If we are firm I have great confidence in our success and almost on our own terms, much better than those limited above. Be firm also in sustaining our claims to the Rio Bravo. A contrary doctrine should not be listened to."

Monroe also earnestly recommended the immediate suspension of D'Yrujo for its moral effect on Spain, that luckless minister having been guilty of some further indiscretions which had aroused the executive animosity. [1] Pinckney advocated stirring up public feeling in the United States in favor of annexing Florida so as to make the more impression on Spain and induce her to arrange a transfer. [2]

Let us take up the negotiations more in particular and watch their progress.

Demand was made on Spain for indemnity after the close of the first Napoleonic war. Numbers of American vessels had been condemned by French consuls resident in Spain. French privateers had been fitted out in Spanish ports to capture American vessels. Under pretense of a blockade of Gibraltar, Spanish subjects had seized every American vessel that had come for a convoy through the Mediterranean. Spain was ready to make redress for the depredations of her own subjects but she absolutely declined to consider the question of paying for the French misdemeanors. Finally the American minister, unable to secure better terms, gave way and the convention was

---

1. Vol. VII, p. 269, Monroe to Madison, June 30, 1805.
2. Pinckney to Madison, Aug. 24, 1805.

framed. This provided for the spoliations by the Spanish subjects but left the question of French spoliations for future settlement. The senate refused to ratify the convention thus drawn up and the American minister was directed to press negotiations at Madrid for a broader treaty. Again Spain refused to consider the American demand. Meanwhile D'Yrujo, noting the attitude of the senate upon the subject, submitted the questions in dispute to five eminent lawyers of this country for their decision. Jared Ingersoll and William Rawle, leaders of the Philadelphia bar, Stephen du Ponceau, Edward Livingston, and Joseph B. McKean, governor of Pennsylvania and brother-in-law of D'Yrujo, constituted the notable tribunal to which was referred the justice of the demand of the United States.

Concealing the names of the powers, D'Yrujo stated the case:

"The power A (Spain) lives in perfect harmony and friendship with power B (United States). The power C (France) either with reason or without reason commits hostilities against the subjects of the power B, takes some of their vessels, carries them into the ports of A, friend to both, where they are condemned and sold by the official agents of power C without power A's being able to prevent it. At last a treaty is entered into by which the powers B and C adjust their differences and in this treaty the power B renounces and abandons to power C the right to any claim for the injuries and losses occasioned to its subjects by the hostilities from power C."

Having thus stated the case, D'Yrujo asked:

"Has the power B any right to call upon the power A for indemnities for the losses occasioned in its ports and coasts to its subjects by those of the power C after the power B has abandoned or relinquished by its treaty with C its right for the damages which could be claimed for the injuries sustained from the hostile conduct of the power C?"

Each of these five lawyers replied in an unqualified negative. To the Spanish arguments the United States replied:

"The only supposition on which Spain could turn us over to France would be that of her being in a state of absolute duress, of her being merely the staff by which the blow was given by France. But even on this supposition the injuries done by France through Spain could not by any interpretation be confounded with the injuries released to France by which could be meant such injuries only as proceeded from her own immediate responsibility and as were in the ordinary course of things chargeable on her.

"The last plea under which refuge has been sought by Spain against the justice of our claims is the opinion of four or five American lawyers given on a case stated, without doubt, by some one of her own agents: an argument of this sort does not call for refutation: but for regret that the Spanish government did not see how little such an appeal from the ordinary and dignified discussions of the two governments by their regular functionaries, to the authority of private opinions and of private opinions so obtained, was consistent with the respect it owed to itself or with that which it owed to the government of the United States: that it did not even reflect on the reply so obvious that four or five private opinions, however respectable as such, could have no weight against the probability that others had been consulted whose opinions were not the same and that if the government here could descend to the experiment, little difficulty could be found in selecting more numerous authorities of the same kind not only in the United States but among the jurists of Spain." [1]

When the convention and the letters showing the course of D'Yrujo were laid before the senate in December, 1803, that body was indignant and less than ever disposed to ratify the instrument. The question of the Floridas was now urgent and to render possible new negotiations with Spain the treaty was at length approved,

1. Vol. VI, Instructions, p. 199, Madison to Pinckney, Feb. 6, 1804.

though not without many eloquent expressions of disapproval and indignation. [1]

Duly signed and ratified it was shortly dispatched to Charles Pinckney at Madrid. He at once carried it to Don Pedro Cevallos, the Spanish minister of foreign affairs, expecting its prompt approval as a matter of course. True to his Spanish training, Cevallos hesitated and delayed. Meanwhile a copy of the Mobile act had come to hand. Cevallos at once declared it a violation of Spanish sovereignty, demanded an explanation from Pinckney and consumed a month in a profitless interchange of notes. [2] At length he agreed to name definitely the conditions on which Spain would consent to ratify the convention. Time must be given to the subjects of Spain having claims against the United States, to prepare and submit them: the sixth article in reference to damages inflicted by French cruisers upon American shipping must be eliminated, the act setting up the custom district in West Florida must be repealed. [3]

Pinckney, losing all sense of diplomacy and policy, in a delirium of rage wrote a threatening and insolent letter to Cevallos seeking enlightenment on "just one question." If the sixth article were not suppressed would Spain refuse to ratify the convention? An early reply was demanded as he proposed immediately to send messengers to all the American consuls in Spain and to the commander of the American squadron in the Mediterranean, to inform them of the critical posture, to bid them warn all ships and be prepared to quit Spain at a minute's warning. [4] Cevallos, though doubtless impressed by our minister's attitude, coolly replied that he did not believe Pinckney's instructions war-

1. January 9, 1804. Journal of Executive Proceedings of the Senate, Vol. I, pp. 461, 462.
2. Cevallos to Pinckney, May 31, 1804.
3. Cevallos to Pinckney, July 2, 1804.
4. Pinckney to Cevallos, July 5, 1804.

ranted such action and transferred all negotiations from Madrid to Washington.[1] Not in the least perturbed by Cevallos's answer, Pinckney dispatched the couriers and gave notice that as soon as his affairs could be arranged he should demand his passports and quit the Spanish court.

In October news of the developments at Madrid reached Washington followed by a request for Pinckney's recall; this request was granted and Monroe ordered to Madrid.[2] But Monroe was already on his way. After the Louisiana treaty of 1803 had been concluded Monroe prepared to join Pinckney at Madrid. But the reception of that treaty at the Spanish court led the French officials to insist that he alter his course.[3] Following their advice he remained at Paris and while there, was commissioned minister plenipotentiary at London in place of Rufus King. In July he reached London and immediately took up the impressment question with the English government. Orders now came to proceed to Madrid.

Four things he was directed to accomplish; induce Spain to recognize the Perdido as the eastern boundary of Louisiana; persuade her to sell her possessions east of the Perdido for $2,000,000; secure the payment of our claims for condemnations by the French courts on Spanish soil; insist on the right of the United States to Texas. If Spain refused to yield the last point he was authorized to waive the question of the western boundary of Louisiana and consent to establish a neutral zone into which people of neither power should be permitted to emigrate. The eastern limit of this belt should be the Sabine River from its mouth to its source; a straight line to the junction of the Osage and Missouri, and a line parallel to the Mississippi River to the northern boundary. On the west side the

1. Cevallos to Pinckney, July 8, 1804.
2. Madison to Monroe, Oct. 26, 1804.
3. Monroe to Madison, July 20, 1805. Monroe to Talleyrand, Nov. 8, 1804. Foreign Relations, Vol. II, p. 634.

limit was fixed at the Rio Colorado to its source; thence
a line to the most southwesterly branch of the Red River;
the highlands parting the beds of the Missouri and Mississippi from those of the Rio Bravo as far as the source
of the Rio Bravo and a meridian to the northern
boundary.   No inducement should prevail upon him
to give up our claim to the Rio Bravo nor to consent
that the neutral belt should exist for more than twenty years;
later he was instructed to secure the Rio Bravo as the limit
of Spanish, and the Rio Colorado of American settlement
but not to give up the intervening territory forever. [1]

Proceeding to Madrid by way of Paris, Monroe there
sought to enlist French assistance for his undertaking.   He
was not long in learning the attitude of the French government on the question.   He saw that it was a financial matter.   "Spain," he was told, "must cede territory; the United
States must pay money."   Marbois informed him that for
a suitable compensation Spain might be induced to comply.
No official encouragement was given him; in fact he saw
that France was unmistakably hostile to his mission.   Hastening to Madrid he lost no time in presenting to Cevallos
a project for a treaty in line with his instructions.   Politely
refusing the project which had been submitted to him,
Cevallos replied that a plan of treaty should result from a
negotiation on the points in issue under three heads — general spoliation claims, the subject of the damages caused by
the suspension of the deposit at New Orleans, and the Louisiana boundaries.

After a fruitless discussion of the subject of indemnity
that matter was passed and the eastern boundary of Louisiana taken up.   After several weeks of profitless conferences they passed to a discussion of the western boundary.
Cevallos proposed to fix a point on the gulf of Mexico
between the Calcasieu and Marmenton rivers and draw a

---

1.   Madison to Monroe and Pinckney, July 8, 1804.

line northward between the Spanish post of Nuestra Senora
de los Adaes and the French post of Natchitoches on the
Red River, where the line should then run to be determined
by a commission.[1] The reply was, while the United States
were persuaded that they owned to the Rio Bravo, they
would nevertheless accept the Rio Colorado on two conditions; if Spain would ratify the convention of 1802 and
cede the two Floridas, the United States would waive all
other claims for damages and as a western boundary establish a neutral zone thirty miles wide on one or both sides
of a line to be the Colorado to its source, to the most southwesterly source of the Red River, thence along the high
lands parting the Missouri and Mississippi rivers from the
Rio Bravo, and a meridian to the northern boundary of
Louisiana.[2] Cevallos declaring these terms to be utterly
unreasonable, the correspondence terminated. Monroe demanded his passports, and was within a few days well on
his way to London.

The most favorable terms which he could secure were
manifestly of French dictation; a loan of seventy million
livres to be given to Spain and when Spain had transferred
it to France the United States should receive from Spain
the disputed territory; the money was to be repaid by in-
stalments in seven years.[3] Pinckney having received his
recall prepared to leave but was delayed some months, for
every mule had been seized for the use of the king and
other means of transportation could not be secured. In the
meantime James Bowdoin of Massachusetts was appointed
to take his place as minister to the court of Spain.

Jefferson, having been informed that all negotiations at
Madrid were broken off, turned first to Madison and

---

1. Cevallos to Pinckney and Monroe, April 13, 1805.
2. Pinckney and Monroe to Cevallos, May 12, 1805. Foreign Relations, Vol. II, p. 665.
3. Monroe's Diary at Aranjuez, April 22, 1805. MSS. State Department.

then to the other members of his cabinet for advice. Madison favored dropping the questions which had caused the dispute, taking up others as yet untouched by the mission and reopening negotiations anew at Madrid. Gallatin counseled peace — a war would cost more than Florida was worth. He thought the boundaries should have been settled when the Louisiana treaty was made; since this had not been done the Sabine and Perdido should be accepted, the militia improved and one million dollars appropriated for building ships of the line, and, with this as a threat, negotiations renewed.[1] Smith advised more gun-boats, twelve new seventy-fours, and, if necessary, an English alliance with war against France and Spain.[2] Jefferson himself inclined strongly to an alliance with England, stipulating that peace should not be made with France and Spain until West Florida and the spoliation claims had been secured.[3]

Various other counsels were offered. Armstrong, from Paris, urged Jefferson to seize Texas and break off all intercourse with Spain. This plan seemed most feasible to the president. Congress was to be asked for power to drive the Spanish out of Texas, to sever diplomatic relations at will, and provide a commission to determine the amount of our spoliation claims. Monroe, Livingston, and Pinckney offered similar advice — their single theme was a bold and determined line of conduct. Jefferson's decision was strengthened by news from the southwest. From Claiborne, governor of the Mississippi Territory, and Wilkinson, commander of the army, came reports that the garrisons of Mobile and Baton Rouge had been strengthened; that a fort had been erected in Trinity River; a new governor general had reached San Antonio; a large number of families from old Spain

---

1. Gallatin to Jefferson, Sept. 12, 1805. Gallatin's Works, Vol. I, p. 241.
2. Robert Smith to Jefferson, Sept. 10, 1805.
3. Jefferson to Madison, Aug. 4 and 17, 1805. Madison MSS. Department, Aug. 27, 1805. Jefferson's Works, Vol. IV, p. 585.

were on the way to settle in Texas; troops were being massed at Nacogdoches and Matagorda; that Spanish soldiers had led foraging expeditions into Louisiana and Mississippi, stealing horses and abusing Americans; that every American vessel attempting to pass through the Mobile was forced to pay duty of twelve per cent. on the value of the cargo even when it belonged to the United States.

But before Jefferson's plan could be definitely formulated and communicated a sudden combination of circumstances changed everything. Each day brought word of some new outrage committed by England upon our citizens. Our seamen were impressed, our ports blockaded, and our ships overhauled and examined; Monroe was neglected at London, and Armstrong insulted at Paris, and, to determine finally the question, a London packet brought the news that an added restriction had been placed upon neutral trade, that eighteen American merchantmen had been already condemned, and that the condemnation of thirty more was immediately expected. No English alliance could now be considered. The policy of overawing Napoleon must be given up. After a conference with the members of his cabinet he decided to appeal to France for assistance in the Spanish negotiations. Armstrong was to inform Napoleon that one more attempt would be made to secure a peaceable settlement and to ask him to lay before Spain three propositions:

To sell the two Floridas for five million dollars; the United States to cede to Spain Louisiana from the Rio Grande to the Guadeloupe; Spain to pay to the United States all spoliations committed under her flag. A letter was dispatched to Governor Claiborne directing that the Marquis de Casa Culvo and all other persons holding commissions or retained in the service of his Catholic Majesty

11

be ordered to quit New Orleans as soon as possible, and in such terms as to leave no room for further discussion.[1]

Word from Armstrong at this time encouraged Jefferson in his determination to reopen negotiations. During the summer an anonymous agent of the French government came to him with an unsigned letter from Talleyrand suggesting another note to Spain of no uncertain tone and calculated to rouse that country from her lethargic indifference. She should be warned that to persist in her refusal to treat could only mean war, and arbitration should be suggested. Should Spain agree to this, Armstrong, according to the program, should address Talleyrand asking the Emperor Napoleon to serve as arbitrator. Napoleon would decree, it was intimated in unmistakable terms, that the Floridas should go to the United States in return for ten million dollars; the Rio Colorado to its source and the northwest line heading all the waters flowing into the Mississippi should be the western boundary of Louisiana; a strip thirty leagues each side of this line should be a neutral zone forever; the spoliation claims were to be settled by Spain and she should have the same commercial rights in Florida that she then enjoyed in Louisiana and New Orleans. Armstrong after decidedly rejecting these terms — refusing even to communicate them to his government — was a few days later given an audience with the emperor and informed that the sum should be seven millions instead of ten. This offer appearing more reasonable, Armstrong agreed to forward it to America. The matter was laid before the cabinet and debated most carefully; the Spanish troubles were reviewed and discussed from alpha to omega. All of Napoleon's propositions except one were finally approved; after mature consideration it was determined that five million dollars should be the limit of the consideration

---

1. Vol. XV, Domestic Letters, p. 52, Madison to Governor Claiborne, Nov. 18, 1805.

to emanate from this government. Further a portion of this should be canceled by the spoliation claims which approximated, it was believed, three million dollars.

The other two millions must be secured from congress. Secrecy above all things was essential. To name publicly the inducements would be to invite a refusal. Gathering the Spanish papers Jefferson transmitted them to congress without any hint of his purpose. Summoning various members of the committee in charge of the message, the president initiated them into the secret and even drew up resolutions which he desired them to report. Congress assembled the second of December and on the following day received the message treating at length on the subject of outrages inflicted, upon the Spanish indisposition to a friendly arrangement of boundary disputes, upon their violation of our sovereignty by invading Louisiana and Mississippi and murdering our people in that quarter. More complete details he promised would shortly follow and three days later another collection of Spanish papers was submitted to a breathless and expectant house.

In obedience to the injunction of secrecy, the galleries were promptly cleared and behind closed doors the members eagerly listened to the further disclosures. But their expectation and curiosity were disappointed. To the surprise and astonishment of all, the president suggested no line of action. Neither did he make any requests. Unable to fathom the mystery, the curious house referred the papers to a select committee of which the brilliant but eccentric John Randolph of Roanoke was the chairman. Hastening to interview the president he was informed that two million dollars was wanted immediately to purchase the Floridas. A proceeding which seemed to him so irregular, Randolph declared he could not and would not support. Money he said had not been requested; and indeed if it had been, he would still have opposed such a course, for, after negotia-

tions had been suspended, to offer money would be an
everlasting disgrace to the country.[1] Some of the committee however enjoyed Jefferson's confidence to a greater
degree. Nicholson already had in his possession the resolutions which the president had· drawn up. Barnabas Bid-
well, intimating that to his mind the proper course was an
appropriation, moved a suitable grant. His motion was
lost and an adjournment of two weeks followed.

During this interval the members of the cabinet strove
manfully to turn Randolph from his obdurate course, but all
to no avail. The gentleman from Roanoke denounced the
whole plan in no measured terms. Jefferson, he declared,
should not be permitted to have two sets of principles — the
one ostensible, the other real. He should not be tolerated
publicly to urge vigorous measures while secretly advising
tame ones. He should not be allowed to appear as an
energetic executive thwarted by an unpatriotic and hesitat-
ing congress. Between losing all hope of securing the
Floridas and openly breaking with Randolph, Jefferson
chose the latter alternative, and the discerning public was
shortly aware of a schism in the dominant party. A secret
report of the committee was soon made denouncing the
hostile attitude of Spain. To a government of rulers such
a course would be considered ample cause for war. But
to a government such as ours where the rulers and people
were so closely identified, and especially to a government
with a debt which absorbed so large a portion of its revenue,
an honorable peace must ever be preferred to war. Cultivate the interests of the Union by peace until such time as
the national debt should be extinguished, that as many
troops be voted as the president should deem necessary to
defend the southern frontier and render our territory im-
mune to all incursions.

---

1. Letters of Decius No. 1, Richmond Inquirer, Aug., 1806.

Jefferson realizing the failure of his original course took a new tack and communicated his desires to other trusted members of the house who, when the report had been presented to the committee of the whole, mustered the friends of the administration and immediately submitted three resolutions. The first of these provided for a sum of money to meet such extraordinary expenditures as might be incurred in connection with our intercourse with foreign countries. This money was to be borrowed if the amount was not in the treasury. The second provided for the perpetuation of the two and one-half per cent. ad valorem duty constituting what was termed the Mediterranean fund. The third stated that congress would look with favor upon any settlement of the boundary which, while it gave Spain ample territory on the Mexican side, at the same time secured to this country the territory east of the Mississippi and the regions watered by that river. Randolph's committee report having been defeated, a bill was passed appropriating two million dollars for our negotiations with foreign powers; this was accompanied by a resolution explaining that the appropriation was made with a view to purchasing the Floridas. The senate promptly concurring, Jefferson signed the bill on the thirteenth of February.[1]

On the last day of March the injunction of secrecy was removed and the doors of congress were thrown wide open that the long confined news might sweep across the land. There had been rumors wild and incredible, but yet finding credence. In some quarters it was believed that the Louisiana stock would be confiscated, for what had seemed to be the conduct of Spain was generally credited to French domination. Others were confident that, with the removal of the mask of secrecy, would come the declaration of war. When therefore the announcement was made that two million dollars had been appropriated for the purchase of

---

1. Annuals of Congress, 1805-06, pp. 1226-27.

Florida it is said that disappointment and disgust were vividly pictured on the faces of the crowd thronging about the capitol. And as the expectant and dissatisfied multitude slowly separated, many and loud were the mutterings that Jefferson was truckling to France and bringing dishonor upon the nation.

In 1804 the hapless D'Yrujo became involved in certain transactions in this country which increased his unpopularity and resulted in instructions to our minister at Madrid to insist upon his recall. He was accused of "an attempt to debauch a citizen of the United States into a direct violation of an act of congress, and into a combination with a foreign functionary, in favor of a foreign government against the supposed measures of his own." D'Yrujo, it seems, approached Mr. Jackson, editor of the Political Register of Philadelphia, with a proposition for printing in his paper certain pro-Spanish articles. Having been so often made a target for the attacks of the newspapers and having sufficiently perused our constitution to know that there existed therein some sort of a provision for the liberty of the press, D'Yrujo conceived that its use must be a "shield of defense as it had been an instrument of attack." Having on a previous occasion been taught the futility of bringing the authors of these attacks into the courts of justice, D'Yrujo concluded to take up the same weapons. "Were the foreign ministers to be deprived of this right, enjoyed by every individual who breathes the air of the United States, they would be reduced to the sad condition of distinguished slaves in the very center of the Land of Liberty," wrote D'Yrujo to Madison. Summoning Mr. Jackson, D'Yrujo, according to his official explanation, sought to impress upon him the fact that the interests of both Spain and the United States dictated peace but that the spirit being engendered in this country forboded war. D'Yrujo requested him to publish certain "explanations and

elucidations which could not fail to be favorable to the cause
of peace and that for his trouble he would have the acknowledgment that would be proper." Jackson in sworn
affidavits promptly declared that he had detected the "infamous purpose" of the Spanish minister, crediting the
indiscreet D'Yrujo with all manner of Machiavellian deviltry. D'Yrujo blandly insisted that the acknowledgment was
intended merely as a just compensation, "which is due an
editor of a newspaper full of advertisements — for the room
that my intended essays would have occupied in his gazette,
or a reward for his labor if he was to take upon himself to
couch my ideas in a more correct language than I could do
myself." "Surely," continues D'Yrujo, "the honor of a
man who is in the habit of retailing the space of his paper
by lines should not be hurt at a just compensation which
was offered when it was a question of occupying some
columns."

To D'Yrujo it seemed comprehensible that a foreign
minister might risk an intrigue with a high officer of a
crown, depositary of the secrets of state and director of its
measures, but bribing the editor of a newspaper whose
sheets were scarcely to be seen beyond the borders of his
own city, a man without a place in the government, and
without personal influence, seemed such perfect folly as in
itself to establish his innocence. The offer of a reward
he placed in the same category as the payment of a fee to a
lawyer or a physician. [1]

Whatever may have been his purpose in this matter and
however guiltless his intentions his course was at any
rate indiscreet and his explanation was not such as to
increase his standing with the government or proclaim his
innocence to the people. D'Yrujo was further charged with
publishing certain correspondence in the papers of the day

---

1. Vol. I, Spanish Minister to Secretary of State, D'Yrujo to
Madison, Oct. 3, 1804.

and using expressions "grossly disrespectful" to the executive of the United States. The request for his immediate recall was submitted by Monroe and Pinckney to Cevallos, the Spanish foreign minister, in April, 1805.[1] Although succeeded in his official capacity by Valentine de Foronda, D'Yrujo lingered in the United States until 1807, to the indignation of Jefferson who all the while contemplated vigorous steps to relieve the country of the presence of "this troublesome foreigner."

In the spring of 1806 instructions were sent to Armstrong and Bowdoin, at Paris, to guide them in their task of securing a Spanish treaty under French auspices.

"The object of the United States," wrote Madison "is to secure West Florida which is essential to their interest and to obtain East Florida which is important to them; procuring at the same time equitable indemnities from Spain for the injuries for which she is answerable, to all of which the proposed exchange of territory and arrangement of the western boundary, may be made subservient."[2] The ministers were directed to seek, if possible, an arrangement which would involve no pecuniary consideration on the part of the United States; the project of a convention which was forwarded to them indeed made no provision for a money payment. By that instrument Spain was to confirm West Florida and cede East Florida to this country. On the west side the Colorado River should be the boundary; provision was made for a neutral zone in the southwest.

It could hardly be supposed that Napoleon would manifest any particular enthusiasm in persuading Spain to accept such a treaty. It must be conceded that his sole motive for desiring an arrangement was the idea that the United States would pay a large sum of money which would naturally gravitate into his coffers.

---

1. Vol. VII, p. 199, Pinckney and Monroe to Cevallos, April 13, 1805.
2. Vol. VI, Instructions, p. 315, Madison to Armstrong and Bowdoin, March 13, 1806.

A few months later Madison, suspecting the rejection of the terms which he had suggested, sent instructions that in such an event an arrangement be sought providing that the status quo, taking the date of the transfer of Louisiana to the United States, should be established with respect to the disputed territories on both sides of the Mississippi; neither country to strengthen or advance its military force or positions or make any other innovations unsatisfactory to the other party. The navigation of the Mobile and other rivers running from our territories through those of Spain, should be freely enjoyed by our citizens in like manner as that of the Mississippi was enjoyed by the subjects of Spain inhabiting the territory adjoining. Further that the convention of August, 1802, be allowed by Spain to go into effect. Such an arrangement, intimated Madison, could alone insure peace between the two countries and would, without any dishonorable concessions on the part of either nation, afford a time for further consideration "and for that increase of the relative power of the United States for which time alone is wanted," the last an expression pregnant with meaning. [1]

In the meantime alarming reports of the movements of Spanish forces to our southwest had reached Washington. Castilian troops had taken post at Lanans between Nacogdoches, their former most advanced post, and Natchitoches, our frontier post. Large reinforcements were said to be moving toward our forts in that quarter. Parties of dragoons were reconnoitering the disputed country and troops had been ordered from the Havana for Pensacola and Mobile. Whatever might be the motives, such activity, it was felt, could not be favorable to the tranquillity of the two nations. Even though Spain insisted that they were merely precautionary steps against the pos-

---

1. Vol VI, Instructions, p. 357, Madison to Armstrong and Bowdoin, May 26, 1806.

sibility of an attack by England, Madison declared that the cordial relations existing between this country and Great Britain were a sufficient guarantee that no hostile intrusions would be attempted, seeking to show some ulterior and hostile purpose on the part of the Spanish authorities.[1] Moreover the conduct of the Spanish in obstructing the Mobile was kindling a flame which must soon acquire proportions not to be easily resisted. The United States may soon "have no other choice than between a foreign and an internal conflict."

The conspiracy of Aaron Burr was at this time foremost in the public mind and served to call attention to our Spanish connections. What his famous plot really was cannot be definitely known. In the later years of his life he declared that he had planned to do what Houston and others later did in Texas. Andrew Jackson, notoriously hostile to Spain, being approached, gave the plan his approval, persuaded that some design against Spanish provinces was being contemplated. Otherwise we know, from his intense patriotism, that he would never have gone so far with Burr as to call out his Tennessee militia for the invasion of Texas and Mexico. With three hundred Tennessee militiamen Jackson declared he would "cut his way through those d—d greasers to the heart of Mexico." The conferences at Blennerhasett's Island, the purchase by Burr of the large Spanish grant, point in the same direction. D'Yrujo, it was confidently believed, plotted with Burr with the idea that a dismemberment of the Union was the object. The silence and manner of Turreau convinced Madison beyond doubt that he did not regard Mexico as the object. Merry, the English minister, was in the secret of the plot against the Spanish possessions and relished it, though without committing his government. These overtures to

---

1. Vol. XIV, Domestic Letters, p. 479, Madison to Governor Claiborne, Feb. 25, 1805.

Spain and France disclose a plan to sever the Union. It may be safely concluded that Burr would have stopped at nothing in an effort to retrieve his shattered fortunes and that he would adopt such a plot as augured most for success. [1]

There was much secret meeting and planning, much approaching of various western officials, much sending of cipher dispatches, purchasing of supplies and boats, and much sailing and counter-sailing on the Mississippi and Ohio rivers. And indeed for Burr's success there was too much talk and too little action, too much time spent in vain social frivolities when the cry should have been, "up and doing." Had Burr concentrated his time and his talents upon the Spanish plot and shown the ability to act quickly and decisively, history would tell a different story of the southwest. Burr's scheme was popular in that section, and familiar withal, ever since the early days of our national existence. Genet had proposed that George Rogers Clarke should call for volunteers and march upon New Orleans and the volunteers had not been slow to offer their services, nay to demand that they be accepted. And there had been other plots of a similar nature concocted in dark by-ways and conjured up in secret meetings but which had never seen the light of day. To crystallize that sentiment, organize an expedition quietly yet rapidly, and strike suddenly, before the enemy could be informed, was to spell success.

Unfortunately for himself, Burr became connected with General James Wilkinson, the commanding officer in that region, a man of whom historians even in the charity of patriotism are able to say little good. The revealed secrets of Spanish archives leave no doubt that in 1787-89, Wilkinson had contracted to devote his influence and his life to

---

1. Burr insisted that his plan against Mexico was feasible only in case of war between Spain and the United States. After Trafalgar, in 1805, Spain was helpless and war with the United States impossible. Pitt was a necessary factor in Burr's anti-Spanish plots, and with his death in 1806 they were harmless.

the end that Kentucky should be delivered to Spain. In the critical days of the Union a Castilian agent, receiving pay for his iniquity, later working against Spain, setting up brazen claims, and stooping to all manner of contemptible treachery, this is the man who later wore the epaulettes of commanding·general of the American army, when justice, with the bandage torn from her eyes, should have seen him standing before the execution squad, a condemned traitor, the companion of Benedict Arnold in the popular execration of later generations. A general of the army, an agent in Spanish pay, yet listening eagerly withal to the plots of Burr — and prepared to renounce both Spain and the United States, if Burr's schemes promised him more of personal glory or pecuniary gain. Guilty of treason, cowardly, treacherous, and corrupt, this was the man who might reveal the conspiracy and who did reveal it.

Andrew Jackson, from certain well defined rumors, was convinced of Wilkinson's traitorous conduct towards this government and wrote Governor Claiborne a letter of warning.

"Put your town in a state of defense. Organize your militia and defend your city as well against internal enemies as external. My knowledge does not extend so far as to authorize me to go into detail but I fear you will meet with an attack from quarters you do not at present expect. Be upon the alert; keep a watchful eye upon our General (Wilkinson) and beware of an attack as well from our own country as Spain. . . . . You have enemies within your own city that may try to subvert your government and try to separate it from the Union. You know I never hazard ideas without good grounds and you will keep these hints to yourself. But I say again be on the alert; your government I fear is in danger. I fear there are plans on foot inimical to the Union. Whether they will be attempted to be carried into effect or not I cannot say; but rest assured they are in operation, or I calculate boldly. Beware of the month of December. I love my country

and government. I hate the Dons; I would delight to see
Mexico reduced, but I will die in the last ditch before I
would yield a foot to the Dons or see the Union disunited.
This I write for your own eyes and for your own safety;
profit by it and the Ides of March remember." [1]

Wilkinson having betrayed his chief, the lesser associates adopted the discreet if cowardly course of seeking
shelter. And Burr, if it ever was his intention to attack the
United States, was now helpless, and, a disguised fugitive,
hoping only to reach the gulf. Detected and captured in
Alabama he was returned to Richmond to become the principal in one of the most bitter and partisan trials the country has ever known. With one accord the Federalists, the
chief fomenters of the proposed Miranda expedition, yet,
such the anomaly of events, forgetful of their great Hamilton, rushed to his defense, and sought, through this means,
to convict Jefferson of all manner of crimes and misdemeanors.

The affair took on the appearance of a worthy welcome to a returning hero rather than the trial of a man
who had been, a few-short weeks before, a hunted fugitive
in the wilds of the South. A suite of rooms was especially
prepared for his confinement and his jailers became rather
his servants. Magnificent levees were held where the leading citizens paid court to dominant high treason. Judge
and prisoner sat down together at a brilliant banquet.
Choice fruits, beautiful flowers, daintily scented notes, the
fair ladies showered upon this notorious seducer of their
sex. And can even Marshall's most ardent admirer claim
that the decisions of that eminent jurist were wholly un-
tainted by party prejudice and political passion? It must
ever remain a problem to future generations, the manner
in which leading Federalists rallied to the rescue of the
murderer whose hands were yet wet with the blood of their

1. Parton's Jackson, Vol. 1, p. 319. Jackson to Governor Claiborne, Nov. 12, 1806.

distinguished and adored Hamilton. Yet a great tribute they paid to the power of hatred, for their abhorrence of Jefferson rather than their love of Burr was the salvation of the brilliant but dissolute arch-conspirator.

But a short time before Burr's conspiracy came to a head, apparently wholly disconnected with it, Nathaniel Kemper with a body of volunteers invaded the Spanish territory to the south, arrested several alcaldes, published a proclamation calculated to excite the Spanish against their king, and endeavored to obtain possession of Baton Rouge by a *coup de main;* being driven back this knight errant had taken refuge in the territories of the United States.[1] In answer to our protest against the erection of a military road from Pensacola to Baton Rouge, on the ground that the United States claimed West Florida, the Spanish minister justified this course in part on the ground of the Kemper affair and similar incursions which had repeatedly been made into that province. The United States also found grounds for protesting to the Spanish officials, that the records and documents of Spain relating to grants of land in Louisiana had not been delivered but had been sent to Pensacola. Governor Claiborne was directed to take such legal measures as might be necessary to secure possession of them. Further reason for complaint was found in the Spanish settlements which were being established in the disputed territory to the southwest. Rumors reached Washington in the spring of 1807 of strenuous efforts on the part of the Marquis of Carondolet to alienate the people of Kentucky from their connection with the United States. These accusations, however, failed of substantiation.

In 1806 General Miranda, of uncertain fame, whom the reader will recall in connection with the plots of 1798,

1. Vol. XIV, Domestic Letters, p. 405. Madison to Governor Claiborne, Nov. 10, 1804.

appears again on the Spanish-American stage. Reaching
this country in the winter of 1805-06 he sought some encouragement and assistance in instituting a revolution in
South America. He evidently had in mind the probability
of a rupture between the United States and Spain. But
receiving scant notice from the officials of this government,
he organized and recruited a company of militia, purchased
cannon and other stores, loaded them on a chartered ship,
and, eluding the now watchful officers, set boldly to sea.
Having fitted out as on a commercial trip to San Domingo,
the true character of this venture was not known. Touching first at a French port, Miranda headed for the Spanish
possessions and military fame. This, together with the
Burr expedition, served naturally to irritate Spain who communicated to this country her determination to demand
damages. Jefferson proposed to offset the complaints of
Spain with their intrigues for the detachment of the Mississippi region from the United States and suggested the
balancing of this account and the unsettled claims of the
convention of 1802 by taking Florida. "I had rather have
war against Spain than not if we go to war with England,"
said the president. In 1808 he favored taking "our own
limits of Louisiana and the residue of the Floridas as re-
prisals for spoliations." European complications however
exerted a chastening influence upon him and decided him
to still keep peace and hold the favor of the United States
wavering between France and England.

In the spring of 1806, France was undoubtedly anxious
to secure a settlement of the Spanish-American difficulties
and arrange a sale of the Floridas. Spain was in most
desperate financial straits. Bowdoin was approached unofficially by French officers desiring to arrange a cession
of those territories to the United States for six million dollars. Their intimations induced him to believe they might
even be secured for four million. Spain owed subsidies to

Napoleon and this amount must soon find its way to Paris. But she stubbornly refused to contribute more to the French war chest. Further, the United States wished to secure the Floridas either by way of satisfaction for spoliation claims or by exchange rather than by purchase. Thus the effort of Napoleon to continue negotiations at Paris came to naught.

The Spanish government was loath to enter into any sort of a treaty or convention. To postpone a treaty and yet avoid a war, making a treaty only as a last recourse was the aim of Spanish diplomacy. As Erving, our chargé at Madrid, wrote Bowdoin, they felt "that they must sacrifice something by an arrangement, and they trust without it they will sacrifice nothing."[1] It is evident that in the fall of 1806 Napoleon had lost all interest in any settlement. In fact, he did not really care to arrange the dispute, for, after Jena, Spain lay prostrate at his feet, in short, was his own. Further, from D'Yrujo's reports, Spain was confident that she need have no fear of war with the United States owing to the diversity of interests in this country. The northern states would never consent to a war for anything which concerned southern territory, it was believed. That this impression had great weight in Spain cannot be doubted. And this, with the mercurial variations of her position in Europe, changed her manner toward this country. She became more conciliatory to the United States as her fortunes in Europe were less favorable, more firm as they brightened. Bowdoin, appreciating the failure of our representations at Paris, advocated more decisive measures and suggested seizing the Floridas. Like Monroe, Livingston, and Pinckney, he felt that we must present a decided front, else give up forever our claims to West Florida and Spanish spoliations. The publication of a Spanish paper at New Orleans which might have a

---

1. Erving to Bowdoin, Sept. 12, 1806.

circulation in the Floridas had suggested itself as a scheme likely to arouse in those territories a desire to become a part of this nation.

In the year 1807, the depredations committed by the English fleet off the Virginia capes and the prospect of immediate war with that country determined the president not in any way to apply "the public funds to objects not immediately connected with the public safety." Accordingly Armstrong and Bowdoin were instructed to suspend the negotiations for the purchase of the Floridas "unless it shall be agreed by Spain that payment for them shall, in case of a rupture between Great Britain and the United States, be postponed till the end of one year after they shall have settled their differences; and that in the meantime no interest shall be paid on the debt." These terms it was felt would be agreeable to her by reason of the advantages which Spain and her allies would derive from such a contest. Indeed such considerations it was felt ought to lessen the price we should pay for the Floridas. For, in the event of war, our pecuniary faculties would be materially benumbed while those of Spain would be essentially aided by giving that country once again the command of her South American treasury through the United States. Further, such a war might remove the objections hitherto felt by Great Britain to enterprises against the Floridas and even lead to a military occupation of them with views decidedly adverse to the policy of Spain.[1]

In 1807 information was received in Washington that the people of West Florida meditated an attempt to liberate themselves from the Spanish government. With this in view they intended, if the manner of this government did not promise taking them by the hand, to address themselves to England. Confident of their ability to overpower

---

1. Vol. VI, Instructions, p. 430, Madison to Armstrong and Bowdoin, July 15, 1807.

the Spanish garrisons, the external aid they sought related solely to subsequent support against whatever force Spain might employ to regain possession. This development was one which must interest both Spain and the United States. Great Britain had not hitherto deemed it politic to direct any of her forces to the easy conquest of the Floridas, fearing thereby to add the United States to the number of her enemies. The present crisis with Great Britain might alter the course on the part of England and thus compel this country, either promptly to occupy the territory in question, or see it pass into the hands of a conqueror from whom it might not be easily secured in the future. General Armstrong was directed to make suitable representations on this subject with a view either to stimulating Spain to an immediate concurrence in the plan of adjustment proposed by the United States, or to prepare her and her ally for any sudden measures which the approach of war with Great Britain might prescribe to this government.[1]

Napoleon at this juncture made overtures for an accession of the United States to the war against England, as an inducement to which his interposition would be employed with Spain to obtain for us the Floridas. Many historians consider this the time when we should have fought our war which came four years later. Here we would have secured a virile and powerful ally, who was nearly able to humble the haughty Briton and thus we might have derived much benefit from the startling victories of Napoleon. Unfortunately we were doomed to wait until France lay exhausted and defeated on the field of battle, when England might turn her whole force and divert her battle-scarred veterans to our shores and there bring confusion and panic upon our untrained militia. Let it suffice to say that no man knows the future, and to Jefferson the

---

1. Vol. VI, Instructions, p. 436, Madison to Armstrong and Bowdoin, Aug. 2, 1807.

muse of history had not confided the virgin pages yet un-
written. To Napoleon's advances Madison replied that
"the United States having chosen as the basis of their
policy a fair and sincere neutrality among the contending
powers, they are disposed to adhere to it as long as their
essential interests will permit, and are more especially dis-
inclined to become a party to the complicated and general
warfare which agitates another quarter of the globe, for
the purpose of obtaining a separate and particular object
however interesting to them."[1]

It was now out of the question to think of negotiations between the United States and Spain. Harassed by
Napoleon, drained of men and money, Godoy, the dissolute
Prince of Peace, fallen, her king had abdicated and his son
had been crowned amidst the joyful demonstrations of his
insanely patriotic subjects. The French armies were in
Madrid and shortly the imprisoned Charles and Ferdinand
had both surrendered their rights at the dictation of Napoleon. In May, 1808, at first dazed with this kaleidoscopic
change of sovereigns, the people in every part of the Spanish kingdom were in arms, and anarchy seemed complete
in that wretched country. Governed by Joseph Bonaparte
as king and a miserable though native junta, who
claimed in their peripatetic movements to be the true rulers,
all questions of diplomacy were forced to give way to the
sterner considerations of war and pillage.

In the United States the accredited chargé continued
to conduct the ordinary diplomatic intercourse. Foronda
found cause for complaint in various irregularities in the
south and southwest. Negroes and Indians were attacking Florida and shutting off provisions from the province.
The commandant of American gunboats captured Spanish
vessels within the jurisdiction of East Florida. This government under its Embargo Act, forbidding exportation by

---

1. Vol. VI, Instructions, p. 458, Madison to Armstrong, May 2, 1808.

land as well as sea, had shut off supplies from Florida and was causing untold hardship and suffering. The Georgians were raiding Florida, stealing slaves and personal property. The Spanish territory was being violated by men in the naval and military service of the United States. They were encouraging an uprising at Mobile; Spanish vessels were being shut out of the Mississippi in violation of treaty rights. Certain citizens of New Orleans were plotting revolutionary movements in Mexico and Vera Cruz and setting on foot filibustering expeditions. Such was the burden of Foronda's letters to the secretary of state in the years of 1808 and 1809. That many of his complaints were ill-founded is probably true, but that there were constant incursions into Spanish territory, and constant violations of Spanish sovereignty and that our southern ports, particularly New Orleans, were being made the headquarters of revolutionary plotters and filibusters seems equally certain.

In the fall of 1808 the report gained credence in Spain that Napoleon intended to sell the Floridas to the United States. This caused the utmost concern and consternation in Madrid and the Spanish junta protested vigorously to Mr. Erving against such an act. It was rumored that negotiations with this in view had already been opened by the French minister at Washington. There seems to have been no foundation for this *canard* and Erving promptly disclaimed all knowledge of it.

During the struggle then being waged for the possession of the Spanish throne, the United States insisted on observing absolute neutrality, refusing to recognize either claimant until the question should be definitely settled. In 1810 Ferdinand VII having gained at least a temporary success, was nominally at the head of the Spanish government and as such appointed De Onis minister at Washington to succeed D'Yrujo. The United States, true to its declaration, refused to recognize Ferdinand or receive De Onis.

As one reads the history of bleeding Spain during these years of national misfortune he must needs nominate it a "hapless, miserable country." And yet he cannot fail to admire those peasants, priest-ridden and ignorant though they were, who rose as one man to fight for their legitimate sovereign and drive out the hated despot — the people who taught other nations that even Napoleon was vulnerable, and inspired them to rise against the curse of Europe. For in Spain it was that Napoleon received the first reverses which culminated six years later in an overwhelming Waterloo. The Spaniards were a people — hitherto Napoleon had attacked governments and defeated them. At Jena he had fought a government and Europe lay prostrate at his feet — at Waterloo he fought a people and St. Helena was his grave. Let the future applaud the Spanish patriotism, unworthy though the beneficiaries were, which released Europe from the bonds of cruel slavery forged to satisfy the insatiable ambition of a heartless warrior.

CHAPTER VI.

FLORIDA DURING THE WAR OF 1812.

THE anarchy which existed in the mother country, the downfall of the Spanish monarchy, and the elevation of Joseph Bonaparte to the throne had given a show of legitimacy to a series of revolutions which gradually infected most of the Spanish provinces of South America. Nor had the organization of the Spanish junta succeeded in restoring any degree of order in these countries. The downfall of legitimacy at Madrid was rather the excuse than the justification of the rebellions which now sprang up in the South American colonies, like toad-stools in a night. Encouraged and assisted by English emissaries the people of Buenos Ayres rose and expelled the viceroy commissioned by the Spanish junta. The worthy people of Caraccas were not slow in imitating their neighbors and soon Venezuela, New Granada, and Mexico were in arms and the discerning eye could readily detect the signs of imminent trouble in Cuba and West Florida. In the latter territory the germs of rebellion first bore fruit in the district of New Feliciana which lay along the Mississippi just across the boundary line of 31°. The immediate cause may have been a widely circulated rumor that Napoleon intended to seize and hold West Florida. A curious population, that of this province, since the purchase of Louisiana — a notable congregation of evil-doers; Englishmen, Spaniards, renegade Americans, traders, land speculators, army deserters, fleeing debtors, fugitives from justice, fili-

busters, pirates, and others of like ilk. Taking advantage
of the confusion in Spain and the difficulties in the other
provinces these people determined to seize the opportunity
to set up a free government — which meant simply substi-
tuting their own misrule for that of Spain. In the spring
of 1810 they issued a call for a convention which with the
consent of the governor, Don Carlos Debault Delassus, met
at St. John's Plains in July. Delegates from San Feliciana,
Baton Rouge, St. Helena, and Tauchipaho responded to
the call.

The settlers were, generally speaking, divided into
three classes. One, mostly the people of New Feliciana,
wanted an independent government; another faction insisted
that the province should support Ferdinand VII; but the
largest number sought annexation to the United States,
in which they were stoutly supported by the press of
Tennessee and Kentucky. It was argued by these papers
that if the United States did not take West Florida, England would. In that event the people of Kentucky and
Tennessee and the territories of Indiana, Mississippi, and
Louisiana would never tolerate being cut off from access
to the Gulf of Mexico and trade on the Atlantic. Those
desiring a separate government issued a manifesto, — a
combination of queer political philosophy and grandilo-
quent literature, — a blending of our Declaration of Independence and constitution with certain other features
making it radically different.

This innovation proved too bold and when the convention reassembled after a short adjournment, the delegates merely suggested a few reforms which Delassus
promised to put into execution. They recommended a provisional government in the name of Spain; courts of justice modeled after those of the United States, a militia,
the naturalization of aliens and a printing press under
the control of the judiciary. Such a scheme was manifestly

unsatisfactory to both those who favored annexation to the United States and those who, with greater temerity, wished to take their place in the world as an independent nation — in short these two factions vowed they would never submit to such a government as the one proposed, and soon they had a declaration of independence, a state, a constitution, a lone-star flag, a standing army of one hundred and four men and a president of their own. Philemon Thomas, an American, was ordered by the convention to take the Spanish fort at Baton Rouge. Rapidly getting together a motley crowd of boatmen, Thomas moved upon the fort which was garrisoned by about twenty half-sick, incapacitated men under the command of Louis Grandpré. Storming the works, the insurgents captured the town taking prisoner, among others, Governor Delassus.

The convention thereupon declared West Florida a free and independent state and instructed John Rhea, its president, to offer terms of annexation to the United States; West Florida should be admitted into the Union as a state or territory with the power to govern itself, or at least as part of Orleans; it should be recognized as having full title to its public lands and that one hundred thousand dollars should be loaned to it by the United States. [1]

The requests of the revolutionary party were refused and Madison replied to their offer of annexation by a proclamation taking possession of territory in the name of the United States, by virtue of the treaty of 1803, and annexing it to Orleans. An order was drawn up addressed to the governor of Orleans to carry out the terms of the proclamation. Spain and Great Britain, at that time allies, protested strongly against Madison's course. Claiborne was directed to hold a consultation with the governor of Mississippi and the commander of the troops, and proceed im-

1. American Papers, Foreign Affairs, Vol. III, p. 395.

mediately to West Florida and take possession as far as the
Perdido River. This done, he was to organize the government, mark out parish limits, set up parish courts, organize
militia, and take other necessary steps to secure to the
people the "peaceful enjoyment of their lives, property,
and religion." By the first of December, Claiborne was
scattering copies of the president's proclamation broadcast
through the towns and hamlets of West Florida much to
the indignation of the newly chosen governor, Fulwar
Skipwith, who pompously declared that his dignity had
been insulted, that a copy of the proclamation should have
been brought to him before being thus indiscriminately scattered among the people. Then he took the mirth provoking course of recalling Philemon Thomas from a projected assault upon Mobile, shutting himself up in the
fort at Baton Rouge and defying Governor Claiborne to do
his worst.

Colonel Pike was ordered at the head of a force
to proceed by land to Mobile, and the commander of several of Jefferson's famous gunboats was directed to proceed from New Orleans to the same point. Claiborne
hastened to Francisville. There, raising the American
flag, he addressed the people. He was followed on the
program by General Thomas who delivered a passionate
harangue. The United States he declared had refused assistance and protection when it was needed, and now, when
it was unnecessary, sought to force it on them; the claim
of the United States to West Florida was bad in law and
morals; Madison's proclamation he characterized as a
declaration of war; his oration, if we may thus term an
harangue delivered amidst such settings, he concluded by
theatrically announcing his determination of hastening to
Baton Rouge and on the ruins of that fort giving up his
life, if need be, for the sake of his country. The challenge
was accepted; the troops were recalled from Mobile; gun-

boats were ordered from New Orleans and in forty-eight hours Claiborne was in Baton Rouge and the United States flag was flying over the city. Trouble ensued. The malcontents tore down the stars and stripes and in its stead ran up the lone-star flag. Providentially the troops and gunboats appeared and those disposed to create trouble quickly subsided. Even the fort quietly surrendered and there were no ruins and no generals immolated on the altar of patriotism. In the other sections even less opposition was offered to the American occupation and by the close of the year we were in possession of the districts of Baton Rouge, New Feliciana, St. Helena, St. Ferdinand and Tauchipaho.

But beyond the Pearl, conditions were even worse. Here, for years, there had been no pretense of enforcing law or preserving order. The character of the people of that section was even more hopeless than those of West Florida. Now had come their opportunity. They sought a government of their own with themselves as officials. Under the command of Reuben Kemper they proceeded against Mobile. At first repelled by the Spanish, the insurgents returned to the attack. So exhausted and disgusted was Governor Folch at the neglect of his own government that in a letter to Robert Smith, our secretary of state, he offered to give up both Floridas to the United States if assistance did not arrive from Havana or Vera Cruz before January 1, 1811. This letter did not reach Washington until the first of January but immediately upon its arrival Madison sent it to Congress with a secret message. He asked a declaration from that body that the United States could not, without concern, see the Floridas pass from the ownership of Spain to that of any other foreign power; and he requested authority to take possession of the province with the consent of the Spanish officials.

The senate was already in secret session considering a bill on West Florida. A committee to which had been referred that portion of the president's message relating to that province had reported a resolution declaring all the region south of the Mississippi Territory, east of the Mississippi River and west of the Perdido, to be part of the territory of Orleans; other sections of the bill related to claims and titles to land. The discussion was bitter and prolonged and the arguments presented varied and novel. The proclamation was unconstitutional and illegal as an act of legislation and a declaration of war; an act of legislation in that it joined the province to a territory of the United States and gave Claiborne governmental authority over it; a declaration of war in that it directed the occupation of the country by a military force. The remnants of the Federalist party were particularly bitter in their characterization of the course of the administration. With the battle taunt of French influence they eloquently dilated upon the respectful treatment of Spain when an ally of France and enemy of England, and compared it with the high-handed treatment of her now that she was the ally of England and the enemy of France. That it was a piece of robbery was their final judgment. The Republicans taking the negative declared that the proclamation was not an act of legislation and that the president had not assumed a war power; Florida was rightfully ours and its occupation was an act of prudence and necessity; the Federalists, they delared, were Anglophiles who had never been able to free themselves of the English influence.

In the midst of the debate, congress received the secret message accompanied by the letters of Governor Folch. A fortnight later Madison attached his signature to a bill and a joint resolution. The resolution declared that in view of the situation of Spain and her American colonies and the influence which Florida must ever exert on the peace, tranquillity, and commerce of the United States this country must view with grave alarm any act by which any part of that province might pass into the hands of a foreign power; that a due regard for our own national safety made it necessary to occupy the territory; the occupation, however, should be temporary and subject to future negotiation. The bill which they passed was based on the letter of Governor Folch and authorized the president to receive and hold Florida east of the Perdido River, if the local authorities were willing to deliver it up or if any foreign power attempted to occupy it. The president was authorized, if necessary, to use the army and navy and expend one hundred thousand dollars. He was further empowered to set up a temporary government and vest the civil, military, and judicial powers in such persons as he might see fit.[1] Madison, in conformity with this resolution, appointed General George Matthews and Colonel John McKee commissioners to carry out the law and ordered their instructions immediately prepared.

While the United States claimed all the territory from the Mississippi to the Perdido her authority did not extend to the Mobile and it is doubtful if she was recognized beyond the Pearl. To the Pearl even, congress was not ready to enforce its authority and by the act granting the people of Orleans the power to frame a constitution and seek admission as a state, the Mississippi, the Iberville, Lake Maurepas, Lake Pontchartrain, and the Gulf of Mexico were made the eastern boundary of the state of Louisiana.

There has been much discussion among historians on the right of the United States thus to seize West Florida. Jefferson who consistently followed, and urged upon Madison, the policy of using the intrigues and combinations

---

1. Before adjournment an act was passed forbidding the promulgation of this resolution and law before the end of the next session of congress.

of Napoleon to obtain Florida and even Cuba for the United States, was anxious to "maintain in Europe a correct opinion of our political morality." He believed that the documentary history would prove the conscientiousness of the United States. The question of title to West Florida arose in the case of Foster and Elam against the United States, but the supreme court, without deciding on the merits as to what had passed by that convention, held that it was bound by the legislative construction that the territory passed to the United States by the treaty of Paris of 1803.[1]

The course of the United States called forth a bitter protest from the Spanish representative at Washington, Juan B. Bernabue. He complained that French emissaries were permitted to stop in the United States contrary to the neutrality laws at the very time that France was confiscating American vessels; that these French emissaries moreover were charged to stir up revolution in the Spanish territories. On the other hand Spain allowed American vessels to trade freely in her ports; had assisted the United States in her revolutionary war, and was the first to send an accredited agent to this government. "Spain, notwithstanding this conduct," wrote Bernabue, "is treated by the United States as an enemy, her frontiers in this quarter of the world are invaded without any other reason or motive being assigned saving the convenience of the acquisition of those territories to the views and interests of the invaders, or perhaps because it has been presumed that Spain, who has dared to face and arrest the progress of the most formidable power in the world, is in such a state of weakness as not to be able to defend her rights whenever they may be violated and infringed in the most

1. Vol. II, Peters, p. 253.

open manner." [1] Complaint was also made that the insurrections in West Florida, Buenos Ayres, and Caraccas were publicly favored, that a consul had been appointed who resided at and exercised his consular functions among the rebels at Caraccas permitting a considerable remittance of arms and ammunition from the United States to the provinces in rebellion; further, that agents and emissaries of these revolting colonies were admitted to this country; and that French cruisers were tolerated in our ports and those of Joseph Bonaparte were permitted to cruise against the commerce of Spain. In short, concluded Bernabue, the Spanish troubles in this hemisphere were largely due to the fact that the United States did not restrain her "factious citizens."

To General Matthews and Colonel McKee were sent instructions for carrying into effect the provisions of the act of congress relative to that portion of the Floridas east of the River Perdido. The purpose of the United States was to take possession of East Florida for fear that, in the present chaotic condition of Spanish affairs, some foreign power might seize it. The country was to be held subject to future diplomatic negotiations. The commissioners were directed to proceed immediately to that province "concealing from general observation the trust . . . . with that discretion which the delicacy and importance of the undertaking required."

Did Governor Folch or the local authority seem inclined to surrender in an amicable manner, General Matthews was to accept his abdication in behalf of the United States and if the Spanish officials should insist on a stipulation for the future re-delivery of the country, such a demand should be complied with. Thus much for an "amicable surrender." "Should there be room," writes

---

1. Juan B. Bernabue to Secretary of State, Vol. II. Spanish Ministers to Secretary of State.

Robert Smith, "to entertain a suspicion of an existing design of any foreign power to occupy the country in question you are to keep yourselves on the alert and, on the
first undoubted manifestation of. the approach of a force
for that purpose, you will exercise with promptness and
vigor the powers with which you are invested by the president to pre-occupy by force the territory to the entire
exclusion of any armament that may be advancing to take
possession of it."[1] These instructions at the present day
seem extraordinary.

Hastening to St. Mary's, a small place on the American side of the line, Matthews encountered a condition
of affairs which, as he construed his instructions, demanded
that immediate possession be taken on the plea of self-
preservation. The river was alive with British shipping
engaged in smuggling goods into the United States in
manifest violation of the non-importation law. Amelia
Island which was situated at the mouth of the St. Mary's
River just off the coast of Florida, was a notorious resort of smugglers. Fernandina, the Spanish town on the
island, was merely an entrepot for their illicit trade. Spanish authority existed there more in fiction than in fact.
No law of any kind was in force.

After making diligent inquiries, Matthews concluded
that to obtain quiet possession was impossible. The profits
of the illegal traffic were far too alluring to be thus tamely
surrendered. Inferring that the country was to be taken
at all events, he recommended the employment of force.
The course of West Florida furnished to his mind a suitable criterion. The people of East Florida should be encouraged to revolt, declare the province independent, and
then apply for annexation to the United States. Two
hundred stand of arms and fifty horsemen's swords would

---

1. Vol. XVI, Domestic Letters, p. 1. Robert Smith to Gen.
George Matthews and Col. John McKee, Jan. 26, 1811.

be necessary and he would guarantee that they reached the people without in any manner compromising the United States. These suggestions were more fully enlarged upon to Senator William H. Crawford of Georgia and by him communicated to President Madison. Mistaking silence for consent Matthews began to organize the revolution. In the order of General Eustis, a hint had been given to create a new local authority friendly to the United States. For this the conditions were ripe. Adventurous spirits — the stuff of which filibusters are made — abounded along the St. Mary's. It was familiarly termed the "jumping place" of criminals and desperate characters from Georgia and Florida. The "moccazin boys" were even then making their slave and cattle stealing raids into the Indian country. Outlawry was everywhere the dominent influence. The weak Spanish government could offer no effective protection to the planters in the northeast. Many of the nominal subjects of Spain were disaffected, first among whom was General John McIntosh, an ideal leader for such a revolution as the one contemplated. After his release from Moro Castle he had returned to Florida, gathered together his former adherents and quit the province after wreaking vengeance by destroying a small Spanish post at the Cow Ford, and some Spanish boats near the site of Jacksonville. By 1811 he had become a man of importance on the lower St. John's. He owned large numbers of negroes, horses, and boats and was extensively engaged in cutting pine timber under a lucrative contract. The insurrection was acomplished through his influence under the protection of General Matthews. He devoted all his property to the "sacred" cause under the guarantee by Matthews that the United States would make good any loss he might suffer. The two other leading agents there were the postmaster at St. Mary's and the United States deputy marshal.

By the spring of 1812 some two hundred of these adventure-seeking "patriots" were assembled near St. Mary's. Organizing themselves they announced as their purpose the establishment of republican institutions in Florida. A provisional government was formed and officers duly elected. General John H. McIntosh was chosen governor or director of the republic of Florida, and Col. Ashley was named as military chief. One day in March, 1812, found them across the St. Mary's River on Florida soil, and there on a bluff six miles above Amelia Island they camped and ran up a white flag decorated with a soldier with bayonet charged and the motto "Salus populi — suprema lex."

Fernandina had been occupied as a Spanish port for three or four years and had rapidly grown to be a place of importance. During the existence of the embargo, particularly, the town had flourished and as many as a hundred and fifty vessels might be seen at one time in her harbor. In 1812 a Spanish garrison of ten men under the command of Don José Lopez held the place. It was deemed of vital necessity to secure possession of the town.

On the fifteenth of March, Colonel Ashley sent an ultimatum to Lopez. The determination of the United States to seize East Florida had led the inhabitants to do it themselves. Therefore under the patronage and protection of the United States they had taken possession of the country from the St. Mary's River to the St. John's; and now they summoned Fernandina to surrender. It is certain, beyond all peradventure, that General Matthews having determined upon the occupation of Amelia Island, used the patriot organization as a cover to effect his purpose. Nine American gunboats under the command of Hugh Campbell had come into the harbor with the avowed purpose of preventing smuggling and enforcing the non-importation law. To Commander Campbell, Lopez dispatched messengers informing him of the demands of the insur-

13

gents and inquiring whether he had orders to aid them. Messengers were similarly dispatched to Major Laval who was in command of the American troops at Point Peter. Laval replied that he had no such orders, while Campbell referred the whole affair to General Matthews. General Matthews was at the time, so the commandant informed the messengers, in the camp endeavoring to persuade the troops to join the patriots.

In an interview which followed, the messengers informed him plainly that the patriots were Americans brought into Florida under the promise of five hundred acres of land to each of them in the event of the success of the revolution. In the eyes of Spain, they declared, it was an American invasion. After having thus delivered themselves of these expressions, for which there could be no denial, the messengers proceeded to the patriot camp and informed the commanding officer that under no circumstances would they surrender to him, but that they would treat with the United States. According to agreement all three parties, Spanish, Americans, and patriots met the next day at the patriot camp on Belle River.

The conference, however, proved barren of results and the messengers set out for Amelia Island, there to find the American gunboats drawn up in line in front of Fernandina with their guns trained upon the fort. The patriots dropped down the river in boats and Lopez, seeing the line of war ships with strings on their cables, their guns bearing upon the town, matches lighted and flying the flag of a neutral power, but prepared to enforce the demands of the soi-disant patriots, had no alternative but to surrender. The Spanish garrison, ten strong, marched out and grounded arms, Lopez gave up his sword, McIntosh hauled down the Spanish flag and hoisted the patriot banner. The articles of capitulation, entered into March 17, 1812, stipulated that within twenty-four hours after the capitulation the island should be surrendered to the United States and should be exempt from the operation of the non-importation law. By noon of the following day the stars and stripes were flying over the fort and a company of United States soldiers were doing garrison duty. The manner and the pretences under which this was done reflect but little credit on the United States government and the transparent sham of taking possession of the country by "patriots" supported by the United States troops was both a reproach upon our dignity and a stain upon our honor.

The patriots themselves sought other fields to conquer, other worlds to win, and, still encouraged and led by citizens and officers of the United States, began the march to St. Augustine. With them, it appears, went a detachment of United States regulars. Taking possession of old fort Moosa, about two miles distant, they invested the place. Dislodged from this site by a Spanish gunboat, they still hovered about the city and cut off all supplies. The courage and bravery of a company of negroes, led by a free black, alone saved the town from starvation. The Indians of Florida were aroused to attack the Americans and patriots, and for a year the unhappy province was scourged by these contending parties.

The occupation of Fernandina and the subsequent movement upon St. Augustine brought forth a vigorous remonstrance from the Spanish minister at Washington. He learned that Matthews had seduced the inhabitants by offering to every free white male inhabitant fifty acres of land, the free exercise of his religion, the undisturbed possession of his estates, assuring them that the American government would pay to individuals whatever debts might be due to them from the Spanish authorities on account of salary or otherwise.[1] The British minister also presented

---

1. De Onis to Secretary of State, Vol. III, Sept. 5, 1811.

a protest against this "flagrant violation of neutral territory."

President Madison was placed in an embarrassing position. General Matthews was his accredited commissioner and had been instructed in writing to occupy the country, if there should be room to entertain a suspicion that any other power contemplated taking possession. The alternative was presented of sacrificing his agent and disowning his acts or of boldly justifying his course, assuming the responsibility, and accepting the consequences. Pursuing the usual course of those in authority, he sacrificed another. Declaring that General Matthews had transcended his authority, he regretted the occurrence and promised to restore conditions to their status quo ante. Matthews was relieved of his position and Governor Mitchell of Georgia appointed in his stead. The letter of disavowal which Matthews received must have read painfully after his zealous efforts "to promote the welfare of the country."[1]

The conduct of our officials in Florida furnishes a sad contrast to what Monroe at that time declared to be the policy of this country towards Spain. In a letter to Governor Howard he had written, "The United States are at peace with Spain. The convulsions of the Spanish monarchy have produced no effect on this policy towards her. The disorganized condition of that power and its embarrassments have afforded motives rather to forbear to press claims of right founded on positive wrongs than to seek redress by force which under other circumstances might have been done."[2]

Had our conduct been dictated by the principles thus proclaimed, the task of the historian would be far more pleasant, for it is more agreeable to praise than to apolo-

---

1. Vol. XVI, Domestic Letters, James Monroe to Gen. George Matthews, April 4, 1812.
2. Vol. XVI, Domestic Letters, p. 199, Sept. 3, 1812.

gize for the deeds of one's own country. Governor Mitchell was directed to withdraw the American troops if, on reaching St. Mary's, he saw no prospect of foreign occupation. He was further instructed to restore Amelia Island and, above all, take care to secure from molestation or harm those men, who had been induced by General Matthews to embark in the revolution. Accepting the mission, Mitchell hastened to St. Mary's, there to find affairs in a serious condition. The patriots firmly declined to retire; and at a meeting at their headquarters before St. Augustine, they issued a call for additional recruits and pledged their honor not to lay down their arms until absolute independence had been won. Without money, they promised to pay all volunteers in land or such property as might be captured from their enemies. [1]

Having been attacked by the Spanish gunboats they were forced gradually to retire to St. John's. The governor of Florida declined to make any agreement with Mitchell for the immunity of these self-seeking "patriots." Alarmed by the attacks upon the revolutionists, indignant at the refusal of Governor Estrada to accept the proffered arrangement, and desirous of ousting Spain from this province, Governor Mitchell determined upon bold measures and sent to Savannah for aid. The Republican Blues and Savannah Volunteer Guard were soon on their way to St. Mary's. Simultaneously with their arrival came an express bearing news of the declaration of war against England. Seventeen British ships lying at anchor were immediately seized, a large quantity of floating timber cut for the use of the British navy was confiscated, and a call issued to Georgia for more troops. One hundred men from the vicinity quickly responded.

Aroused by Indian attacks, the Georgia legislature, in the fall, passed an act providing that a state force be

---

1. May 2, 1812.

raised to reduce St. Augustine and chastise the hostile redskins. They further resolved that the occupation of East Florida was essential to the safety of their state whether congress should approve or not. Thus the state of Georgia apparently came into conflict with the Federal government, but, as it happened, its measures were consistent with the policy of the administration which was compelled to resort to military operations both against the hostile Indians and the British forces now in Spanish territory. With this complication, Governor Mitchell was relieved of further duty after having received the thanks of Madison for the "ability and judgment" which he had displayed "in the important and delicate transaction."[1] The trust was again transferred, this time to General Thomas Pinckney. Like his predecessors he was to take possession of the province only upon the peaceable surrender by the Spanish authorities or in view of its possible seizure by some other foreign power.[2]

To the Spanish representations upon our course in East Florida a characteristic answer had been returned. Spain owed the United States more than the province was worth for spoliations and for the suppression of the deposit at New Orleans. The United States looked to East Florida for their indemnity. They would permit no power to take it and would take it themselves at the invitation of the inhabitants or to prevent its falling into the hands of another nation. As for West Florida, that belonged to the United States by a title which could not be improved, and, it might have been added, which could not be proved.[3]

In the meantime the question of the revolted South

---

1. Vol. XVI, Domestic Letters, p. 72, Madison to Governor Mitchell of Georgia, Oct. 13, 1812.
2. Vol. XVI, Domestic Letters, p. 204, Madison to Gen. Thomas Pinckney, Dec. 8, 1812.
3. Vol. VII, Instructions, p. 173, Monroe to Joel Barlow, Nov. 21, 1811.

American colonies had become a burning one between this country and Spain. The provinces of Venezuela had declared their independence and a similar step was imminent at Buenos Ayres and in other quarters. The Departments of Venezuela had proposed to the United States the recognition of their independence and the reception of a minister from them. Though such a recognition in form was not made, a friendly and conciliatory answer was given to them. They were also informed that the ministers of the United States in Europe would be instructed to avail themselves of suitable opportunities to promote their recognition by other powers, an object "thought to be equally due to the just claims of our southern brethren, to which the United States cannot be indifferent, and to the best interests of this country." [1]

The fate of West Florida was soon determined by congress. That portion south of 31° and between the Mississippi and Pearl rivers was added to the new state of Louisiana. [2] The portion between the Pearl and the Perdido was annexed to the Mississippi Territory. This act differed little from a declaration of war. For when, by Madison's signature, it became a law, the Spanish banner floated over Mobile and Spanish troops held the city in the name of Ferdinand.

In the war of 1812 it was hardly to be expected that Spain would or could maintain order in her Florida possessions or that she would perform the duties of a neutral power. Her throne was the plaything of Napoleon, her king was his prisoner. Without any force capable of commanding obedience to law it was natural that the Floridas should become, more than ever, the breeding ground of pirates, smugglers, and privateers. Further, in the Euro-

---

1. Vol. VII, Instructions, p. 183, Monroe to Joel Barlow, Nov. 27, 1811.
2. Act of Congress, April 14, 1812. Act of Congress, April 8, in effect April 30, 1812.

pean alliance against Napoleon, Spain and her armies were completely under English domination. It was probable that now, in view of the war, England would seize the Floridas and use them as a base of supplies, a plan which had often seemed so seductive to that power but which had never been pursued because of the attitude of the United States. That the United States should forestall her enemy by first occupying the country was a course which to President Madison admitted of no argument. Nor did he doubt that it would appeal to congress in the same light and that that body would promptly authorize it. He intended to be prepared for immediate compliance with the expected order.

The governor of Tennessee was requested to prepare a militia force of fifteen hundred men for "the defense of the lower country." General Pinckney, who had been named as Governor Mitchell's successor, was informed that when congress should consent to the proposed seizure of the Floridas, troops would be dispatched to him for the capture of St. Augustine.[1] Wilkinson, the weakling, the traitor to both friend and country, was commanded to hold himself in readiness to lead an army into West Florida.[2]

It seemed to the people of the Mississippi Valley that the authorities at Washington had at last begun to see the light, and there was much rejoicing among those Westerners at the projected turn of affairs. At length their dreams were to be realized — were to become fact rather than fancy. They were not afflicted with any mental troubles about the "defense of country" and "extra-territorial service" such as had reflected so little credit upon their brothers of the Canadian border. Conquest was their purpose and to them no peace was desirable, nay, no peace was tolerable, that did not recognize American sovereignty

---

1. Monroe to Pinckney, Jan. 13, 1813. War Department Archives.
2. Monroe to Wilkinson, Jan. 30, 1813. *Ibid.*

from the Sabine to the St. Mary's, from Canada to the Gulf of Mexico.

Governor Blount's order to General Jackson to call out two thousand men found every fighting man in Tennessee eager for the fray. The troops, having been mustered in on the seventh day of January, 1813, set out from Nashville. They were the men for the purpose. Their leader, Jackson, whose heart was ulcerated with hatred for the Dons, wrote: "They are the choicest of our citizens. . . . . They go at our country's call to do the will of the government. No constitutional scruples trouble them. Nay, they will rejoice at the opportunity of placing the American eagle on the ramparts of Mobile, Pensacola, and Fort St. Augustine."[1] Their principal heritage had been a hardy constitution and a bitter hatred for the Spanish. Now at last had come the hour when they might wipe out with blood and fire the insults of former days which they had suffered at the hands of those whom they despised. The cavalry, if such it may be called, rode through the Indian country, while the remainder of the force embarking on boats slowly made their way down the Ohio, the Cumberland, and the Mississippi. On the fifteenth of February, in obedience to instructions from Wilkinson, they put in at Natchez and camped on the neighboring cliffs impatiently awaiting orders to move on the enemy.

In the meantime the senate had declined to countenance the occupation of East Florida and orders were hastily dispatched to the intrepid Jackson; "the cause for marching the corps under your command to New Orleans no longer exists. You will therefore consider it as dismissed from public service."[2] Jackson's indignation knew no bounds and in contempt of his instructions he marched his men back to Nashville, making himself personally respon-

---

1. Parton's Jackson, Vol. II, p. 372. Jackson to Secretary Eustis.
2. Armstrong to Jackson, Feb. 6, 1813.

sible for their rations and pay, and defying all attempts to enlist his volunteers into the regular regiments.

Though demurring to the seizure of East Florida, congress consented to the invasion of West Florida and, on February 20, Madison signed an act to accomplish that purpose. Orders were immediately hastened to Wilkinson and by the middle of May that officer had organized an expedition at Pass Christian, had led it against Mobile, had taken Fort Charlotte and the city (April 15), had begun the erection of Fort Bowyer at the entrance to the bay, and had returned to New Orleans (May 19). There he found awaiting him orders to proceed to the Canadian border to retrieve the failures of our generals in that region. May 16 General Pinckney withdrew from Amelia Island and quiet reigned along the coast.

In the early months of 1813 came the proffered mediation of the Russian czar, an offer which Madison gladly embraced. Quickly appointing a joint commission composed of Albert Gallatin, John Quincy Adams, and James A. Bayard, Madison provided them with instructions and dispatched them to St. Petersburg where they arrived in July to the consternation, if not embarrassment, of Alexander who had been at least politely discouraged in his pacific efforts by Lord Castlereagh.[1] Aware of the friendly relations existing between Russia and Spain, and the interest which Alexander took in behalf of Ferdinand, our commissioners were instructed to broach cautiously the question of the Floridas at St. Petersburg.[2] Fearful lest our warlike course in East Florida might injure the American cause in the eyes of Europe, particularly with Russia, besides its exasperating effect on the protesting northern peace men, it was decided not to endanger the outcome of the Russian

1. Adams was already at St. Petersburg as minister to Russia.
2. Vol. VII, Instructions, pp. 276, 279. Monroe to J. Q. Adams, etc., April 27, 1813.

mediation because of East Florida. Orders were issued for the evacuation of that province, but possession was retained of West Florida together with Mobile.

A rude awakening was in store. British emissaries were in the meanwhile at work stimulating the southern Indians to make war upon the United States. Tecumseh with his passionate eloquence had visited the southern tribes in the fall of 1811. After his departure there appeared certain miraculous emblems of his mighty power and wrath. With counsels divided, surrounded by white settlements and friendly Choctaws and Chickasaws, the infatuated Creeks took the war path. Arms and supplies were furnished them from a British fleet in the gulf and some assistance seems to have been given by the Spanish governor at Pensacola.

Approaching Fort Mimms, an American stockade east of the Alabama River and ten miles above its junction with the Tombigbee, they terrified the white settlers who in wild alarm had taken refuge there from all parts of the surrounding country. On the thirtieth of August the setting sun cast its rays upon the most revolting scenes of savage cruelty as the hostile Creeks completed one of the bloodiest massacres history has to record. The buildings of the fort were in ashes and out of five hundred and fifty persons, four hundred were scalped or roasted to death. Neither age nor sex was spared.

Mingled with the wail of grief and despair there arose from the southern border a cry for vengeance. Tennessee instantly responded with her ready volunteers, now pledging the faith of the state without awaiting arrangements with the federal authorities. General Jackson was again in command. The East and West Tennessee troops uniting in the upper Alabama country, after many sanguinary encounters drove back the foe, who, in utter disregard of the most elementary tactics of warfare, instead of turning to threaten Mobile had advanced northward from Fort Mimms.

Finally at the battle of the Horseshoe (March 27-29, 1814) the Creek nation was annihilated and the few surviving warriors abjectly sued for life and peace. After signing a treaty with the Indians at Fort Jackson, August 9, 1814, the trip was resumed. Floating down the Alabama River, Mobile was reached a few days later and preparations were at once under way for the invasion of Florida.

The possession of that province was to Jackson's mind absolutely necessary to the national peace and welfare. He welcomed the chain of circumstances which seemed likely to make him the instrument for wresting it from those despised Dons for whom he had long entertained an ill concealed contempt and hatred. When appointed major general he had written to Armstrong begging for orders to attack and reduce Pensacola. These orders did not materialize and when he reached Fort Jackson he determined to go about the matter in another though equally effective way. With an ungovernable temper Jackson had a faculty, amounting really to a talent, for provoking quarrels. Seizing upon every opportunity to drag the Spanish into an attitude of open hostility toward the United States, he demanded from the governor of Pensacola the delivery of those Red Stick Indians who had escaped into Florida. In August when he reached Mobile he was more than ever hot for an attack upon Pensacola, for the English were already there.

Spain was absolutely at the mercy of England and with the disorganized state of affairs existing in the Iberian Peninsula, England exercised complete mastery and dominion over her. There is nothing to show that Spain did not act in good faith. She was unable, from her impotency to preserve her neutrality and give force to her desires. Together with her colonies she was a mere puppet in the hands of our enemies, and surely not to be held accountable as a nation acting of her own volition. It is claimed that the obligations of gratitude and the prospect that England might soon have possession of Louisiana, and be able to dispose of it, led Spain to violate her neutrality in Florida, but these suspicions fail of documentary proof. Certainly it cannot be disproved that Spain protested both to London and to other courts of Europe against England's summary course in the province of Florida.

The English fleet sent to capture Savannah lay many weeks under Amelia Island whence it must soon have departed but for the provisions and supplies claimed to have been furnished by the citizens and authorities of East Florida. The Spanish governor is said to have congratulated the victorious Weathersford upon his successes against the Americans and to have received the surviving warriors of the now broken chief into the friendly shelter of Pensacola. The harbor of Pensacola was the finest in all Florida. Fort Barrancas, six miles from the town, poorly garrisoned, guarded, together with Fort St. Michael, the entrance to the bay. This place the English selected as the *point d'appui* for their operations in the Gulf of Mexico, as a rendezvous for their fleet and a convenient point whence they might operate against Mobile and New Orleans.

Maintaining at least the outward forms of neutrality, which was reciprocated by the United States, unwilling then to add another to its enemies, the governor general of Cuba refused to permit the British to land at Pensacola. The town, then but the grave of its former splendor, was peopled with Indians, half breeds, West Indian traders, smugglers, buccaneers, fugitive slaves, and white men "with a past" who had fled from the States for cause. Despite the refusal of the Spaniards, late in July there was sighted from the lookouts an approaching British fleet, the forerunner and vanguard of the great expedition — Major Edward Nicholls with four officers, eleven non-commissioned officers, ninety-seven marines, two howitzers, a thousand stand of

arms and three thousand suits of clothing, and Captain
Percy commanding the sloops "Hermes" and "Carron."
Landing without ceremony, Nicholls seized Forts Barrancas and St. Michael, hoisted the English flag beside that of
Spain, built barracks for his soldiers, took up his quarters
in the governor's house and began a rapid issue of sonor-
ous proclamations to the people of Louisiana and Kentucky.

"Natives of Louisiana," began one of these bombastic
productions of his pen, "on you the first call is made to
assist in liberating your paternal soil from a faithless, imbecile government. The American usurpation of this country must be abolished. I am at the head of a large body of
Indians well armed, well disciplined and commanded by
British officers. Be not alarmed at our approach. The
same good faith which distinguished the Britons in Europe
accompanies them here. A flag over any door, whether
Spanish, French, or English, will be a sure protection; nor
dare any Indian put his foot on the threshold thereof under
penalty of death. Inhabitants of Kentucky, you have too
long borne with grievous impositions. The whole brunt of
the war has fallen on your brave sons. Be imposed on no
longer. Range yourselves under the standard of your fore-
fathers or observe a strict neutrality. After the experience
of twenty-one years can any of you longer support those
brawlers for liberty who call it freedom when they themselves are free?"[1] As an additional stimulus to the zeal
of the Indians the bounty on American scalps was raised
from five to ten dollars. We may imagine the spirit with
which these proclamations were received on the Kentucky
borders. True it might be, that they felt their treatment
at the hands of the eastern states had been contemptuous, but
in their hearts they harbored an undying hatred for both
Briton and Spaniard — the former for having instigated the
hostile savages to bloody attacks upon defenseless settle-

---

1. Niles Weekly Register, Vol. VII, pp. 134-135.

ments, the latter from the days of the Mississippi blockade.

Meanwhile Captain Woodbine, one of the English officers was busy with his new recruits. Some seven hundred warriors in full paint and feather were soon enrolled, with the expectation of drilling them into serviceable soldiers as the Indians of the East Indies are drilled. A truly comical yet pathetic scene they must have presented in their red army uniforms, divided into companies and battalions, those denizens of the forest used to the single file and the ambush. "Such scenes of preposterous costuming, of tripping over swords, of hopeless drilling and mad marching and counter-marching as the common of Pensacola then witnessed can be imagined only by those who know precisely what sort of creatures Indians are. Captain Woodbine might as well have attempted to train the alligators of the Florida lagoons for the British artillery service." [1]

Captain Percy, to take his part in this farcical exhibition, dispatched a ship, the "Sophie," to Jean Lafitte, the "pirate of the gulf," leader of the Barratarian privateers — to use a euphemism for their real character. An alliance was sought with these robbers who carried on their nefarious trade under the semblance of authority, for they had secured letters of marque and reprisal from the various revolted colonies of Spanish-America, particularly that of Cartagena. Failing to secure the assistance of the wily Lafitte, whose stronghold was within a few days destroyed by the Americans under Commander Daniel Patterson, Nicholls determined immediately to attack Jackson at Mobile. Fort Bowyer, a diminutive earthen affair built by Wilkinson on a low sand pit at the entrance to Mobile Bay, was defended by twenty guns, only eight of which were serviceable, with a garrison of one hundred and sixty men under Major William Lawrence. Captain Percy proceeded against this fort with the "Hermes" of twenty-two

---

1. Parton's Jackson, Vol. I, p. 579.

guns, the "Sophie" of twenty guns, the "Carron" and "Childers" of eighteen guns each, and a large force of marines and Indians under Colonel Woodbine. The marines and Indians with two light guns were landed in the rear of the fort behind the sand hills, on September 12.

Three days later the fleet, headed by the "Hermes," sailed for the bay in line of battle. Adopting the battle cry of "Don't give up the fort," the officers solemnly swore never to surrender until the ramparts were in ruins, and only then under the assurance of protection from an Indian massacre. At about four in the afternoon the "Hermes" followed by the rest of the fleet ran into the narrow channel leading into the bay, dropped anchor off the fort, and the attack was on. The superior American marksmanship soon left the final issue in no doubt. The "Hermes" with her cable cut, and her bow swinging toward the fort, was slowly swept down the stream exposed to a raking fire until she finally grounded. She was immediately deserted and fired by her officers and crew. The other ships, suffering badly, drew off and at daybreak of the sixteenth were making sail for Pensacola while the Indians and marines beat a hasty land retreat towards the same town.

Jackson, in command of only parts of three regiments of regulars, with a thousand miles of coast to defend, without a fort garrisoned or well armed, would gladly have pursued the enemy and carried the attack to Pensacola; but he was forced to await the arrival of the twenty-five hundred men he had summoned from Tennessee. Here was a wild borderer, "of fiery word and ready blow," with a genius for quarreling, who had never met a civilized foe, in supreme command, and practically without instructions, left to solve intricate questions of diplomacy and superintend the puzzling affairs of internal government, with a powerful expedition of a great nation to meet and conquer. While awaiting reinforcements and chafing under the enforced delay the unlettered Jackson took to the proclamation business himself. He addressed to the Louisiana settlers a reply to that of Nicholls and much in the style employed by the Briton, and another to the free negroes exhorting them to enlist against the common enemies.

At this time a messenger arrived with letters from Washington warning him of the intended attack upon New Orleans. Word was received shortly before that the enemy was preparing an expedition against Louisiana and that five thousand troops had been ordered from Tennessee and twenty-five hundred from Georgia to reinforce those now under his command and that one hundred thousand dollars in treasury notes had been given to Governor Blount to pay the cost of the armament.[1] Scarcely heeding these orders, Jackson, following a course long in his mind, set out with a force of from three to four thousand men for Pensacola as soon as the Tennessee troops had arrived. Leaving Mobile November 3, he conducted the expedition with all that impetuous zeal for which he later became famous. Demanding the surrender of Pensacola on the night of the sixth, he carried it by storm the following day, witnessed the destruction of Fort Barrancas by the British on the eighth and was again in Mobile on the eleventh, there to find fresh instructions awaiting him.[2]

Applauding his conduct of the expedition against Mobile the authorities cautioned him against any attack upon Pensacola. "Do not, at present," wrote Monroe, "involve the United States in a contest with Spain. The conduct of the Pensacola governor is for complaint rather through the diplomatic channels than an attack on the place. Great trust is reposed in you."[3] Jackson's conduct likewise be

---

1. Monroe to Jackson, Sept. 25, 1814. MSS War Department Archives.
2. Lossing's War of 1812, p. 1023.
3. Monroe to Jackson, Monroe Correspondence, Oct., 1814.

14

came a subject for complaint through the diplomatic channels. Pensacola fallen, Jackson in sad contrast with his
former zeal, appeared to ignore the threatened attack upon
New Orleans. Leaving twelve hundred men at Mobile, dis-
patching one thousand more to attack the Indians and British on the Yellow River and the Escambia, he ordered General Coffee to march with two thousand by easy stages to
Baton Rouge. Sending one regiment direct to New Orleans,
he himself, suffering in body and mind, slowly made his
way to that city arriving on the second of December. But of the subsequent events culminating in the battle
of New Orleans and the utter discomfiture of the British
expedition the historian of Florida has little concern.

During the war many complaints were received of expeditions fitted out in America against the Spanish forces
in the colonies now in revolt. In the spring and fall of
1812 numerous complaints were made that the Mexican
insurgents were procuring arms from the United States and
that a filibustering expedition against that province was
being planned and organized. Further, American privateers were indiscriminately plundering Spanish vessels. The
principal offenders named were the "Revenge" under Captain Butler, and the "Saratoga."

In the fall of 1813 a proclamation published in bombastic and passionate language by a certain Dr. John H.
Robinson appeared at Pittsburgh. Dr. Robinson had already figured in the letters which De Onis, the unrecognized
Spanish envoy, filed at the state department complaining of
the insurgent junta representing the revolutionists of Mexico at New Orleans. The object of the Pittsburgh proclamations was to secure men for service in Mexico against
the Spanish army. Dr. Robinson, it seems, had lately been
in the employ of the United States in making a report of
the conditions in the internal provinces of Spain. His relations with the government made his present activity a cause

for stronger suspicions upon the part of De Onis. With him were operating General Toledo, the late commander of the revolutionists of Texas, and General Humbert, a French adventurer, all engaged in organizing and equipping a force in Louisiana, and elsewhere within the United States, for Mexican service.[1] In July De Onis again protested against the activity of these insurgent representatives in this country. With the aid of the pirates of Barataria, whose suppression and extinction he requested, a force of some six hundred men had been publicly and notoriously recruited and armed in the territory of New Orleans, and under General Humbert and General Gutierres had departed against Matagorda and Tampico.[2] Furthermore banditti from Georgia, under the orders of General Harris of the Georgia militia and Colonels Alexander and MacDonald, had been making hostile incursions into Florida, burning the houses and establishments of the Spanish citizens and robbing them of their slaves and stock.

During the progress of the war efforts had constantly been made at the different courts of Europe to impress upon their governments — particularly those of the maritime nations, including Spain — that we were fighting for their cause as well as our own, against the right of search and impressment. It was hoped that they might realize that it was to their interest that we should not be forced to yield up our rights on the sea. After the fall of Napoleon it was believed from persistent rumors that England and the allies would dispatch large forces to the United States and that Spain in particular was hostile to this country. The council of state it seems recommended to the king of Spain a declaration of war against the United States upon the general grounds of our proceedings relative to Louisiana

---

1. Monroe to Governors of Louisiana and Mississippi Territories, Feb. 14, 1814. Vol. XVI, Domestic Letters, pp. 230, 231.
2. De Onis to Secretary of State, July, 1814, Volume II.

and Florida.   Expeditions were even then preparing at
Cadiz, their destination supposed to be Mexico and Buenos
Ayres though many, expecting an Anglo-Spanish alliance
against this country, looked to see them sail for the United
States.   A fortunate peace rescued America from these
perils.

During the negotiations the envoys of the United States,
in the early stages, insisted upon the cession of the lower
part of the Canadas arguing that by such a cession only
could a lasting peace be secured with Great Britain.[1]   This
representation, quite in keeping with similar pleas at the
court of Spain — for this had been one of the reasons advanced for the sale of the Floridas — indicated that only by
the absence of foreign neighbors could peace be maintained
with this country, a rather unfortunate commentary, it would
seem, upon the character and disposition of this government
and our border settlers.   Carried to its logical conclusion
we must have a continental nation embracing both Americas
or a *reductio ad absurdum.*

---

1.   Vol. VII, Instructions, p. 373.

CHAPTER VII.

IN July, 1810, De Onis had been appointed minister from Spain, but that country, being then torn by factional and civil war, and her throne variously claimed by Joseph Bonaparte, Ferdinand VII, and the junta, the United States determined to become in no manner connected with any of the aspirants to the royal power, and declined either to recognize Ferdinand or receive De Onis. Until some ruler should be recognized as legitimate and obeyed by all factions, the United States declined to receive any representative in an official capacity from that country. De Onis however proceeded to the United States where he was acknowledged merely as a private or unaccredited personage; once in this country he directed at Monroe a rapid fire of protests at this refusal to receive him. Ferdinand and the junta were in control of all Spain and her armies and navies, while Joseph Bonaparte could only be considered in the light of a foreigner invading the country. Other nations had recognized the junta and for the United States to follow their lead could scarcely be considered a violation of neutrality.

Exception was taken by this government to the manner in which the Chevalier de Onis had conducted himself since his advent in this country. Gardoqui had endeavored to promote a dismemberment of the western from the Atlantic states and had pursued, with the co-operation of the Spanish authorities at New Orleans, certain measures

of a highly odious and reprehensible nature.   D'Yrujo's
conduct had been similar to that of Gardoqui with the
difference that it was less masked and more indecent and
insulting to the United States.   He had been a party to the
Burr conspiracy against the Union, and he had sought to
debauch and seduce the Western people.   De Onis it was
insisted had followed in the footsteps of his unfortunate
predecessors, had attempted repeatedly to excite discontent,
had publicly manifested decidedly hostile views towards the
United States and had even suggested the means by which
their dismemberment might be accomplished.   Such was
the nature of the replies made to the protestations of Barnabue and De Onis.   In short De Onis was held to be
persona non grata.

Barnabue filed with Monroe a complete disclaimer and
denial of these charges.   The character of De Onis was the
highest and his feelings to the United States most friendly.
Further it was probable, maintained Barnabue, that those
papers, which it was said proved De Onis's complicity in
plots against the United States, were forgeries.   Of late,
Spanish passports had been repeatedly forged and even the
seal of office and exequaturs of the Spanish consuls in Philadelphia, Baltimore, and New York had been counterfeited.
And there had come into his possession a copy of a letter
from De Onis forged by the French revolutionary party in
the United States. [1]

George W. Erving, who was our chargé at Madrid,
owing to the war and chaotic condition of affairs in
Spain, quit that country in May, 1810, and went to
England.   The United States had no direct intercourse
with the Spanish nation during the terms of the cortes
and regency, but throughout these years this country
was unofficially represented by Anthony Morris, and
Thomas L. Brent who had been secretary of legation.

---

1.   Barnabue to secretary of state, Vol. II, p. 3, July, 1811.

Affairs had not progressed smoothly even before Erving's departure in 1810, for we find him complaining that the papers and letters of the legation were being searched and scrutinized by Spanish officials. On some charge, it is not clear just what, the Reverend Thomas Gough, agent and chancellor of the legation, had been arrested. And Erving found cause to felicitate himself upon foiling an attempt made in 1808, by one Ravarra, to assassinate him.

After Erving left Madrid there seems to have been much friction, much scheming, much working at cross purposes in the American legation. Thomas Brent and Anthony Morris and Thomas Gough, among the three, generated an over-supply of friction. Brent in his letters to the United States spoke always in most disparaging and contemptuous terms of Morris whom he accused of seeking the appointment of minister to Spain. Mr. Morris advanced his knowledge of the Spanish language as an inducement for his nomination to the coveted post. But Gough, failing to be properly impressed, wrote: "Mr. Morris may talk of his proficiency in the Spanish language and his diplomatic career, but of both I think as highly as of the progress of Cato in the Greek who began to learn this tongue at the age of sixty."[1] At any rate Morris was party to a discreditable intrigue, in which figured certain Spanish officials, to make himself minister — one feature of which was to discredit Erving with the ministry of Spain who would protest against his appointment. In 1814 the government of Spain was re-established and Ferdinand seated on the throne with the consent of the nation. In August of that year Erving was named as our minister to that country.

Cevallos, the Spanish minister of foreign affairs, however, announced that certain wrongs committed by the United States must be redressed before a minister from this country could be received. De Onis, who, as we have

---

1. Thomas Gough to Thomas Brent, Feb. 29, 1816.

seen, was personally disagreeable to our president, was
to be received, the posts in both Floridas were to be returned to the Spanish officials, and due satisfaction made for
their seizure.[1] De Onis moreover was to be recognized
under and by virtue of his appointment and letters of 1809,
when, from the position taken by the United States, the government of Spain was practically in abeyance. The United
States declined to enter into any discussion of the events
in the Floridas during the recent war, until ministers had
been reciprocally received, when these affairs might be
made the subject of diplomatic interchanges. As for the
refusal to receive De Onis under the appointment of 1809,
that, it was insisted, was imputable to the state of Spain at
that time, her territory being in the possession of contending
armies nearly equal, victory sometimes favoring both and
the result altogether precarious. It was the interest of the
United States to take no part in that controversy and they
were under no obligation to do so. Had they acknowledged
either party, as would have been done by the acceptance of a
minister, just cause of offense would have been given to the
other. As soon as Ferdinand was recognized and received
as the sovereign of Spain the president had appointed a
minister to him, instructed to explain why that measure
had not been sooner adopted.

There were serious objections to De Onis personally
but "in a spirit of amity," it was declared that, "if his
Catholic Majesty after knowing them should request your
recognition as an act of accommodation to himself it would
be complied with." Much was made of the fact that the
Chevalier de Onis had produced no letter of credence from
Ferdinand, and that his appointment by the central junta
was in itself not a sufficient authority. Monroe was indignant at the repeated requests for the acceptance of De Onis

---

1. George W. Erving to Monroe, Paris, Dec. 4, 1814, Vol. XIII.

"not as an act of accommodation to your sovereign but of concession on the part of the United States," and further took occasion to communicate to De Onis certain of his views upon the course of one power pressing another, equally independent, to recognize against its will a minister to whom objections of a personal nature were entertained. [1]

A vast amount of undignified quibbling, alike discreditable to both nations, was indulged in over this question of the recognition of ministers and renewal of diplomatic intercourse. Each nation insisted upon the acceptance of its minister as the condition precedent to its reception of the representative of the other. And when, in June of 1815, De Onis received new letters of credence from Ferdinand the United States still refused to receive him until Ferdinand should expressly state that he desired his acceptance as a personal favor to himself. Ferdinand having at length complied with this condition, that gentleman was received by the president, December 19, 1815, as a "distinguished proof of his high consideration" for the Spanish monarch. Diplomatic intercourse was thus at length renewed after irritating higgling and splitting of hairs, partaking too much of the child's method of quarreling.

Diplomatic relations having been resumed, the questions of years' standing were again taken up. Anthony Morris, during that gentleman's sojourn at Madrid, having authority to receive "informal communications" from the Spanish government, as early as 1814, expressed the opinion that East and West Florida could be purchased. He intimated that $10,000 for douceurs would be indispensable as the different departments of the Spanish government were not sufficiently "regenerated" to allow great hopes of success without the use of such means. Spain was at that time practically bankrupt and corruption was rampant in public office. The suggestion of Morris seems to have

---

1. Vol. II, Foreign Letters, p. 86, Monroe to De Onis, May 5, 1815.

elicited neither consideration nor reply from this government. In the fall of 1815 it was persistently rumored in Europe that the Floridas had been ceded to England but, in response to a pointed inquiry from Morris, Cevallos asserted in the most positive terms that no such cession had been made. [1]

After his reception in December, 1815, De Onis entered feelingly into a series of protests against our course in the Floridas during the war of 1812, and our relations with the revolted Spanish provinces, in permitting filibustering expeditions to be fitted out in this country. He first imperatively demanded that West Florida be returned before any discussion as to its ownership could be considered. He bitterly and repeatedly protested against that "gang of seditious, incendiary profligates who were carrying on with impunity, in the state of Louisiana and New Orleans especially, an uninterrupted system of raising and arming troops for the purpose of lighting the torch of revolution in the kingdom of New Spain (Mexico)." All the state of Louisiana had witnessed, he declared, those armaments, the public recruitings, the transportation of arms, the meetings of the seditious and their hostile and warlike march from the territory of this republic against the dominions of their friendly and neighboring power.

Joseph Alvarez de Toledo and Joseph Manuel de Herrera, the latter calling himself "minister near the United States" of the self styled Mexican congress, were the ringleaders in these recruiting expeditions. De Onis requested that orders be issued to the collectors of the custom houses prohibiting the admission into our ports of vessels sailing under the insurgent flag of Cartagena, the Mexican congress, Buenos Ayres or any other place in insurrection against Spanish authority. Vessels, flying the flags of these revolted colonies, were constantly armed in our harbors

1. Vol. II, Foreign Letters, p. 86, Monroe to De Onis, May 5, 1815.

with the object of destroying and plundering Spanish vessels, and then returning to our ports to find a mart for the
spoils of their piracies. [1]

Without doubt a serious breach of international law
was committed by the United States during these years,
although this nation exercised what it declared to be great
diligence against these abuses.   To the impartial critic
there seems to have been a highly damaging and incriminating amount of connivance and blindness on the part of many
of the government officials.   These so-called revolutionary
governments could have no communication with any power
in amity with Spain for neither that government nor any
other had acknowledged their independence.   That a
stronger, more virile nation than Spain would have taken
more decisive measures than recourse to mere diplomatic
protests, we cannot doubt.   As it was, the United States
might well have been liable for damages and spoliations on
the very principle by which we enforced the Alabama claims
against England half a century later.   The Spanish complaints against the filibustering expeditions and armaments
fitted out in our ports covered a period of ten years from
1812.

In a vigorous protest, which followed closely upon the
heels of his first, De Onis announced to Monroe that he
had received positive information that two bodies of troops
of one thousand men from Kentucky and three hundred
from Tennessee, commanded by American citizens holding
Mexican commissions, were about to set out for Mexico to
enlist in the revolutionary service.   Toledo, Humbert,
Amaya, Bernado, Gutierres, Urtui, Dr. Robinson, and Majors Peive and Priere were the leaders against whom the
Spanish minister sought executive action.   Unless the insurgent activity in this country be immediately suppressed,
"the king, my master," declared De Onis, "will have reason

---

1.   Vol. III, De Onis to Monroe, Dec. 30, 1815.

to suspect that if those meetings are not authorized by the government, they are at least tolerated; all the assurances I may give to my sovereign of the friendly disposition of the president will not stand any competence when compared with the evident proofs I had the honor to communicate in this and my former note; particularly when his Majesty is well convinced of the resources and authority of the federal government and the promptitude with which their orders are strictly observed in the whole Union." [1]

This he followed with an explanation of the violation

---

1. Vol. III, De Onis to secretary of state, p. 2, Jan., 1816.

In this letter De Onis seeks to show the short-sightedness of the people of our southern and western states in helping to secure the freedom of New Spain, or Mexico, and helping to there build up a new and independent nation. The statements and conclusions of the Spanish minister are most interesting in view of our later history, and the present condition of Mexico. "Grant that the new government and constitution would be all that could be desired: the climate of Mexico is more temperate than that of the United States, the soil richer and more productive; the productions and fruits more abundant, wealthy and of a superior quality, and that provisions, hand work, wood, houses, clothing, etc., are in consequence of the mildness and regularity of the climate exceeding cheaper than in this country. If this event should take place do you not think, sir, as I do, that so many alluring prospects and so many evident advantages would deprive this republic of the successive emigrations from Europe and, what is more, of a very considerable part of the most useful and industrious inhabitants of this confederation who would carry with them to Mexixo their flour and saw mills, machines, manufactures, their enterprising genius, in a word their general instruction and all the means that actually promote and vivify the commerce of these states. I flatter myself that this event will not happen; but I am fully convinced that all the consequences of this hypothesis can be demonstrated almost with a mathematical certainty; and that if the citizens of Kentucky, Louisiana and Georgia should reflect deeply on this subject, far from giving any aid to these incendiaries, thirsty of gold and regardless of the happiness of their country, would unite themselves with the authorities of the king, my master, to punish that gang of perfidious traitors that hide themselves in their territory with the criminal design of devastating their country."

That Mexico today has an excellent constitution no one questions. So indeed has Venezuela and many of the other periodically revolutionizing southern nations. It seems to be not the form of government so much as the genius of the people that constitutes a nation great or insignificant. The climatic conditions must be considered largely as a factor entering into the character and disposition of the people.

of the neutrality of Florida in the war of 1812. De Onis declared that Spain had protested to Great Britain and to
Europe against the forcible occupation of Florida and violation of her neutrality, and that it was due to personal
misconduct of the governor of West Florida. As a proof
of this he called attention to the fact that the strictest neutrality was observed in Cuba, East Florida and other
Spanish possessions, thus absolving from all blame the
Spanish ministry and government. Then began a long and
tedious interchange of views and presentation of arguments
on the western and eastern boundaries of Louisiana.

De Onis insisted that the territory extending to the
Rio Bravo or del Norte had been under the dominion of
Spain both before and since the treaty by which France
had ceded Louisiana to his Catholic Majesty, that it had
been under Spanish dominion from the time of the discovery and conquest of Mexico, without ever having passed
by treaty to any other nation. He declared, in 1816, that
the two Floridas had passed into the hands of England by
cession from France and Spain in 1763, and were in the
legitimate possession of England from 1763 to 1783, and
therefore France could not cede them — together with
Louisiana — to Spain, by the treaty of 1764, nor could Spain
retrocede them to France, France not having received them
from her, unless there should have been an article on this
point, in which express and direct mention was made of that
cession. Further the claim of the United States to any of
the Floridas seemed to De Onis wholly intangible, for the
two contracting parties, Spain and France, had declared in
the most solemn manner, the first that she did not cede to
France any part of the Floridas, the second that she had
not acquired them by the treaty of San Ildefonso nor had the
least intention to set up a claim to them. De Onis maintained that according to all the principles of justice no one
could be ousted from what he holds until the right of the

claimant should be proved and recognized — that Spain
having been in possession of West Florida when the United
States claimed it, she should keep it until in a friendly negotiation this republic had shown a better right to it.

Taking an analogous case in private law, if A should
say that he never sold B a certain plot of land, and B says
that he never claimed ownership of it, would C, a purchaser
from B, simply enter and take possession of the premises
which A says he never bought? De Onis forwarded to Monroe copies of several letters confirming his representations
on the filibustering expeditions which were continually being
organized in the southwest. These implicated the former
leader, John McIntosh, in a plot to recruit in Georgia a
number of vagabonds to invade again East Florida.[1] Despite presidential proclamations these violations of our
neutrality became constantly more flagrant.

In reply to the representations of De Onis, Monroe entered into a careful review of the grounds of complaint of
the United States against Spain. He rehashed the Spanish
spoliation claims — the losses sustained by the seizure and
condemnation of vessels in Spanish ports — the failure to
ratify the convention of 1802, the suppression of the deposit
at New Orleans, the negotiations preliminary to the purchase of Louisiana and the consequent dispute over boundaries, our unsuccessful effort to secure Florida by purchase or trade and thus remove the dangerous element of
jealousy and the resultant injuries to the two countries —
how every proposition of the American envoys had been
rejected and none made in return. Such conduct on the
part of Spain, insisted Monroe, would have justified, if it
did not even invite, decisive measures on the part of the
United States. It left this nation free to pursue such a
course as, in their judgment, a just regard to the honor,

---

1. Vol. III, De Onis to Monroe, Feb. 22, 1816. A translation
of these letters bears out the charges made by De Onis. The question
then arises whether the letters are authentic.

the rights, and the interests of the nation might dictate. For the condition of affairs in the Spanish Peninsula and the Spanish provinces in America excited no apprehension of any serious consequences that might follow even a decisive action on our part. Besides the injuries already catalogued there were the breaches of neutrality, which the Spanish government permitted, if indeed it did not authorize, by British troops and British agents in Florida and through the Creeks and other Indian tribes in the late war.

"In reply to your demand for the exclusion of the flag of the revolting provinces," wrote Monroe, "I have to observe that in consequence of the unsettled state of many countries and repeated changes of the ruling authority in each, there being at the same time several competitors, and each party bearing its appropriate flag, the President thought it proper some time past to give orders to the collectors not to make the flag of any vessel a criterion or condition of its admission into the ports of the United States. Having taken no part in the differences and convulsions which have disturbed those countries, it is consistent with the just principles, as it is with the interests of the United States, to receive the vessels of all countries into their ports, to whatever party belonging and under whatever flag sailing, pirates excepted, requiring of them only the payment of the duties and obedience to the laws while under their jurisdiction: without adverting to the question whether they had committed any violation of the allegiance or laws obligatory on them in the countries to which they belonged either in assuming such flag or in any other respect."

In answer to the complaints of De Onis that the United States was offering assistance to the revolted provinces and that, but for the support which the revolutionists received from the people of this nation, they must have long since miserably failed, Monroe wrote: "All that your government had a right to claim of the United States was that they should not interfere in the contest or promote by any active service the success of the revolution, admitting that they continued to overlook the injuries received from Spain and remained at peace. This right was common to the colonists. With equal justice might they claim that we would not interfere to their disadvantage; that our ports should remain open to both parties as they were before the commencement of the struggle; that our laws regulating commerce with foreign nations should not be changed to their injury. On these principles the United States have acted." [1]

De Onis intimated that in a general treaty, which would settle all differences between the two countries, Spain might be willing to cede her claim to territory east of the Mississippi, in satisfaction of claims and in exchange for territory west of that river. [2] However the king of Spain was unwilling to deprive himself of East Florida and the important port of Pensacola, the key to the Gulf of Mexico. In support of the contention that West Florida did not pass into the hands of France with the cession of Louisiana, De Onis quoted the sixth article of the treaty of 1778 between France and the United States, by which the former power engaged never to acquire West Florida or any of the territories ceded to England in 1763. In answer to our claims against Spain for spoliations by French cruisers and French prize courts, De Onis argued that these claims had been settled by France in her treaty with the United States in 1803, wherein the United States had released France from all liability by the provision for indemnification. At any rate Spain could in no way be held liable and, if the treaty of 1803 did not settle those claims, the responsibility rested with France alone.

Months were consumed in an exchange of arguments

1. Vol. II, Foreign Legations, p. 121, Monroe to Chevalier de Onis, Jan. 19, 1816.
2. Vol. VIII, Instructions, p. 32, Monroe to Erving, March 11, 1816.

concerning the Louisiana boundaries, without arriving at
any conclusion.   Each party to the controversy presented
some few new deductions in its own favor, but it was mostly
a tiresome reiteration of the correspondence of a decade
before, able neither to convince nor persuade.   Monroe
argued, with much show of reason, that had it been intended
to exempt any portion of the former province of Louisiana
from the operation of the treaty of San Ildefonso, it would
have been easy to do so and in a manner to preclude all
doubt of the intention of the parties.   It might have been
stated that Spain ceded back to France such part of the
province as France had ceded to Spain.   Or they might have
defined the extent of the cession by a natural boundary
which would have been equally distinct, concise, and satisfactory, and thus there could have arisen no controversy
between France and Spain, nor between the United States
and Spain respecting the eastern limits. [1]   It is not necessary to review the arguments, already given at length, advanced by the two nations.

We find the communications of De Onis to the secretary of state at this time, teeming with complaints against
the unjust rulings of the American prize courts and the
armament of vessels in our ports — filibustering expeditions.
The "Fairy," the "Romp," the "Chasseur" and the "Comet"
— the same vessel often sailing under different names —
were frequently mentioned as offenders.   One vessel in particular, the "Caledonia," was being fitted out by a Xavier
Mina, at Baltimore, to assist the Mexican insurgents.   Her
cargo consisted of twenty-five hundred muskets, fifty pair
of pistols, two cases of swords and cutlasses, one hundred
saddles, bridles and complete equipment for one hundred
cavalry, a quantity of cavalry uniforms, barrels of powder,
nine eight-pounders, a printing press for striking off procla-

---

1.   Vol. II, Foreign Legations, p. 142, Monroe to Chevalier de Onis,
June 10, 1816.

15

mations, etc., and all manner of provisions. In the same
connection De Onis filed charges against the officer commanding the naval forces of the United States on the New
Orleans station, for encouraging and conniving at this filibustering. That many of the complaints of De Onis were
misrepresentations and exaggerations we can well believe,
but at the same time we are forced to admit that there was
good cause for his protests.

It can scarcely be denied that except for the assistance
rendered, directly or indirectly through the United States,
most of the Spanish American revolutions must have miserably failed. It is also true that many Spanish vessels
fell a prey to these South American privateers within fir-
ing distance of our shores — a violation of the territory of
the United States. And in many instances, particularly at
Baltimore, Norfolk, and New Orleans, the fitting out of
these armaments was only too clearly connived at by the
American customs officials. Many of the charges of De
Onis were substantiated by affidavits of American citizens
who had been asked to enlist for service on these vessels,
being assured "that they were being fitted out for the purpose of fighting the Spaniards." Nor did these privateers
hesitate in the most wanton manner to prostitute the flag
of the United States. As an instance, we may cite the
case of the "Patricia Mexicana," commanded by José Esta-
fanos, manned with citizens of the United States, and covered by the American flag, under which they chased and
brought to the Spanish polacre, the "Santa Maria," until,
having effected her capture, the insurgent flag was
hoisted. An unparalleled audacity these buccaneers displayed by such predatory acts, in trampling under foot national rights and removing themselves from the protection
of international law.

The so-called "Napoleon Propaganda" in the late summer of 1817 aroused alike the French and Spanish ambas-

sadors. This was a plot, it seems, on the part of certain people who had emigrated to this country from Europe — ostensibly to settle western lands — to seduce the western inhabitants and organize, under color of forming a colony, an expedition to invade Mexico and there proclaim Joseph Bonaparte. The plot was supported by the very riches of which Joseph had plundered Spain. This matter was laid before the secretary of state by the French minister but, like many of the wild schemes so prevalent in that day and region, it seems to have rapidly vanished into thin air or to have died in the imaginations of those adventurous empire builders in whose minds alone it may have had its only existence.

We now come to treat of one of the most audacious and surprising incidents of American history.

The treaty of Fort Jackson, which terminated the Creek war of 1814, ceded to the United States several million acres of Indian land purposely selected so as to separate the Indian settlements of Georgia and Alabama — an arrangement which it was expected would insure peace and order in that section. But, unfortunately for these hopes, many of the Creeks, still unsubdued and refusing to recognize the treaty, had fled to Florida and joined the Seminole Indians under their chief Boleck, or more popularly "Billy Bowlegs." Here as the allies of Great Britain, and relying upon the promises of that nation, they fully expected the restoration of their lands upon the conclusion of peace between England and the United States.

In this contention they were supported by a former British officer and adventurer, Colonel Edward Nicholls, who, claiming to be "on his Majesty's service," concluded an offensive and defensive alliance between England and the Seminoles, rebuilt an old fort on the Appalachicola some fifteen miles from its mouth, supplied it with arms, made a demand on Colonel Hawkins for the evacuation of the Creek lands under the ninth article of our treaty with England, and requested the arrest of certain men charged with murder. Early in the summer of 1815 Nicholls with his troops, the Indian prophet Francis, and many of the leading Creeks, departed for London, leaving in the fort some 750 barrels of cannon powder, 2,500 muskets, casks of gunpowder, and many hundred carbines, pistols, swords and various accoutrements. These English officers, not under direct responsibility, and operating on foreign territory, acted with much arbitrary self will, seizing the opportunity to gratify their personal malice without being held to strict account. It is impossible to understand many of their actions consistently with any theory and it is certain that England would not have sanctioned much that was done in her name.

Besides the refugee Creeks there were in Florida at that time, many runaway slaves — probably a thousand or more — who had escaped from their Georgia owners. They had adopted the manner of life of the redskins. They were commanded by chiefs and had farms and grazing lands stretching fifty miles either way along the Appalachicola from the British post. After the departure of Nicholls and his followers these negroes seized the British post and it was henceforth known as the "Negro Fort." The blacks rapidly degenerated into an army of outlaws and plunderers. The Georgia frontier was especially the scene of their efforts. They harried the country, drove off cattle, freed slaves, rescued criminals, murdered those who resisted, fired upon boats passing up and down the river and became the terror of the region. General Jackson was directed by the secretary of war to demand of the Spanish governor of Pensacola the suppression of this nuisance.[1] Jackson promptly complied with the orders and intimated at the

---

1. Crawford to Jackson, March 15, 1816, State Papers, 2nd Session, 15th Congress, No. 122, p. 5.

same time that if Spain did not destroy the fort and break up the outlaws, the United States would.[1]

General Edmund Gaines had been instructed to take possession of the lands secured under the Fort Jackson treaty, build forts and block-houses and furnish suitable and sufficient protection for the surveyors engaged in running the township and section lines. Colonel Clinch was deputed to undertake these duties. As Clinch moved down the Chattahoochee, General Gaines, fearing danger from the Negro Fort, asked and secured authority from General Jackson to build a fort on the Appalachicola, near the boundary, so as to effectively overawe the hostile negroes.[2] Jackson gave this permission to Gaines in no uncertain terms: "The growing hostility of the Indians," he said, "must be checked by prompt and energetic measures. Half peace and half war is a state of things which must not exist. I have no doubt that this fort has been established by some villains for the purpose of murder, rapine, and plunder, and that it ought to be blown up regardless of the ground it stands on. If you have come to the same conclusion destroy it and restore the stolen negroes to their rightful owners."[3]

Gaines immediately set about building the fort, afterwards called Fort Scott, near the junction of the Flint, Chattahoochee and Appalachicola rivers. Owing to the cost and hazards of land transportation he decided to bring his supplies from New Orleans by water. This of course necessitated passing the Negro Fort. Fearful of an attack at this point, Gaines requested Daniel Patterson, commander of the New Orleans station, to provide a convoy.[4] Jairus

---

1. Jackson to the Governor of Pensacola, State Papers, 2nd Session, 15th Congress; No. 122, p. 8.
2. Gaines to Jackson, March 20, 1816, *ibid.*, pp. 14, 15.
3. Jackson to Gaines, April 8, 1816.
4. Gaines to Patterson, May 22, 1816, State Papers, 2nd Session, 15th Congress, No. 122, pp. 118, 119.

Loomis was accordingly ordered to rendezvous with two
gunboats at Pass Christian prepared to escort up the river
two transports laden with ordnance and provisions. On
July 10, 1816, the fleet arrived at the mouth of the Appalachicola.

In the meantime, hearing that the Indians were drink-
ing the war medicine, and celebrating their martial dances,
and confident that the passage of the fleet would be disputed
at the Negro Fort, General Gaines ordered Colonel Clinch,
with sufficient troops to move down the river, take a position
near the Negro Fort and raze it at the first sign of an attack.
Clinch and Loomis prepared to move at the same time.
During the delay a boat crew, while seeking fresh water,
was attacked by the negroes and three men were killed and
one made prisoner.

Floating down the river from Fort Scott, Clinch met a
party of negro-hunting Seminoles who joined him, hoping
to secure possession again of their fort. A negro with a
white scalp at his belt was captured. From him was learned
the attack on the boat crew. Clinch now determined on
his course, pushed forward and invested the fort. A demand for its surrender was answered by the hoisting of a
red flag and the English Union Jack with a defiant discharge of cannon. Loomis, in response to the request of
Clinch, came up with his boats and on the morning of July
27 opened fire. The ramparts were strong enough to withstand unscathed the light guns of the vessels. It was then
determined to burn the fort. After securing the range, a
ball, red hot from the cook's galley, was sent sputtering over
the wall into the magazine. The scene that followed defies
description and the mind must take the place of the pen.
There is no imagination so torpid as not to be able to conceive at once all the frightful colorings of the picture.
Seven hundred barrels of gunpowder tore a vast hole in
the ground, and hurled the wretched, screaming, mangled

victims through the air.[1] The scene was of hell in all its fury. The tortures were of the damned. Some two hundred and seventy men, women, and children were instantly killed, while of the sixty or more taken alive the greater number soon found death a welcome relief from their sufferings. Garçon, the leader, and a Choctaw chief, taken alive, were consigned to the cruel tortures of the infuriated Seminoles.

As the curtain fell on this awful scene, peace and quiet along the frontier were secured, temporarily at least. The Seminoles were duly impressed with the strength of the federal power and the awful visitation upon the enemies of the United States which they had witnessed. With peace seemingly assured, and the prospect of an early acquisition of the province of Florida by the United States, many of the more prominent men of Tennessee started a wild speculation in Pensacola property. But the Seminole Indians could not forget the wrongs they had suffered at the hands of the whites and awaited but a new provocation and an able leader to induce them to take the war-path and show that quiet is not pacification, nor is desolation peace.

The story now shifts to the east and for the next act the curtain rises upon Amelia Island. We need no effort of the mental faculties to realize the condition into which that island had fallen since the withdrawal of the American troops, who had earlier taken the place in conjunction with the so-called East Florida "patriots." We have further seen that this was essentially an era and community of filibustering and privateering. The expedition of General Miranda who had sailed from New York to Cartagena in 1806 was probably the first. His example was persistently followed. Amelia Island, from its location and its utter freedom from all law or recognized authority, was an

---

1. Jairus Loomis to Daniel Patterson, Aug. 13, 1816, State Papers, 2nd Session, 15th Congress, No. 119, pp. 15, 16.

admirable depot for such undertakings. The people there had become quite accustomed to adventurers of all sorts, pirates, admirals, generals, and dignitaries of every kind and description suddenly appearing to assume authority, presently to vanish silently away. The island long feasted its eyes on the prodigious galloping and curvetting of red-sashed majors, gold laced colonels and epauletted generals.

Since the termination of the war of 1812, a motley and miscellaneous crew it was that had congregated there — British adventurers who had followed in the wake of the English army, Irish and French refugees; Scotch enthusiasts, Mexican and Spanish insurgents; graduates of the Baratarian school; relics and remnants of a negro squad that had served in Mexico under Aury; privateersmen, slavers, traders and all manner of scoundrels — in short the nobility of deviltry were all there. And that they included many Americans we cannot for a moment doubt when we learn that among the first acts of the filibusters was the establishment of a newspaper. One of this brand of adventurers who had gravitated to the South American scenes of rebellion and revolution was a Gregor MacGregor, who claimed to be a brother-in-law of General Simon Bolivar. After an unsuccessful attempt against the Spanish possessions in Mexico, having recruited at Baltimore an expedition to "wrest the Floridas from Spain," MacGregor arrived in Fernandina harbor late in June of 1817, and within a few days captured the fort.[1]

Colonel Morales, the Spanish officer in command, sailed for St. Augustine while MacGregor took possession of the lower St. Johns and established a blockade of the city. MacGregor was, like most of those leaders, a man of intelligence and fine appearance. In demanding the surrender of Fernandina he had addressed a communication to Mor-

---

1. July 14 and 21, 1817.

ales to which he had signed himself: "Gregor MacGregor, Brigadier General of the armies of the United Provinces of New Granada and Venezuela, and General-in-chief of that destined to emancipate the provinces of both Floridas, under the commission of the Supreme Government of Mexico, and South America, etc., etc."

The series of proclamations which followed the advent of this Scotchman was truly formidable. Official documents gay and impressive with chromatic seals and jaunty ribbons were daily promulgated. In one of them his followers were directed to wear, each on his left arm a shield of red cloth with the words "Venredores de Aurala" and a wreath of oak and laurel leaves embroidered in yellow silk. In another he promised soon to plant the "green cross of Florida on the proud walls of St. Augustine." A third declared all Florida in a state of blockade beginning at the south side of the island of Amelia and extending to the Perdido.[1] But nature in endowing MacGregor with the talent of producing proclamations exhausted her gifts and denied him the ability to carry them out. Wearied in the effort of composition, he achieved nothing more.

There may have been some honest intention in their announced plans for freeing Florida but it seems more reasonable to conclude that it was his purpose to supplant Spanish misrule in those regions by his own. Those who fight for freedom, to avenge their wrongs or even to retaliate for the grievances of their country, enlist us in their cause at once. But we find little in the affair at Amelia to awaken our sympathy or merit our support. The people of Florida did not appear to have any love for the self-styled patriots, nor did the insurgents display any marked zeal in joining the Scotchman's standard.

Abundantly supplied with money, MacGregor entertained at lavish dinners and entertainments the worthy fam-

---

1. Niles Register, Vol. XIII, p. 28, Sept. 6, 1817.

ilies of Fernandina. But affairs went badly. Disease and desertions played havoc with his already depleted forces. Supplies were scarce. His paper money did not inspire confidence and rapidly depreciated. The proposed expedition to St. Augustine was abandoned. In September Mac-Gregor sailed for New Providence to secure recruits and supplies, leaving in command one Hubbard, lately sheriff of New York.

One day, about the first of October, a small fleet appeared in the harbor under the command of Louis Aury, a man of the MacGregor stripe. A short account of Aury's career will help the reader to a clearer understanding and appreciation of these filibusters, then in the zenith of their power and glory. According to his own narration, being filled with a burning desire to immolate himself on the altar of freedom, Aury had gone to Cartagena to devote his life to the cause of liberty. The Spanish fleet and troops arriving at that point most inopportunely for his ambitions, he had managed, with a few ships, to run the blockade and reach San Domingo. After laying in stores and recruiting his forces he and his followers eagerly scanned the horizon for an available spot where they might "spill their blood in the cause of American independence and freedom."

Texas seemed the most profitable field for these seekers of gory fame and they were not long in reaching Galveston Bay where Aury was hailed with delight by Don Manuel de Herrera whom we recognize as the "Minister Plenipotentiary from the Republic of Mexico to the United States." Galveston was declared the Puerto Habillitado, of the Republic of Mexico, Aury was made military governor, letters of marque were issued, courts of admiralty established. A horde of vagabonds promptly assembled like vultures gathering for the feast. Negroes, smugglers, Baratarian refugees, freebooters, escaped criminals and others of the same type — on they came — a motley horde they were.

This patch of sand however was not to Aury's taste and in April, 1817, the place was abandoned by that fickle leader, with no one left to assume the authority so lavishly bestowed upon him. But within a few days these noble buccaneers had formed a new government — a travesty to be sure; the governor, admiralty judges, prize courts, collector, notary public, secretary and all the other functionaries necessary for carrying on a good intentioned state. They too sought to execute another weird bit of drollery, tragically saluting liberty and prospective spoils. What mattered Mexico to them, should they be blamed because they had never heard of such a nation? Were they not assembled in the sacred cause of plunder and loot?

Their only object was to capture Spanish ships and Spanish property, and could they be censured if in their zeal they occasionally made mistakes in distinguishing national flags and thus fell into a way of plundering every sort of property, and capturing all manner of ships so presumptuous as to appear on the high sea?

But what good all their plunder if they possessed no market or no clearing house? To obviate this difficulty they raised the Mexican flag and declared that they were acting under authority of that republic — for this sophistry might indeed save many a well curved neck from the vengeful and profane gallows. In their courts of admiralty the captured ships were adjudged good prizes and the plunder was hurried to New Orleans through this mock obedience to the troublesome forms of international law. There the market was kept stocked with "jewelry, laces, silks and linens, muslins, britannias, seersuckers, china, crockery, glass and slaves," and every other conceivable commodity.

But to return to Aury. Entering Fernandina he was appealed to for assistance, which, with proper magnanimity, he refused, unless the green cross should give way to the Mexican flag and he be made governor and commander-in-chief. Compliance was rendered easy by necessity, and October 4th Amelia Island, formally declared a part of the Republic of Mexico, passed into the hands of "General" Aury. But his rule was brief in this volatile community.

Acting under the joint congressional resolution of January, 1811, the president of the United States ordered troops and ships to suppress the "liberation" movement. Resistance being futile, Aury, protesting against such interference, quietly surrendered Fernandina and the American navy took possession while he sailed away out of the history of Florida. A second time was Fernandina thus under the stars and stripes, garrisoned by United States troops, in trust for the king of Spain. But the place was soon abandoned by the American marines who evacuated in the face of a superior enemy — the yellow fever, that rapidly depopulated the town.

In the meantime the Seminole Indian question had become critical. The failure to recover the lands ceded by the treaty of Fort Jackson had made them ugly and vengeful, and when they saw white settlements and forts on their ancestral domains and hunting grounds they sullenly determined to take an early opportunity of regaining by force what they felt to be rightfully their own. During 1817 collisions between the Indians and white settlers were frequent. The Indian agents, Hawkins and Mitchell — the latter a former governor of Georgia — undoubtedly the fairest and best informed witnesses who appeared before the congressional committee in 1818-19, testified that the blame for these collisions was equal, that the white settlers were as much the aggressors as the Indians, and that the lawless persons in Georgia and Florida were particularly to be censured for acts which provoked retaliation. The Indians with the Bible theory of "an eye for an eye and a tooth for a tooth" navely claimed that four Indians had been killed to one white and that they must insist upon a proper balancing of accounts. With the usual inaccuracy and perversion in the reports which were sent north, the blame was laid upon the redskins. Harrowing stories were rife of men, women, and children murdered, cabins burned, cattle run off, and of unwonted warlike preparations on the part of the savages.[1] That most of these reports were true there can be little doubt, but that the whites had brought much of it upon themselves by their treatment of the unfortunate redskins there is as little question.

A settlement of about twoscore Indians, known as Fowltown, some fifteen miles from Fort Scott, near the national boundary became particularly inflamed. War paint was used in crude and inartistic abundance, the war dance was celebrated, the red war pole erected and notice sent to Major Twiggs in command of Fort Scott "not to cross or cut a stick of timber on the east side of the Flint." The warning was met with silent contempt but when General Gaines arrived with reinforcements it was determined to summon the Fowltown chief to a conference. The invitation having met with a defiant refusal, Major Twiggs was dispatched with two hundred and fifty men to bring the chief and leading warriors, or, in case he met with resistance, to treat them as enemies. As the Americans approached the town they were fired on; most of the Indians having found refuge in the swamps, the town was taken and burned. "This fact," said Mitchell, "was, I conceive, the cause of the Seminole war." The whole country arose and war was on.

In accordance with a decision reached at a meeting of some twenty-seven hundred warriors, shortly before, the Indians considered war as an accepted fact now that the American troops had crossed the Flint River. While the soldiers were burning Fowltown a large open boat under Lieutenant Scott, containing seven women, four children

1. American State Papers, Military Affairs, Vol. I, pp. 681-685.

and forty soldiers, was slowly wending its way up the Appalachicola toward Fort Scott. Fearing trouble, Scott had sent to the fort for help. There were, however, no signs of hostility until, in picking its course, the boat came close to the shore of a densely wooded swamp when suddenly a volley of musketry was poured upon the party at point-blank range. Lieutenant Scott and almost every soldier fell. Boarding the helpless craft the Indians retaliated for the Fowltown ruins by an indiscriminate slaughter. The historian would gladly draw the curtain on the scene. A grewsome play of savage deviltry was enacted there. Women cut down and scalped, children taken by the heels and their brains dashed out, the dead mutilated by savages drunk with the sight of blood. Of the whole boatload only five survived the horrible orgy. One woman was carried into captivity and four men, leaping overboard, succeeded in reaching the other shore able to convey the awful news to an indignant audience.

In response to Lieutenant Scott's appeal for help, two covered boats with forty men were hastily dispatched. Too late to be of any assistance, the reinforcements pushed on and rescued Major Muhlenburg who was coming up from Mobile with three boats laden with military stores. For four days these boats were obliged to remain at anchor in mid-stream for no man could raise his head above the bulwarks without offering himself as a target for the fire of the Indians. [1]

By the time that reports of these outrages reached Washington General Gaines, in obedience to orders from Calhoun, had gone to Amelia Island. Instructions were immediately dispatched to Andrew Jackson, directing him to proceed to Fort Scott, assume command of the forces stationed there, call on the governors of adjacent states for the necessary militia, and push the war to an end. This

---

1. American State Papers, Military Affairs, Vol. I, pp. 690, 691.

order, dated December 26, 1817, was passed on its way south by a letter from Jackson to Monroe.

Hatred of the Spanish was Jackson's cloud and his pillar of fire which guided his days and nights. In Nashville it was generally understood and expected that Jackson was moving against Florida when he set out for the Seminole war, and it was for this expedition that most of the volunteers enlisted. "To storm the walls of St. Augustine" was the battle cry in Tennessee.

CHAPTER VIII.

JACKSON, after reading the orders to Gaines to prosecute the war against the Indians, wrote a confidential
letter to President Monroe on the subject. "The executive
government has ordered," said he, "and, as I conceive, very
properly, Amelia Island to be taken possession of. This order ought to be carried into execution at all hazards and simultaneously the whole of East Florida seized, and held as
indemnity for the outrages of Spain upon the property of
our citizens. This done, it puts all opposition down, se-
cures our citizens a complete indemnity and saves us from
a war with Great Britain or some of the continental powers
combined with Spain. This can be done without implicat-
ing the government. Let it be signified to me through any
channel (say Mr. J. Rhea) that the possession of the Floridas would be desirable to the United States and in sixty
days it will be accomplished." [1]

Of the history of this famous letter there are two
utterly irreconcilable stories. According to that of Monroe he was sick in bed when it arrived. Glancing at it he
observed from a perusal of the first one or two lines that
it related to the Seminole War. Handing it to Calhoun
who came in shortly, that gentleman replaced it with the
remark that it would require Monroe's personal attention,
but without explaining the contents. Crawford, who hap-

---

1. Andrew Jackson to Monroe, Jan. 6, 1818. Benton's Thirty
Years' View, Vol. I, p. 170.

pened in soon afterwards, likewise read it but made no
comments. The letter was then laid away and forgotten,
according to Monroe, and he did not read it until after the
conclusion of the war. Why the letter should have been thus
submitted to Crawford, with whose duties it had no relation, unless it had been to secure his views on its expressions and sentiments is not quite clear. Nor is it to be
credited that Calhoun should have read such startling statements from the officer in command, likely to involve the
nation in serious difficulties without even a comment or expression of opinion.

In his exposition, prepared during his lifetime but
published after his death, Jackson said: "Availing himself of
the suggestion contained in the letter, Mr. Monroe sent for
Mr. John Rhea (then a member of congress), showed him
the confidential letter and requested him to answer it. In
conformity with this request Mr. Rhea did answer the letter and informed General Jackson that the president had
shown him the confidential letter and requested him to state
that he approved of its suggestions. This answer was received by the general on the second night he remained at
Big Creek, which is four miles in advance of Hartford,
Georgia, and before his arrival at Fort Scott to take command of the troops." [1]

The production of the Rhea letter would have solved
the whole question. Its absence was thus explained by
General Jackson: "About the time (February 24, 1819)
Mr. Lacock made his report (to the senate), General Jackson and Mr. Rhea were both in the city of Washington.
Mr. Rhea called on General Jackson, as he said, at the request of Mr. Monroe and begged him on his return home
to burn his reply. He said the president feared that by
the death of General Jackson or some other accident, it
might fall into the hands of those who would make an

---

1. Exposition, Benton's Thirty Years' View, Vol. I, p. 179.

improper use of it. He therefore conjured him by the friendship which had always existed between them (and by his obligations as a brother Mason) to destroy it on his return to Nashville. Believing Mr. Monroe and Mr. Calhoun to be his devoted friends, and not deeming it possible that any incident could occur which would require or justify its use, he gave Mr. Rhea the promise he solicited, and accordingly, after his return to Nashville, he burnt Mr. Rhea's letter and on his letter book, opposite the copy of his confidential letter to Mr. Monroe made this entry: 'Mr. Rhea's letter in answer is burnt this 12th April, 1819.' " [1]

Mr. Rhea was an aged member of congress from Tennessee, an intimate friend of Jackson, and counsellor of Monroe. But three persons ever saw the Rhea letter, namely, General Jackson, Rhea himself, and Judge Overton. The two latter both wrote statements supporting the contention of General Jackson though neither of the gentlemen attempted to give the substance of the destroyed letter.

Mr. Monroe claimed, on the other hand, never to have read the letter until after the war and denied having authorized Mr. Rhea to answer it. There are no allusions to the matter in any of Mr. Monroe's correspondence. This silence may of course be credited to forgetfulness or discretion. At any rate, granted that the letter was not answered, the course of the administration upon that hypothesis was highly reprehensible. General Jackson had meanwhile received orders vesting him with discretionary powers. Mr. Calhoun wrote to Governor Bibb, that General Jackson was "authorized to conduct the war as he thought best." Jackson's letter of January 6th clearly indicated the course that he "thought best."

Any sane man must have seen that, in the absence of express orders to the contrary, General Jackson would seize East Florida. Silence then meant tacit consent. If

---

1. Benton's Thirty Years' View, Vol. I, p. 179.

Mr. Rhea really did write, under Monroe's direction, Jackson had the express approval of the administration. If Jackson's letter received no reply but he was to "conduct the war as he thought best" then Jackson had the implied approval of the administration. Jackson's character and disposition were even at that time matters of common knowledge. Were his sentiments and intimations to be so lightly considered? On the twenty-fifth of March Jackson informed Calhoun that he intended to occupy St. Marks and on April 8th informed him that it was done, yet he received no word of disapprobation. On the fifth of May he wrote to Mr. Calhoun saying that he was about to move on Pensacola to occupy that town. Still no word of criticism. On the second of June he wrote to the secretary of war that on May 24th he had entered Pensacola and on the 28th received the surrender of the Barrancas, yet no breath of censure.

Not until the receipt of Monroe's private letter of July 19th did Jackson receive any intimation that his Florida operations were other than what Monroe and Calhoun expected. [1] The confidential understanding and express agreement, or if it be preferred the tacit consent, made Jackson's instructions as effectually orders "to take and occupy the province of Florida as if that object had been declared on their face." Under any hypothesis it is impossible to do otherwise than hold the administration responsible for Jackson's wild career in Florida. That for reasons of policy Monroe and Calhoun sought to absolve themselves from all blame can scarcely concern the historian. That certain of Jackson's acts in connection with the invasion would have been thoroughly disapproved by Monroe and Calhoun no one will deny, but for them, however, the impartial critic must reserve the censure for the general event.

---

1. Benton's Thirty Years' View, Vol. I, p. 172.

Calhoun's order to proceed to Fort Scott was received at Nashville, January 11th. It gave Jackson power to call on the governors of the adjacent states for militia. The Georgia militia had been called out by Gaines before starting for Amelia Island. Jackson therefore concluded to secure a thousand mounted volunteers from West Tennessee and Kentucky, the men with whom he had fought in 1813 and 1814. But the governor of Tennessee was absent from the state — none knew where he was or when he would return. Taking the responsibility upon himself Jackson privately summoned to Nashville a number of his old volunteer officers and laid the scheme before them. The officers separated to carry out the measures. The general issued one of his characteristic addresses and within twelve days of the meeting, such was the popularity of the cause and the leader, two regiments of mounted men numbering more than a thousand were assembled at the old rendezvous at Fayetteville, Tennessee. The governor of Tennessee approved General Jackson's measures, irregular though they were. So did Mr. Calhoun in his letter of January 24th. We may pass lightly over the ensuing incidents.

On the tenth of March General Jackson assumed command at Fort Scott. He ordered part of his provisions sent to the fort (Scott) by the Appalachicola on which the Spanish had no fortifications. On the site of Negro Fort he erected Fort Gadsden and sent word to the Spanish commander at Pensacola that if the fort at Barrancas hindered his supply boats from ascending the Escambia he would consider it an act of hostility to the United States. An arbitrary and aggressive course this, to the representative of an independent nation with whom we were at peace. But Jackson knew nothing of red tape and cared less for diplomatic niceties. All through the military correspondence there was talk of marching into East Florida and attacking the Indians through that province as though no possible question could be raised as to orders or the restrictions of international law.

He immediately advanced towards St. Marks. Captain McKeever in command of the squadron agreed to coöperate with him in the movement on St. Marks. The following is a portion of a remarkable and characteristic order delivered by the general to McKeever: "It is reported to me that Francis, or Hillis Hago, and Peter McQueen, prophets, who excited the Red Sticks in their late war against the United States and are now exciting the Seminoles to similar acts of hostility, are at or in the neighborhood of St. Marks. United with them it is stated that Woodbine, Arbuthnot, and other foreigners have assembled a motley crew of brigands — slaves enticed away from their masters, citizens of the United States, or stolen during the late conflict with Great Britain. It is all important that these men should be captured and made examples of, and it is my belief that on the approach of my army they will attempt to escape to some of the sea islands. . . . You will therefore, cruise along the coast, eastwardly, and as I advance, capture and make prisoners all, or every person, or description of persons, white, red, or black, with all their goods, chattels, and effects, together with all crafts, vessels or means of transportation by water. . . . Any of the subjects of his Catholic Majesty, sailing to St. Marks, may be permitted freely to enter the said river. But none to pass out, unless after an examination it may be made to appear that they have not been attached to or in any wise aided and abetted our common enemy. I shall march this day and in eight days will reach St. Marks, where I shall expect to communicate with you in the bay." There is no precedent in all modern history for such a high handed course. Let the mind for one moment contemplate the fleet of a nation with whom we were at peace maintaining a blockade of one of our ports and compelling our citizens to submit to search. For what principle was fought the war of 1812? In defense of what right did Jackson himself beat back the English at New Orleans? International law and American consistency were violated at the same stroke.

In his forward march Jackson came upon a number of Indians engaged in the innocuous pursuit of "herding cattle." Upon these redskins an attack was ordered. Many were killed but some succeeded in escaping and fled to St. Marks. As Jackson understood his orders he was to pursue the Indians until he caught them wherever they might go. That Spanish rights were to be respected so far as was consistent with that purpose. That the Spanish inability to police her own territory and maintain order therein was to be the justification of his course. His proceedings were based on two positive and arbitrary assumptions. First that the Indians received aid and encouragement from St. Marks and Pensacola. That the Spanish denied this was of no matter to Jackson for his presumption had always been that every Spanish official was a consummate prevaricator. His second assumption was that Great Britain kept paid emissaries in Florida hostile to the United States. This latter presumption, prevalent in the United States at that time, seems upon a careful consideration of the facts to have been wholly groundless. England had without doubt made some connection with the Indians during the late war and had encouraged them to believe that with the treaty of peace they would be reimbursed for their losses, but there is no evidence that after the termination of the war she did not act in good faith. She promptly disavowed the acts of Colonel Nicholls and firmly refused to either aid or encourage the deputation of Indian chiefs that were shipped to London. But the inaccuracy of Jackson's assumption did not save the lives of two English subjects so unfortunate as to fall in the hands of that fire eating officer.

Alexander Arbuthnot, a Scotchman seventy years of

age, a man of considerable ability and education, had come to Florida in 1817 attracted by the prospect of a flourishing Indian trade. He established as friendly relations as possible with the Indians for his own security and advantage. By fairer treatment and more equitable prices he secured a large part of the Indian trade to the indignation and loss of an older firm who had habitually cheated and swindled the savages. He soon received from the Creek chief power of attorney to act for him in all affairs which concerned the tribe. At the request of the Indian chief, he wrote letters to the governor of the Bahamas, the British minister at Washington, to Colonel Nicholls at London, the governor of Florida, the officers commanding the neighboring United States forts, General Mitchell and others. The treaty of Ghent had been violated, for the lands taken from the Creeks by the treaty of Fort Jackson had not been restored. The Georgians were murdering and plundering the Indians. The English government ought to send an agent to report upon the American course in Florida. Thus trading with the redskins, by a mere chance he reached St. Marks in April of 1818. There, hearing for the first time of the approach of Jackson and the arrival of McKeever's fleet, he dispatched a letter to his son, in charge of his schooner lying at anchor in the Suwanee River below the towns of Boleck — and bade him hurry his goods to a place of safety, get them on the ship if possible and sail for Cedar Keys Bay.

On April 6th, after having burned Fowltown where he found the redpole decorated with the scalps of a year's accumulation, Jackson halted near St. Marks and sent his aide-de-camp to demand admittance to the town. To prevent in the future such gross breaches of neutrality, as had characterized the past, Jackson informed the governor that it was necessary that St. Marks should be occupied and garrisoned by United States troops and held until the termination of the war. The Spanish officer in command, Don Francisco Casa y Luengo, replied that he would have to write for authority to admit the troops, to do so personally was beyond his power. This answer was delivered to General Jackson on the morning of April 7th. He instantly replied by taking possession of the fort, replacing the Spanish flag with that of the United States, and quartering the American troops within the fortress. The governor could and did offer no resistance. He was forced to content himself with a formal protest against such unusual and unwarranted proceedings. Arbuthnot was found within the fort, preparing to leave the town, and was promptly seized by order of General Jackson.

In the meantime Captain McKeever had captured two more prisoners of note. Violating all rules of national law and by a ruse as disgraceful as it was exceptional, McKeever entered the bay with the English flag at his masthead and thus lured on board his ship the Indian prophet Francis and his companion Himollemico — the latter the savage who had attacked Lieutenant Scott's expedition. These Indians, supposing the ship to be the one long looked for from England with supplies and munitions of war, had boarded her and upon being enticed into the cabin were seized and bound. The next day they were sent up to the fort and hung by Jackson's order. For the capture of St. Marks, history and investigation are unable to present an adequate justification. But we must stand aghast at Jackson's imperial assumption of the dread prerogative of arbitrarily dooming men to death without a trial. The prophet Francis was an educated man of pleasing manners, humane disposition, well versed in English and Spanish — indeed a model chief. Himollemico was the type of the cruel, morose, bloodthirsty savage, who probably richly deserved his fate, but no one has ever explained by what law or custom, observed in the service of the United States, they were put to death, when thus captured by an ignoble stratagem, not even on the field of battle, and without the bare formality of a trial of any sort.

Jackson pushed on as rapidly as possible for Suwanee, the headquarters of Boleck ("Billy Bowlegs"), the Seminole chief, and the refuge of the troublesome negroes, half breeds, and fugitive slaves. Arbuthnot had a trading post here, and it was to this place that he had written the letter to his son directing him to remove the stock of goods. In the afternoon of April 17th Jackson, forming his army into three divisions, rushed on to overwhelm the village, but found it abandoned.

Arbuthnot's warning to his son had been read to Bowlegs who was thus able, with his women and children, to escape into the swamps, so inaccessible and so plentiful in that region. Jackson was baffled and, we need not be told, enraged. The town was burned. Nearby were taken prisoners an Englishman by the name of Robert Ambrister and three companions, two of them negroes, who, unaware of the course of events, had accidentally stumbled upon the American camp.

On one of the negroes was found Arbuthnot's letter to his son. From Cook, the white man, it was learned that the letter had been read to Bowlegs and was responsible for the escape of the Indians and the evacuation of the town. Ambrister was found to be an agent of Arbuthnot, with headquarters on Arbuthnot's schooner then at the mouth of the Suwanee River. Lieutenant Gadsden was hastily dispatched to capture the schooner. Jackson had considered Arbuthnot an English emissary. The escape of the Indians enraged him and, we may say, bemuddled his mind. He now considered Arbuthnot's letter an overt act of interference in the war.

The Seminole war was now ended. It had been contemptible and meager in military results, but it was prolific

in its surprising complications.   On April 20th, the
Georgia troops marched homeward to be disbanded.   On
the 24th General McIntosh and his brigade of Indians were
dismissed.   On the 25th General Jackson with his Tennessee militia and his regulars was again at Fort St. Marks.

Having accepted the cession of West Florida to the
United States, General Jackson further assumed the authority of constituting a provisional government for the conquered province.   He appointed one of his officers, Colonel
King, civil and military governor.   He extended the revenue laws of the United States over the country and appointed another of his officers, Captain Gadsden, collector
of the port of Pensacola, with authority to execute those
laws.   He declared what civil laws should be enforced and
provided for the preservation of the archives as well as
for the care and protection of what had been the property
of the Spanish crown but which now, in the general's conception, had become the property of the United States.

The war was over, but one more act of imperial authority remained to complete the cycle of Jackson's astounding conduct.   At St. Marks was convened a "special court"
of fourteen officers to try Ambrister and Arbuthnot and
determine what punishment, if any, should be meted out to
them.   That they were not unceremoniously hanged or shot,
as were the Indians, we must admit was a concession on
the part of Jackson hardly to have been expected.   Of all
the tribunals convened to sit on cases, the court-martial is
without doubt the least likely to dispense any measure of
equity.   To mete out vengeance rather than justice seems
to be their purpose.   The constituent members are not
selected by reason of any special fitness for their task or because they possess in any measure the judicial qualities.
And of all the iniquities which may be credited to this
form of tribunal, it is doubtful whether any were ever more
reprehensible than those perpetrated by the one which was

convened that twenty-eighth of April, over which General Gaines presided and before which Arbuthnot was arraigned.

Three charges were filed against the unfortunate Scotchman:

1. Inciting the Creeks to war against the United States.

2. Acting as a spy and supplying them with munitions of war.

3. Inciting the Indians to murder William Hambly and Edmund Doyle.

The third charge was so absurd that it was withdrawn after the court had determined that it possessed no jurisdiction in the matter. Such a violation of all known or accepted methods of procedure and rules of evidence has seldom been seen, in even the most arbitrary tribunals. There was no real evidence against Arbuthnot on any charge, that would stand in an ordinary court of law. His business and presence in Florida were open and obvious. He had, while using his influence and ability in behalf of the Indians, always advised them to peace and submission rather than to a course which he well knew would lead to their certain defeat and extinction. For his construction of the treaty of Ghent there is much to be said. Indeed diplomatic measures were necessary to set it aside. As for his letter to his own son, written entirely in the line of his business, it could hardly be ground for censure though it did render Jackson's march of two hundred miles all but fruitless. To the question, can traders be executed if their information, not transmitted through the lines, frustrate military purposes, we imagine there can be but one answer. At any rate Arbuthnot was found guilty by a two-thirds vote of the court and sentenced to be hanged.

Ambrister was tried on the charge of aiding and comforting the enemy and waging war on the United States. He had no ostensible business in Florida — an adventurer in short. It was proved that he had come to Florida on "Woodbine's business," that he had captured Arbuthnot's schooner and plundered his store, that he had sent into New Providence for arms and that he had sent a party "to oppose" the American invasion. Ambrister made no formal defense but put himself on the mercy of the court. He was promptly pronounced guilty and sentenced to be shot. A member of the court, however, securing a reconsideration of the sentence, he was awarded fifty lashes on the bare back and confinement with ball and chain at hard labor for one year.

In his orders of April 29th, Jackson, disapproving the revised sentence of Ambrister, ordered the first finding carried out. Accordingly Arbuthnot was hanged from the yard arm of his schooner, and Ambrister took his place as a target before an execution squad.

Jackson had committed a murder all the more atrocious because done under the guise of legal form. Arbuthnot was executed upon the testimony of men who had the strongest interest in his conviction, and upon evidence of a nature which would not today be tolerated in any proceeding, criminal or civil, in any court of this country. The presiding officer of that court was the officer whose arrogant, unreasoning treatment of the Fowltown Indians precipitated the war. And yet the war was concluded and the enemy crushed and obliterated before these two lives were sacrificed. Did the rules of war demand instant death? Would it not have been the part of charity, nay of reason, to forward the case to Washington?

With his dying breath Arbuthnot declared that his country would avenge his execution. Political reasons alone, we may believe, prevented the fulfillment of the unfortunate victim's prophecy. The executions produced the most intense indignation in England, and all Europe stood aghast. At an entertainment given by the French ambassador on July 30, 1818, the foreign ambassadors and ministers crowded about our Mr. Rush in eager curiosity to know of this matter of Pensacola and of the probable war with Spain. That the whole affair smacked of hostilities, with either Spain or England or both, was the general impression. And to Europe long drunk with the mad Napoleonic carnival of fire and slaughter another war would prove an object of unalloyed pleasure at least to those nations which might stand at the ringside, as it were, and be the spectators. After the kaleidoscopic metamorphoses which had marked the days of the great conqueror a few years of peace had greatly bored the *ennuye* continent.

The executions became the subject of parliamentary inquiry. The excitement was at fever heat. Stocks fell. The newspapers were particularly bitter in their denunciation of the United States and the offending general was addressed in their columns by the opprobrious names of "tyrant," "ruffian," and "murderer," and was placarded about the streets of London. "We can hardly believe that anything so offensive to public decorum could be admitted even in America" was the comment of one journal. After a full deliberation the cabinet however declared that the conduct of Arbuthnot and Ambrister had been unjustifiable, and did not therefore call for the special interference of Great Britain. And in the ensuing days of seething popular passion when war would have been certain "if the ministry had but held up a finger," the cabinet stood firm for peace. We may well believe with the traditional jealousy with which Great Britain has ever guarded the interests and the lives of her subjects that there was some ulterior motive which had determined Lord Castlereagh and his compeers in their decision.

Since the termination of the Napoleonic wars and the second treaty of Paris England had become isolated and now

stood alone against the continental powers. [1] To the United
States only could she look for support against the reaction-
ary doctrines promulgated in the holy alliance. For England to go to war with the United States would have left
the European powers free to pursue their purposes without
a single restraining force and would leave Great Britain
without one ally to whom she might turn for either
moral or material support in those principles for whose
recognition she was then working. To declare war then
would be merely to accentuate her isolation and invite worse
calamities. At any rate the inquiry was not pressed by
England as all patriotic citizens must hope the United States
would push a similar one.

The two Indians who had been hanged had no friends
to demand an explanation or reparation, but their execution
was a most awkward thing to justify before the world.
The Creeks were not a nation in contemplation of international law — not the possessors of the soil on which they
had lived and fought, because enjoying only what, by a
suitable stretch of national ethics or morals, may be termed
the right of temporary use or occupation, subject to the
higher and ultimate title which vested in the nation. There
had been no declaration of war, yet the Indians were not
rebels against the United States and in the eyes of any but
Jackson they possessed some belligerent rights. Though
there never was any proof that anybody incited the Indians
yet, whatever rights the redskins possessed, the Englishmen,
even had they been complete allies, must have been entitled
to. If the Indians were not to be slain like wild beasts or
executed by court-martial for levying war on the United
States, the Englishmen were done to death without legal or
moral right.

Learning that some five hundred hostile Indians were
receiving friendly asylum at Pensacola, Jackson hurried

1. November 20, 1815.

off to that place with a small detachment of regulars and militia. On his march he was met by a messenger from the governor of that town, protesting against his summary course and ordering him either to quit the province of West Florida or be prepared to meet force with force. If this notice was intended to overawe Jackson and induce him to withdraw it failed of its purpose most signally. It only aroused and excited him, and on May 24th he entered Pensacola without the slightest opposition beyond that of the quill. Capturing Fort Carios de Barrancas, whither the Spanish had retreated, and leaving a garrison of American troops, some five days later Jackson was marching homeward. On his way he learned of an attack by the Georgia militia on the villages of friendly and allied Indians. A fiery correspondence between Governor Rabun of Georgia and General Jackson ensued in which, though the general was undoubtedly right, he provoked anger and discord by his violent, impetuous manner where a temperate remonstrance, judiciously administered, would have better gained the object in view.[1]

In the whole Florida campaign we have seen that prejudice and assumption took the place of evidence and information. Jackson's theory "of making the United States as uncomfortable a neighbor to Spain as he could," had borne fruit. His only regret was that when he took Pensacola he "had not stormed the works, captured the governor,

---

1. The following is an abstract from a sarcastic letter written by Governor Rabun to General Jackson, Sept. 1, 1818: "I hope you will now permit me in turn to recommend to you that before you undertake to prosecute another campaign you examine the orders of your superiors with more attention than usual. . . . . Indeed, sir, we had expected that your presence at the head of an overwhelming force would have afforded complete protection to our bleeding and distressed frontier, but our prospect was only delusive, for it would seem that the laurels expected in Florida was the object that accelerated your march far more than the protection of the 'ignorant Georgians.'" Andrew Jackson MSS., Congressional Library.

put him on his trial for the murder of Stokes and his family, and hung him for the deed."[1]

Thus terminated the Seminole war, insignificant and trivial in the forces involved and the actual military operations. On the American side there were engaged about eighteen hundred whites and fifteen hundred friendly Indians. The hostile Indians numbered not more than about one thousand, of whom not over one half were at any one time before Jackson. What fighting there was, was largely done by the allied Indians. They lost twenty men, the whites lost one man and the hostile Indians sixty. Yet this petty Indian campaign was one of the most pregnant and important events in our national history.

The Seminole war was soon made the subject of a congressional investigation. In both the house and the senate the question was submitted to committees. That of the house presented two reports. The majority report condemned the proceedings of the trial and execution of Arbuthnot and Ambrister. The minority report declared that where there was much in the conduct of the campaign to praise, there was little to censure and when the incalculable benefits resulting to the nation were considered it was their sense that Jackson and his officers deserved the thanks of the nation.

In due time the report of the majority was taken up in the committee of the whole and the resolution "That the house of representatives of the United States disapproves the proceedings in the trial and execution of Alexander Arbuthnot and Robert Ambrister" was debated. William C. Cobb of Georgia opened the discussion. He could conceive of no law, martial, municipal, or national, that had been violated by the luckless Englishmen. Martial law subjected spies to the death penalty. But although these men, or one of

---

1. For this remarkable statement see Jackson's letter to George W. Campbell, then minister to Russia, Parton's Jackson, Vol. II, p. 500.

them, was accused of this, he was acquitted of the charge. Admitting the truth of the charges for which they were executed, yet they were not declared penal in any of the rules of war, neither were they declared to be the subject matters for trial before a court-martial. The evidence of papers not produced or accounted for, the belief of persons whose testimony of undoubted facts ought to have been suspected, hearsay, and that of Indians, negroes, and criminals who, had they been present, could not have been sworn, were all indiscriminately admitted and acted upon.

Did not the reconsideration of the sentence in Ambrister's case render null and void the first decree of the court? Can it be said that there was any other sentence than the one last passed in the case? The whole proceeding on its very face manifested a cruelty that must excite the greatest disapprobation of all impartial men. In his official orders Jackson had justified the execution of Ambrister in these words — "It is an established principle of the law of nations that any individual of a nation making war against the citizens of another nation, they being at peace, forfeits his allegiance, and becomes an outlaw and a pirate." No one had ever heard or dreamed of such a rule of international law. Reason, propriety, justice, and humanity all cry aloud against such a principle. If Jackson's statement stood unchallenged, LaFayette, De Kalb, Pulaski, Steuben, and the large host of foreigners who joined the standard of our fathers in the revolution, and with their life's blood baptized the infant nation, were "outlaws and pirates," and had they been captured were subject to trial by court-martial and sentence to an ignominious death.

Jackson had usurped the power of congress to declare war. International law permits us to cross the lines in fresh pursuit of the enemy, but does not sanction razing forts, conducting sieges, receiving capitulations, mounting bat-

17

teries, and granting terms of surrender to such places. The reasons for invading Florida were many of them ridiculous and such as, to say the most, are but causes of war. They may contain wrongs which demand redress but that through diplomatic channels, and not by any such methods as those employed by Jackson. A certain mystery appeared on the face of the documents which, Cobb declared, quite staggered him. The perfect confidence shown by Jackson in the correctness of his proceedings, in which he had clearly violated what appeared to be his orders, seemed quite unaccountable and suggested something ulterior. Jackson did not attempt to excuse himself, did not seem to think he had overleaped his orders, and had neither apprehension nor fear as to the opinion that the executive might form of his proceedings. Did it not seem a suspicious circumstance that General Jackson had not been called to account for thus transcending his orders? Let it be admitted that Spain was too weak and had forfeited her right of sovereignty, yet to whom had it been forfeited and why to the United States rather than to some other nation? Cobb took the occasion to declare that he was personally hostile to Spain and felt that that nation had done us many wrongs, but that his feelings upon that subject could not render him callous to the stain which Jackson had inflicted on our national honor.

Let it be granted that a nation had broken a treaty, as we insisted Spain had done, is it usual for the commanding general to go in and inaugurate a war? Moreover Vattel, in his "Law of Nations," declares that a nation's breach of a treaty may be excused by the other nation especially, as in this case, when it proceeds from weakness. There existed no proofs of a warlike association between the Spanish and the Indians which would identify them as equally our enemies according to the definition given of this compact by international law. Had we been dealing with Great Britain instead of Spain, a virile instead of a weak nation, would we have proceeded in this manner? Was Jackson's declaration that "St. Marks was necessary as a depot for the success of his future operations," in any sense a justification? Gibraltar might be the same if we contemplated an attack on the Barbary States. His feelings and dignity having been injured by the "insulting letter of the governor of Pensacola," Jackson "hesitated no longer and exposed the nation to war." "But sir," concluded Cobb, "I have done with this disagreeable subject — I turn with disgust from this nauseous scene."

In the course of his speech Cobb introduced three amendments; one instructed the committee on military affairs to report a bill forbidding the execution of any captive of the army of the United States in time of peace, or in time of war with any Indian tribe unless the president approved. Another declared that the house of representatives disapproved of the seizure of St. Marks, Pensacola, and the Barrancas, as contrary to orders and the constitution. The third instructed the proper committee to frame a bill prohibiting United States troops marching into foreign territory unless ordered to do so by congress, or when in hot pursuit of an enemy beaten and flying for refuge across the border.

Holmes of Massachusetts then took up the cudgels in behalf of Jackson and was in turn followed by Henry Clay. Beginning with a disclaimer of all hostility to either Jackson or the administration, this eloquent speaker launched forth in a wonderful oration. Strengthened by his perfect diction, vivified by his stirring appeals, and marked by his acute reasoning, apt illustrations, and glowing peroration, this effort strongly affected the house and won for its author the bitter and undying hatred of Jackson. For to the doughty fighter those who approved his acts were his friends, those who criticised, his enemies, and that, too, whether or no any personal feeling was brought into the discussion of either law or fact. At any rate Clay was in opposition to the administration because he had not been appointed secretary of state. His hostility is generally declared to have been factious, despite his disclaimer. There are some facts which lend color to the theory that Clay and Crawford had already begun to regard Jackson as a possible competitor for the presidency.

Clay began his speech with a bitter denunciation of the treaty of Fort Jackson. He blushed with shame at the ignoble and unworthy ruse by which Francis and Himollemico were captured and the unceremonious manner in which they were executed, under the guise of retaliation for the crimes which had been committed by their followers. Even admitting the guilt of Arbuthnot and Ambrister he ridiculed and riddled Jackson's argument by which their execution had been justified. He likened their treatment to that accorded by Napoleon to the Duc d'Enghien, and found a duplicate for the seizure of Pensacola and St. Marks in the bombardment of Copenhagen and capture of the Danish fleet by England. To Jackson's statement that Arbuthnot and Ambrister had been legally condemned and justly punished, Clay remarked, "The Lord preserve us from any such legal convictions and such legal condemnations."

While acquitting Jackson of any intention of violating the laws, as he said, Clay accused him of seizing forts, usurping the exclusively congressional power of making war, and took occasion to warn the people against the military hero covered with glory. The eloquent Kentuckian closed with incomparable ability. "They may bear down all opposition," he declared, "they may even vote the general public thanks. They may carry him triumphantly through this house. But if they do, in my humble judgment, it will be the triumph of insubordination, a triumph of the military over the civil authority, a triumph over the powers of this house, a triumph over the constitution of the land. And I

pray devotedly to heaven that it may not prove, in its ultimate effects and consequences, a triumph over the liberties
of the people."

Other speakers followed in much the same general
strain. Jackson had committed an act of war. He himself had said that the articles of capitulation of Pensacola,
"with the exception of one article, amounted to a complete
cession of the country to the United States." If this did not
constitute war the speakers earnestly demanded a suitable definition of that term. Granted, as Jackson's adherents claimed, that the law of nations authorizes retaliation,
yet the same law says, "where severity is not absolutely
necessary, clemency becomes a duty." The war against the
Indians being at an end, where was the necessity? Arbuthnot was punished upon the testimony of his admitted personal enemies as the papers show. "The judgment of a
court-martial is always under its own control," declares
Macomb, "until it is communicated to the officer by whom it
was convened." The final judgment of Ambrister was the
only judgment of the court. And, by appointing the court-
martial, Jackson was morally bound to accept its verdict. A
notable example, they declared, of the maxim that when a
man acquires power he forgets rights. It was even directly
intimated that the court-martial was irregularly formed, and
its verdict prepared beforehand.

The treaty of Fort Jackson of 1814, came in for a bitter
arraignment. In its terms it was most harsh and severe;
it was made with a minority of the Creek chiefs who had
remained either friendly or passive. There were at the
time manifest signs of its disapproval by the majority of
Indians. They were robbed of a large portion of their
territory, and unromantic roads, trading houses, etc., were
inflicted upon the portion left to them. Not a single hostile
chief had either signed or acquiesced in the pact, which was
declared to be quite like the most of our Indian treaties.

According to the principles of international law, it is not permitted to cross a neutral line after an enemy, scattered and broken up, fleeing from death and destruction, as were the Seminoles, but only after one retreating with the idea of again renewing the attack. Vattel laid it down that "extreme necessity may even authorize the temporary seizure of a place (in a neutral country) and the putting a garrison therein, for defending itself against an enemy or preventing him in his designs of seizing this place when the sovereign is not able to defend it. But when the danger is over it must be immediately surrendered." Where was the necessity which had justified Jackson's course, the opposition demanded. After the Indians had been conquered, with whom was the general waging war? Not with Spain and not with the Indian tribes — because they had been already subdued.

Jackson's letter of the second of June to the secretary of war was bitterly denounced. It read in part: "The Seminole war may now be considered at a close, tranquillity again restored to the southern frontier of the United States, and as long as a cordon of military posts is maintained along the Gulf of Mexico, America has nothing to apprehend from either foreign or Indian hostilities. Captain Gadsden is instructed to prepare a report on the necessary defenses of the country as far as the military reconnoissance will permit, accompanied with plans of the existing works; what additions or improvements are necessary, and what new works should in his opinion be erected to give permanent security to this important territorial addition to our republic." Unsparing were the terms in which this report was characterized.

But Jackson was not without his defenders. Johnson, Tallmadge, Poindexter, Alexander Smyth of Virginia, and Barbour ably met the onslaught of his detractors. They tore to pieces the speech of Clay, they quoted Vattel and

Martens in support of their hero. They enumerated precedents in our own national history which vindicated the defendant.

Yet after nearly a century Jackson's conduct stands out in bold relief, while their alleged precedents have paled into oblivion. The case of Major Andre and the conduct of Washington were cited repeatedly as though there could have been any real analogy between the conduct of the unfortunate Englishman of our revolutionary days and that of his equally unfortunate countrymen of later date.

For twenty-seven days, without interruption, and to the exclusion of all business, flowed this stream of oratory. No attack upon any public man up to that time had so interested and aroused the country. The sensations at the trial of Samuel Chase and of Aaron Burr were as nothing compared with this. Popular feeling was with Jackson. His hold upon the country had already begun to exert a wonderful dispensating influence for him and his misdoings. He possessed an extraordinary combination of those qualities calculated to arouse the imagination and sentiment of the people. The strange magic of military success had carried him to a height from which to attempt to drag him down would have been to invite ruin. Official Washington knew this only too well, and so did Jackson.

The battle of New Orleans, the one brilliant land feat of our armies in the war of 1812, had given him a firm hold upon the hearts of the people. Niles, representing the popular sentiment and believing in the emissary theory, exactly summarized the general attitude in this paragraph: "The fact is that ninety-nine in a hundred of the people believe that General Jackson acted on every occasion for the good of his country, and success universally crowned his efforts. He has suffered more hardships and encountered higher responsibilities than any man living in the United States to serve us and has his reward in the sanction of his government and the approbation of the people." [1]

On both sides of the question were the finest orators, the most skillful debaters, the shrewdest and most consummate politicians of the generation. This and the feeling that on the outcome might depend a Spanish war, brought all Washington to the daily feast of words and reason. Even the minority of the house committee, friendlier to Jackson, declared that after considering the documents submitted it would have been "more correct" to acquiesce in the final verdict of the court-martial in Ambrister's case. At length on the eighth of February a vote was taken on the amendments and on the resolution. In each case Jackson was sustained both by the committee of the whole and by the house.

In the senate the question had been referred to a committee early in December, but no report was made until February 24th. The document then submitted declared that the general's ideas of international law were entirely unfounded on any recognized authority, that his actions were "calculated to inflict a wound on the national character," and condemned his conduct at every point. After an order to print, the report was laid on the table where it remained when the second session of the fifteenth congress ended on March 4th.

While the senate committee was in session preparing their report, wild stories were current in Washington of Jackson's wrathful denunciations of different members of the committee. It was commonly stated that he proposed to lie in wait and inflict summary vengeance upon his critics. Mr. Lacock of the senate committee wrote: "General Jackson is still here and by times raves like a madman. He has sworn most bitterly he would cut off the ears of every member of the committee who reported against his conduct. This bullying is done in public, and yet I have passed

---

1. Vol. XVI, Niles Register, p. 25.

his lodgings every day and still retain my ears. Thus far I consider myself fortunate. How long I shall be spared without mutilation I know not, but one thing I can promise you, that I shall never avoid him a single inch. And as the civil authority here seems to be put down by the military, I shall be ready and willing to defend myself and not die soft." After Jackson's return from his northern trip and after the report of the committee, his threats and menaces were repeated with increased violence, and there was more talk of ears as the reward of vengeance. There is good foundation for the story that Commodore Decatur with difficulty succeeded in preventing Jackson from entering the senate chamber to attack Mr. Eppes. Members of the committee went armed prepared to resist bodily assault with powder and bullets.

General Jackson, after his return from Florida and during the congressional investigation, received many letters of fulsome praise and sickening flattery from unworthy sycophants — men who swore by the gods that they "adored" him, and lived for the opportunity to "feast their eyes on their favorite soldier and peacemaker." The Jackson correspondence teems with these letters from that class of men who ascribe to themselves something of glory or fame in communicating with those prominent in the public eye. In April, 1819, Ex-Governor Blount wrote Jackson a highly disgraceful letter in which he traduced the opposition and referred to Cobb and Clay in disgustingly indecent terms.

Jackson's friends characterized Lacock's report as a "most malicious and iniquitous production where facts were suppressed and circumstances exhibited in a light to mislead and pervert the judgment," while General Jackson himself spoke of Crawford's "depravity of heart" and departure from that "strictly honorable deportment" in opposing him through congress. An "infamous report of un-

godly scoundrels" — such the Jackson coterie of flatterers
nominated the senate committee resolution.

Captain Gadsden, a devoted personal friend of General
Jackson, spoke of the "whole conduct of the executive as
mysterious, and characterized with a degree of indecision
and imbecility disgraceful to the nation" — a remark worthy
of a court-martial and dismissal from the army. [1] Governor
McMinns of Tennessee was "prodigiously pleased" to learn
that Florida was in the hands of "the Americans out of
which I trust in God they never will be taken." [2] One John
B. White wrote a drama, "The Triumph of Liberty" in
honor of the failure of Jackson's enemies in congress, and
sent a copy to the general accompanied by a nauseating
letter of adulation. [3]

It is generally conceded that had there been less decla-
mation and more convincing argument in support of the
majority report in the house, Jackson would not have been

---

1. Capt. Gadsden to Gen. Jackson, Sept. 28, 1818.
2. Governor McMinns to Gen. Jackson, June 20, 1818.
3. The following is a fair sample of the letters received by General Jackson from fawning individuals throughout the country:

Boone County, State of Kentuck, February 20, 1819.
To Major General A. Jackson, Sir:—
Indulge one of the American revolution, while you are surrounded
by an approving multitude, to offer his mite of gratitude to the protector of female innocence and helpless infancy, and his country's
wrongs, against the wily hand of the savage instigated by, and supplied with the means to perpetrate their cruel acts by the imbecile
Spaniard and the vile Briton.
I hope ere this "the long agonies are o'er," of your quondam friends!
and when time shall have obliterated their sickliness and the forked
tongue of envy and malice shall be at rest, the children, yet unborn,
shall sound the praises of the man who had the fortitude, courage,
virtue, and obedience to the call of necessity to step forward, with a
gallant band to encounter every privation, hardship, and danger to
rectify that country's wrongs. I am a simple, plain man in my habits
and manners, no courtier. But here claim the privilege to give my
sentiments in favor of patriotism, fortitude, courage, virtue, and morals
when mingled with glorious deeds; of every man who nobly steps
forward in the cause of Humanity, Justice, and his country's freedom;
in opposition to the enemies of the Human race!!! Accept the respect
of my rational homage and very high consideration.
JOHN BROWN.

sustained. Parton says: "If there had been but one hard-headed, painstaking, resolute man in the house who had spent ten days in reading and comparing the evidence relating to the invasion of Florida and the execution of the prisoners, and two days more in presenting to the house a complete exposition of the same, hammering home the vital points with tireless reiteration, the final votes would not have been what they were. The cause, despite the month's debate, was, after all, decided without a hearing." [1]

When the news of Jackson's Florida exploits reached Washington all was excitement among the officials and the public. The administration was in a quandary. It was ignorant of the fact that Jackson had been authorized to violate neutral territory. Moreover, this administration, like those which had preceded it was timid, and, without precedents, knew scarcely anything of its powers. The cabinet was certainly anxious to secure Florida, but by purchase not by conquest. Monroe was weak, to say the least, and possessed little of the "defiant patriotism" of the younger Adams. The whole matter came up in the cabinet on the question of what disposition to make of Jackson and his conquests. On the fifteenth of July Adams records in his diary that there was a cabinet meeting lasting from noon until near five. The president and all the members of the cabinet except himself were of the opinion that Jackson should be disavowed and suitable reparation made.

Calhoun, "generally of sound, judicious, comprehensive mind," was offended with Jackson's insubordination to the war department and insisted that he be roundly censured. The secretary of war, was convinced that we would certainly have a Spanish war, and that such was Jackson's object that he might be able to command an expedition against Mexico. Crawford feared that if Pensacola were not at once restored and Jackson's acts disavowed, war would

---

1. Parton's Andrew Jackson, Vol. II, p. 550.

follow and that our ships and commerce would become the
prey of privateers from all parts of the world sailing under
the Spanish flag, and that the administration would not be
sustained by the people.[1]   Jackson had to face the Indians
but the cabinet was compelled to face Spain and England,
congress, the hostile press, the people and not least, Jackson
himself.   The question was indeed embarrassing and complicated.

During July and August, cabinet meetings were held
almost daily and the question was hotly debated.   In all of
these conferences Jackson's sole friend and only defender
was Adams, the secretary of state, the man upon whom
would fall the labor of vindicating the general diplomatically, should the administration decide to assume the responsibility.   Adams declared that there was no real though an
apparent violation of instructions and that his proceedings
were justified by the necessity of the case and by the misconduct of the Spanish commanding officers in Florida.
He insisted that if Jackson were disavowed he (Jackson)
would immediately resign his commission and turn the
attack upon the administration and would carry a large part
of the public with him.   With the overwhelming majority
against Jackson, the question arose as to the degree to
which his acts should be disavowed.

The entry in Adams's diary under date of July 19, is of
interest as indicating something of the struggle in the cabinet.   Having presented a new point in justification of
Jackson, Adams commented upon the ensuing arguments:

"It appeared to make some impression upon Mr. Wirt,
but the president and Mr. Calhoun were inflexible.   My
reasoning was that Jackson took Pensacola only because
the governor threatened to drive him out of the province
by force if he did not withdraw; that Jackson was only
executing his orders when he received this threat; that he

1.   Memoirs of J. Q. Adams, Vol. IV, pp. 107-109.

could not withdraw his troops from the province consistently with his orders and that his only alternative was to prevent the execution of the threat. I insisted that the character of Jackson's measures was decided by the intention with which they were taken, which was not hostility to Spain but self defense against the hostility of Spanish officers. I admitted that it was necessary to carry the reasoning upon my principles to the utmost extent it would bear, to come to this conclusion. But if the question was dubious, it was better to err on the side of vigor than of weakness — on the side of our own officer who had rendered the most eminent services to the nation, than on the side of our bitterest enemies and against him. I glanced at the construction which would be given by Jackson's friends and by a large portion of the public to the disavowal of his acts. It would be said that he was an obnoxious man, that after having the benefit of his services he was abandoned and sacrificed to the enemies of his country; that his case would be compared with that of Sir Walter Raleigh. Mr. Calhoun principally bore the argument against me insisting that the capture of Pensacola was not necessary upon the principles of self defense and therefore was both an act of war against Spain and a violation of the constitution, that the administration by approving it, would take all the blame of it upon themselves; that by leaving it upon his responsibility, they would take away from Spain all pretext for war and for resorting to the aid of other European powers — they would also be free from all reproach of having violated the constitution; that it was not the menace of the governor of Pensacola that had determined Jackson to take that place; that he had really resolved to take it before; that he had violated his orders and, upon his own arbitrary will, set all authority at defiance."

After many days of argument, when Adams continued to oppose the unanimous opinions of the president, the secre-

tary of the treasury, Crawford, the secretary of war, Calhoun, and the attorney general, Wirt, a draft of a note to
De Onis was prepared and a newspaper paragraph was submitted to the press for publication. With a sigh at this
"weakness and confession of weakness" Adams set himself
to the task of meeting the protests and threats of De Onis
and the inquiries of Bagot.

CHAPTER IX.

ADAMS VERSUS DE ONIS.

WE have seen that on the renewal of diplomatic relations with Spain in December, 1815, De Onis demanded the surrender of so much of West Florida as Madison had organized under the congressional act of 1811, and that this demand had been followed by an interchange of views upon the title to that province which Spain claimed never to have ceded to France, since she had received it from England and not from his Christian Majesty.

In 1816 Monroe expressed his surprise and regret that De Onis should bring up these troubles when he was without authority to settle them and declared that full power to conclude a treaty had been sent to George W. Erving, the minister of the United States at Madrid. Cevallos, the Spanish foreign minister, repeatedly complained of the number of Americans to be found officering the insurgent privateers and fighting in the ranks of the revolutionists against Spain; and of the export of arms from the United States to the insurgent forces. In answer to our complaints against the British occupation of East Florida during the late war, Cevallos denied that it had been done "with the acquiescence of the Spanish government. On the contrary it had remonstrated repeatedly and in the most energetic terms to the cabinet of St. James on this violation of its territory."[1] But Cevallos had no intention of troubling

---
1. Letters from Ministers Abroad, Vol. XIII, p. 30, Erving to Secretary Monroe, Aug., 1816.

himself with such a negotiation and gave De Onis full power to treat, referring the whole matter back to Washington.

In January, 1817, an offer was made by Monroe of so much of Texas as lies between the Rio Grande and Colorado in exchange for the two Floridas, to which De Onis replied that the territory offered was already the property of Spain and could not therefore be made the basis of an exchange. And further that he had no instructions covering the entire cession of the two Floridas. De Onis declared that he could consent to no arrangement by which Spain should cede her claims to territory east of the Mississippi unless the United States ceded their claims to all the territory west of that river. And that even such an agreement would be restricted to a recommendation to his government to adopt such an arrangement. Monroe, declaring such terms utterly inadmissible, commented with considerable indignation upon the Spanish minister's lack of powers, and announced that this government had no motive to continue the negotiation on the subject of boundaries. De Onis was then requested to state whether he would enter into a convention similar to that of 1802, which had never been ratified, providing compensation for spoliations and for the suppression of the deposit at New Orleans.[1] The negotiation on the matter of boundaries being thus abruptly terminated, De Onis despatched his secretary of legation to Madrid for more definite powers.

Erving at this time wrote a letter to our secretary of state giving his impression of the status of our affairs with Spain. "I would not intimate," said he, "that Spain is disposed to war — on the contrary I believe its dispositions, though not friendly, to be pacific — this of necessity, for it has not the means of making war on us with any effect and

---

1. Vol. II, Foreign Legations, p. 197, Monroe to De Onis, Jan. 14, 1817; *ibid.*, p. 198, same to same, Jan. 25, 1817.

it cannot in the present state of England count upon her
assistance. But there are innate vices which no experience
can correct and there is an obstinacy in error which defies
all policy or persuasion . . . they have had a long experience of our forbearance which they attribute to our weakness — they suppose that expedients, evasions, and palli-
atives will answer now as well as ever — they do not regard
affairs in the concrete but are satisfied if they do not find
immediate danger in every separate one — for the rest they
trust to time and accident, and think it will never be too
late to ward off the blow."[1]

In his next letter home, Erving treated at length of
the apparent Russian-Spanish understanding. Heretofore
Spain had hoped for an alliance with England as the most
likely to sustain and increase her power. A strict alliance
between Great Britain and Portugal, and the views of the
former power on the subject of the revolted Spanish colonies, furnished the proper instruments for Mr. Tatischoff,
the Russian minister at Madrid, a man bitterly hostile to
England and everything English, by which he gained the
entire confidence of the Spanish king and succeeded in
withdrawing Spain from her connection with England.
Rumors were abroad of a Russian plot which were given
some credence because of comporting with the well known
inordinate ambition of the czar, and yet so extravagant and
absurd as, on their face, to be incredible. Russia wished
to secure a footing in the Mediterranean and would endeav-
or to wheedle Spain out of Majorca or Minorca. Russia
might secure Texas in America. A cession of Louisiana
by Spain was proposed. And for these magnificent acqui-
sitions what should be the consideration? Her mediation
with Austria respecting Parma, etc., which as yet had
produced no results. Her mediation with Brazil who, with

---

1. Letters from Ministers Abroad, Vol. XIV, G. W. Erving to
secretary of state, March 2, 1817.

18

the revolted colonies, would only ridicule the idea: "But," concluded Erving, "Mr. Tatischoff is adroit, and the king in his weakness imagines that if he has the great Emperor Alexander for his friend he has nothing to fear."[1]

Another letter of Erving's tends to show the relations of Spain with the European powers and their bearing upon a Spanish-American treaty. In part it follows: "Upon the whole, sir, I conclude that the course which this government will take — the more or less zeal with which it will act — the more or less moderation and good faith which it will display — will very principally depend on its always fluctuating hopes and fears on the side of England; should its disputes with the king of Brazil ripen into a serious rupture, it will certainly make an attempt on Portugal; then a breach with England of course; but this I consider to be a remote possibility — the question as to the slave trade has created considerable discussion between the two governments. England as I understand has offered to his Catholic Majesty a certain sum for the relinquishment of the traffic and he has demanded a larger sum — the question turning upon this point cannot be considered as one of great difficulty; with respect to the colonies I believe it to be very certain that England has offered her mediation but here these governments cannot agree; Spain in the true spirit of her system insists on their returning to their ancient unqualified allegiance — England, besides the reasonable objections which she has to oppose to such absurd and hopeless overtures, cannot find that she has any interest in making them; she does not wish to separate the colonies from Spain — on the contrary; but she desires that the trade to them may be open."[2]

Although the Russian influence continued to prepon-

---

1. Letters from Ministers Abroad, Vol. XIV, Erving to secretary of state, April 6, 1817.
2. *Ibid.*, Erving to secretary of state, No. 30, April 6, 1817.

derate at Madrid, England soon succeeded in settling the
trade question with Spain upon a fair and satisfactory basis.

"Whether Russia, England, or France have given any
encouragement to Spain in her disputes with the United
States or not," writes Erving, "it is quite certain that in case
of a rupture Spain will appeal to one or all of them. . . .
Of their ministers here I am inclined to think that the
Russian Tatischoff, at least (certainly not the English),
who meddles with everything, has interfered with his advice
and that I see the influence of it. . . . Upon the whole
however I do not think that the hopes of Spain founded
upon the interference of others are so strong as to induce
her to decline reasonable overtures." [1]   At this time Spain
resolved to use heroic measures to force her American colonies to return to their allegiance.   With this in view and to
organize a suitable armament she purchased a fleet of ships
from Russia which, to Russia's lasting disgrace, proved
a lot of rotten hulks unable even to sail out of the harbor
of Cadiz.   One of the fruits, this was, of Tatischoff's influence over the Spanish monarch.

The arrival at Madrid of De Onis's secretary of legation was made the occasion for a proposition by Don José
Pizarro, the new foreign minister, that the negotiations be
again transferred to Madrid. [2]   Erving having consented
to this plan, after an exchange of views, Pizarro submitted
to our minister the outline of a treaty by the terms of which
Spain agreed to cede the Floridas in return for every inch of
territory the United States owned or claimed to own west
of the Mississippi from its source to the Gulf of Mexico. [3]
This was promptly and unequivocally rejected and the secretary of De Onis was immediately dispatched with new
instructions and negotiations again transferred to Wash-

1.   Letters from Ministers Abroad, Vol. XIV, Erving to J. Q.
Adams, Aug. 27, 1817.
2.   Pizarro to Erving, July 16, 1817.
3.   Pizarro to Erving, Aug. 17, 1817.

ington.[1] The Spanish council of state and principal officials were mostly grandees and priests, bigoted and narrow minded, who lived and talked only of the glories of the days of Charles V., unable to realize the present decrepit condition of the kingdom. "The ancient policy of never conceding," wrote Erving, "still prevails in the council of state before which all such matters are discussed — the members of this council, for the most part inveterate in the prejudices of former times, are wholly unfit for the direction of state affairs in this day."[2]

After an exchange of notes reciting in detail the various claims of the two parties in dispute, Adams, in January, 1818, proposed an adjustment of all differences by an arrangement on the following terms:

1. Spain to cede all her claims to territory east of the Mississippi.

2. The Colorado from its mouth to its source and from thence to the northern limits of Louisiana to be the western boundary.

3. The claims of indemnities for spoliations, whether Spanish, or French within Spanish jurisdiction, and for the suppression of the deposit at New Orleans, to be arbitrated and settled by commissioners in the manner agreed upon in the unratified convention of 1802.

4. The lands in East Florida to the Perdido to be made answerable for the amount of the indemnities which may be awarded by the commissioners under this arbitration. With an option to the United States to take the lands and pay the debts, distributing the amount received equally, according to the amount of their respective liquidated claims among the claimants. No grants of land subsequent to August 11, 1802, to be valid.

1. Pizarro to Erving, Aug. 30, 1817.
2. Letters from Ministers Abroad, Vol. XV, Erving to J. Q. Adams. Adams entered upon his duties as secretary of state September 22, 1817.

5. Spain to be exonerated from the debts or any part of them. [1]

These proposals did not differ materially from those made to Cevallos in May, 1805.

De Onis had protested against the seizure and occupation of Amelia Island by General Gaines; and the determination thus manifested by the American government "that the adjoining territories of Spain should not be misused by others for purposes of annoyance to them," it was felt would convince Spain of the necessity for coming to an immediate arrangement. There followed another elaborate and tedious discussion of the grounds on which each nation rested its claims, concluding with a statement from De Onis that the demands of the United States were so extraordinary that he must again dispatch a messenger to Madrid for additional instructions. That Adams was irritated at the course of the negotiations soon became apparent. De Onis was truly a finished scholar in the Spanish procrastinating school of diplomacy. Of him Adams said, "He has more of diplomatic trickery in his character than any other of the foreign ministers here." In his letter of March 12, 1818, in reply to the statement of De Onis that his arguments were the same as they had been for the past fifteen years "because truth is eternal," Adams said: "The observation that truth is of all time and that reason and justice are founded upon immutable principles has never been contested by the United States, but neither truth, reason, nor justice consist in stubbornness of assertion nor in the multiplied repetition of error." [2]

Adams in the same note remarked that the discussion had been "sullied by unworthy and groundless imputations" on the part of De Onis, who had declared that the United States did not herself believe in the validity of the state-

1. Vol. II, Foreign Legations, p. 273, Adams to De Onis, Jan. 16, 1818.
2. *Ibid.,* p. 282, same to same.

ments and arguments used by her ministers in support of her claims, and further that these arguments were "vague and groundless."

In March Erving noticed that the Spanish attitude toward the United States had become decidedly more favorable: "I must attribute (this) in part to the failure of the hopes which he (Pizarro) once entertained of receiving support from other quarters in the disputes between the United States and Spain, in part to the little prospect offered by the Russian memorial of a prompt and vigorous interference of the allies in the disputes between Spain and her colonies — but most principally to the prompt and vigorous course taken by our government in regard to Amelia Island and Galveston, in fine to the menacing attitude of the United States." [1]

The negotiations with Spain were also being helped along by the friendly services of the new French government. Erving seemed no less out of patience with De Onis than Adams had been, and characterized his plea of requiring new powers, as indeed the most extraordinary device for delay that could have been hit on: "It is to be hoped that it is the expiring struggle of procrastination as it is the very apex of shuffling diplomacy or the dregs of a worn out capacity." [2]

After much haggling, Erving's efforts finally succeeded in securing from Pizarro by the end of June an offer to ratify the old convention of 1802 without qualification.

In January of 1818 Mr. Bagot, the British minister in Washington, showed to Mr. Adams a copy of a dispatch from Lord Castlereagh to Sir Henry Wellesley dated August 27, 1817, and being an answer to one from him which had enclosed a detailed statement by the Spanish minister of the state of the controversies between the United States

1. Vol. XV, Letters from Ministers Abroad, Erving to J. Q. Adams, March 16, 1818.
2. *Ibid.*, same to same, June 12, 1818.

and Spain, for the mediation of Great Britain. Lord Castle-reagh declined to intervene unless it should be requested by both parties. In making the communication, Bagot expressed the willingness of Great Britain to mediate if the United States should concur with Spain in requesting it. In a letter to Erving upon the subject Adams made the following comments: "But in reflecting upon these transactions it could not escape observation,

"1. That this overture from Mr. Pizarro to Sir Henry Wellesley must have been made early in August last, between the first and the fifteenth and precisely while Mr. Pizarro was professing an intention to conclude immediately a treaty with you.

"2. That no notice was given to you either by Mr. Pizarro or by Sir Henry Wellesley, of this very important incident in a negotiation to which the United States were a party, and in which the step ought not to have been taken without first consulting you. Mr. De Onis, however, privately insinuates that the offer of mediation did really first come from Great Britain. That it was not requested by Spain but resulted from an intimation by Spain that she had resolved to cede the Floridas to the United States, to which she requested the assent of England; having been, as he further hinted, under previous engagements to England that she would not cede any of her territories to them. Instead of acquiescing in the pretended cession Great Britain now, according to Mr. De Onis, offered her mediation. However the fact may be, it is evident that Spain and Great Britain have some serious misunderstandings with each other, and it can scarcely be expected that the policy which England is adopting in relation to South America will tend to reconcile them." [1]

---

1. Vol. VIII, Instructions, p. 178, J. Q. Adams to Erving, April 20, 1818.

In the meantime Adams, convinced of the desirability of recognizing the South American colonies, had sent officials to report upon the conditions prevailing in those provinces. After their return he was more than ever anxious not only to recognize some of them, particularly Buenos Ayres, which had held out against Spain since 1816; but of persuading certain of the European powers to take a similar course. England had sought to dissuade the United States from this step, as likely to frustrate her plan of mediation between Spain and the revolutionists, by which Spanish sovereignty should still be recognized, but the colonies were to be opened to the trade of the world and granted certain rights of self-government. This failing, Adams addressed a note to Richard Rush, our minister at the court of St. James, inquiring what part he thought the "British government would take in regard to the dispute between Spain and her colonies, and in what light they will view an acknowledgment of independence of her colonies by the United States. Whether they will view it as an act of hostility to Spain and, in case Spain should declare war against us in consequence, whether Great Britain will take part with her in it?" [1]

War with Spain then seemed imminent, even more probable, than it had upon many occasions since 1789. The South American colonies had been taught by the United States something of the manner in which a hated yoke might be thrown off, and were now looking to this country for sympathy and assistance. Their efforts to obtain official recognition and an exchange of ministers were eager and persistent. The constant violations of our neutrality by the organization of filibustering expeditions inspired the first neutrality act, which has since served to establish the princi-

---

1. Vol. VIII, Instructions, p. 246, J. Q. Adams to Richard Rush, Aug. 15, 1818.

ple of international obligation in such cases, and has been the basis of all subsequent legislation on the subject in this country and Great Britain. Continental Europe, still oppressed by the reaction of the era of revolution and the imperial Napoleon, had banded together to crush out republicanism as some noxious serpent. Thus, naturally hostile to rebellions and convinced that Spain would ultimately prevail, they formed the holy alliance to help the Spanish Bourbons, to the extent even of subduing her rebellious colonies. It was far different on this side of the ocean. Apart from a natural sympathy in such conflicts, it was generally believed that the revolted provinces were destined to drive the hated Spaniards back to their ships. After many a long and anxious cabinet discussion, the part of caution and reason prevailed and it had been determined to postpone a recognition, until circumstances should clearly warrant such a course. But Clay ever alert, now that he had failed to secure the office of secretary of state -- in direct line for succession to the presidential chair — found in this an excellent opportunity to harass the administration. Moreover the question was one which appealed to him and offered an excellent opportunity wherein he might at the same time abuse the heads of the government, and laud liberty and freedom with his matchless eloquence and superb oratory.

The United States, thus, if not duly cautious in her Florida negotiations, might find herself face to face not alone with Spain but with all continental Europe. Nor indeed could she afford to offend England and thus risk the failure of negotiations, then under way with that country, for a treaty of friendship, boundaries, and commercial concessions — at this time, under circumstances demanding extreme caution and circumspection on the part of the United States, had Jackson violated Spanish sovereignty and murdered English subjects.

De Onis was strenuously protesting against the intolerable use of our ports by the privateers of Buenos Ayres and the filibustering parties which were being fitted out to fight against Spain, when reports reached Washington of Jackson's campaign. Upon receipt of the report of the governor of West Florida, he entered a vigorous and indignant protest, demanding that St. Marks be delivered to the Spanish commander with all the arms and stores, that the American troops be withdrawn and full indemnity be made for damages done by the American army in Florida.[1] Reports of the capture of Pensacola were not long in reaching the capital, and De Onis, now thoroughly aroused, demanded of Adams to be informed "in a positive, distinct, and explicit manner, just what had occurred." Fuller accounts soon arrived and he once more addressed Adams. He protested vigorously against Jackson's invasion. The Spanish officials had neither incited nor aided the Indians, and, even had they done so, the proper course was for the United States to make a demand on these officers for such Indians and criminals as had escaped to Florida. "These facts (the capture of the Spanish posts) need no comment; they are notorious and speak for themselves. Their enormity has filled even the people of this Union with wonder and surprise and cannot fail to excite the astonishment of all nations and governments. The American general can have neither pretext nor subterfuge of which he can avail himself to give the least color for this invasion and excessive aggression — unexampled in the history of nations. Whatever pretexts may be resorted to, to mislead and impose on the vulgar, will be frivolous, contradictory, and falsified by the very course of events, public and notorious." He demanded the prompt restitution of St. Marks, Pensacola, Barrancas and all other places wrested by Jackson

---

1. De Onis to J. Q. Adams, June 17, 1818. American State Papers, Foreign Relations, Vol. IV, p. 495.

from the crown of Spain, together with all artillery, stores, and property and indemnity for losses, "together with the lawful punishment of the general and the officers of this republic by whom they were committed." [1]

Adams's reply to De Onis was dated July 23. It reminded him that by the treaty of 1795 both Spain and the United States were bound to keep peace along the frontier. That neither power was to permit the Indians dwelling on its soil, to cross the boundaries and molest subjects or citizens of the other. "Notwithstanding this precise, express, and solemn compact of Spain, numbers, painful to recollect, of the citizens of the United States inhabiting the frontier, numbers not merely of persons in active manhood, but of the tender sex, of defenseless age and helpless infancy, had at various times been butchered with all the aggravations and horrors of savage cruelty, by Seminole Indians, and by a banditti of negroes sallying from within the Spanish border and retreating to it again with the horrid fruits of their crimes."

Jackson had, in 1816, in accordance with the treaty provision, called upon the governor of Pensacola [2] to break up a stronghold of which this horde of savages and fugitive slaves had possessed themselves in Florida, and the answer acknowledged the obligation but pleaded a lack of force for its fulfilment; and that the United States had finally been compelled with its own force to accomplish its destruction. With this in mind, when Indian hostilities broke out in 1817, among others, the following orders were issued to the American general in command: "On the receipt of this letter should the Seminole Indians still refuse to make reparation for their outrages and depredations on the citizens of the United States, it is the wish of the president that you consider yourself at liberty to march across

1. American State Papers, Foreign Relations, Vol. V, De Onis to J. Q. Adams, July 8, 1818.
2. Maurico de Zuniga.

the Florida line and to attack them within its limits, should it be found necessary, unless they should shelter themselves under a Spanish fort — in the last event you will immediately notify this department." The right of pursuing an enemy who seeks refuge from actual conflict within a neutral territory could not be denied. But in this case the territory of Florida was not even neutral, for it was the abode of the Indians, and Spain was bound to restrain them. The capture of St. Marks and Pensacola were Jackson's own acts rendered necessary by the "immutable principles of self defense" and the hostility of the governor of Pensacola. Further, that the governor of Pensacola had caused it to be directly reported to the American general that Fort St. Marks was in imminent danger from the Indians and negroes. Then, with surprising audacity, which must have taken De Onis off his feet, Adams in the name of the United States called upon his Catholic Majesty for the punishment of all the Spanish officers concerned. The letter closed with the intimation that "Pensacola will be restored to the possession of any person duly authorized on the part of Spain to receive it; and that Fort St. Marks being in the heart of the Indian country and remote from any Spanish settlement, can be surrendered only to a force sufficiently strong to hold it against the attack of the hostile Indians, upon the appearance of which it will also be restored." [1]

In reply De Onis asserted that the Indians had repeatedly complained to the Spanish officers in East Florida of the "incessant injuries and vexations committed on them by the citizens of this republic inhabiting the frontiers." "Strange indeed, it must appear to the whole world," continued De Onis, "that General Jackson should arrogate to himself the authority of issuing orders and imposing re-

---

1. Vol. II, Foreign Legations, p. 328, Adams to De Onis, July 23, 1818.

strictions on the governor of Pensacola." The matters of complaint should have been referred to the two governments for settlement. The reasons assigned by Jackson only increased the enormity of his offense. The governor of Pensacola had not in any manner intimated that he was fearful lest St. Marks might fall into the hands of the Indians and negroes. Again demand was made for the punishment of Jackson. [1]

In the meantime, De Onis having received notice of the action of the Spanish council of state upon the convention of 1802, announced that he was prepared to exchange the ratifications of that convention. It was, however, determined to postpone the exchange of ratifications with the view of securing a more general and satisfactory adjustment of all the other subjects in controversy between the two nations. [2]

An account of the occurrences in Florida had been sent to Spain by De Onis, and with the first news Pizarro began to address Mr. Erving on the subject. As fuller details reached him Pizarro became more and more insistent upon an explanation, until in August, by the order of the king, all negotiations with the United States were suspended, "until satisfaction should be made by the American government" for the proceedings of Jackson which were considered "acts of unequivocal hostility against him, and as outrages upon his honor and dignity, the only acceptable atonement for which would consist of a disavowal of the American general, the infliction upon him of a suitable punishment for his conduct," and the restitution of the posts and territories taken by him from the Spanish authorities, with indemnity for all the property taken and all damages and injuries, public or private, sustained in conse-

---

1. Vol. V, Foreign Relations, De Onis to Adams, Aug. 5, 1818.
2. Vol. II, Foreign Legations, p. 341, Adams to De Onis, Oct. 23, 1818.

quence of it. [1] Negotiations however were soon renewed, [2]
and Adams sent to Erving, for presentation to the Spanish
foreign minister, one of the most wonderful state papers
ever conceived — a full statement of the American case.

This document, destined to become so famous, was
narrative in form. Beginning with the violation of Spanish neutrality by the English forces in the late war, Adams
went on to speak of Colonel Nicholls and his crew, consisting of "all the runaway negroes, all the savage Indians, all
the pirates, and all the traitors to their country," collected
for the purpose of waging an "exterminating war against
that portion of the United States." He treated with ridicule and scorn the pretensions of Colonel Nicholls that the
United States had failed to observe that article of the
treaty of Ghent which related to the Indian lands, since our
Creek war had terminated by the treaty of Fort Jackson,
concluded some four months before the close of the war of
1812, and that we were at peace with those Indians at the
time of the treaty of Ghent. He then derided the "treaty
of alliance, offensive and defensive, and a treaty of navigation and commerce with Great Britain" which Colonel Nicholls had concluded with the ignorant and credulous Indians.
He referred to the occupation of the Negro Fort.

Then he fell upon poor Arbuthnot whom he characterized as the successor of Nicholls, as a foreign incendiary in
the employment of instigating the Seminole and outlawed
Red Stick Indians to hostilities against the United States.
Even his "intrusion" as a trader he declared was without
excuse or justification and contrary to the policy of all
European powers in this hemisphere. His "infernal instigations" were but too successful and his arrival was followed by the visitation upon the peaceful inhabitants of
the border, of "all the horrors of savage war." He then pro-

---

1. Pizarro to Erving, Aug. 29, 1818.
2. De Onis to Adams, Oct. 18, 1818.

ceeded to justify Jackson in crossing the boundary and in seizing St. Marks. It needed "no citations from printed treatises on international law" to prove his contentions for "it is engraved in adamant on the common sense of mankind." He applauded the arrest of Arbuthnot, "the British Indian trader from beyond the sea, the firebrand by whose torch this Negro-Indian war against our borders had been kindled."

Adams disclosed the fact that councils of war had been held within the very walls of St. Marks by the savage chiefs and warriors. That the Spanish storehouse had been appropriated to their use. That it was an open market for cattle known to have been stolen by them from citizens of the United States, and which had been contracted for and purchased by the officers of the garrison. That information had been sent from this fort by Arbuthnot to the enemy, of the strength and movements of the American army. That ammunition, munitions of war, and all necessary supplies had been furnished to the Indians. He then enlarged upon the hostility of the governor of Pensacola, and justified Jackson in the capture of that town.

"The president," declared Adams, "will neither inflict punishment nor pass censure upon General Jackson for that conduct — the vindication of which is written in every page of the law of nations, as well as in the first law of nature, self-defense." On the contrary, "suitable punishment," it was demanded, should be inflicted upon Don José Mazot, governor of Pensacola, and Don Francisco Luenzo, commandant of St. Marks, for their "defiance and violation of the engagements of Spain with the United States." If these officers were powerless, Adams declared, the "United States can as little compound with impotence as with perfidy, and Spain must immediately make her election, either to place a force in Florida, adequate at once to the protec-

tion of her territory and to the fulfilment of her engagements or cede to the United States a province of which she
retains nothing but the nominal possession, but which is
in fact a derelict, open to the occupancy of every enemy,
civilized or savage, of the United States, and serving no
other earthly purpose than as a post of annoyance to
them."

To Pizarro's complaint of the "shameful invasion of
his Majesty's territory," Adams inquired "What was the
character of Nicholls's invasion of his Majesty's territory,
and where was his Majesty's profound indignation at that?
. . . Has his Majesty suspended formally all negotiation
with the sovereign of Colonel Nicholls for this shameful invasion of his territory without color of provocation, without
pretence of necessity, without shadow or even avowal of
pretext? Has his Majesty given solemn warning to the
British government that these were incidents 'of transcendent moment, capable of producing an essential and thorough change in the political relations of the two countries?' . . . Against the shameful invasion of the territory,
against the violent seizure of the forts and places, against
the blowing up of the Barrancas, and the erection and maintenance under British banners of the Negro Fort on Spanish soil; against the negotiation by a British officer in the
midst of peace, of pretended treaties, offensive and defensive, and of navigation and commerce upon Spanish territory, between Great Britain and Indians, Indians which
Spain was bound to control and restrain? If a whisper of
expostulation was ever wafted from Madrid to London it
was not loud enough to be heard across the Atlantic, nor
energetic enough to transpire beyond the walls of the palaces from which it issued and to which it was borne."

Next the affair of Amelia Island and MacGregor and
his crew of patriots was discussed in no uncertain terms
of indignation and wrath. Ambrister and his career were

glowingly depicted. "Is this narrative," he questioned, "of dark and complicated depravity; this creeping and insidious war; this mockery of patriotism, these political philters to fugitive slaves and Indian outlaws; these perfidies and treacheries of villains, incapable of keeping their faith even to each other; all in the name of South American liberty, of the rights of runaway negroes, and the wrongs of savage murderers; all combined and projected to plunder Spain of her provinces and to spread massacre and devastation along the border of the United States; is all this sufficient to cool the sympathies of his Catholic Majesty's government excited by the execution of these 'two subjects of a power in amity with the king?' The Spanish government is not at this day to be informed, that cruel as war in its mildest forms must be, it is, and necessarily must be doubly cruel when waged with savages. That savages make no prisoners but to torture them; that they give no quarter; that they put to death without discrimination of age or sex. That these ordinary characteristics of Indian warfare have been applicable in their most heart-sickening horrors to that war, left us by Nicholls as his legacy, reinstigated by Woodbine, Arbuthnot, and Ambrister, and stimulated by the approbation and encouragement and aid of the Spanish commandant at St. Marks, is proof required?"

By way of illustrating the horrors which he had so eloquently described Adams cited three occurrences, two of which took place before Arbuthnot reached Florida and the third, one with which there exists no reason for connecting the unfortunate trader. The first was the case of the sailor Daniels, who had been captured by the occupants of the Negro Fort and tarred and burned alive in July, 1816. The second was the murder of Mrs. Garret and her children, in February, 1817, which General Mitchell expressly testified was an act of retaliation for the murder of Indians by the

19

whites. The third was the massacre of Lieutenant Scott and his party, which we know to have been the Seminole revenge for the attack of General Gaines upon Fowltown, and which occurred while Arbuthnot was at New Providence.

"Contending with such enemies, although humanity revolted at entire retaliation and spares the lives of their feeble and defenseless women and children, yet mercy herself, surrenders to retributive justice the lives of their leading warriors taken in arms, and still more the lives of the foreign white incendiaries who, disowned by their own governments, and disowning their own natures, degrade themselves beneath the savage character by voluntarily descending to its level. . . . It is thus only that the barbarities of Indians can be successfully encountered. It is thus only that the worse than Indian barbarities of European impostors, pretending authority from their governments, but always disavowed, can be punished and arrested. Great Britain yet engages the alliance and co-operation of savages in war. But her government has invariably disclaimed all countenance or authorization to her subjects to instigate them against us in time of peace. Yet so it has happened to this day, all the Indian wars with which we have been afflicted have been distinctly traceable to the instigation of English traders or agents. Always disavowed yet always felt; more than once detected but never before punished. Two of them, offenders of the deepest dye, after solemn warning to their government, and individually to one of them, have fallen, *flagrante delicto,* into the hands of an American general. And the punishment inflicted upon them has fixed them on high as an example, awful in its exhibition but we trust auspicious in its results, of that which awaits unauthorized pretenders of European agency to stimulate and interpose in wars between the United States and the Indians within their control."

Adams also embodied in the note a demand for the punishment of the Spanish officers for their misconduct, and a further demand "of Spain for a just and reasonable indemnity to the United States for the heavy and necessary expenses which they have been compelled to incur by the failure of Spain to perform her engagement to restrain the Indians, aggravated by this demonstrated complicity of her commanding officers in their hostilities against the United States."

Then followed further justification of the execution of Arbuthnot and Ambrister, declaring that Jackson would have been warranted in summarily hanging them without the formality even of a trial. That the latter had confessed his guilt and that the defense of the former consisted "solely and exclusively of technical cavils at the nature of part of the evidence against him."

Adams wound up the document with an open threat. "If the necessities of self defense should again compel the United States to take possession of the Spanish forts and places in Florida," it was fitting that the United States should "declare, with the frankness and candor that becomes us, that another unconditional restoration of them must not be expected. That even the president's confidence in the good faith and ultimate justice of the Spanish government will yield to the painful experience of continual disappointment. And that after unwearied and almost unnumbered appeals to them for the performance of their stipulated duties, in vain, the United States will be reluctantly compelled to rely for the protection of their borders upon themselves alone." [1]

Such was the answer to Pizarro, and with it was dispatched a forbidding mass of documents. Adams's defense was plausible and was fortified with references to doc-

---

1. Vol. VIII, Instructions, p. 257, J. Q. Adams to George Erving, Nov. 28, 1818. Also see Appendix C.

uments which, when examined with care, however, fail to bear out his statements. For example he quotes a letter as proving that Arbuthnot was not a trader but had certain ulterior plans. The letter, on the contrary, bears no testimony whatever to the assertion. Some essential facts were omitted. Many were misstated and others perverted. Nothing was said of the tragedy of the Negro Fort — the awful career of that hot shell. Scarcely an allusion to the Fowltown attack which precipitated the war. The "firebrand" Arbuthnot, mild mannered man of seventy summers, peace loving and submission-counselling, it was he who had taught the Indians to slaughter and pillage, to murder defenseless women, and take little children by the heels and dash their brains out on the side of the boat. No reference was made to Jackson and his notoriously anti-Spanish sentiments; or to the surprise and opposition to the course of the general so widely prevalent in the United States.

There was no intimation of what every fair and impartial student must admit, that the Seminole war was inspired by the attacks and ravages committed upon the redskins by the white border settlers. There was no hint that the attacks of the Indians were retaliatory; and that they were induced by that same treatment which, we blush to admit, has ever been accorded the doomed race that stands in the path of the white man's advance to something that he desires. The letter made no allusion to the pitiable and defenseless condition of the Seminole Indians, and the size of the army and the amount of armament collected by Jackson for the contest with so weak and contemptible a foe; or of the conclusions to be drawn from such suspicious circumstances. There was no comment upon the articles of capitulation of Pensacola which showed most clearly that the reasons assigned by Jackson for his expedition were but a pretext, and that the real motive was a provisional cession of the province as the first step to a permanent acquisition.

It was indeed a highly ingenious instrument and did credit to the author's legal acumen. To quote Parton, it stands as "the most flagrant piece of special pleading to be found in the diplomatic records of the United States." To one who is not acquainted with the facts its perusal is a pleasure and, admitting its premises, there can be no answer to its conclusions. Never has a diplomatic paper met with more signal success. It averted war. It silenced the English government and warranted that country in ignoring the execution of its subjects, though it was anxious for such an excuse. It gave the continental powers ground for refusing to assist Spain in making war against the United States. It convinced the people of the United States, and even well nigh persuaded Pizarro and the Spanish council of state. In this country it won for its author universal applause. [1] "Adams has done honor to his country and himself," was the verdict of all, irrespective of party or principle. The document as if by magic cleared the air so heavily surcharged with rumors and threats of war, and on the convening of congress the president was able to announce that our relations with Spain did not differ materially from what they had been a year before.

It was also necessary to appease General Jackson for the disavowal of certain of his acts. A long letter, a happy blending of mild rebuke and pleasing compliment, was written by President Monroe explaining the necessity of surrendering the Spanish posts. One paragraph in particular was noteworthy as showing the prevalent feeling upon the subject of a Spanish war. "Should we hold the posts it is impossible to calculate all the consequences likely to result from it. It is not improbable that war would im-

---

1. Jefferson thought that a translation of the note should be sent to all of the courts of Europe.

mediately follow. Spain would be stimulated to declare it; and once declared the adventurers of Britain and other countries would, under the Spanish flag, privateer on our commerce. The immense revenue which we now receive would be much diminished, as would be the profits of our valuable productions. The war would probably soon become general; and we do not foresee that we should have a single power in Europe on our side. Why risk these consequences? The events which have occurred in both the Floridas show the incompetency of Spain to maintain her authority; and the progress of the revolutions in South America will require all her forces there. There is much reason to presume that this act will furnish a strong inducement to Spain to cede the territory, provided we do not wound too deply her pride by holding it. If we hold the posts, her government cannot treat with honor, which, by withdrawing the troops, we afford her an opportunity to do. The manner in which we propose to act will exculpate you from censure, and promises to obtain all the advantages which you contemplated from the measure, and possibly very soon. From a different course no advantage would be likely to result, and there would be great danger of extensive and serious injuries." [1]

In a similar vein Calhoun wrote to Jackson: "A war with Spain, were it to continue with her alone, and were there no great neutral powers to avail themselves of the opportunity of embarrassing us, would be nothing. But such a war would not continue long without involving other parties, and it certainly would in a few years be an English war." [2]

Gallatin, then our minister at Paris, had written that the capture of Pensacola and the execution of the two Englishmen, as well as that of the Indian chiefs, had excited

1. Monroe to Jackson, July 19, 1818.
2. Calhoun to Jackson, Sept., 1818.

in France and even in other parts of Europe "sensations peculiarly unfavorable" to the United States. To Rush, at London, Adams wrote: "The impression produced upon the public mind in England, throughout Europe, and even partially in this country has been, that this was, on our part, a wanton and unprovoked war upon the Indians and that the execution of Arbuthnot and Ambrister were acts of sanguinary cruelty in violation of the ordinary usages of war." [1]

Pizarro, commenting upon the Florida affair, referred to the executions as an "act of barbarity glossed over with the forms of justice and thereby rendered, on considering the nature of the plan and other circumstances, a refinement of cruelty." On the whole he had concluded "that it appears that a forcible occupation was preferred to a peaceful acquisition — no claim to the territory invaded by General Jackson, whether founded or unfounded, has been advanced by the American government — no revolution of the inhabitants real or supposed offered a pretext — no previous aggressions by banditti, as was urged on the occasion of the unjust occupation of Amelia Island." [2] There could be no doubt in their eyes that the invasion of Florida "was a premeditated act of hostility" and that "General Jackson, trampling under foot all laws, has committed in the territory of his Majesty outrages and excesses, of which there are few examples in the civilized world." "It will," Pizarro continued, "one day or other be stated with surprise that the theatre of such devastation and unprovoked offense, in the midst of peace, was the very same, on which Spain, not many years since, shed her blood and poured out her treasures for the United States in the

---

1. Vol. VIII, Instructions, pp. 204-205, J. Q. Adams to Richard Rush, Dec. 1, 1818.
2. Letters from Ministers Abroad, Vol. XVI, Pizzaro to Erving. Aug. 29, 1818.

days of their calamity."[1]   Spain had protested to France,
England, and other continental courts against the conduct
of Jackson and the action of the United States.   Adams in
his valuable diary refers to an interview with Bagot upon
the execution of Arbuthnot and Ambrister in which some
quotations were made from Jackson's letters. "He (Bagot)
said," writes Adams, "he should think little of anything said
or written by General Jackson because he thought there
were evident marks in his conduct of personal bitterness
and inveteracy."

In September, Pizarro and the other ministers, as a
result of a court intrigue, were dismissed and banished and
Casa D'Yrujo named as foreign minister in his stead.
On Pizarro, Erving commented, "his intelligence and good
sense, his moderate and conciliatory temper and his honor
and good faith recommended him to every one — no Spanish
minister of late years has done so much to repair the dis-
ordered state of affairs as he has done, and none has received more marks of the satisfaction of the foreign cabinets
with whom he has treated."   Of the new minister, Erving
wrote, "I expect no good from D'Yrujo in our affairs and
shall be very happy if I can only keep him from undoing
whatever Pizarro has done favorable to an amicable adjustment of them."[2]

For reasons of public policy, France had been anxious
to secure a friendly settlement between Spain and the
United States and thus prevent hostilities.   Again then did
European complications and dynastic aliances come to the
rescue of the United States and prevent awkward complications.   "France," wrote Erving to Adams, "is very
reasonably alarmed at the least symptom of discord any-
where.   It knows that the smallest spark may produce con-

---

1. Letters from Ministers Abroad, Vol. XVI, Pizzaro to Erving.
Aug. 11, 1818.
2. *Ibid.*, Erving to J. Q. Adams, Sept. 20, 1818.

flagration and that France is most combustible. The evacuation of the allies cannot but increase that tremor; not like besotted Spain who has flattered herself so long that she was under the protection of a special providence, who has expected support from all quarters and has relied with entire confidence on that of England, the enlightened government of France sees that in the event of a rupture between the United States and Spain, the natural progress of things will necesarily lead to an alliance or at least to a very dangerous concert of measures between the United States and Great Britain. The separation of the congress of Aix-la-Chapelle without the least demonstration of a disposition to listen to the 'jerémiades' of Spain naturally confirms this apprehension. This then is probably the most favorable moment for treating with Spain which has yet occurred, and I do not doubt but that even Mr. Casa D'Yrujo is now fully convinced of the necessity of making what he would consider considerable sacrifices to procure an arrangement." [1]

---

1. Letters from Ministers Abroad, Vol. XVI, Erving to J. Q. Adams (private), Oct. 22, 1818.

CHAPTER X.

THE TREATY OF 1819.

IN accordance with our agreement, the Spanish posts, which had been captured by Jackson, were delivered over to the proper officials.

It might seem at first, that the reoccupation of Florida by the Spanish was a mere matter of form in which a proud and sensitive nation consulted its dignity and satisfied its honor by being placed in a position to make a voluntary surrender of the province instead of submitting to a conquest. The course of Jackson had wounded her pride and exposed her weakness to the world. But the delay of Spain in ratifying the treaty, after the pressure of conquest had been removed, forces us to the conclusion that the mailed fist of Jackson was as much responsible for its final cession as the diplomatic pen of the secretary of state.

Enraged and humbled Spain, and rapacious and determined United States — these Adams must bring together and that too when there was so much of wrong on both sides and such realm for honest differences. Nor was De Onis unworthy of Adams's mettle. Of him we read Adams's opinion: "Cold, calculating, wily, always commanding his temper, proud because he is a Spaniard but supple and cunning, accommodating the tone of his pretensions precisely to the degree of endurance of his opponents, bold and overbearing to the utmost extent to which it is tolerated, careless of what he asserts or how grossly it is proved to be un-

founded, his morality appears to be that of the Jesuits as
exposed by Pascal. He is laborious, vigilant, and ever
attentive to his duties; a man of business and of the world."
We are inclined to wonder whether this was not written by
an irritated author after a long hard day of unsuccessful
attempt to persuade the skillful Spaniard.

But De Onis was scarcely less solicitous than his adversary for a treaty and certainly the difficulties which he encountered were no less grave. He was anxious to
return home and to crown his mission to this country by
a treaty which would be acceptable to his king and becoming
to his fame. The Spanish nobles, three thousand miles away,
were unable to appreciate the true situation. Arrogance
and Spanish strength had not declined *pari passu*. The
concessions demanded by the United States were to them
humiliating and intolerable. De Onis must have been often
exasperated and discouraged, for, after a long attempt to
persuade Adams to meet him on a boundary line, he declared that he had taken infinite pains "to prevail upon his
government to come to terms of accommodation, and
insisted that the king's council was composed of such ignorant and stupid niggards, grandees of Spain, and priests,"
that Adams "could have no conception of their obstinacy
and imbecility."

In October of 1818 De Onis informed Adams of the
arrival of new instructions, and offered as the western
boundary a line from the Gulf of Mexico between the Mermenteau and Calcasieu rivers to the Red River at latitude
32°, thence due north to the Missouri and along that river
to its source.[1]

---

1. De Onis to Adams, Oct. 24, 1818: "A line beginning on the
Gulf of Mexico between the rivers Mermenteau and Calcasieu following the Arroyo Hondo between the Adaes and Natchitoches, crossing
the Rio or Red River at 32° of latitude and 93° of longitude from London—and thence running directly north, crossing the Arkansas, White
and Osage rivers and then following the middle of that river to its
source."

This, the first sign of concession on the part of Spain, was met by an offer on the part of the United States, which, abandoning the Rio Grande, proposed the Sabine from its mouth to 32°; a line due north to the Red River; the channel of that river to its source in the mountains, then to the summit and along the crest to latitude 41° and by it to the Pacific Ocean. De Onis, accepting the Sabine line, declared that he had no authority to go to the Pacific whereupon Adams withdrew his offer and declared that the United States stood by the Rio Grande.

A further difficulty presented itself in the question of the grants of land which had been made in Florida. Adams wrote to De Onis that the United States could not "recognize as valid all the grants of land until this time, and at the same time renounce all their claims and those of their citizens for damages and injuries sustained by them and for the reparation of which Spain is answerable to them. It is well known to you, sir, that notice has been given by the minister of the United States in Spain to your government that all the grants of land alleged to have been made by your government within those territories must be cancelled, unless your government should provide some other adequate fund from which the claims . . . of the United States and their citizens may be satisfied."[1] The United States in return for the cession of Florida, would exonerate Spain from all claims and agree to make satisfaction for them to an amount not exceeding five million dollars — the amount and validity of the claims to be determined by a commission which should meet at Washington within three years.

De Onis replied that the demand that the Spanish land grants in Florida after 1802 be declared null and void, was "offensive to the dignity and imprescriptible rights of the

1. Adams to De Onis, Oct. 31, 1818, Vol. II, Foreign Legations, p. 360.

crown of Spain" which, as the legitimate owner of both
Floridas, had a right to dispose of those lands as it pleased
— and further as the said modification would be productive
of incalculable injury to the bona fide possessors who have
acquired, settled, and improved these tracts. However he
agreed that the grants made since January 24, 1818, "the
date of my first note announcing his Majesty's willingness
to cede them to the United States . . . shall be declared null
and void in consideration of the grantees not having complied with the essential conditions of the cession, as has
been the fact." [1]

The question of the South American colonies was likewise an embarrassing feature in the negotiations. Monroe
was anxious not only to recognize the revolted provinces of
Spain, but also to persuade England and other European
countries to take the same step. Under date of July 25,
1818, we find the following entry in the diary of John
Quincy Adams: "Two days ago he (Monroe) had very
abruptly asked me to see Mr. Bagot and propose through
him to the British government an immediate co-operation
between the United States and Great Britain to promote the
independence of South America. 'All South America and
Mexico and the islands included.' I told him I thought
Great Britain was not yet prepared for such a direct proposition."

The first of the following year representations were
made to the English government upon this subject. These
consisted of a statement of the attitude of this country
toward the belligerents and an effort to secure some con-
certed action in the matter. Adams declared that it was
the purpose and the policy of this government to "remain
neutral;" to award to both of the contestants "equal
and the same treatment, recognizing neither the supremacy

---

1. Vol. V, Foreign Relations, De Onis to J. Q. Adams, Nov. 16,
1818.

contended for by Spain nor the independence contended for by the South Americans." An entire equality of treatment was not possible. As Spain, being an acknowledged sovereign power, has "ministers and other accredited and privileged agents to maintain her interests and support her rights," the American government considered it among the obligations of neutrality to obviate this inequality and "we listen therefore to the representations of their deputies·or agents and do them justice as much as if they were formally accredited." Adams had the grace to admit that "by acknowledging the existence of a civil war the right of Spain as understood by herself is no doubt affected. She is no longer recognized as the sovereign of the provinces in revolution against her."

This state of things was declared to be merely temporary. Any guarantee of the restoration of Spanish sovereignty in South America on the part of the allied powers would have been a departure from neutrality by them. No mediation ought to be undertaken without the consent of both parties in the contest. "Whether we consider the question of the conflict between Spanish colonial dominion and South American independence upon principles, moral or political, or upon those of the interest of either party to the war, or of all other nations as connected with them, whether upon grounds of right or of fact, they all bring us to the same conclusion that the contest cannot and ought not to terminate otherwise than by the total independence of South America. . . . Convinced as we are that the Spanish authority can never be restored at Buenos Ayres, in Chili, or in Venezuela, we wish the British government and all the European allies to consider how important it is to them, as well as to us, that these newly formed states should be regularly recognized," both because of their just right to such recognition, and that they may be held to an observation of the rules of the laws of nations. For that course seemed to present the only effectual means of "repressing the excessive irregularities and piratical depredations of armed vessels under their flags and bearing their commissions. . . . It is hardly to be expected," declared Adams, "that they will feel themselves bound by the ordinary duties of sovereign states while they are denied the enjoyment of all their rights." The letter then stated the determination of President Monroe to recognize the government of Buenos Ayres "at no remote period" and concluded that, "if it should suit the views of Great Britain to adopt similar measures at the same time and in concert with us, it will be highly satisfactory to the president." [1]

After the refusal of De Onis to accept the Sabine boundary proposition in full, there was a lull in the negotiations. Early in January the president and his cabinet conferred upon the advisability of securing from congress an act authorizing the seizure of Florida upon certain contingencies. The secretary of state favored such a bill and desired that it should extend to the power of taking and holding the entire province, "in the event of any further failure on the part of Spain to fulfill her engagement of restraining by force the Indians within her territory from hostilities against the United States, formal notice having been given her that such would be the result." Crawford declared that it would give the nation the appearance of acting in bad faith and lose the credit we had obtained in Europe by restoring the places captured by General Jackson. Calhoun did not consider the necessity sufficiently urgent. That to suppose Spain unable or unwilling to fulfill her treaty engagements would be, in the least, insulting. That congress ought to "pass laws only upon existing facts and not upon speculative anticipations."

---

1. Vol. VIII, Instructions, p. 296. J. Q. Adams to Richard Rush, Jan. 1, 1819.

Wirt stated that if it were *res integra* it might be insulting to Spain to assume that she would not fulfill her treaty, and asked if all prospect of obtaining Florida by an arrangement seemed hopeless. Adams answered in the affirmative unless such a law should pass; that that might bring Spain to it but that nothing else would. The matter was then laid aside for future consideration. [1]

Agreeably to his instructions and the policy of his government, Hyde de Neuville, the French minister at Washington, took a warm interest in the negotiations. He served as a channel of communication and carried propositions and counter-propositions, arguments and denials between the two negotiators — messages which could pass better through a third party than directly from hand to hand. He even expostulated and argued in turn with De Onis and with Adams imploring the one to yield a point, the other to be reasonable in his demands. England's proffered services were rejected. Adams neither needed nor desired any mediation. He was willing to take upon himself the entire responsibility for the success or failure of his efforts.

But Adams was forced to contend with lukewarm support, nay even active opposition in his own ranks. Crawford, apart from seeking to disgrace Jackson and thus make him an impossibility for the presidency, sought steadily to discourage a Spanish treaty on the ground that, if it were a success, it would add too much strength and popularity to Monroe's administration. This secretary of the treasury, of whom Adams said, "He has a talent for intrigue only," did not hesitate to intimate indirectly to De Neuville and De Onis that the French should demand special commercial privileges in Louisiana, and that Spain should insist upon a boundary line west of the Mississippi more favorable to her than that offered by Adams. The cabinet of Monroe at

1. J. Q. Adams's Diary, Jan. 2, 1819.

that time was innately vicious, the various members fighting
the administration and one another, all playing for the
presidential stake, utterly indifferent to the demands of the
country and the pledges of their oaths. There was every
reason to expect that Clay would fight any treaty which
did not satisfy the wildest demands of the United States
and of his romantic mind. Crawford desired to see Adams
fail in his negotiations or conclude an unpopular treaty.

In Spain, D'Yrujo, the foreign minister, was hostile
to the United States, and was still controlled by the "unex-
tinguished rancorous feelings . . . of ancient date." The
king was probably more anxious for a treaty and more
ready to make the necessary sacrifices to obtain it, than any
member of his council. Erving wrote home that however
sincere may be the disposition of the Spanish government to
treat at that time, a dissolution of congress before a treaty
was concluded, "or without taking some very strong resolution with regard to the Floridas," would produce a most
unfavorable change. If the independence of the South
American colonies should be acknowledged the greatest
evil which Spain apprehended would thus come to pass,
and the temptation to any sort of an arrangement would be
diminished. Should the independence not be acknowledged
and the Floridas be restored, Spain would "lapse into security or indifference," for twelve months would thus be
gained for the operation of chances in her favor. "But in
either of the supposed cases," concluded Erving, "should the
president be authorized to take and to hold possession of
the Floridas till the claims of the United States be satisfied,
this pressure may produce a final adjustment."[1]

In January, 1819, De Onis, announcing the receipt of
new instructions, offered the old line to the source of the
Missouri, with a new one thence to the Columbia, and so to

---

1. Vol. XVI, Letters from Ministers Abroad, Erving to J. Q.
Adams, Jan. 4, 1819.

20

the sea. Monroe anxious for a treaty — though long in accord with Adams — as De Onis gradually conceded point by point, began to fear lest Adams by insisting on extreme measures would not only fail in a treaty but might invite war. But Adams seems to have correctly measured the exact line to which the pressure of Spanish misfortunes would compel De Onis to advance. Gradually yielding, but bitterly protesting, and imploring Adams to concede here or there and advance to meet him, the Spanish minister slowly approached the demands of our secretary of state. Yet so slowly was this done that we find Adams noting in his diary that he "could not express the disgust with which he was forced to carry on a correspondence with him upon subjects which it was ascertained that we could not adjust." And even saying to De Onis that he "was so wearied out with the discussion that it had become nauseous," and that he "really could discuss no longer and had given it up in despair." [1] And yet during all this time the other members of the administration and the members of congress talked freely both with De Neuville and De Onis intimating how far they may urge their pretensions and how far we might "be prevailed upon to concede." [2]

There were many alarming pauses and Adams was ever anxious as to the outcome and fearful lest De Onis might make a firm stand and refuse absolutely to yield more. But as they approached nearer to an agreement Adams records that the president was inclined to give up all that remained in contest. On February 11, Monroe declared decidedly for agreeing to the 100° of longitude and 43° of latitude and taking the middle of the rivers (Arkansas, Red, and Multnomah). The other members of the administration all inclined the same way, but Adams was convinced that more might be obtained by adhering

---

1. Adams's Diary, Feb. 11, 1819.
2. *Ibid.*, Feb. 15, 1819.

steadily to our demands.[1] De Onis objected strongly to
having the United States name five million dollars in the
treaty, to be paid for claims, lest it should appear that he
was selling Florida for that sum, while it was worth ten
times that amount; that to name that figure would arouse
indignation in Spain and endanger the ratification of the
treaty.[2]

The proposed line of De Onis to the South Sea was the
beginning of the end. For each receded gradually until
on the twenty-second of February, 1819, the two negotiators
signed and sealed the counterparts of the treaty — consum
mating the diplomatic efforts of this country for nearly a
score of years.

The result justified Adams and was a great personal
triumph, although Erving is authority for the statement
that the Spanish cabinet was "highly delighted with the
treaty."[3] No concession had been made except as to
accepting the Sabine as the boundary. The United States
received the Floridas in return for an agreement to settle
the disputed claims of certain of her citizens against Spain
to an amount not more than $5,000,000; while the Spanish
claims against the United States, provided for in the convention of 1802, were wholly expunged. The western
boundary secured for this country the coveted outlet to the
shores of the "South Sea." The line ran along the south
banks of the Red and Arkansas rivers leaving all the islands
to the United States, although granting to Spain a common
right of navigation.

Let us quote from the famous diary under date of
February 22, 1819: "It was near in the morning when I
closed the day with ejaculations of fervent gratitude to the
Giver of all good. It was, perhaps, the most important day

1. Adams's Diary, Feb. 11, 1819.
2. *Ibid.*, Feb. 15, 1819.
3. Vol. XVI, Letters from Ministers Abroad, Erving to J. Q.
Adams, April 28, 1819.

of my life. What the consequences may be of the compact this day signed with Spain is known only to the all-wise and all-beneficent Disposer of events, who has brought it about in a manner utterly unexpected and by means the most extraordinary and unforeseen. Its prospects are propitious and flattering in an eminent degree. May they be realized by the same superintending bounty that produced them. May no disappointment embitter the hope which this event warrants us in cherishing, and may its future influence on the destinies of my country be as extensive and as favorable as our warmest anticipations can paint. Let no idle and unfounded exultation take possession of my mind, as if I could ascribe to my own foresight or exertions any portion of the event. It is the work of an intelligent and all-embracing cause. May it speed as it has begun, for without a continuation of the blessings already showered down upon it, all that has been done will be worse than useless and vain.

"The acquisition of the Floridas has long been an object of earnest desire to this country. The acknowledgment of a definite line of boundary to the South Sea forms a great epoch in our history. The first proposal of it in this negotiation was my own and I trust it is now secured beyond the reach of revocation. It was not even among our claims by the treaty of independence with Great Britain. It was not among our pretensions under the purchase of Louisiana — for that gave us only the range of the Mississippi and its waters. I first introduced it in the written proposal of 31st October last, after having discussed it verbally both with De Onis and De Neuville. It is the only peculiar and appropriate right acquired by this treaty in the event of its ratification."

A protest against the treaty, particularly against the boundary line, appeared the following day in one of the Washington papers, and was believed to have been written or inspired by Clay. However his opposition was practically without effect, and on the twenty-fourth the treaty was unanimously ratified. It was proclaimed a day later by President Monroe.

But troubles soon appeared. In February, 1818, while the negotiations for the cession of the Floridas were under way, Erving wrote to Madison that the king had made three vast grants of land in that province — one to the duke of Alagon, captain of the bodyguards; another to the Count de Punon Rostro, one of his Majesty's chamberlains; the third, which it was believed contained all the land in Florida and the adjacent islands not already disposed of, was to Don Pedro de Varges, the treasurer of the household. There can be no doubt that this was a highly disgraceful act of bad faith and that the intention of the king was to deprive the United States of the ownership of the crown lands. Adams, with these grants in mind, we will recall, had insisted in October of 1818 that all grants made since 1802 in the Floridas should be declared null and void. De Onis in a counter-proposition suggested rather the date of January 24, 1818, that being the date when Spain first expressed her willingness to cede the Floridas. Adams finally accepted this date, but not knowing the exact date of the grants referred to by Erving, distinctly declared to De Onis that he did so with the express understanding that these three grants should be held void. Adams cannot be absolved from blame, for he was undoubtedly guilty of carelessness in not examining the original grants. He accordingly wrote to De Onis that he understood it to be the intent of the treaty to nullify the grants. De Onis at first evaded and quibbled, but a few days later he candidly declared that it was his understanding that these three grants were, by the eighth article of the treaty, to be null and void whatever their dates may have been.

In April, in consequence of a long expressed desire, the Chevalier de Onis returned home and was succeeded at Washington by General Don Francisco Dionisio Vives. On the twenty-ninth of April Erving held his farewell audience with the king and princes of Spain and gave way to his successor, John Forsyth of Georgia. [1]

That no doubt might exist upon the point of the land grants, Forsyth received special instructions to deliver a written declaration upon the subject when he exchanged the ratifications of the treaty. On reaching Madrid, in May, he applied to Marquis Casa d'Yrujo for a date for exchanging ratifications. Receiving no reply, he wrote again, two weeks later, reminding him of the presence of the sloop of war, "Hornet," in the harbor of Cadiz, that the time for her departure was nearly at hand, and that if she returned without the ratified treaty a most unfavorable impression would be created in the United States. [2]   This brought a reply. "The importance of the treaty made necessary an extended deliberation on the part of the king." [3] Before a decision could be reached there must be certain explanations on the part of the United States; that a person enjoying the fullest confidence of his Majesty would be sent to Washington for that purpose. August twenty-second being the last day on which, by the terms of the treaty, ratifications could be exchanged, Forsyth served formal notice on the twenty-first, that matters were in precisely the same condition as before the consummation of the convention, and the United States were free to enforce and maintain their claims in such manner as might seem best.

In the meantime the "Hornet" had reached the United

---

1. Forsyth as a member of the senate was ever inveterate in his attacks upon General Jackson for his course in Florida.
2. Forsyth to D'Yrujo, May 18 and June 4, 1819.
3. Gonzales Salmon to Forsyth, June 19, 1819.

States. Full instructions were dispatched to Forsyth. The United States would hold Spain responsible "for all damages and expenses which may arise from the delay or refusal of Spain to ratify, and from the measures to which the United States may resort to give efficacy to their rights, and that for the indemnities to which they will be justly entitled for this violation of faith by Spain, the United States will look to the territory west of the Sabine River." From the powers given to De Onis, after the signature of that minister and the ratification of the United States the treaty was as binding upon the honor and good faith of the Spanish king and nation as it would be after its ratification by the king.

De Onis had declared that he was ashamed that the grants had been made and wished them declared void because of certain remarks publicly made that he was personally interested in them. These grantees were not named in the treaty (1) to save the honor of the king, and (2) because there were other grants made at the same time and to have named these would presumptively have raised an inference in favor of others. De Onis had expressly stated (1) that the grants in question were all, in his belief, included among those positively annulled by the date of January 24, 1818; (2) that these grants had been made by the king with the view of promoting population, cultivation, and industry, and not with that of alienating the territory and, (3) that the grants were all null and void because the grantees had not complied with the essential conditions of the grants.

Adams continued: "When the government of a nation degrades itself by flagrant and notorious perfidy, those who are constrained to entertain political relations of neighborhood are justified by the law of nature, and it is their duty to themselves in subsequent transactions with such a state, to take pledges of security for the performance of its engagements more effectual than confidence in its good faith. Such pledges are amply within the reach of the United States, in their intercourse hereafter with Spain, nor is it to be presumed that those who are entrusted with the maintenance of the rights and interests of this nation, will over-look or neglect the duty which may be devolved upon them of taking them." [1] Forsyth was also to announce that, although six months had elapsed, the ratification by Spain would still be received on two conditions. It must be within one week, and must be accompanied by the avowal that the three land grants in question were null and void. This demand having been explicitly stated, the note was returned to Forsyth with the statement that it could not be laid before the king. Forsyth insisted that it be delivered, and wrote to Adams that in the event of its failing he should leave Madrid. [2]

The situation was now considered so critical that Count Bulgary, the Russian chargé d'affaires, was sent to explain matters and request that the returned note be withheld, and to say that a minister would be immediately sent to the United States to ask for certain explanations. The minister selected for this mission was Mariscal de Campo Don Francisco Dionisio Vives and with his departure Forsyth was notified that all discussion of the difficulty at Madrid must cease.

Vives with the undoubted purpose of consuming as much time as possible, traveled by easy stages from Madrid to Bayonne, thence to Paris, and from Paris to England, reaching the United States in April, 1820.

---

1. Vol. VIII, Instructions, p. 343, J. Q. Adams to Forsyth, Aug. 18, 1819. See also De Onis to Adams, Oct. 24, 1818, and answer Oct. 31, 1818. De Onis to Adams, Nov. 16, 1818. De Onis to Adams, Feb. 9, 1819. Adams to De Onis, Feb. 13, 1819.

2. Forsyth to Duke of San Fernandino and Quirago, Oct. 18, 1819. Answer to Forsyth, Nov. 12, 1819. Forsyth to Duke of San Fernandino,·etc., Nov. 20, 1819. Forsyth to Adams, Nov. 27, 1819.

In the United States the course of Spain aroused intense indignation. There was a wide feeling that the United States should forcibly possess Florida, that Spain had paltered long enough with us. Adams, long before desirous of an act of congress authorizing the seizure of Florida and Galveston, now thoroughly indignant, advised that the United States prepare at once to take and hold the disputed territory and some undisputed territory as well. Monroe and the other members of the cabinet advocated a milder course. France and England expressed hopes to this country that no violent action would be precipitately taken.

The agitation of the slavery question, already exerting a great power in American politics, had its influence on the still pending and rather dubious Spanish treaty. The south was desirous of seizing not only the Floridas but as much as possible towards Mexico to carve into more slave states. But the north was no longer eager for an extension of the Union on the southern side. Sectional predominated national interests. The question was not without its effect upon the presidential aspirations of Adams.

Poor Spain, with her vast American empire in open and successful revolt, was in no humor to add to her losses by the cession of Florida. The announcement that a special envoy would be sent to the United States to treat further in the case created, in this country, a sensation of the most profound disgust. Jackson, fuming at the Spanish breach of faith, wrote to Senator Eaton: "I deprecate the idea of waiting longer for an explanation from unfaithful Spain. Can we receive a minister from that power, under present circumstances, without compromising in some degree our national character? Under the bad faith of Spain, as I believe, the only good explanation that can be given is from the mouth of American cannon."[1] The general was ex-

---

1. Jackson to Eaton, Dec. 28, 1819.

pecting soon to have the pleasure of leading another expedition into Florida.[1]

In April of 1820, Vives arrived in Washington and immediately addressed Adams upon the reasons which had induced the delay in ratifying the treaty. The system of hostility so prevalent in many parts of the Union against the Spanish dominions was a cause of grave dissatisfaction. The "scandalous system of piracy" carried on from the ports of this country induced Spain to demand: That satisfactory and effectual measures be taken to repress "the barbarous excesses and unexampled depredations committed upon Spain, her possessions and properties; that in order to put an entire stop to any future armaments and to prevent all aid whatsoever being afforded from any port of the Union which may be intended and employed in the invasion of the possessions of his Catholic Majesty in America, the United States will agree to give security that their integrity shall be respected. And finally that they will form no relations with the pretended governments of the revolted provinces of Spain lying beyond the sea, and will conform to the course of proceeding adopted in this respect by other powers in amity with Spain." In addition Vives took occasion to comment upon the "disrespectful" manner in which Forsyth had conducted himself in Madrid.[2] During the interim between the departure of De Onis and the arrival of Vives, the chargé of the Spanish legation had constantly complained of the filibustering expeditions from the ports of the United States and of the vessels which had been brought into our ports and adjudicated prizes. Strong proofs were also presented of the connivance of the American officials and men-of-war.

---

1. In January, 1819, even, Jackson had considered the plans for another attack upon Florida, and was making preparations with that in view. Gaines to Jackson, Jan. 16, 1819.

2. Don Vives to J. Q. Adams, Volume VI, Foreign Relations, April 14, 1820.

Adams, in reply to the representations of Vives, asserted that by the universal usage of nations nothing could release a sovereign from the obligation to ratify such a treaty except the proof that his minister, empowered to conduct the negotiations, had been faithless to his trust by transcending his instructions — that this the Spanish king did not even allege. [1]

To this contention Vives took exception and declared that there might be other reasons sufficiently valid to exonerate a sovereign from the obligation of ratifying a treaty. "The scandalous proceedings of a number of American citizens; the decisions of several of the courts of the Union and the criminal expeditions set on foot within it, for the invasion of his Majesty's possessions in North America, when the ratification was still pending, were diametrically opposite to the most sacred principles of amity and to the nature and essence of the treaty itself. . . . So that the belief generally prevailed throughout Europe that the ratification of the treaty by Spain and the acknowledgment of the independence of her rebellious trans-Atlantic colonies by the United States would be simultaneous acts. . . . It is therefore," he concluded, "not possible to assign reasons more powerful or more completely justificatory of the sovereign resolution of the king to suspend his ratification of that instrument." [2]

Vives was told in reply that the representations made to his government of the hostility of our courts, people, and administration were unfounded. That in the war between Spain and her South American provinces an impartial neutrality had been constantly avowed and faithfully maintained. That whenever the laws enacted for the preservation of neutrality were found defective they had been strength-

---

1. Vol. II, Foreign Legations, p. 385, J. Q. Adams to Don Vives, April 21, 1820.
2. Vol. VI, Foreign Relations, Don Vives to J. Q. Adams, April 24, 1820.

ened by new provisions. That Spanish property, illegally taken, had been constantly restored by the decisions of our tribunals and that even life itself had not been spared when individuals had been found guilty of piracy against Spain. But that the United States would not contract any engagement with regard to the revolted provinces. That it would be inconsistent with the obligations of neutrality and had not been done even by any of the European nations, ·and further that the United States could not, "consistently with what is due themselves, stipulate new engagements as the price of obtaining the ratification of the old." That if there were any further delay in the ratification of the treaty by Spain this country could not hereafter accept either the five million dollars for indemnities nor the Sabine for the boundary line. [1]

In answer to certain observations made by Vives upon the subject of our proposals to European powers for recognizing the South American colonies, Adams wrote: "The proposal which at a prior time had been made by the government of the United States to some of the principal powers of Europe for a recognition in concert of the independence of Buenos Ayres was founded . . . upon an opinion then and still entertained that this recognition must and would, at no very remote period, be made by Spain herself. That the joint acknowledgment by several of the principal powers of the world at the same time might probably induce Spain the sooner to accede to that necessity in which she must ultimately acquiesce, and would thereby hasten an event propitious to her own interests by terminating a struggle in which she is wasting her strength and resources without a possibility of success; an event ardently to be desired by every friend of humanity, afflicted by the continual horrors of war, cruel and sanguinary almost beyond example; an

---

1. Vol. II, Foreign Legations, p. 387, J. Q. Adams to Vives, May 3, 1820.

event, not only desirable to the unhappy people who are suffering the complicated distresses and calamities of this war, but to all nations having relations of amity and commerce with them.

"This proposal, founded upon such motives, far from giving Spain the right to claim of the United States an engagement not to recognize the South American governments ought to have been considered by Spain as a proof at once of the moderation and discretion of the United States; as evidence of their disposition to discard all selfish or exclusive views in the adoption of a measure which they deemed wise and just in itself, but most likely to prove efficacious by a common adoption of it, in a spirit entirely pacific, in concert with other nations, rather than by a precipitate resort to it, on the part of the United States alone." [1]

Vives denied the assertion that the laws of the United States were or had been competent to prevent the excesses of which he had complained, and asserted that the European nations so far from being disposed to recognize the insurgent governments of South America, had declined the invitation thus extended. He further declared that the question of the land grants had not been the chief motive for suspending the ratification of the treaty, but rather the question of the South American provinces. "I shall submit it," he concluded, "to the general sense of the reflecting part of mankind to decide whether the reasoning you rely on to show the motives of the American government for proposing to the powers to acknowledge the revolted provinces of Spanish America and in exhibiting them as favorable not only to suffering humanity but to the interests of Spain herself, is not in the highest degree specious. For if such maxims were to be adopted, nations could no longer

---

1. Vol. II, Foreign Relations, p. 398, J. Q. Adams to Don Vives, May 8, 1820.

count upon the integrity of their possessions or on the maintenance of that mutual amity and good understanding which it is equally their duty and their interest to cultivate in their mutual relations." [1]

In the meantime, by a change in the government of Spain, and the adoption of a constitution, the sovereign was prohibited from alienating any portion whatever of the Spanish territory without the consent of the cortes. Vives informed Adams that the king would lay the treaty before that body at its next meeting in July. [2]   Adams maintained that the solemn pledge of the nation had already been given before the change and could not be affected by any subsequent engagement of the king.- Forsyth was instructed to manifest no peculiar earnestness to obtain the ratification; but to announce that, in the event of further delay, an additional provision for indemnity would be demanded and that the right of the United States to the western boundary of the Rio del Norte "will be re-asserted and never again relinquished." [3]

On the ninth of May the papers on the Florida treaty were sent to both houses of congress. Adams had assumed an air of effective indifference. In view of the prevailing public opinion, the secretary of state maintained a decisive bluntness and stubbornness scarcely calculated to invite further discussion. Spain might make the treaty or take the consequences, and congress was about to declare upon the consequences. No other course than this obvious indifference could have been more effective.

In congress the question went over to the next session, but in the house much had already been said on the subject. Several attempts had been made to secure vigorous action. A member from Virginia, impressed with the idea

---

1. Vol. VI, Foreign Relations, Vives to Adams, May 5 and 9, 1820.
2. *Ibid.*, Vives to Adams, May 28, 1820.
3. Vol. IX, Instructions, p. 7, Adams to Forsyth, May 25, 1820.

that De Onis had been authorized to cede more territory than provided in the treaty, moved that the president be asked to inform the house how much the Spanish minister had been empowered to cede. At one time the committee on foreign affairs reported a bill authorizing the president to take possession of both East and West Florida, and if necessary to use the army, navy, and militia. The motion and bill were both ignored and, as the house showed a strong disposition to do nothing, Clay made a vigorous attack on the treaty.

He introduced two resolutions which were referred to the committee of the whole. The first declared that, by the constitution, congress alone had the power to dispose of territory belonging to the United States and that no treaty alienating any part thereof was valid unless approved by congress. The second declared that as the equivalent offered by Spain for the territory of the United States west of the Sabine was inadequate, it would be inexpedient to renew the treaty. Clay declared that he did not desire to renew a discussion of the treaty making power. But as congress alone had power to dispose of the territory of the United States, and, as the constitution contained specific grants of power to congress, they controlled, and it must follow that no treaty disposing of territory could be valid without the consent of the house as well as the senate. A treaty fixing limits or establishing boundaries might be valid without the intervention of the house. The treaty of 1794 with England had done so. So had that of 1795 with Spain. And the provisions of the treaty of Ghent for determining the northeast boundary of Maine — they did not mark out a new boundary, they merely established or proclaimed the location of the old line. The Florida treaty differed from these. It had fixed a new and arbitrary line with a large cession of territory to Spain. "What do we get for Florida?" demanded Clay. "We get Florida loaded and encumbered with land grants which leave scarcely a foot of soil for the United States. What do we give? We give Texas free and unencumbered. We pay five million dollars and we surrender all our claims for damages not included in that five million dollars."

Several members replied to Clay asserting that Texas had always been disputed territory, and that our claim to it had always been questionable. That Clay's construction of the treaty making power would prevent any question of limits ever being settled without the consent of the house, as such questions always involved the cession of territory by one or both parties. The resolutions failed to pass the committee of the whole, and the question was dropped for the time. Monroe in his message transmitting the correspondence with General Vives had requested that no action be taken till Spain had once more been heard from. With this congress willingly complied, though many radicals were for forcing immediate action.

While negotiations were pending Adams received little support in his efforts to push the boundary line westward. Monroe and the cabinet cared little for Texas. Jackson who was consulted, thought that the Sabine should be accepted if thereby we could acquire the Floridas. His interests were then centered in the Floridas and he was indifferent as to Texas. Jackson afterwards denied this in a violent and insulting manner.[1] In a letter to President Monroe, the general wrote: "I am clearly of your opinion that, for the present, we ought to be contented with the Floridas. . . . . With the Floridas in our possession, our fortifica-

---

1. In 1836 General Jackson denied having been consulted in regard to the boundary line. When told that Adams's diary showed that he had approved of the line of the Sabine, he vehemently replied: "His diary. Don't tell me anything more about his diary. Sir, that diary comes up on all occasions—one would think that its pages were as immutable as the laws of the Medes and Persians. Sir, that diary will be the death of me. . . . . Sir, I did not see it; I was not consulted about it." Vol. II, Parton's Life of Jackson, p. 587.

tions completed, New Orleans, the great emporium of the West, is secure. The Floridas in possession of a foreign power, you can be invaded, your fortifications turned, the Mississippi reached, and the lower country reduced. From Texas an invading enemy will never attempt such an enterprise. If he does, notwithstanding all that has been said on the floor of congress on this subject, I will vouch that the invader will pay for his temerity." [1]

On the fifth of October Forsyth's efforts were rewarded by the Spanish cortes, who, after annulling the three land grants, advised the king to ratify the treaty, which he did October 24, 1819. At the same time the cortes declared that they "had observed with great mortification and pain that besides the alienation of valuable provinces of the Spanish monarchy. . . . . the Spanish negotiator of the treaty had left altogether unprovided for and had renounced all the just claims of Spanish subjects upon the United States for which indemnity had been stipulated by the convention of 1802." [2]

The treaty was ratified despite the opposition of Clay who had declared that Florida must come to us sooner or later; "that ripened fruit will not more surely fall. Florida is enclosed between Georgia and Alabama and cannot escape. Texas may." Only four votes were cast against it: Brown of Louisiana, a brother-in-law of Clay; Richard M. Johnson of Kentucky from mere political subserviency to Clay; Williams of Tennessee from a violent hatred of General Jackson; and Trimble of Ohio from "some maggot of the brain."

Mr. Benton was bitter in his regrets that the western boundary had not been extended much further westward into Texas. Besides cutting off Texas, the treaty, he declared, dismembered the Mississippi, mutilated two of its

1. Gen. Jackson to President Monroe, June 20, 1820.
2. Vol VI, Foreign Relations, Memorandum of Interview between Adams and Vives, Feb. 12, 1821.

noblest rivers, and brought a non-slave-holding foreign dominion to the neighborhood of New Orleans. He declared that "the Spanish government had offered us more than we had accepted" and that our policy and not hers had deprived us of Texas and the vast territory between the Red River and Upper Arkansas. Political considerations had entered into the question, for the repugnance in the northeast was not merely to territorial aggrandizement in the southwest but to the subsequent extension of slavery in that quarter. To prevent the slavery extension question from becoming a test in the presidential election was, he declared, the true reason for thus giving away Texas.

But the treaty met with popular approval and Mr. Benton was forced to admit that he stood "solitary and alone" in the matter, not a paper in the United States supporting his opposition. [1] Jefferson remained inflexibly opposed to its ratification.

---

1. Benton's Thirty Years' View, Vol. I, p. 16.

CHAPTER XI.

THE FLORIDA TREATY.

EAST Florida was delivered by Governor Coppinger to Lieutenant Robert Butler of the United States army, July 10, 1821, and on that day the Spanish flag was finally lowered from the walls of St. Augustine, where it had so long and so proudly waved. The stars and stripes announced the second acquisition to the young nation of the New World.

Before the end of the cession during which the Florida treaty was ratified, congress did not have time to legislate for the new territory. An act was passed, however, extending to it the revenue law and the laws against slave trade which had already existed in the United States. In April, General Jackson was appointed governor of Florida, possessing all the powers of the captain generals of Cuba and the Spanish governors of Florida, except those of granting lands and laying taxes. An American governor under Spanish law, of American territory not under the constitution — an anomalous position pregnant with possibilities for complications of serious import. With what was attributed to the traditional Spanish policy, the actual cession of Florida was not accomplished until July 17. In the meantime Jackson fumed, and his fury and his hatred for Spain and things and people Spanish increased in geometric proportion.

In September through a trifling misunderstanding respecting some papers in the hands of the Spanish officials, Jackson sent Callava, the Spanish commissioner, and several of his associates, to the calaboose in that same unreasoning manner and with that same contempt for all law and form which had characterized his conduct of affairs in the Seminole war. Somebody had crossed his path and incurred his wrath and that somebody must pay the penalty. Then Elgin Fromentin, judge of the western district of Florida, in due form issued a habeas corpus for Callava. Jackson's wrath knew no bounds. He summoned Fromentin, to show cause why he had not interfered with the governor and thus become liable. A stormy interview followed and each side sent a statement to the authorities at Washington. Meanwhile some of Fromentin's friends, with less discretion than loyalty, published a defense of the judge. Again Jackson waxed warm and they were ordered out of Florida at four days' notice on pain of arrest for contempt and disobedience.

Worthington, the secretary and acting governor of East Florida, was meanwhile embroiled with Coppinger, the former Spanish governor, over papers which had been seized under Jackson's orders. These were a few of the problems which the headstrong Tennesseean prepared for his friends at Washington within six months' service. Small wonder that Adams dreaded the arrival of mails from Florida lest some new difficulty of Jackson's brewing be presented for solution. In fact his whole conduct, based only upon a snap judgment, was in open disregard and contempt of all diplomatic obligations, propriety, law, or procedure, and his course only failed of being atrocious by being ludicrous.[1] In short Jackson played the fool. Yet again his personal popularity saved him. But why have

---

1. For a detailed account of the whole miserable farce, see Vol. II, Parton's Jackson, p. 638.

trusted so dangerous, so irresponsible a man in so delicate a position? Only because of his personal popularity we presume, for everybody had been taught what to expect of Jackson. When he was sent to Florida as governor there was ringing in Monroe's ears Jefferson's remark upon the subject of sending Jackson on the Russian mission, "Why, good God, he would breed you a quarrel before he had been there a month." Yet he was sent south and the nation was made ridiculous in the eyes of the world.

Now that Florida was actually ours, all reason for delay in recognizing the South American countries seems to have disappeared and in March, 1822, congress passed an appropriation for missions to these revolted provinces.

* * * * *

Thus ends the history of the acquisition of Florida and our relations with Spain. No sooner were we a nation than we cast our eyes about. We coveted Florida, and we talked of manifest destiny, and the falling of ripened fruit, and eased our conscience by like casuistry. Spain was weak, she was entangled in the Herculean grasp of European complications — all of which materially assisted this ever favorable manifest destiny. The nation's leaders, Hamilton, Jefferson, Madison, Monroe, Livingston, Pinckney, and a score of others all insisted that we must possess the Floridas. They wanted Louisiana, they even talked of Mexico and South America — they were to be ours, peaceably if possible, forcibly if necessary. [1]

True, we suffered much at the hands of Spain in our early years. She had sought to confine us to the Atlantic seaboard, and when that became impossible, she attempted to hold the east bank of the Mississippi and prevent the advance of the frontiersmen. She sought to seduce our Western territory from its connection with the Union, and

---

1. Hamilton in 1799 had considered the acquisition of Louisiana and the Floridas as "essential to the permanency of the Union."

many of our officers, notably the contemptible Wilkinson, were guilty of corrupt connections with these plots. This not by way of justification — but England was doing the same thing and France was not innocent.

Then we acquired Louisiana. France, admittedly, had no right to sell it to us, yet we desired it, it was possible to secure it, and so it became ours. Spain vigorously protested but was obliged to acquiesce lest even worse misfortune come upon her. A strong, powerful nation we may well believe would have done something more than weakly protest. We were in a position to profit by the troubles of Europe and we cared naught for the ineffectual anger of deceived and injured Spain. And we must blush with shame when we note that the great Fisher Ames was not alone in thinking the purchase of Louisiana mean and despicable when the province might have been seized by violence — or to use the synonymous expression, have come to us by manifest destiny. To secure by purchase what might soon have yielded to force, they deemed cowardly and unstatesmanlike.

Louisiana secured, we deliberately set about to acquire the two Floridas. We systematically stirred up trouble for Spain. We advanced a claim to West Florida that was wholly untenable. Spain, nay, all Europe, considered our pretensions founded on a sophistry in words, though there was an evident perspicuity in sense. Then we proceeded to seize the territory by arms under the shameful pretence that we would give it up when we found the seizure wrong — a dangerous and astounding theory, supported neither by law nor morals. In 1811 Congress passed a resolution and an act authorizing the seizure of the Floridas under certain contingencies, leaving the widest latitude to executive discretion. This was a bold defiance of the law of nations and individuals. Spain had every right to either hold or sell her territory, and to whatever nation she pleased. The

United States forbade her doing either. We announced that we would wage war upon Spain if she attempted to sell, and upon whatever nation might become the vendee.

Every American citizen knows in his heart that nothing of the kind would have been conceived or attempted if Spain had been able to defend by force her unquestionable rights. Nor did we stop there. To all intents and purposes we served notice upon her that she must dispose of the territory to us or prepare for war. We were determined to possess Florida. What did we offer in return? We would release her from the claims which we held against her. We presented huge bills for damages, many of which would never have been allowed in any court in this country. We held her responsible for the losses inflicted by French vessels and French prize courts after we had expressly released France from all liability. We brought forward claims for the losses of our citizens along the Florida line, losses which by their own misconduct they had expressly invited — for the white settlers of Georgia were responsible for most of the Indian ravages in that section, apart from the losses which they themselves had inflicted in their constant raids across the Florida line.

We thus presented enormous claims to bankrupt Spain and we well knew that in only one way could she liquidate them — by surrendering her territories. Then we took further advantage of the confusion in Spanish affairs by fomenting insurrections in her territories and under this miserable and humiliating guise sought to extend our power. How gross the artifice, how shallow the deception! We seized Amelia Island under the pretext of breaking up a nest of pirates and bandits — a proceeding particularly disgraceful to us because it was principally American freebooters who had congregated there.

During all these years, had England, Russia, or France supported the wishes of Ferdinand, he would probably have defied the United States.

Then the Seminole war, our own fault, because largely the direct result of instructions from our government to the officers in that region. Jackson with his genius for arranging diplomatic controversies, this inveterate don-hater with his intense and notorious anti-Spanish sentiments, was sent to conduct the war. This man, whose desire it had long been to seize Pensacola and occupy the Floridas as indemnity for our claims, was dispatched on a mission where infinite tact and self control were imperatively demanded. Then followed what might have been expected and what appears to have been desired, a series of violations of international law which astounded the whole world and incurred the hostility of Europe. No more here of Arbuthnot and Ambrister. The Spanish governor at St. Marks may have been an accomplice of the Seminoles; but there was nothing calculated to implicate other Spanish commandants, and even if all were guilty, self preservation did not require a summary seizure of the posts, or Jackson's presumption, or Adams's either, that Spain sanctioned the treachery of her provincial agents.

And in the meantime we were tearing at the vitals of Spain in another direction. All South America was in revolt and we were giving the revolutionists something more than our mere sympathy. Monroe admitted in his confidential letters that the policy of his administration had been to throw the moral weight of the United States in the scale of the colonies, without so deeply compromising the nation as to make it a party to the war. Our ports were opened to them; filibustering expeditions were organized in this country; our harbors were filled with their prizes; our good offices had been exercised for them, and to good purpose, with every power in Europe; and by the policy thus pursued more real service had been done them than recognition could possibly have procured. We feared to acknowledge their independence lest it ruin our purposes with regard to the Floridas, but those once in our hands, with singular bad faith, ministers were immediately dispatched to their governments. For nearly a year Spain had held up the treaty of 1819 in an effort to secure from this country a pledge not to recognize the South American countries. True, we had refused, but a strict adherence to the rules of international ethics — if in truth there be any such thing — hardly countenanced our course in the matter.

The question then presents itself for candid, honest consideration: How far was the cession of Florida due to the fact that we wanted it and were determined to have it at all hazards, and how far to the "grievances" of one kind and another which we urged against Spain, and then how far were these "grievances" due to the acts of our own citizens? Had we been unselfish and shown a disposition, as a friendly power, to help Spain out of her difficulties, were there any troubles which could not have been removed without our threats of war and without our insisting upon a transfer of territory? Had our claims to that province been even weaker, which is difficult to conceive, or those of Spain a hundredfold stronger than they actually were, would we not have acquired the territory all the same — would not this same manifest destiny have exercised its all-potent influence?

Consider for a moment the position of Spain on this continent at the opening of the nineteenth century, and that of the United States at the same time. One great fact stands out above all this intervening century of diplomacy with its dark intrigues and chicanery on one side and the other — those vast territories which were then in the possession of Spain now recognize our sovereignty — and that transfer has been effected without any appreciable cost to ourselves. There is no American today who is not ashamed of our wholly unwarranted method of despoiling Mexico; can he feel any prouder of the Florida acquisition? Or are we the especial pet of manifest destiny, and when will she cease to honor our nation with her lavish gifts?

At the time of the acquisition of Florida, Crawford suggested that England and France regarded the United States as ambitious and encroaching, and he counselled moderation. Adams cared naught for foreign opinion and replied that "if the world do not hold us for Romans, they will take us for Jews, and of the two vices I would rather be charged with that which has greatness mingled in its composition." He deemed it proper that the world should be "familiarized with the idea of considering our proper dominion to be the whole continent of North America." This was a "law of nature" and could not fail. To suppose that Spain and England could, through lapse of time, retain their possessions on this side of the Atlantic was to his way of thinking a "physical, moral, and political absurdity." More talk then of manifest destiny and its miracles or, more accurately, manifest determination and strength on the one side, and manifest weakness on the other. It was the right of might — the triumph of force.

THE END.

APPENDICES

APPENDIX A.

VOL. VI, INSTRUCTIONS, P. 137.

James Monroe.   July 29, 1803.

On the presumption . . . . that you will have proceeded to Madrid it is thought proper to observe to you that although Louisiana may in some respects be more important than the Floridas and has more than exhausted the funds allotted for the purchase of the latter, the acquisition of the Floridas is still to be pursued, especially as the crisis must be favorable to it.

You will be at no loss for the arguments most likely to have weight in prevailing on Spain to yield to our wishes. These colonies separated from her other territories on this continent by New Orleans, the Mississippi and the whole of Western Louisiana are now of less value to her than ever, whilst to the United States they retain the peculiar importance derived from their position and their relation to us through the navigable rivers running from the United States into the Gulf of Mexico. In the hands of Spain they must ever be a dead expense in time of peace, indefensible in time of war, and at all times a source of irritation and ill blood with the United States. The Spanish government must understand in fact that the United States can never consider the amicable relation between Spain and them as definitely and permanently secured without an arrangement on this subject which will substitute the manifest indications of nature for the artificial and inconvenient state of things now existing.

The advantage to be derived to your negotiations from the war which has just commenced will certainly not escape you. Powerful and effectual use may be made of the fact that Great Britain meant to seize New Orleans, with a view to the anxiety of the United States to obtain it — of the inference from that fact, that the same policy will be pursued with respect to the Floridas. Should Spain be in the war it cannot be doubted

that they will be quickly occupied by a British force and held
out on some condition or other to the United States. Should
Spain be still at peace and wish not to lose her neutrality she
should reflect that the facility and policy of seizing the Floridas
must strengthen the temptations of Great Britain to force her
into the war. In any view it will be better for Spain that the
Floridas should be in the hands of the United States than of
Great Britain and equally so that they should be ceded on beneficial terms by herself than that they should find their way to
us through the hands of Great Britain. . . . .

By the enclosed note of the Spanish minister here you will
see the refusal of Spain to listen to our past overtures, with
the reasons for the refusal. The answer to that communication is also enclosed. The reply to such reasons will be very
easy. Neither the reputation nor the duty of his Catholic
Majesty can suffer from any measure founded in wisdom and
the true interests of Spain. There is as little ground for supposing that the maritime powers of Europe, will complain of,
or be dissatisfied with, a cession of the two Floridas to the
United States more than with the late cession of Louisiana by
Spain to France or more than with the former cession through
which the Floridas themselves have passed. What the treaties
are subsequent to that of Utrecht, which are alleged to preclude
Spain from the proposed alienation have not been examined.
Admitting them to exist in the sense put upon them, there is
probably no maritime power who would not readily acquiesce
in our acquisition of the Floridas as more advantageous to itself,
than the retention of them by Spain shut up against all foreign
commerce and liable at every moment to be thrown into the
preponderant scale of Great Britain. Great Britain herself
would unquestionably have no objection to their being transferred to us: unless it should be drawn from her intention to
conquer them for herself, or from the use she might expect to
make of them in a negotiation with the United States and with
respect to France. Silence at least is imposed on her by the
cession to the United States of the province ceded to her by
Spain: not to mention, that she must wish to see the Floridas
like Louisiana kept out of the hands of Great Britain and has
doubtless felt that motive in promising her good offices with
Spain for obtaining these possessions for the United States. Of
this promise you will of course make the proper use in your
negotiations.

For the price to be given for the Floridas you are referred
generally to the original instructions on this point. Although
the change of circumstances lessens the anxiety for acquiring
immediately a territory which now more certainly than ever,
must drop into our hands and notwithstanding the pressure of
the bargain with France on our treasury; yet for the sake of
a peaceable and fair completion of a great object you are permitted by the president, in case a less sum will not be accepted,
to give $2,250,000, the sum heretofore apportioned to this pur-
chase. It will be expected however that the whole of it, if
necessary, be made applicable to the discharge of debts and
damages claimed from Spain—as well those not yet admitted
by the Spanish government as those covered by the convention
signed with it by Mr. Pinckney on the eleventh day of August,
1802.

These claims include those arising from privateers' depredations along Florida and Mississippi lines and losses arising from
violation of our deposit at New Orleans.

If it be impossible to bring Spain to a cession of the whole
of the two Floridas a trial is to be made for obtaining either
or any important part of either. The part of West Florida
adjoining the territories now ours and including the principal
rivers falling into the gulf will be particularly important and
convenient.

It is not improbable that Spain in treating on a cession of
the Floridas may propose an exchange of them for Louisiana
beyond the Mississippi or may make a serious point of some
particular boundary to that territory. Such exchange is inadmissible. In intrinsic value there is no equality: besides the
advantage, given us by the west bank of the entire jurisdiction
of the river. We are the less disposed also to make sacrifices
to obtain the Floridas because their position and the manifest
course of events guarantee an early and reasonable acquisition
of them. With respect to the adjustment of a boundary between
Louisiana and the Spanish territories, there might be no objection to combining it with a cession of the Floridas, if our
knowledge of the extent and character of Louisiana were less
imperfect. At present any arrangement, would be a step too
much in the dark to be hazarded, and this will be a proper answer
to the Spanish government. . . .

Should no cession whatever be obtainable, it will remain
only, for the present, to provide for the free use of the rivers

running from the United States into the gulf. A convenient deposit is to be pressed as equally reasonable there as on the Mississippi.

The free use of those rivers for our external commerce is to be insisted on as an important right.

APPENDIX B.

FROM MAJORITY REPORT OF COMMITTEE ON MILITARY AFFAIRS—CON-
GRESS (H. OF R.), JANUARY, 1819. ANNALS OF CONGRESS, P. 515.

Your committee can find no law of the United States authorizing a trial before a military court for such offenses as are
alleged against Arbuthnot and Ambrister (except so much of
the second charge as charges Arbuthnot with "acting as a spy" of
which part of the charge the court found him "not guilty"), nor in
the opinion of our committee does any usage authorize or ex-
igency appear from the documents accompanying the report of
the trial which can justify the assumption and exercise of power
by the court-martial and the commanding general on this occasion. It is admitted as a maxim of the law of nations that where
the war is with a savage nation which observes no rules and never
gives quarter we may punish them in the person of any of their
people whom we may take (belonging to the number of the
guilty) and endeavor by this vigorous proceeding to force them to
respect the laws of humanity. Wherever severity is not a
necessity mercy becomes a duty. In vain has your committee
sought for a shadow of a necessity for the death of the prisoners
arraigned before the court. The war was at an end to all intents and purposes, the enemy's strongholds had been destroyed—
many of them killed or taken prisoners, and the remainder a
feeble band dispersed and scattered in every direction. The
Spanish fort of St. Marks which it was supposed (and no doubt
justly) had protected them was also in our possession and so
entirely was the war considered to be terminated that the Georgia
militia under General Glascock had returned to their homes.
Then where was the absolute necessity which alone could warrant a departure from the exercise of that clemency of which
the United States has heretofore so justly boasted?

Your committee find in the general order of the twenty-ninth
of April, in which General Jackson orders the execution of Arbuth-

22

not and Ambrister this remarkable reason, intended as a justification of the executions, principally of Ambrister but applying
to both Arbuthnot and Ambrister: "It is an established principle
of the law of nations that any individual of a nation making war
against the citizens of another nation, they being at peace, forfeits
his allegiance and becomes an outlaw and a pirate." It may be
asked by what system of interpretation the offenses charged
could be considered as piracies which imply in common accepta-
tion offenses upon the high seas, of which the court could not assume cognizance; and it is equally difficult to understand the propriety of the application of the term "outlaw" to the offenders —
a term which applies only to the relations of individuals with
their own governments. It will not be pretended that Lafayette
who volunteered his services in the cause of America in the
war which established our independence forfeited his allegiance,
became an outlaw, and subjected himself to an ignominious death
had he fallen into the hands of the English, or can it be believed
that one voice could be heard in justification of Spain if she
were to execute such of our countrymen as she may make
prisoners, while fighting in the armies of the South American
patriots? And if these cases should not be considered of such a
nature as to warrant a resort to so severe a measure while they
occurred with a people in a state of revolution and considered
by the parent countries to be in a state of rebellion, much less
could these (Arbuthnot and Ambrister) be considered liable to
it who were acting with a power acknowledged and treated as
sovereign and independent by us.

Your committee beg leave to call your attention particularly
to the case of R. C. Ambrister who, after having been subjected
to a trial before a court which had no cognizance or jurisdiction
over the offenses charged against him was shot by the order of
the commanding general contrary to the forms and usages of
the army and without regard to the finding of that court which
had been instituted as a guide for himself. . . .

Nor can your committee forbear including in their strictures
the court-martial who sat on the trial of Arbuthnot and Ambrister. A court-martial is a tribunal invested with limited
jurisdiction having for its guidance the same rules of evidence
which govern courts of law; and yet Arbuthnot is refused by the
court-martial, before whom he was on trial for his life, the
benefit of the testimony of Ambrister who had not been put upon
his trial at that time and whose evidence would have been re-

ceived by any court of law as legal, if not credible. Many other exceptions might be made to the evidence recorded in these proceedings: particularly to the question put to the witness, Hambly, namely: "Do you believe the Seminoles would have commenced the business of murder and depredation on the white settlements had it not been at the instigation of the prisoner (Arbuthnot) and a promise on his part of British protection?" Answer: "I do not believe they would, without they had been assured of British protection." A leading question is expressly forbidden to be used by a court-martial by Macomb on martial law, and of which the court must have been apprised as it is a work common in the army and usually referred to by every court-martial when in session: and the question was calculated to elicit an expression of opinion and belief from the witness rather than a statement of facts upon which alone could the court act. Hearsay evidence, in a case of life and death, your committee will venture to assert, was never before received against the accused in any court of this country and yet on the face of the record of the proceedings of the court-martial, hearsay testimony is admitted which had been received from an Indian who, if present, would not have been allowed to give evidence himself. After mature deliberation your committee beg leave to submit the following resolution: Resolved that the honor and right of the United States disapproves the proceedings in the trial and execution of Alex. Arbuthnot and Robert C. Ambrister.

To George W. Erving.   November 28, 1818.

In the fourth and last of these notes of Mr. Pizarro he has given formal notice that the king, his master, has issued orders for the suspension of the negotiation between the United States and Spain until satisfaction shall have been made by the American government to him for those proceedings of General Jackson: which he considers as acts of unequivocal hostility against him and as outrages upon his honor and dignity, the only acceptable atonement for which is stated to consist in a disavowal of the American government thus complained of: the infliction upon him of a suitable punishment for his supposed misconduct: and the restitution of the posts and territories taken by him from the Spanish authorities with indemnity for all the property taken and all damages and injuries, public or private, sustained in consequence of it.

Within a very few days after this notification Mr. Pizarro must have received with copies of the correspondence between Mr. De Onis and this department the determination which had been taken by the president to restore the place of Pensacola with the Fort of Barrancas to any person properly authorized on the part of Spain to receive them: and the Fort of St. Marks to any Spanish force adequate to its protection against the Indians by whom its forcible occupation had been threatened, for purposes of hostility against the United States. The officer commanding at the post has been directed to consider two hundred and fifty men as such adequate force and in case of their appearance with proper authority to deliver it up to their commander accordingly.

From the last mentioned correspondence the Spanish government must likewise have been satisfied that the occupation of these places in Spanish Florida by the commander of the American forces was not by virtue of any orders received by him from this government to that effect with any view of wresting the province from Spain nor in any spirit of hostility to the Spanish government. That it arose from incidents which occurred in the prosecution of the war against the Indians, from the imminent danger in which the Fort of St. Marks was of being seized by the Indians themselves; and from the manifestations of hostility to the United States by the commandant of St. Marks, and the governor of Pensacola, the proofs of which were made known to General Jackson and impelled him from the necessities of self defense to the steps of which the Spanish government complains.

It might be sufficient to leave the vindication of these measures upon those grounds and to furnish, in the enclosed copies of General Jackson's letters and the vouchers by which they are supported, the evidence of that hostile spirit on the part of the Spanish commanders, but for the terms in which Mr. Pizarro speaks of the execution of a British subject taken, one at the Fort of St. Marks and the other at Suwany and the intimation that these transactions may lead to a change in the relations between the two nations which is doubtless to be understood as a menace of war. It may be therefore proper to remind the government of his Catholic Majesty of the incidents in which this Seminole war originated: as well as of the circumstances connected with it in the relations between Spain and her ally, whom she supposes to have been injured by the proceedings of General Jackson: and to give the Spanish cabinet some precise information of the nature of the business peculiarly interesting to Spain in which these subjects of her allies, in whose favor she takes this interest, were engaged, when their projects of every kind were terminated in consequence of their falling into the hands of General Jackson.

In the month of August, 1814, while a war existed between the United States and Great Britain to which Spain had formally declared herself neutral, a British force — not in the fresh pursuit of a defeated and flying enemy, not overstepping an imaginary and equivocal boundary between their own territories and those belonging in some sort as much to their enemy as to Spain, but approaching by sea and by a broad and open invasion of the Spanish province, at a thousand miles or an ocean's distance from any British territory — landed in Florida; took possession of Pensacola and the Fort of Barrancas and invited by public proclamations all the runaway negroes, all the savage Indians, all the pirates and all the traitors to their country whom they knew or imagined to exist within reach of their summons to join their standard and wage an exterminating war against the portion of the United States immediately bordering upon this neutral and thus violated territory of Spain. . . . The land commander of the British forces was a certain Colonel Nicholls who, driven from Pensacola by the approach of General Jackson, actually left to be blown up the Spanish Fort of Barrancas when he found it could not afford him protection, and evacuating that part of the province landed at another, established himself on the Appalachicola River, and there erected a fort from which to sally forth with his motley tribe of black, white, and red combatants against the defenseless borders of the United States in that vicinity. A part of this force consisted of a corps of colonial marines, levied in the British colonies, in which George Woodbine was a captain and Robert Chrystie Ambrister was a lieutenant. As between the United States and Great Britain we should be willing to bury this transaction in the same grave of oblivion with other transactions of that war, had the hostilities of Colonel Nicholls terminated with the war. But he did not consider the peace which ensued between the United States and Great Britain as having put an end either to his military occupations or to his negotiations with the Indians against the United States. Several months after the ratification of the treaty of Ghent he retained his post and his party-colored forces in military array. By the ninth article of that treaty the United States had stipulated to put an end to hotilities immediately after its ratification with all the tribes or nations of Indians with whom they might be at war at the time of the ratification and to restore to them all the possessions which they had enjoyed in the year 1811. This article had no application to the Creek nation with whom the United States had already made peace by a treaty concluded August 9, 1814, more than four months before the treaty of Ghent was signed. Yet Colonel Nicholls not only affected to consider it as applying to the Seminoles of Florida and the outlawed Red Sticks whom he had induced to join him there, but actually persuaded them that they were entitled, by virtue of the treaty of Ghent, to all the lands which had belonged to the Creek nation within the United States in the year of 1811, and that the government of Great Britain would support them in that pretension. He asserted also this doctrine in a correspondence with Colonel Hawkins, then the agent of the United States with the Creeks, and gave him notice in their name, with a mockery of solemnity, that they had concluded a treaty of alli-ance offensive and defensive and a treaty of navigation and commerce with Great Britain of which more was to be heard after it should be ratified in England. Colonel Nicholls then evacuated his fort which in some of the enclosed papers is called the Fort of Prospect Bluff, but which he had denominated the British post on the Appalachicola, took with him the white portion of his force, and embarked for England with several of the wretched savages whom he was thus deluding to their fate: among whom was the Prophet Francis or Hillis Hadjo, and left the fort, amply supplied with military forces and ammunition, to the negro department of his allies. It afterwards was known by the name of the Negro Fort.

Colonel Hawkins immediately communicated to this govern-ment the correspondence between him and Colonel Nicholls . . . upon which Mr. Monroe, then secretary of state, addressed a letter to Mr. Baker, the British chargé d'affaires at Washington complaining of Nicholls's conduct and showing that his pretence that the ninth article of the treaty of Ghent could have any appli-cation to his Indians was utterly destitute of foundation. Copies of the same correspondence were transmitted to the minister of the United States then in England with instructions to remon-strate with the British government against these proceedings of Nicholls and to show how incompatible they were with the peace which had been concluded between the two nations. These remonstrances were accordingly made. First, in personal in-terview with Earl Bathurst and Lord Castlereagh and afterwards in written notes addressed successively to them. . . . Lord Bath-urst in the most unequivocal manner confirmed the facts and dis-avowed the misconduct of Nicholls and declared his disappro-bation of the pretended treaty of alliance, offensive and defensive, which he had made: assured the American minister that the British government had refused to ratify that treaty: and would send back the Indians whom Nicholls had brought with him, with advice to make their peace on such terms as they could obtain. Lord Castlereagh confirmed the assurance that the treaty would not be ratified: and if at the same time that these assurances were given certain distinctions of public notoriety were shown to the Prophet Hillis Hadjo and he was actually honored with a commission as a British officer, it is to be presumed that these favors were granted him as rewards of past services and not as encouragement to expect any support from Great Britain in a continuance of savage hostilities against the United States; all intention of giving any such support having been repeatedly and earnestly disavowed.

The Negro Fort however, abandoned by Colonel Nicholls, remained on the Spanish territory, occupied by the banditti to whom he had left it and held by them as a post from whence to commit depredations, outrages, murders, and as a receptacle for fugitive slaves and malefactors to the great annoyance both of the United States and of Spanish Florida. In April, 1816, General Jackson wrote a letter to the governor of Pensacola calling upon him to put down this common nuisance to the peaceable inhabitants of both countries. That letter with the answer of the governor of Pensacola have been already communicated to the Spanish minister here and by him doubtless to his government. Copies are nevertheless now again enclosed; particularly as the letter from the governor explicitly admits that this fort constructed by Nicholls in violation both of the territory and neutrality of Spain was still no less obnoxious to his government than to the United States: but that he had neither sufficient force nor authority without orders from the governor general of the Havanna to destroy it. It was afterwards, July 27, 1816, destroyed by a cannon shot from a gun vessel of the United States which in its passage up the river was fired upon from it. It was blown up with an English flag still flying at its standard: and immediately after the barbarous murder of the boat's crew, belonging to the navy of the United States by the banditti left in it by Nicholls.

In the year 1817 Alexander Arbuthnot of the island of New Providence, a British subject, first appeared as an Indian trader in Spanish Florida: and as the successor of Colonel Nicholls in the employment of instigating the Seminole and outlawed Red Stick Indians to hostilities against the United States by reviving the pretence that they were entitled to all the lands which had been ceded by the Creek nation to the United States in August, 1814. As a mere Indian trader the intrusion of this man into a Spanish province was contrary to the policy observed by all the European powers in this hemisphere, and by none more rigorously than by Spain, of excluding all foreigners from intercourse with the Indians within their territories. It must be known to the Spanish government whether Arbuthnot had a Spanish license for trading with the Indians in Spanish Florida or not, but they also knew that Spain was bound by treaty to restrain by force all hostilities on the part of those Indians against the citizens of the United States: and it is for them to explain how, consistently with those engagements, Spain could, contrary to all the maxims of her ordinary policy, grant such a license to a foreign incendiary whose principal if not his only object appears to have been to stimulate those hostilities which Spain had expressly stipulated by force to restrain. In his infernal instigations he was but too successful. No sooner did he make his appearance among the Indians accompanied by the Prophet Hillis Hadjo, returned from his expedition to England, than the peaceful inhabitants on the borders of the United States were visited with all the horrors of savage war — the robbery of their property and the barbarous and indiscriminate murder of women, infancy, and age.

After the repeated expostulations, warnings, and offers of peace through the summer and autumn of 1817, on the part of the United States, had been answered only by renewed outrages and after a detachment of forty men under Lieutenant Scott accompanied by seven women had been waylaid and murdered by the Indians, orders were given to General Jackson and an adequate force was placed at his disposal to terminate the war. It was ascertained that the Spanish force in Florida was inadequate for the protection even of the Spanish territory itself against this mingled horde of lawless Indians and negroes, and although their devastations were committed within the limits of the United States they immediately sought refuge within the Florida line and there only were overtaken. The necessity of crossing the line was indispensable: for it was from beyond the line that the Indians made their murderous incursions within that of the United States. It was there that they had their abode: and the territory belonged in fact to them though within the borders of the Spanish jurisdiction. There it was that the American commander met the principal resistance from them: there it was that they found still bleeding scalps of our citizens, freshly butchered by them: there it was, that he released the only woman who had been suffered to survive the massacre of the party under Lieutenant Scott. But it was not anticipated by this government that the commanding officers of Spain in Florida, whose especial duty it was, in conformity to the solemn engagements contracted by their nation, to restrain by force those Indians from hostilities against the United States, would be found encouraging, aiding, and abetting them and furnishing them supplies for carrying on such hostilities. The officer in command immediately before General Jackson, was therefore specially instructed to respect as far as possible the Spanish authority, wherever it was maintained, and copies of those orders were also furnished to General Jackson upon his taking command.

In the course of his pursuit as he approached St. Marks he was informed, direct from the governor of Pensacola, that a party of the hostile Indians had threatened to seize that fort and that he apprehended the Spanish garrison was not in strength sufficient to defend it against them. This information was confirmed from other sources and by the evidence produced upon the trial of Ambrister is proved to have been exactly true. By all the laws of neutrality and of war as well as of prudence and humanity, he was warranted in anticipating his enemy by the amicable, and that being refused, by the forcible occupation of the fort. It will need no citations from printed treatises on international law, to prove the correctness of this principle. It is engraved in adamant on the common sense of mankind, no writer upon the laws of nations ever pretended to contradict it. None of any reputation or authority ever omitted to assert it.

At Fort St. Marks, Alexander Arbuthnot, the British Indian trader from beyond the sea, the firebrand, by whose touch this negro Indian war against our borders had been rekindled, was found an inmate of the commandant's family. And it was also found that by the commandant, himself, councils of war had been permitted to be held within it by the savage chiefs and warriors: that it was an open market for cattle known to have been robbed by them from citizens of the United States and which had been contracted for and purchased by the officers of the garrison: that information had been afforded from this fort by Arbuthnot to the enemy of the strength and movements of the American army: that the date of departure of express had been noted by the Spanish commissary and ammunition, munitions of war, and all necessary supplies furnished to the Indians.

The conduct of the governor of Pensacola was not less marked by a disposition of enmity to the United States and by an utter disregard to the obligations of the treaty by which he was bound to restrain by force the Indians from hostilities against them. When called upon to vindicate the territorial rights and authority of Spain by the destruction of the Negro Fort, his predecessor had declared it to be not less annoying and pernicious to the Spanish subjects in Florida than to the United States, but had pleaded his inability to subdue it. He himself had expressed his apprehensions that Fort St. Marks would be forcibly taken by the savages from the Spanish garrison; yet at the same time he had refused the passage up the Escambia River, unless upon the payment of excessive duties, to provisions destined as supplies for the American army which by the detention of them was subjected to the most distressing privations. He had permitted free ingress and egress at Pensacola to the avowed savage enemies of the United States. Supplies of ammunition, munitions of war, and provisions had been received by them from thence. They had been received and sheltered there, from the pursuit of the American forces, and suffered again to sally thence to enter upon the American territory and commit new murders. Finally on the approach of General Jackson to Pensacola the governor sent him a letter denouncing his entry upon the territory of Florida as a violent outrage upon the rights of Spain, commanding him to depart and withdraw from the same, and threatening, in case of his non-compliance, to employ force to expel him.

It became therefore, in the opinion of General Jackson, indispensably necessary to take from the governor of Pensacola the means of carrying his threat into execution. Before the forces under his command the savage enemies of his country had disappeared. But he knew that the moment those forces should be disbanded, if sheltered by Spanish fortresses, if furnished with ammunition and supplies by Spanish officers and if aided and supported by the instigation of Spanish encouragement, as he had every reason to expect they would be, they would reappear and, fired, in addition to their ordinary ferociousness, with revenge for the chastisement they had so recently received, would again rush with the war-hatchet and scalping knife into the borders of the United States and mark every footstep with the blood of their defenseless citizens. So far as all the native resources of the savage extended, the war was at an end and General Jackson was about to restore to their families and their homes the brave volunteers who had followed his standard and who had constituted the principal part of his force. This could be done with safety leaving the regular portion of his troops to garrison his line of forts and two small detachments of volunteer cavalry to scour the country round Pensacola and sweep off the lurking remnant of savages who had been scattered and dispersed before him. This was sufficient to keep in check the remnant of the banditti against whom he had marched so long

as they should be destitute of other aid and support. It was
in his judgment not sufficient, if they should be suffered to rally
their numbers under the protection of Spanish forts and to
derive new strength from the impotence or the ill will against
the United States of the Spanish authorities.

He took possession therefore of Pensacola and of the fort of
Barrancas as he had done of St. Marks, not in a spirit of hostility
to Spain but as a necessary measure of self defense: giving notice
that they should be restored whenever Spain should place commanders and a force there able and willing to fulfill the engagements of Spain towards the United States of restraining by force
the Florida Indians from hostilities against their citizens. The
president of the United States, to give a signal manifestation of
his confidence in the disposition of the king of Spain to perform
with good faith this indispensable engagement and to demonstrate
to the world that neither the desire of conquest nor hostility
to Spain had any influence in the councils of the United States,
has directed the unconditional restoration to any Spanish officer,
duly authorized to receive them, of Pensacola and the Barrancas,
and that of St. Marks to any Spanish force adequate for its defense against the attack of the savages. But the president will
neither inflict punishment nor pass a censure upon General Jackson for that conduct for which he had the most immediate and
effectual means of forming a judgment: and the vindication of
which is written in every page of the law of nations as well as
in the first law of nature, self defense. He thinks it, on the contrary, due to the justice which the United States have a right
claim from Spain, and you are accordingly instructed to demand
of the Spanish government, that inquiry shall be instituted in
the conduct of Don José Mazot, governor of Pensacola, and of
Don Francisco C. Luengo, commandant of St. Marks, and a
suitable punishment inflicted upon them for having, in defiance
and violation of the engagements of Spain with the United
States, aided and assisted these hordes of savages in those very
hostilities against the United States which it was their official
duty to restrain. This inquiry is due to the character of those
officers themselves and to the honor of the Spanish government.
The obligation by Spain to restrain by force the Indians of
Florida from hostilities against the United States and their
citizens is explicit, is positive, is unqualified. The fact, that for
a series of years, they have received shelter, assistance, supplies,
and protection, in the practice of such hostilities, from the

Spanish commander in Florida is clear and unequivocal. If, as the commanders both at Pensacola and St. Marks, have alleged, this has been the result of their weakness rather than of their will, if they have assisted the Indians against the United States, to avert their hostilities from the province which they had not sufficient force to defend against them, it may serve in some measure to exculpate, individually those officers; but it must carry demonstration irresistible to the Spanish government, that the right of the United States can as little compound with impotence as with perfidy and that Spain must immediately make her election either to place a force in Florida adequate at once to the protection of her territory and to the fulfilment of her engagements or cede to the United States a province of which she retains nothing but the nominal possession, but which is in fact a derelict, open to the occupancy of every enemy, civilized or savage, of the United States and serving no other earthly purpose, than as a post of annoyance to them.

That the purposes, as well of the Negro-Indian banditti with whom we have been contending, as of the British invaders of Florida who first assembled and employed them, and of the British intruding and pretended traders, since the peace, who have instigated and betrayed them to destruction, have not been less hostile to Spain than to the United States, the proofs contained in the documents herewith enclosed are conclusive. Mr. Pizarro's note of the 29th of August speaks of his Catholic Majesty's profound indignation at the "sanguinary executions on the Spanish soil of the subjects of powers in amity with the king" — meaning Arbuthnot and Ambrister. Let Mr. Pizarro's successor take the trouble of reading the enclosed documents and he will discover who Arbuthnot and Ambrister were and what were their purposes, that Arbuthnot was only the successor of Nicholls, and Ambrister the agent of Woodbine and the subaltern of MacGregor. Mr. Pizarro qualifies General Jackson's necessary pursuit of a defeated savage enemy beyond the Spanish Florida line as a shameful invasion of his Majesty's territory. Yet that territory was the territory also of the savage enemy and Spain was bound to restrain them by force from hostilities against the United States; and it was the failure of Spain to fulfill this engagement which had made it necessary for General Jackson to pursue the savage across the line. What was the character of Nicholls's invasion of his Majesty's territory and where was his Majesty's profound indignation at that? Mr. Pizarro says, his

Majesty's forts and places have been violently seized on by General Jackson. Had they not been seized on, nay had not the principal of his forts been blown up by Nicholls and a British fort on the same Spanish territory been erected during the war and left standing as a negro fort in defiance of Spanish authority after the peace? Where was his Majesty's indignation at that? Has his Majesty given solemn warning to the British government that these were incidents "of transcendent moment capable of producing an essential and thorough change in the political relations of the two countries?" Nicholls and Woodbine in their invitations and promises to the slaves to run away from their masters and join them did not confine themselves to the slaves of the United States. They received with as hearty a welcome and employed with equal readiness the fugitives from their masters in Florida and Georgia. Against this special injury the governor of Pensacola did earnestly remonstrate with the British Admiral Cockburn, but against the shameful invasion of the territory; against the blowing up of the Barrancas, and the erection and maintenance under British banners of the Negro Fort on Spanish soil; against the negotiation by a British officer in the midst of peace, of pretended treaties, offensive and defensive, and of navigation and commerce, upon Spanish territory between Great Britain and Spanish Indians whom Spain was bound to control and restrain; if a whisper of expostulation was ever wafted from Madrid to London it was not loud enough to be heard across the Atlantic nor energetic enough to transpire beyond the palaces from which it issued and to which it was borne.

The connection between Arbuthnot and Nicholls and between Ambrister, Woodbine and MacGregor is established beyond all question by the evidence produced at the trials before the court-martial. I have already remarked to you on the very extraordinary circumstance that a British trader from beyond the sea should be permitted by the Spanish authorities to trade with the Indians of Florida. From his letter to Hambly dated May 3, 1817, it appears that his trading was but a pretence and that his principal purpose was to act as the agent of the Indians of Florida and outlaws from the Creeks to obtain the aid of the British government in their hostilities against the United States. He expressly tells Hambly there that the chiefs of those outlaws was the principal cause of his (Arbuthnot) being in the country; and that he had come with an answer from Earl Bathurst, delivered to him by Governor Cameron of New Providence, to certain Indian talks in which this aid of the British government had been solicited. Hambly himself had been left by Nicholls as the agent between the Indians and the British government; but having found that Nicholls had failed in his attempt to prevail upon the British government to pursue this clandestine war in the midst of peace, and that they were not prepared to support his pretence that half a dozen outlawed fugitives from the Creeks were the Creek Nation; when Arbuthnot the incendiary came and was instigating them by promises of support from Great Britain to commence their murderous incursions into the United States, Hambly at the request of the chiefs of the Creeks themselves, wrote to him, warning him to withdraw from among that band of outlaws and giving him a solemn foreboding of the doom that awaited him from the hand of justice, if he persevered in the course that he pursued. Arbuthnot nevertheless persisted; and while he was deluding the wretched Indians with the promise of support from England he was writing letters from them to the British minister in the United States, to Governor Cameron of New Providence, to Colonel Nicholls to be laid before the British government and even to the Spanish governor of St. Augustine and the governor general of the Havanna, soliciting in all quarters aid and support, arms and ammunition for the Indians against the United States, bewailing the destruction of the Negro Fort, and charging the British government with having drawn the Indians into war with the United States and deserting them after the peace.

You will remark among the papers produced on his trial a power of attorney, dated June 17, 1817, given him by twelve Indians, partly of Florida and partly of the fugitive outlaws from the United States. He states that this power and his instructions were to memorialize the British government and the governor general of the Havanna. These papers are not only substantially proved as his handwriting on the trial, but in the daily newspapers of London of the 24th and 25th of August, his letter to Nicholls is published (somewhat curiously garbled) with a copy of Hambly's above mentioned letter to him and a reference to this Indian power of attorney to him aproved by the commandant of St. Marks, F. C. Luengo. Another of the papers is a letter written in the name of the same chiefs by Arbuthnot to the governor general of the Havanna asking of him permission for Arbuthnot to establish a warehouse on the

Appalachicola; bitterly and falsely complaining that the Americans had made settlements on their lands within the Spanish lines, and calling upon the governor general to give orders to displace them and send them back to their own country. In this letter they assign as a reason for asking the license for Arbuthnot their want of a person to put in writing for them their talks of grievances against the Americans; and they add "the commander of the fort of St. Marks has heard of all our talks and complaints. He approves of what we have done and what we are doing and it is by his recommendation we have thus presumed to address your excellency." You will find these papers in the printed newspapers enclosed and in the proceedings of the court-martial and will point them out to the Spanish government, not only as decisive proof of the unexampled compliance of the Spanish officers in Florida to foreign intrusive agents and instigators of Indian hostilities against the United States, but as placing beyond a doubt that participation of this hostile spirit in the commandant of St. Marks, which General Jackson so justly complains of and of which we have so well founded a right to demand the punishment. Here is the commandant of the Spanish fort, bound by the sacred engagement of a treaty to restrain by force the Indians within his command from committing hostilities against the United States, conspiring with those same Indians and deliberately giving his written approbation to their appointment of a foreigner, a British subject, as their agent to solicit assistance and supplies from the governor general of the Havanna and from the British government for carrying on those same hostilities.

Let us come to the case of Ambrister. He was taken in arms, leading and commanding the Indians in the war against the American troops; and to that charge upon his trial pleaded guilty. But the primary object of his coming there was still more hostile to Spain than to the United States. You find that he told three of the witnesses who testified at his trial that he had come to this country upon Mr. Woodbine's business at Tampa Bay, to see the negroes righted, and one of them that he had a commission in the patriot army under MacGregor, and that he expected a captaincy. And what was the intended business of MacGregor and Woodbine at Tampa Bay? It was the conquest of Florida from Spain by the use of those very Indians and negroes whom the commandant of St. Marks was so ready to aid and support in war against the United States. The chain of proof that establishes this fact is contained in the documents communicated by the president to congress at their last session relating to the occupation of Amelia Island by MacGregor. From these documents you will find that while MacGregor was there Woodbine went from New Providence in a schooner of his own to join him; that he arrived at Amelia Island just as MacGregor, abandoning the companions of his achievement there, was leaving it; that MacGregor, quitting the vessel in which he had embarked at Amelia, went on board that of Woodbine and returned with him to New Providence; that Woodbine had persuaded him they could yet accomplish the conquest of Florida with soldiers to be recruited at Nassau, from the corps of colonial marines which had served under Nicholls during the late war with the United States, which corps had been lately disbanded, and with negroes to be found at Tampa Bay, and 1,500 Indians already then engaged to Woodbine, who pretended that they had made a grant of all their lands to him. Among the papers, the originals of which are in our possession, are, in MacGregor's own handwriting, instructions for sailing into Tampa Bay, with the assertion that he calculated to be there by the last of April or first of May of the present year; a letter, dated December 27 last, to one of his acquaintances in this country which was to have been issued at Tampa Bay, to the inhabitants of Florida, by the person charged with making the settlement there, before his arrival, announcing his approach for the purpose of liberating them from the despotism of Spain and of enabling them to form a government for themselves. He had persuaded those who would listen to him here, that his ultimate object was to sell the Floridas to the United States. There is some reason to suppose that he had made indirect overtures of a similar nature to the British government. This was Ambrister's business in Florida. He arrived there in March, the precursor of MacGregor and Woodbine, and immediately upon his arrival he is found seizing upon Arbuthnot's goods and distributing them among the negroes and Indians; seizing upon his vessel and compelling its master to pilot him with a body of armed negroes toward the fort of St. Marks; with the declared purpose of taking it by surprise in the night; writing letters to Governor Cameron of New Providence urgently calling for supplies of munitions of war and of cannon for the war against the Americans, and letters to Colonel Nicholls renewing the same demands of supplies and informing him that he is with 300 negroes, "a few of our

23

Bluff people" who had stuck to the cause and were relying upon the faith of Nicholls's promises. "Our Bluff people" were the people of the Negro Fort, collected by Nicholls's and Woodbine's proclamations during the American and English war, and "the cause" to which they stuck was the savage, servile, exterminating war against the United States.

Among the agents and actors of such virtuous enterprises as are here unveiled, it was hardly to be expected that there would be found remarkable evidences of their respect, confidence, and good faith towards one another. Accordingly, besides the violent seizure and distribution by Ambrister of Arbuthnot's property, his letters to Governor Cameron and to Nicholls are filled with the distrust and suspicions of the Indians, that they were deceived and betrayed by Arbuthnot; while in Arbuthnot's letters to the same Nicholls, he accuses Woodbine of having taken charge of poor Francis the prophet, or Hillis Hadjo, upon his return from England to New Providence, and under pretence of taking care of him and his affairs, of having defrauded him of a large portion of the presents which had been delivered out from the king's stores to him for Francis's use. This is one of the passages of Arbuthnot's letter to Nicholls omitted in the publication of it last August in the London newspapers.

Is this narrative of dark and complicated depravity; this creeping and insidious war, both against Spain and the United States; this mockery of patriotism; these political philters to fugitive slaves and Indian outlaws; these perfidies and treacheries of villains, incapable of keeping their faith even to each other; all in the name of South American liberty, of the rights of runaway negroes, and the wrongs of savage murderers; all combined and projected to plunder Spain of her provinces and to spread massacre and devastation along the border of the United States; is all this sufficient to cool the sympathies of his Catholic Majesty's government excited by the execution of these "two subjects of a power in amity with the king?" The Spanish government is not at this day to be informed that, cruel as war in its mildest forms must be, it is, and necessarily must be, doubly cruel when waged with savages; that savages make no prisoners but to torture them; that they give no quarter; that they put to death without discrimination of age or sex. That these ordinary characteristics of Indian warfare have been applicable in their most heart sickening horrors to that war, left us by Nicholls as his legacy, reinstigated by Woodbine, Arbuthnot, and Ambrister, and stimulated by the approbation, encouragement, and aid of the Spanish commandant at St. Marks, is proof required? Entreat the Spanish minister of state for a moment to overcome the feelings which details like these must excite; and to reflect, if possible, with composure upon the facts stated in the following extracts from the documents enclosed.

Letter from sailing-master, Jairus Loomis to Commodore Daniel T. Patterson, August 13, 1816, reporting the destruction of the Negro Fort: "On examining the prisoners they stated that Edward Daniels O. S., who was made prisoner in the boat on the 17th July, was tarred and burnt alive."

Letter from Archibald Clarke to General Gaines, February 26, 1817. (Messages, Presidents to Congress, March 25, 1818, page 9): "On the 24th instant the house of Mr. Garret, residing in the upper part of this county, near the boundary of Wayne county (Georgia), was attacked during his absence near the middle of the day, by this party (of Indians) consisting of about fifteen, who shot Mrs. Garret in two places and then dispatched her by stabbing and scalping. Her two children, one about three years, the other two months, were also murdered and the eldest scalped; the house was then plundered of every article of value and set on fire."

Letter from Peter B. Cook (Arbuthnot's clerk) to Eliza Carney at Nassau, dated at Suhwahnee, January 19, 1818, giving an account of their operations with the Indians against the Americans; and their massacre of Lieutenant Scott and his party:

"There was a boat that was taken by the Indians that had in thirty men, seven women, four small children. There were six of the men got clear and one woman saved and all of the rest of them got killed. The children were took by the leg and their brains dashed out against the boat."

If the bare recital of scenes like these cannot be perused without shuddering, what must be the agonized feeling of those whose wives and children are from day to day and from night to night exposed to be the victims of the same barbarity? Has mercy a voice to plead for the perpetrators and instigators of deeds like these? Shall inquiry hereafter be made, why within three months after this event the savage Hamathli-Mico, upon being taken by the American troops, was by order of their commander immediately hung, let it be told that that savage was the commander of the party by which those women were butchered and those helpless infants were thus dashed against the boat!

Contending with such enemies, although humanity revolts at entire retaliation upon them and spares the lives of their feeble and defenseless women and children, yet mercy, herself, surrenders to retributive justice the lives of their leading warriors taken in arms and still more the lives of the foreign white incendiaries who, disowned by their own governments and disowning their own natures, degrade themselves beneath the savage character by voluntarily descending to its level. Is not this the dictate of common sense? Is it not the usage of legitimate warfare? Is it not consonant to the soundest authorities of national law? . . . "When at war (says Vattel) with a ferocious nation which observes no rules and grants no quarter they may be chastised in the persons of those of them who may be taken; they are of the number of the guilty and by this rigor the attempt may be made of bringing them to a sense of the laws of humanity." And again: "As a general has the right of sacrificing the lives of his enemies to his own safety or that of his people, if he has to contend with an inhuman enemy, often guilty of such excesses, he may take the lives of some of his prisoners, and treat them as his own people have been treated." The justification of these principles is found in their salutary efficacy for terror and example.

It is thus only that the barbarities of Indians can be successfully encountered. It is thus only that the worse than Indian barbarities of European impostors, pretending authority from their government, but always disavowed can be punished and arrested. Great Britain yet engages the alliance and co-operation of savages in war. But her government has invariably disclaimed all countenance or authorization to her subjects to instigate them against us in time of peace. Yet so it has happened, that, from the period of our established independence to this day all the Indian wars with which we have been afflicted have been distinctly traceable to the instigation of English traders or agents. Always disavowed, yet always felt; more than once detected but never before punished; two of them, offenders of the deepest dye, after solemn warning to their government, and individually to one of them, have fallen, *flagrante delicto*, into the hands of an American general; and the punishment inflicted upon them has fixed them on high as an example, awful in its exhibition, but we trust auspicious in its results, of that which awaits unauthorized pretenders of European agency to stimulate and interpose in wars between the United States and the Indians within their control.

This exposition of their origin, the causes and the character of the war with the Seminole Indians and part of the Creeks, combined with MacGregor's mock patriots and Nicholls's negroes which necessarily led our troops into Florida and gave rise to all those incidents of which Pizarro so vehemently complains, will, it is hoped, enable you to present other and sounder views of the subject to his Catholic Majesty's government. It will enable you to show that the occupation of Pensacola and St. Marks was occasioned neither by hostility to Spain nor with a view to extort prematurely the province from her possession; that it was rendered necessary by the neglect of Spain to perform her engagements of restraining the Indians from hostilities against the United States and by the culpable countenance, encouragement, and assistance given to those Indians in their hostilities by the Spanish government and commandant at those places; that the United States have a right to demand, as the president does demand, of Spain the punishment of those officers for this misconduct and he further demands of Spain a just and reasonable indemnity to the United States for the heavy and necessary expenses which they have been compelled to incur, by the failure of Spain to perform her engagement to restrain the Indians aggravated by this demonstrated complicity of her commanding officers with them in their hostilities against the United States. . . .

That the two Englishmen, executed by order of General Jackson, were not only identified with the savages with whom they were carrying on the war against the United States, but that one of them was the mover and fomenter of the war, which, without his interference and false promises to the Indians of support from the British government, never would have happened; that the other was the instrument of war against Spain as well as the United States; commissioned by MacGregor and expedited by Woodbine, upon their project of conquering Florida with these Indians and negroes; that as accomplices of the savages and sinning against their better knowledge, worse than savages, General Jackson, possessed of their persons and of the proofs of their guilt, might, by the lawful and ordinary usages of war, have hung them both without the formality of a trial; that to allow them every possible opportunity of refuting the proofs, or of showing any circumstances in extenuation of their crimes he gave them the benefit of trial by a court-martial of highly respectable officers; that the defense of one consisted solely and exclusively of technical cavils at the nature of part of the evidence against him and the other confessed his guilt; finally that in restoring Pensacola and St. Marks to Spain the president gives the most signal proof of his confidence, that hereafter her engagement to restrain by force the Indians of Florida from all hostilities against the United States will be effectually fulfilled — that there will be no more murders, no more robberies within our borders by savages, prowling along the Spanish line and seeking shelter within it, to display in their villages the scalps of our women and children, their victims, and to sell with shameless effrontery the plunder from our citizens in Spanish forts and cities — that we shall have no more apologies from Spanish governors and commandants of their inability to perform the duties of their office and the solemn contracts of their country, no more excuses for compliances to the savage enemies of the United States from the dread of their attacks upon themselves, no more harboring of foreign impostors upon compulsion — that strength sufficient will be kept in the province to restrain the Indians by force and officers empowered and entrusted to employ it effectually to maintain the good faith of the nation by the effective fulfilment of the treaty.

The duty of this government to protect the persons and property of our fellow citizens on the borders of the United States is imperative; it must be discharged; and if after all the warnings that Spain has had — if after the prostration of all her territorial rights, neutral obligations by Nicholls and his banditti during war, and all her treaty stipulations by Arbuthnot and Ambrister abetted by her own commanding officers during peace to the cruel annoyance of the United States — if the necessities of self defense should again compel the United States to take possession of the Spanish forts and places in Florida, declare with the frankness and candor that becomes us, that another unconditional restoration of them must not be expected; that even the president's confidence in the good faith and ultimate justice of the Spanish government, will yield to the painful experience of continual disappointment; and that after unwearied and almost unnumbered appeals to them for the performance of their stipulated duties, in vain, the United States will be reluctantly compelled to rely for the protection of their borders upon themselves alone.   JOHN QUINCY ADAMS.

APPENDIX D.

1795.

TREATY OF FRIENDSHIP, LIMITS, AND NAVIGATION.

CONCLUDED OCTOBER 27, 1795; RATIFICATIONS EXCHANGED AT ARANJUEZ
APRIL 25, 1796; PROCLAIMED AUGUST 2, 1796.

His Catholic Majesty and the United States of America,
desiring to consolidate, on a permanent basis, the friendship and
good correspondence which happily prevails between the two
parties, have determined to establish, by a convention, several
points, the settlement whereof will be productive of general advantage and reciprocal utility to both nations.

With this intention, his Catholic Majesty has appointed the
most excellent Lord Don Manuel de Godoy, and Alvarez de
Faria, Rios, Sanchez, Zarzosa, Prince de la Paz, Duke de la
Alcudia, Lord of the Soto de Roma, and of the state of Albala,
Grandee of Spain of the first class, perpetual Regidor of the city
of Santiago, Knight of the illustrious Order of the Golden
Fleece, and Great Cross of the Royal and distinguished Spanish
Order of Charles the V., Commander of Valencia del Ventoso,
Rivera, and Acenchal in that of Santiago, Knight and Great
Cross of the religious Order of St. John; Counsellor of State;
Superintendent General of the Posts and Highways; Protector of
the Royal Academy of the Noble Arts, and of the Royal Societies
of Natural History, Botany, Chemistry, and Astronomy; Gentleman of the King's Chamber in employment; Captain General of
his Armies; Inspector and Major of the Royal Corps of Body
Guards, &c., &c., &c., and the President of the United States,
with the advice and consent of their Senate, has appointed
Thomas Pinckney, a citizen of the United States, and their
Envoy Extraordinary to His Catholic Majesty. And the said
Plenipotentiaries have agreed upon and concluded the following
articles:

ARTICLE 1.

There shall be a firm and inviolable peace and sincere friendship between His Catholic Majesty, his successors and subjects,
and the United States and their citizens, without exception of
persons or places.

ARTICLE 2.

To prevent all disputes on the subject of the boundaries which
separate the territories of the two high contracting parties, it is
hereby declared and agreed as follows, to-wit: The southern
boundary of the United States, which divides their territory
from the Spanish colonies of East and West Florida, shall be
designated by a line beginning on the river Mississippi, at the
northernmost part of the thirty-first degree of latitude north of
the equator, which from thence shall be drawn due east to the
middle of the river Appalachicola, or Catachouche, thence along
the middle thereof to its junction with the Flint; thence straight
to the head of St. Mary's River, and thence down the middle
thereof to the Atlantic Ocean. And it is agreed that if there
should be any troops, garrisons, or settlements of either party in
the territory of the other, according to the above mentioned
boundaries, they shall be withdrawn from the said territory
within the term of six months after the ratification of this
treaty, or sooner if it be possible; and that they shall be permitted to take with them all the goods and effects which they
possess.

ARTICLE 3.

In order to carry the preceding article into effect, one commissioner and one surveyor shall be appointed by each of the
contracting parties, who shall meet at the Natchez, on the left
side of the river Mississippi, before the expiration of six months
from the ratification of this convention, and they shall proceed
to run and mark this boundary according to the stipulations of
the said article. They shall make plats and keep journals of
their proceedings, which shall be considered as part of this
convention, and shall have the same force as if they were inserted
therein. And if on any account it should be found necessary
that the said commissioners and surveyors should be accompanied by guards, they shall be furnished in equal proportions by

the commanding officer of His Majesty's troops in the two Floridas, and the commanding officer of the troops of the United States in their southwestern territory, who shall act by common consent, and amicably, as well with respect to this point as to the furnishing of provisions and instruments, and making every other arrangement which may be necessary or useful for the execution of this article.

ARTICLE 4.

It is likewise agreed that the western boundary of the United States which separates them from the Spanish colony of Louisiana, is in the middle of the channel or bed of the River Mississippi, from the northern boundary of the said States to the completion of the thirty-first degree of latitude north of the equator. And His Catholic Majesty has likewise agreed that the navigation of the said river, in its whole breadth from its source to the ocean, shall be free only to his subjects and the citizens of the United States, unless he should extend this privilege to the subjects of other powers by special convention.

ARTICLE 5.

The two high contracting parties shall, by all the means in their power, maintain peace and harmony among the several Indian nations who inhabit the country adjacent to the lines and rivers, which, by the preceding articles, form the boundaries of the two Floridas. And the better to obtain this effect, both parties oblige themselves expressly to restrain by force all hostilities on the part of the Indian nations living within their boundaries; so that Spain will not suffer her Indians to attack the citizens of the United States, nor the Indians inhabiting their territory; nor will the United States permit these last mentioned Indians to commence hostilities against the subjects of His Catholic Majesty or his Indians in any manner whatever. And whereas several treaties of friendship exist between the two contracting parties and the said nations of Indians, it is hereby agreed that in future no treaty of alliance, or other whatever (except treaties of peace), shall be made by either party with the Indians living within the boundary of the other, but both parties will endeavor to make the advantages of the Indian trade common and mutually beneficial to their respective subjects and citizens, observing in all things the most complete reciprocity; so that both parties may obtain the advantages arising from a good understanding with the said nations, without being subject to the expense which they have hitherto occasioned.

ARTICLE 6.

Each party shall endeavor, by all means in their power, to protect and defend all vessels and other effects belonging to the citizens or subjects of the other, which shall be within the extent of their jurisdiction by sea or by land, and shall use all their efforts to recover, and cause to be restored to the right owners, their vessels and effects which may have been taken from them within the extent of their said jurisdiction, whether they are at war or not with the power whose subjects have taken possession of the said effects.

ARTICLE 7.

'And it is agreed that the subjects of each of the contracting parties, their vessels or effects, shall not be liable to any embargo or detention on the part of the other, for any military expedition or other public or private purpose whatever; and in all cases of seizure, detention, or arrest for debts contracted, or offenses committed by any citizen or subject of the one party within the jurisdiction of the other, the same shall be made and prosecuted by order and authority of law only, and according to the regular course of proceeding usual in such cases. The citizens and subjects of both parties shall be allowed to employ such advocates, solicitors, notaries, agents, and factors, as they may judge proper, in all their affairs, and in all their trials at law, in which they may be concerned before the tribunals of the other party; and such agents shall have free access to be present at the proceedings in such causes, and at the taking of all examinations and evidence which may be exhibited in the said trials.

ARTICLE 8.

'In case the subjects and inhabitants of either party, with their shipping, whether public and of war, or private and of merchants, be forced, through stress of weather, pursuit of pirates or enemies, or any other urgent necessity, for seeking of shelter and harbor, to retreat and enter into any of the rivers, bays, roads, or ports belonging to the other party, they shall be received and treated with all humanity, and enjoy all favor, protection, and help, and they shall be permitted to refresh and provide themselves at reasonable rates, with victuals and all things needful for the sustenance of their persons, or reparation of their ships and prosecution of their voyage; and they shall no ways be hindered from returning out of the said ports or roads, but may remove and depart when and whither they please, without any let or hindrance.

ARTICLE 9.

All ships and merchandize, of what nature soever, which shall be rescued out of the hands of any pirates or robbers on the high seas, shall be brought into some port, in order to be taken care of, and restored entire to the true proprietor, as soon as due and sufficient proof shall be made concerning the property thereof.

ARTICLE 10.

When any vessel of either party shall be wrecked, foundered, or otherwise damaged, on the coasts or within the dominion of the other, their respective subjects or citizens shall receive, as well for themselves as for their vessels and effects, the same assistance which would be due to the inhabitants of the country where the damage happens, and shall pay the same charges and dues only as the said inhabitants would be subject to pay in a like case; and if the operations of repair should require that the whole or any part of the cargo be unladen, they shall pay no duties, charges, or fees on the part which they shall relade and carry away.

ARTICLE 11.

The citizens and subjects of each party shall have power to dispose of their personal goods, within the jurisdiction of the other, by testament, donation, or otherwise, and their representatives being subjects or citizens of the other party, shall succeed to their said personal goods, whether by testament or *ab intestato* and they may take possession thereof, either by themselves or others acting for them, and dispose of the same at their will, paying such dues only as the inhabitants of the country wherein the said goods are, shall be subject to pay in like cases.

And in case of the absence of the representative, such care shall be taken of the said goods, as would be taken of the goods of a native in like case, until the lawful owner may take measures for receiving them. And if questions shall arise among several claimants to which of them the said goods belong, the same shall be decided finally by the laws and judges of the land wherein the said goods are. And where, on the death of any person holding real estate within the territories of the one party, such real estate would by the laws of the land descend on a citizen or subject of the other, were he not disqualified by being an alien, such subjects shall be allowed a reasonable time to sell the same, and to withdraw the proceeds without molestation, and exempt from all rights of detraction on the part of the government of the respective states.

ARTICLE 12.

The merchant ships of either of the parties which shall be making into a port belonging to the enemy of the other party, and concerning whose voyage, and the species of goods on board her, there shall be just grounds of suspicion, shall be obliged to exhibit as well upon the high seas as in the ports and havens, not only her passports, but likewise certificates, expressly showing that her goods are not of the number of those which have been prohibited as contraband.

ARTICLE 13.

For the better promoting of commerce on both sides, it is agreed, that if a war shall break out between the said two nations, one year after the proclamation of war shall be allowed to the merchants in the cities and towns where they shall live, for collecting and transporting their goods and merchandizes; and if anything be taken from them or any injury be done them within that term, by either party, or the people or subjects of either, full satisfaction shall be made for the same by the government.

ARTICLE 14.

No subject of His Catholic Majesty shall apply for, or take any commission or letters of marque, for arming any ship or ships to act as privateers against the said United States, or against the citizens, people, or inhabitants of the said United States, or against the property of any of the inhabitants of them, from any Prince or State with which the said king shall be at war. And if any person of either nation shall take such commissions or letters of marque, he shall be punished as a pirate.

ARTICLE 15.

It shall be lawful for all and singular the subjects of His Catholic Majesty, and the citizens, people, and inhabitants of the said United States, to sail with their ships with all manner of liberty and security, no distinction being made who are the proprietors of the merchandizes laden thereon, from any port to the places of those who now are, or hereafter shall be, at enmity with His Catholic Majesty or the United States. It shall be likewise lawful for the subjects and inhabitants aforesaid, to sail with the ships and merchandizes aforementioned, and to trade with the same liberty and security from the places, ports, and havens of those who are enemies of both or either party, without any opposition or disturbance whatsoever, not only directly from the places of the enemy aforementioned, to neutral places, but also from one place belonging to an enemy, to another place belonging to an enemy, whether they be under the jurisdiction of the same prince or under several; and it is hereby stipulated that free ships shall also give freedom to goods, and that everything shall be deemed free and exempt which shall be found on board the ships belonging to the subjects of either of the contracting parties, although the whole lading, or any part thereof, should appertain to the enemies of either; contraband goods being always excepted. It is also agreed that the same liberty be extended to persons who are on board a free ship, so that although they be enemies to either party, they shall not be made prisoners or taken out of that free ship, unless they are soldiers and in actual service of the enemies.

ARTICLE 16.

This liberty of navigation and commerce shall extend to all kinds of merchandizes, excepting those only which are distinguished by the name of contraband; and under this name of contraband or prohibited goods, shall be comprehended arms,

great guns, bombs, with the fusees, and other things belonging
to them, cannon-ball, gun-powder, match, pikes, swords, lances,
spears, halberds, mortars, petards, granades, saltpeter, muskets,
musket-balls, bucklers, helmets, breast plates, coats of mail, and
the like kind of arms proper for arming soldiers, musket-rests,
belts, horses with their furniture, and all other warlike instruments whatever. These merchandizes which follow shall not
be reckoned among contraband or prohibited goods: That is to
say, all sorts of cloths, and all other manufactures woven of any
wool, flax, silk, cotton, or any other materials whatever; all
kinds of wearing apparel, together with all species whereof they
are used to be made; gold and silver, as well coined as uncoined,
tin, latton, copper, brass, coals, as also wheat, barley, oats, and
any other kind of corn and pulse; tobacco and likewise all manner of spices, salted and smoked flesh, salted fish, cheese and
butter, beer, oils, wines, sugars, and all sorts of salts, and in
general all provisions which serve for the sustenance of life.
Furthermore all kinds of cotton, hemp, flax, tar, pitch, ropes,
cables, pails, sail-cloths, anchors, and any parts of anchors; also
ships' masts, planks, wood of all kind, and all other things
proper either for building or repairing ships, and all other
goods whatever which have not been worked into the form of
any instrument prepared for war, by land or by sea, shall not be
reputed contraband, much less such as have been already wrought
and made up for any other use; all which shall be wholly reckoned among free goods, as likewise all other merchandizes and
things which are not comprehended and particularly mentioned
in the foregoing enumeration of contraband goods; so that they
may be transported and carried in the freest manner by the subjects of both parties, even to places belonging to an enemy, such
towns or places being only excepted as are at that time besieged,
blocked up, or invested. And except the cases in which any ship
of war or squadron shall, in consequence of storms or other accidents at sea, be under the necessity of taking the cargo of any
trading vessel or vessels, and furnish themselves with necessaries, giving a receipt, in order that the power to whom the said
ship of war belongs may pay for the articles so taken according
to the price thereof, at the port to which they may appear to have
been destined by the ship's papers; and the two contracting parties engage, that the vessels shall not be detained longer than may
be absolutely necessary for their said ships to supply themselves
with necessaries; that they will immediately pay the value of the

receipts, and indemnify the proprietor for all losses which he may have sustained in consequence of such a transaction.

ARTICLE 17.

To the end that all manner of dissensions and quarrels may be avoided and prevented on one side and the other, it is agreed that in case either of the parties hereto should be engaged in a war, the ships and vessels belonging to the subjects or people of the other party must be furnished with sea-letters or passports expressing the name, property, and bulk of the ship, as also the name and place of habitation of the master or commander of the said ship, that it may appear thereby that the ship really and truly belongs to the subjects of one of the parties, which passport shall be made out and granted according to the form annexed to this treaty. They shall likewise be recalled every year, that is, if the ship happens to return home within the space of a year.

It is likewise agreed, that such ships being laden, are to be provided not only with passports as above mentioned, but also with certificates, containing the several particulars of the cargo, the place whence the ship sailed, that so it may be known whether any forbidden or contraband goods be on board the same; which certificates shall be made out by the officers of the place whence the ship sailed in the accustomed form. And if any one shall think it fit or advisable to express in the said certificates the person to whom the goods on board belong, he may freely do so. Without which requisites they may be sent to one of the ports of the other contracting party, and adjudged by the competent tribunal, according to what is above set forth, that all the circumstance of this omission having been well examined, they shall be adjudged to be legal prizes, unless they shall give legal satisfaction of their property by testimony entirely equivalent.

ARTICLE 18.

If the ships of the said subjects, people, or inhabitants, of either of the parties shall be met with, either sailing along the coasts or on the high seas, by any ship of war of the other, or by any privateer, the said ship of war or privateer, for the avoiding of any disorder, shall remain out of cannon-shot, and may send their boats aboard the merchant ship, which they shall so meet with, and may enter her to number of two or three men only, to whom the master or commander of such ship or vessel shall exhibit his passports, concerning the property of the ship, made out according to the form inserted in this present treaty; and the ship, when she shall have showed such passports, shall be free and at liberty to pursue her voyage, so as it shall not be lawful to molest or give her chase in any manner, or force her to quit her intended course.

ARTICLE 19.

Consuls shall be reciprocally established, with the privileges and powers which those of the most favored nations enjoy, in the ports where their consuls reside or are permitted to be.

ARTICLE 20.

It is also agreed that the inhabitants of the territories of each party shall respectively have free access to the courts of justice of the other, and they shall be permitted to prosecute suits for the recovery of their properties, the payment of their debts, and for obtaining satisfaction for the damages which they may have sustained, whether the persons whom they may sue be subjects or citizens of the country in which they may be found, or any other persons whatsoever, who may have taken refuge therein; and the proceedings and sentences of the said courts shall be the same as if the contending parties had been subjects or citizens of the said country.

ARTICLE 21.

In order to terminate all differences on account of the losses sustained by the citizens of the United States in consequence of their vessels and cargoes having been taken by the subjects of His Catholic Majesty, during the late war between Spain and France, it is agreed that all such cases shall be referred to the final decision of commissioners, to be appointed in the following manner. His Catholic Majesty shall name one commissioner, and the president of the United States, by and with the advice and consent of their senate, shall appoint another, and the said two commissioners shall agree on the choice of a third, or if they cannot agree so, they shall each propose one person, and of the two names so proposed, one shall be drawn by lot in the presence of the two original commissioners, and the person whose name shall be so drawn shall be the third commissioner; and the three commissioners so appointed shall be sworn impartially to examine and decide the claims in question, according to the merits of the several cases, and to justice, equity, and the laws of the nations. The said commissioners shall meet and sit at Philadelphia; and in the case of the death, sickness, or necessary absence of any such commissioner, his place shall be supplied in the same manner as he was first appointed, and the new commissioner shall take the same oaths, and do the same duties. They shall receive all complaints and applications authorized by this article, during eighteen months from the day on which they shall assemble. They shall have power to examine all such persons as come before them on oath or affirmation, touching the complaints in question, and also to receive in evidence all written testimony, authenticated in such manner as they shall think proper to require or admit. The award of the said commissioners, or any two of them, shall be final and conclusive, both as to the justice of the claim and the amount of the sum to be paid to the claimants; and His Catholic Majesty undertakes to cause the same to be paid in specie, without deduction, at such times and places, and under such conditions as shall be awarded by the said commissioners.

ARTICLE 22.

The two high contracting parties, hoping that the good correspondence and friendship which happily reigns between them will be further increased by this treaty, and that it will contribute to augment their prosperity and opulence, will in future give to their mutual commerce all the extension and favor which the advantage of both countries may require.

And in consequence of the stipulations contained in the fourth article, His Catholic Majesty will permit the citizens of the United States, for the space of three years from this time, to deposit their merchandize and effects in the port of New Orleans, and to export them from thence without paying any other duty than a fair price for the hire of the stores; and His Majesty promises either to continue this permission, if he finds during that time that it is not prejudicial to the interests of Spain, or if he should not agree to continue it there, he will assign to them on another

24

part of the banks of the Mississippi an equivalent establishment.

ARTICLE 23.

The present treaty shall not be in force until ratified by the contracting parties, and the ratifications shall be exchanged in six months from this time, or sooner if possible.

In witness whereof we, the underwritten Plenipotentiaries of His Catholic Majesty and of the United States of America, have signed this present treaty of friendship, limits, and navigation, and thereunto affixed our seals respectively.

Done at San Lorenzo el Real, this seven and twenty day of October, one thousand seven hundred and ninety-five.

(seal)   THOMAS PINCKNEY.
(seal)   EL PRINCIPE DE LA PAZ.

APPENDIX E.

1819.

TREATY OF AMITY, SETTLEMENT, AND LIMITS.

CONCLUDED FEBRUARY 22, 1819; RATIFICATIONS EXCHANGED AT WASH-
INGTON FEBRUARY 22, 1821; PROCLAIMED FEBRUARY 22, 1821.

The United States of America and His Catholic Majesty, desiring to consolidate, on a permanent basis, the friendship and
good correspondence which happily prevails between the two
parties, have determined to settle and terminate all their differences and pretensions, by a treaty, which shall designate, with
precision, the limits of their respective bordering territories in
North America.

With this intention the President of the United States has
furnished with their full powers John Quincy Adams, Secretary
of State of the said United States; and His Catholic Majesty has
appointed the Most Excellent Lord Don Luis de Onis, Gonzales,
Lopez y Vara, Lord of the town of Rayaces, Perpetual Regidor of
the Corporation of the city of Salamanca, Knight Grand Cross
of the Royal Vendee, Knight Pensioner of the Royal and Distinguished Spanish Order of Charles the Third, Member of the
Supreme Assembly of the said Royal Order; of the Council of His
Catholic Majesty; His Secretary, with Exercise of Decrees, and
His Envoy Extraordinary and Minister Plenipotentiary near the
United States of America;

And the said Plenipotentiaries, after having exchanged their
powers, have agreed upon and concluded the following articles:

ARTICLE 1.

There shall be a firm and inviolable peace and sincere friendship between the United States and their citizens and His Catholic Majesty, his successors and subjects, without exception of
persons or places.

ARTICLE 2.

His Catholic Majesty cedes to the United States, in full
property and sovereignty, all the territories which belong to him,
situated to the eastward of the Mississippi, known by the name
of East and West Florida. The adjacent islands dependent on
said provinces, all public edifices, fortifications, barracks, and
other buildings, which are not private property, archives and
documents, which relate directly to the property and sovereignty
of said provinces, are included in this article. The said archives
and documents shall be left in possession of the commissaries or
officers of the United States, duly authorized to receive them.

ARTICLE 3.

The boundary line between the two countries, west of the
Mississippi, shall begin on the Gulf of Mexico, at the mouth of
the river Sabine, in the sea, continuing north, along the western
bank of that river, to the 32d degree of latitude; thence, by a
line due north, to the degree of latitude where it strikes the Rio
Roxo westward, to the degree of longitude 100 west from London and 23 from Washington; then, crossing the said Red River,
and running thence, by a line due north, to the river Arkansas;
thence, following the course of the southern bank of the Arkansas, to its source, in latitude 42 north; and thence by that
parallel of latitude, to the South Sea. The whole being as laid
down in Melish's map of the United States, published at Philadelphia, improved to the first of January, 1818. But if the source
of the Arkansas River shall be found to fall north or south of
latitude 42, then the line shall run from the said source due
south or north, as the case may be, till it meets the said parallel of latitude 42, and thence, along the said parallel, to the
South Sea. All the islands in the Sabine, and the said Red and
Arkansas rivers, throughout the course thus described, to belong
to the United States; but the use of the waters, and the navigation of the Sabine to the sea, and of the said rivers Roxo and
Arkansas, throughout the extent of the said boundary, on their
respective banks, shall be common to the respective inhabitants
of both nations.

The two high contracting parties agree to cede and renounce
all their rights, claims, and pretensions, to the territories described by the said line, that is to say: The United States hereby

cede to His Catholic Majesty, and renounce forever, all their rights, claims, and pretensions, to the territories lying west and south of the above described line; and, in like manner, His Catholic Majesty cedes to the said United States all his rights, claims, and pretensions to any territories east and north of the said line, and for himself, his heirs, and successors, renounces all claim to the said territories forever.

ARTICLE 4.

To fix this line with more precision, and to place the land-marks which shall designate exactly the limits of both nations, each of the contracting parties shall appoint a commissioner and a surveyor, who shall meet before the termination of one year from the date of the ratification of this treaty at Natchitoches, on the Red River, and proceed to run and mark the said line, from the mouth of the Sabine to the Red River, and from the Red River to the river Arkansas, and to ascertain the lati-tude of the source of the said river Arkansas, in conformity to what is above agreed upon and stipulated, and the line of lati-tude 42, to the South Sea; they shall make out plans, and keep journals of their proceedings, and the result agreed upon by them shall be considered as part of this treaty, and shall have the same force as if it were inserted therein. The two govern-ments will amicably agree respecting the necessary articles to be furnished to those persons, and also as to their respective escorts, should such be deemed necessary.

ARTICLE 5.

The inhabitants of the ceded territories shall be secured in the free exercise of their religion, without any restriction; and all those who may desire to remove to the Spanish dominions shall be permitted to sell or export their effects, at any time whatever, without being subject, in either case, to duties.

ARTICLE 6.

The inhabitants of the territories which His Catholic Majesty cedes to the United States, by this treaty, shall be incorporated in the Union of the United States, as soon as may be consistent with the principles of the Federal Constitution, and admitted to

the enjoyment of all the privileges, rights, and immunities of the
citizens of the United States.

ARTICLE 7.

The officers and troops of His Catholic Majesty, in the territories hereby ceded by him to the United States, shall be withdrawn and possession of the places occupied by them shall be
given within six months after the exchange of the ratifications
of this treaty, or sooner if possible, by the officers of His Catholic
Majesty, to the commissioners or officers of the United States
duly appointed to receive them; and the United States shall furnish the transports and escort necessary to convey the Spanish
officers and troops and their baggage to the Havana.

ARTICLE 8.

All the grants of land made before the 24th of January,
1818, by His Catholic Majesty, or by his lawful authorities, in
the said territories ceded by His Majesty to the United States,
shall be ratified and confirmed to the persons in possession of
the lands, to the same extent that the same grants would be
valid if the territories had remained under the dominion of His
Catholic Majesty. But the owners in possession of such lands,
who, by reason of the recent circumstances of the Spanish nation, and the revolutions in Europe, have been prevented from
fulfilling all the conditions of their grants, shall complete them
within the terms limited in the same, respectively, from the
date of this treaty; in default of which the said grants shall be
null and void. All grants made since the said 24th of January, 1818, when the first proposal, on the part of His Catholic
Majesty, for the cession of the Floridas was made, are hereby
declared and agreed to be null and void.

ARTICLE 9.

The two high contracting parties, animated with the most
earnest desire of conciliation, and with the object of putting an
end to all differences which have existed between them, and of
confirming the good understanding which they wish to be forever maintained between them, reciprocally renounce all claims
for damages or injuries which they, themselves, as well as their

respective citizens and subjects, may have suffered until the time of signing this treaty.

The renunciation of the United States will extend to all the injuries mentioned in the convention of the 11th of August, 1802.

2. To all claims on account of prizes made by French privateers, and condemned by French consuls, within the territory and jurisdiction of Spain.

3. To all claims of indemnities on account of suspension of the right of deposit at New Orleans in 1802.

4. To all claims of citizens of the United States upon the government of Spain, arising from the unlawful seizures at sea, and in the ports and territories of Spain, or the Spanish colonies.

5. To all claims of citizens of the United States upon the Spanish government, statements of which, soliciting the interposition of the government of the United States, have been presented to the department of state, or to the minister of the United States in Spain, since the date of the convention of 1802, and until the signature of this treaty.

The renunciation of His Catholic Majesty extends—

1. To all the injuries mentioned in the convention of the 11th of August, 1802.

2. To the sums which His Catholic Majesty advanced for the return of Captain Pike from the Provinces Internas.

3. To all injuries caused by the expedition of Miranda, that was fitted out and equipped at New York.

4. To all claims of Spanish subjects upon the government of the United States arising from unlawful seizures at sea, or within the ports and territorial jurisdiction of the United States.

Finally, to all the claims of subjects of His Catholic Majesty upon the government of the United States in which the interposition of His Catholic Majesty's government has been solicited, before the date of this treaty and since the date of the convention of 1802, or which may have been made to the department of foreign affairs of His Majesty, or to his minister in the United States.

And the high contracting parties, respectively, renounce all claim to indemnities for any of the recent events or transactions of their respective commanders and officers in the Floridas.

The United States will cause satisfaction to be made for the injuries, if any, which, by process of law, shall be established to have been suffered by the Spanish officers, and individual

Spanish inhabitants, by the late operations of the American army
in Florida.

The convention entered into between the two governments,
on the 11th of August, 1802, the ratifications of which were
exchanged the 21st of December, 1818, is annulled.

The United States, exonerating Spain from all demands in
future, on account of the claims of their citizens to which the
renunciations herein contained extend, and considering them
entirely cancelled, undertake to make satisfaction for the same,
to an amount not exceeding five millions of dollars. To ascertain the full amount and validity of those claims, a commission,
to consist of three commissioners, citizens of the United States,
shall be appointed by the president, by and with the advice and
consent of the senate, which commission shall meet at the city
of Washington, and, within the space of three years from the
time of their first meeting, shall receive, examine, and decide
upon the amount and validity of all the claims included within
the descriptions above mentioned. The said commissioners shall
take an oath or affirmation, to be entered on the record of their
proceedings, for the faithful and diligent discharge of their
duties; and, in case of the death, sickness, or necessary absence
of any such commissioner, his place may be supplied by the appointment, as aforesaid, or by the president of the United States,
during the recess of the senate, of another commissioner in his
stead. The said commissioners shall be authorized to hear and
examine suitable authentic testimony concerning the same. And
the Spanish government shall furnish all such documents and
elucidations as may be in their possession, for the adjustment of
the said claims, according to the principles of justice, the laws
of nations, and the stipulations of the treaty between the two
parties of 27th of October, 1795; the said documents to be specified, when demanded, at the instance of the said commissioners.

The payment of such claims as may be admitted and adjusted
by the said commissioners, or the major part of them; to an
amount not exceeding five millions of dollars, shall be made by
the United States, either immediately at their treasury, or by
the creation of stock, bearing an interest of six per cent. per

annum, payable from the proceeds of sales of public lands within the territories hereby ceded to the United States, or in such other manner as the congress of the United States may prescribe by law.

The records of the proceedings of the said commissioners, together with the vouchers and documents produced before them, relative to the claims to be adjusted and decided upon by them, shall, after the close of their transactions, be deposited in the department of state of the United States; and copies of them, or any part of them, shall be furnished to the Spanish government, if required, at the demand of the Spanish minister in the United States.

ARTICLE 12.

The treaty of limits and navigation, of 1795, remains confirmed in all and each one of its articles excepting the second, third, fourth, twenty-first and the second clause of the twenty-second article, which, having been altered by this treaty, or having received their entire execution, are no longer valid.

With respect to the fifteenth article of the same treaty of friendship, limits, and navigation of 1795, in which it is stipulated that the flag shall cover the property, the two high contracting parties agree that this shall be so understood with respect to those powers who recognize this principle; but if either of the two contracting parties shall be at war with a third party, and the other neutral, the flag of the neutral shall cover the property of enemies whose government acknowledge this principle, and not of others.

ARTICLE 13.

Both contracting parties, wishing to favor their mutual commerce, by affording in their ports every necessary assistance to their respective merchant vessels, have agreed that the sailors who shall desert from their vessels in the ports of the other, shall be arrested and delivered up, at the instance of the consul, who shall prove, nevertheless, that the deserters belonged to the vessels that claimed them, exhibiting the document that is customary in their nation; that is to say, the American consul in a Spanish port shall exhibit the document known by the name of articles, and the Spanish consul, in American ports, the roll of the vessel; and if the name of the deserter or deserters who are claimed shall appear in the one or the other, they shall be arrested, held in custody, and delivered to the vessel to which they shall belong.

ARTICLE 14.

The United States hereby certify that they have not received any compensation from France for the injuries they suffered from privateers, consuls, and tribunals on the coasts and in the ports of Spain, for the satisfaction of which provision is made by this treaty; and they will present an authentic statement of the prizes made, and of their true value, that Spain may avail herself of the same in such manner as she may deem just and proper.

ARTICLE 15.

The United States, to give to His Catholic Majesty a proof of their desire to cement the relations of amity subsisting between the two nations, and to favor the commerce of the subjects of His Catholic Majesty, agree that Spanish vessels, coming laden only with productions of Spanish growth and manufactures, directly from the ports of Spain, or of her colonies, shall be admitted, for the term of twelve years, to the ports of Pensacola and St. Augustine, in the Floridas, without paying other or higher duties on their cargoes, or of tonnage, than will be paid by the vessels of the United States. During the said term no other nation shall enjoy the same privileges within the ceded territories. The twelve years shall commence three months after the exchange of the ratifications of this treaty.

ARTICLE 16.

The present treaty shall be ratified in due form, by the contracting parties, and the ratifications shall be exchanged in six months from this time, or sooner if possible.

In witness whereof we, the underwritten Plenipotentiaries of the United States of America and of His Catholic Majesty, have signed, by virtue of our powers, the present treaty of amity, settlement, and limits, and have thereunto affixed our seals, respectively. Done at Washington this twenty-second day of February, one thousand eight hundred and nineteen.

(seal)   JOHN QUINCY ADAMS.

(seal)   LUIS DE ONIS.

RATIFICATION BY HIS CATHOLIC MAJESTY, ON THE TWENTY-FOURTH
DAY OF OCTOBER, IN THE YEAR OF OUR LORD ONE THOU-
SAND EIGHT HUNDRED AND TWENTY.

Ferdinand the Seventh, by the Grace of God and by the
constitution of the Spanish monarchy, King of Spain.

Whereas on the twenty-second day of February, of the year
one thousand eight hundred and nineteen last past, a treaty was
concluded and signed in the city of Washington, between Don
Luis de Onis, my Envoy Extraordinary and Minister Plenipotentiary, and John Quincy Adams, Esquire, Secretary of State of
the United States of America, competently authorized by both
parties, consisting of sixteen articles, which had for their object the arrangement of differences and of limits between both
governments and their respective territories, which are of the
following form and literal tenor:

(Here follows the foregoing treaty, word for word.)

Therefore, having seen and examined the sixteen articles
aforesaid, and having first obtained the consent and authority
of the General Cortes of the nation with respect to the cession
mentioned and stipulated in the 2nd and 3rd articles, I approve
and ratify all and every one of the articles referred to, and the
clauses which are contained in them; promising, on the faith
and word of a King, to execute and observe them, and to cause
them to be executed and observed entirely as if I myself had
signed them; and that the circumstance of having exceeded the
term of six months, fixed for the exchange of the ratifications in
the 16th article, may afford no obstacle in any manner, it is my
deliberate will that the present ratification be as valid and firm,
and produce the same effects, as if it had been done within the
determined period. Desirous at the same time of avoiding any
doubt or ambiguity concerning the meaning of the 8th article of
the said treaty, in respect to the date which is pointed out in it
as the period for the confirmation of the grants of lands in the
Floridas, made by me, or by the competent authorities in my
royal name, which date was fixed in the positive understanding
of the three grants of land made in favor of the Duke of Alagon,
the Count of Punonrostro, and Don Pedro de Vargas, being annulled by its tenor, I think proper to declare that the said three
grants have remained and do remain entirely annulled and in-
valid; and that neither the three individuals mentioned, nor
those who may have title or interest through them, can avail

themselves of the said grants at any time or in any manner: under which explicit declaration the said 8th article is to be understood as ratified. In the faith of all which I have commanded the issuance of these presents. Signed by my hand, sealed with my secret seal, and countersigned by the underwritten my Secretary of the Department of State.

Given at Madrid, the twenty-fourth of October, one thousand eight hundred and twenty.

FERNANDO.

EVARISTO PEREZ DE CASTRO.

APPENDIX F.

BIBLIOGRAPHY.

MSS. State Department.
Instructions to our Ministers.
Domestic Letters.
Letters from Ministers Abroad to the Secretary of State.
Secretary of State to Foreign Ministers.
MSS. State Department, Negotiation Books.
"   "   "   Foreign Letters.
American State Papers.
MSS. State Department, Letters of William Short.
"   "   "   Letters of David Humphreys.
"   "   "   Letters of Thomas Pinckney.
American State Papers, Foreign Affairs.
"   "   "   Military Affairs.
"   "   "   Indian Affairs.
Annals of Congress, Vol. XXXIII. Debates on Seminole War.
Wharton's Diplomatic History of the American Revolution.
Wharton's International Law.
Woolsey's International Law.
Vattel's Law of Nations.
Hall's International Law.
Fiske's Critical Period of American History.
Trescott's Diplomacy of Washington's and Adams's Terms.
Jefferson's Works.
Hamilton's Works.
Hamilton's Republic.
Gallatin's Works.
Jefferson Papers.
John Quincy Adams's Diary.
McMaster's History of the People of the United States.
Schouler's History of the United States.
Hildreth's History of the United States.

Adams's History of the United States.

Benton's Thirty Years' View.

Campbell's Colonial Florida.

Williams's History of Florida.

Memoirs of Florida. R. H. Rerick and Fleming.

Fairbanks's History of Florida.

Green's History of Florida.

Lowry's History of Mississippi.

Stevens's History of Georgia.

Parton's Jackson.

Sumner's Life of Jackson.

Alexander Hamilton. Henry Cabot Lodge.

James Monroe. D. C. Gilman.

Thomas Jefferson. J. T. Morse, Jr.

James Madison. S. H. Gay.

John Quincy Adams. J. T. Morse, Jr.

Life of J. Q. Adams. Josiah Quincy.

Memoirs of J. Q. Adams. Chas. Francis Adams.

Eaton's Jackson.

Niles Register.

Memoranda of a Residence at the Court of London. Richard
    Rush.

Von Holst's Constitutional and Political History of the United
    States.

Acquisition of Florida. American Historical Magazine, Vol. XIX,
    pp. 286-301. Hon. J. L. M. Curry.

Mistake Made as to the East Boundary of Louisiana (1814).
    Benj. Vaughan.

INDEX

Americana

Catalog of the Publications of
THE BURROWS BROTHERS COMPANY
CLEVELAND, OHIO
(and London)

PRINCIPAL CONTENTS

" . . . the enterprising publishers are doing an invaluable service to the literature of American history."—
The Dial, March 16, '04.

*The following pages contain a list of the Publications devoted to American history issued by The Burrows Brothers Company, Cleveland, Ohio. Prices with few exceptions are net, in accordance with the regulations of the American Publishers' Association. Volumes preceded by an * are in limited editions.*

Orth (Samuel P.). Five American Politicians.

Burr — Douglas — Clay — Clinton — Van Buren.
Size, 7½x5¾; 447 pages, photogravure portraits,
cloth (*postage .10*)   **$2.00**

American Politics examined in the light of present
day administration may be said to comprise two distinct
features, i. e., personality and principle. The machinery
of modern politics had its inception in the desire of certain
men to carry out issues and fulfil ambitions highly necessary to their own advancement and success. There have
been many distinct successes in this peculiar field but it
has been Dr. Orth's object to show the beginnings of this
essentially American phase of political life. Each of the
five great names contributed some special feature.

To Aaron Burr may be given the credit of the first
American political machine. It has survived the century
as Tammany Hall. His romantic life and tragic death add
a double interest to the story of his political career.

DeWitt Clinton was the founder of the Spoils System,
the earliest and most pernicious of all forms of graft.
The life of the man was a series of paradoxes; the strong
and weak points constantly in contrast one with the other,
and his final transformation from a "spoils" politician to
one of our greatest constructive statesmen forms an in-
structing as well as interesting chapter in our history.

The system originated by Clinton was deftly carried
by another to Washington. The story of Martin Van
Buren is one of careful plotting and clever manipulation;
his ousting of Jackson to become President, and the
methods used by him to avoid snares and pitfalls is as
fascinating as a romance.

A Master and Victim of Compromise and Coalition,
Henry Clay stands pre-eminent. Five times he stood for
the presidency, either before the convention or the people,
only to be defeated. For half a century he was a leading
actor on our political stage; the organizer of a powerful
party; the originator of great issues.

One other name—Stephen A. Douglas, Defender of
State Rights, must be included, as denoting a man who
lead the old Democracy into the land of promise and the
realm of nationalism. His life was given to that period
which determined for us whether we were to be a nation
or a confederation.

The book is written in a lucid, straightforward manner,
the author's chief object being to bring out the foremost
political episodes in ihe lives of the five men under consideration.

The growth of the spoils system and party machinery;
the origin of the caucus and its decline; the rise and development of the convention plan, and other details of
modern politics are treated exhaustively from an historical
standpoint and moreover the fundamental thought
throughout the book is to show how all the diverse factors
combined to aid in the development of the nation and how
politics and statecraft have united continually in forming
and preserving the Union.

**Douglas (James, LL.D.) Old France in the
New World.** Quebec in the Seventeenth Century.
Second Edition. Size, 6¼x8¾; pages, 597; portraits in photogravure and many full page half-tones,
buckram, gilt, extra (*postage .12*)   **$2.50**

An admirable book on the making of Canada under
the French rule, and especially of the beginnings of Quebec, Dr. Douglas having made a particular study of the
old town ·and its associations. A scholarly and open
minded account, fully illustrated, of the development of
that great country to the north of us. With careful and
comprehensive index.

"The author follows the fortunes of the French settlement on the St. Lawrence with a firm grasp of the philosophy of its history, and with many entertaining details . . .
and is a valuable addition to the increasing literature of
the subject.—*N. Y. Tribune.*

"The illustrations, plans, maps and facsimiles are
numerous, exceedingly well executed, and historically
valuable."—*Cleveland Plain Dealer.*

"It contains a wealth of information, part of which is
new and what is not is told in such an attractive manner
as to give it all the charm of novelty."—*Quebec Chronicle.*

"Dr. Douglas adds a very substantial and comprehensive volume to the literature of the subject . . . in fact he
has achieved a work of value."—*New York Times Satur-
day Review.*

"The history of Canada is well worth reading, and the
book contains one of the best indexes ever seen in a volume of this kind, filling some fifty-four pages. The work
is handsomely printed and bound, and the frontispiece is
a photogravure of the study for a portrait of Cardinal
Richelieu, by Phillippe de Champaigne, in the National
Gallery."—*Boston Transcript.*

"Old France in the New World" will be invaluable to
all those who wish to study, in the formative period, the
people who now form one-third of the population of the
Dominion."—*Manitoba Free Press.*

Descriptive circular on application.

***Leonard (Zenas). Narrative of Adventures,
1839.** Edited by W. F. Wagner. Size 6x9, pages
317; map, portraits, cloth (*postage .14*)   **$5.00**

Since Washington Irving gave us "Capt. Bonneville"
and "Astoria" the interest in the Great West has been unabated: Lewis and Clark were the pioneers through the
country which Leonard describes and here for the first
time is presented in accurate print, one of the most remarkable records of early western adventure (on the prai-
ries and in the Rockies) ever experienced by individuals.
The first description of the Yosemite is here given, of the
redwoods of Mariposa and the big trees of the (then) California Territory. Leonard became a member of the

Walker Expedition and later in 1834, joined Capt. Bonneville at Salt Lake, becoming intimate with the celebrated
Joe Meek and the renegade Edward Rose, of Astorian
fame.

The introduction and very numerous and excellent
annotations are by Dr. W. F. Wagner. There are maps,
fine portraits, and an index of great value. The original
work is one of extreme scarcity and its authenticity is in
no way to be doubted. A limited number of copies are
offered for sale. The present and coming interest in the
Oregon country adds greatly to the value of this book.

"The journal tells a great deal about the western
Indian Tribes."—*American Hist. Review.*

"This reprint is fully and capably annotated. The
value of the publication is increased by an exhaustive
index . . . and a map showing the location of the California missions in 1769-1824."—*Cedar Rapids Republican.*

"A good account is given of the California territory,
its climate, soil, mountains, streams, crops and native
Indians."—*N. Y. Times Sat. Review.*

Guardia (Ricardo Fernandez) Cuentos Ticos.

Short stories of Costa Rica. Translated from the
Spanish by Gray Casement, with an introduction
and many half-tone illustrations. Size 5 x 7¾;
pages 293, cloth, (*postpaid*)   **$2.00**

Costa Rica has its own literature and the above collection—a typical one—of Central American stories has been
carefully and smoothly translated by Gray Casement, a
close student of the Latin-American life, and one who
makes a strong bid for the future of these southern republics. Guardia is considered the leading exponent of
belles-lettres in Costa Rica and his work has exerted a
strong influence over his countrymen. Here for the first
time he is put in English and the illustrations and lengthy
introduction by the translator make the book unique in
the position which it fills.

"Some of the stories are humorous, some tragic; but
all show power and present life vividly."—*New York Sun.*

"Senor Guardia is considered one of the leading literary men of Costa Rica, if not of Central America.
The unusual merit of he short stories in this collection
makes the reader desirous of knowing more of his work.
Mr. Casement, who is responsible for the translation,
has performed a difficult task in a very satisfactory manner."—*New Orleans Picayune.*

"Mr. Casement has been able to retain in his translation the effect of the language in which the stories were
written. He has kept the idiomatic terms of expression
as nearly as possible and the touches of local color make
one of their most pleasing qualities."—*Cleveland Leader.*

"Here is a unique book indeed * * * Tales like these
are not to be found elsewhere."—*The Emporia (Kansas)
Bulletin.*

"The stories are not only good—they are very good. In fact they will remind the reader of the brilliant sketches of Selma Lagerlof, the Swedish impressionist. One feels after reading the book through that he has been making a voyage of discovery, that he has never known Costa Rica before more than a geographical name and a possible space on the map of that neck of woods known as Central America—but that now he knows it well. * * * The short novels that Mr. Casement has translated for us are cut as clean as a cameo. There is not an amateurish line in them."—*Cleveland Town Topics.*

"Mr. Casement's account of the little republic is more thorough and satisfactory than any we have met with."—*Cleveland Plain Dealer.*

* * * "In 'El Clavel' (The Pink) is told the story of a country girl who vainly loves a well-to-do gentleman of the city; although here and there reminiscent of Castilian story tellers, the tales and the style in which they are related, make one wish to know more of Senor Guardia and his works."—*New York Times Sat. Review.*

Descriptive circular on application.

*Wafer (Lionel). A New Voyage to America.
Edited by George Parker Winship. Size 6 x 9, pages 212, two folding maps and three folding plates, cloth (*postage .12*)   **$3.50**

A reprint of one of the most valuable early treatises on Central America and the Isthmus. Published in 1699, the volume has been one of great rarity until now presented with all the original plates, maps and a new chart of the country as it is today. Invaluable as a contribution toward our *canal* literature and the annotations which have been added by Mr. Winship, relating to the ethnology and anthropology of the country, greatly enhance its worth. Edition of 500 copies.

"The publishers have done their full share to produce a book quite in keeping with their well established reputation. The original edition of the work is so scarce that students . . . have hitherto had little opportunity of consulting it."—*American Anthropologist.*

"In the elegant reprints to which the Burrows Brothers Co., Cleveland, Ohio, has devoted itself, timely is Lionel Wafer's 'New Voyage, etc.' The very competent editor, Mr. George Parker Winship . . . has supplemented the text of the narrative with notes drawn from buccaneer literature of the time. . . . The original illustrations are given in facsimile, together with the British Admiralty map."—*The Nation.*

"The work is not only one which should be in every library of Americana, but is highly interesting to the lay reader."—C. F. Lummis, in *Out West.*

"The introduction and annotations of the reprint are valuable contributions to history and anthropology."—*Boston Transcript.*

"As an example of the bookmaker's art, this reprint is almost ideal and the editorial work fully bears out Mr. Winship's reputation for careful scholarship."—*American Hist. Review.*

"Mr. Winship's contribution is a scholarly piece of work."—*N. Y. Times Sat. Review.*

"A delightful story of old buccaneering days, told by a real buccaneer . . . His account should be read with interest now that the Panama canal promises to become a reality."—*N. Y. Sun.*

*Hutchins (Thomas). A Topographical Description of Virginia, Pennsylvania, Maryland, etc. Edited by Frederick Charles Hicks. Size 9⅜ x 6⅜, pages 143, folding maps, portrait and plates, cloth $4.00
On handmade deckle edge paper, super extra (*postage .16*) $6.00

Thomas Hutchins, the author, occupies a unique place in the history of American cartography, being the only incumbent of the civil office of "Geographer of the United States," the position ceasing to exist after his death in 1789.

While directed by him there were executed the first public surveys under the auspices of the Government. He is entitled to commendation not only because of this fact but for the reason of his honorable connection of over twenty-two years, as an officer in the British army, eighteen of which were given to the Engineer Department.

His observations covering the entire southern and western country from West Florida to the Lakes, are embodied in several maps and two books, the earlier of which is now offered to the public in an accurate reprint. The prefatory remarks indicate that the volume is intended more particularly to explain the larger map entitled "The new map of the western parts of Virginia, Pennsylvania, Maryland and North Carolina," etc., published separately but of the same date as the book. This chart, 35 x 45 inches in size, together with the folded maps included in the volume, are reproduced with absolute accuracy. Strange as it may seem, the life of Hutchins who in many respects was vitally connected with the history of the American Colonies, their struggle for independence, and their development after it was attained, has never been written. As an introduction to the volume, the editor, Frederick Charles Hicks, formerly of the Library of Congress, has prepared, entirely from original sources, an extended account of the man, supplemented by a bibliography of his published and unpublished writings. The Topographical Description is copiously annotated and the whole provided with a complete index. Included is the particularly important and exceedingly scarce Journal of Patrick Kennedy, together with a list of the different nations and tribes of Indians then scattered throughout those parts. As an addition to our cartographical literature the work is most acceptable. but in presenting a life drawn from official documents, unpublished correspondence and government records, many new facts are for the first time made public and much of importance, heretofore unknown, is given to the student and historian.

"Mr. Hicks has made scholarly use of the opportunity which he had for several years as a member of the staff of the Congressional Library."—*Bulletin Amer. Geog. Society.*

"The publishers whose reprints of neglected and well nigh forgotten historical documents deserve not only praise but substantial recognition, have done well in reviving the memoirs and work of Hutchins. . . . We regret that the edition is limited, as it is a book which should be in every public library."—*The Nation.*

"An admirable reproduction of a pioneer survey of the Ohio valley. . . . It is a thoroughly creditable performance."—*N. Y. Sun.*

"Mr. Hicks has taken his task seriously, using good source material and collecting his information with commendable care."—*Amer. Hist. Review.*

A descriptive circular on application.

*Eliot (John). The Logick Primer. Edited by Wilberforce Eames. Size 5½ x 6⅝; pages 94, facsimiles, cloth, extra (*postage .10*) $6.00

A reprint of one of the scarcest pieces of Americana, of which there now exists but one original copy in the British Museum. Has both the Indian and English text and is edited by Wilberforce Eames of the Lenox Library. A few copies only remain out of an edition of 150.

"Mr. Eames is an acknowledged authority on matters pertaining to Eliot, and his work will be appreciated by a large number of students and collectors who have known the volume only by report."—*New York Times Sat. Review.*

"The little book contains an excellent introduction by Mr. Wilberforce Eames of the Lenox Library."—*American Anthropologist.*

Paullin (Charles Oscar). The Navy of the American Revolution. Size 7½ x 5¾, pages 426, frontispiece, cloth, (*postage .10*) $1.25

A volume of the highest importance dealing with American naval history in a way entirely unlike that used by any previous historian. The work is divided into two periods, the first dealing exclusively with the Continental Navy or the fleets of the federal government, the second with the several State's navies. Two chapters are devoted to the valuable naval services of Deane, Franklin, Lee and Adams in France. For the first time the duties which devolved upon Washington, Benedict Arnold, the American Commissioners at Paris and the Continental agents at Washington and New Orleans are made clear, as concerned their duty toward the navy. The initial essay considers the Continental Navy under its first and only Commander-in-chief, Esek Hopkins; the celebrated

fight of Jones off Flamborough Head; the bloody engagement between the *Trumbull* and *Watt*, and the mem-
orable cruise of that redoubtable Irishman, Commodore
John Barry, in 1782–1783 are briefly recounted. A critical
and exhaustive bibliography is contained in an appendix,
also a list of the commissioned officers of the Continental
Navy and Marine Corps. The list of Ships supplements
and corrects that by Lieut. T. F. Emmons, while the total
number of officers' names given is 303 or exactly two hundred more than contained in Hamersly. As a concise,
accurate and readable volume on the subject, treating of
the period covered, this little book cannot be excelled.
Descriptive circular on application.

*Jesuit Relations (The). Travels and Explorations of the French Missionaries among the Indians. Edited by Reuben Gold Thwaites, 73 volumes. Size 6 x 9. Average number of pages per volume 300, many, (colored) portraits and full page plates. buckram, deckle edge. Per volume $3.50

Travels and Explorations of the French Jesuit Missionaries among the Indians of Canada and the Northern
and Northwestern States of the U. S., 1610-1791. Taken
from the French, Latin and Italian originals, both manuscript and printed, with a complete English translation.
Portraits, maps, and facsimiles. Of the limited edition
(750 sets) a few only remain for sale. Price to be ad-
vanced at publisher's option.
   "The most important historical enterprise ever under-
taken."—*John Fiske.*
   "The beginnings of American literature."—*Literary
World.*
   "The greatest literary event of the year."—*Chicago
Tribune.*
   "Of the greatest importance for the student of history
and the student of Indian manners."—*Critic.*
   "The documents on which is based the early history
of America."—*Literature.*
   "A work no library should fail to have on its shelves."
—*Canadian Bookseller.*
   "Among our first and best authorities."—*Dial.*
   "The most important historical undertaking of recent
years."—*J. N. Larned.*
   "It makes an epoch in the historical literature of North
America."—*American Historical Review.*
   "The most valuable addition to early American his-
tory that the present decade will see."—*Buffalo Enquirer.*
   "The most important addition to the shelf of access-
ible American history."—*Literary World.*
   "An immense boon to succeeding generations (and
consequently will be called for much more largely in a
few years, when it will be unobtainable)."—*The Month.*
   Descriptive circular on application.

Avery (Elroy McKendree). A History of the United States and Its People. 12 volumes, size 6¼ x 9½, about 400 pages, per volume, colored maps and plates, cloth, super extra **$ 6.25**
Half morocco   **$12.50**
Full levant morocco   **$17.50**

In the treatment of his vast and complicated subject, the author has succeeded, to a remarkable degree, in combining simplicity with fullness, at the same time preserving the proper relation of parts to each other and to the whole, and quite certainly no work has yet appeared that has so masterfully studied the art of condensation. In accomplishing this Doctor Avery has given color and lucidity to his narrative. It takes time to thus write history from the standpoint of exclusion as well as inclusion, but the sure result is that the ideas are not lost in a mere jumble of words.

"The wealth of colored maps is especially commendable."—*Literary Digest.*

"Even a cursory turning of the leaves for purposes of examination constantly presents a temptation to pause and read a bit here and there."—*Brooklyn Eagle.*

"A work that cannot fail to attract the public attention and to compel the favorable judgment even of critics who are prone to look askance at the popular history."—*Boston Transcript.*

"A work which will take high rank with the histories of our country. . . . Dr. Avery writes in a clear, vigorous style and his narration, void of confusing reference notes, is admirable."—*Boston Herald.*

"There is certainly need of a popular history of the United States, better proportioned and more authoritative then Bryant and Gay, and more comprehensive than Fiske. This need Dr. Elroy M. Avery has sought to supply in his 'History of the United States and its People.'—*The Nation.*

Severance (Frank H.) Old Trails on the Niagara Frontier. Second edition. Size 6 x 9; pages 270, map, cloth (*postage .12*)   **$2.50**

Drawn in every instance from such authoritative sources as State Archives, early manuscripts, the Haldimand Papers and other Canadian channels, and woven together after infinite research, the volume has made foritself a place in American local history, though in literary scope it may be called universal. The New York Press termed the first edition "one of the most attractive books of the year."

Frank H. Severance, the author, has long made a study of Eastern pioneer life and has worked carefully and thoroughly on the subject. A few of the chapters taken in the order given present plainly the field covered.

The "Cross Bearers" treats of the Jesuit Missionaries who came to the region, starting with Dallion, in 1626,

"The Paschal of the Great Pinch" is an extract from the hitherto unknown memoirs of the Chevalier de Treygay, of Fort Denonvile (now called Niagara), in 1687, and "With Bolton at Fort Niagara," gives an interesting episode in the life of Lieut. Col. Mason Bolton, of the 34th Royal Artillery.

"What Befell David Ogden" tells the story of one of the thirty-two persons brought captive by the Indians from 1778 to 1783 to Fort Niagara.

In the "Journals and Journeys of an Early Buffalo Merchant" the life of John Lay, who went to that place in 1810, is narrated. One of the most interesting of all chapters is that entitled "The Misadventures of Robert Marsh" during his extraordinary travels. Incredible as it may seem, the actual distance covered by this individual was 77,000 miles, amid hardships and perils, Indians and wild beasts, yet he lived and told the tale. One of the last but far from least interesting events described under the title of "Underground Trails" is that portion of the volume devoted to the flight of the slaves. As a summary the work may be called without hesitancy a contribution, valuable not only as such, but as a faithful descriptive narration of events and filling a long felt want in the annals of border life.

"The book is very handsomely gotten up, and the story form in which the information is put will attract a public that is more than local."—*N. Y. Sun.*

" . . . a work valuable to all interested in early American history."—*N. Y. World.*

"The scholarship, accuracy and local knowledge shown in the treatment of these events described give the book more than a parochial interest."—*The Nation.*

" . . . many articles of interest are to be found in the volume."—*N. Y. Times Sat. Review.*

Rafinesque (C. D.) Ichthyologia Ohiensis.

Size 6½ x 9, cloth, top gilt, deckle edges. . . . (Out of print.)

"It is therefore a source of gratification to note a verbatim reprint of this, the foundation work on fresh water ichthyology.—*Chicago Evening Post.*

The "B B" Reprints.

A select series, devoted entirely to the scarcest pieces of early American history or travel and especially designed for the collector or student. Each volume is beautifully executed and published in a style fitting it to be permanently preserved. Printed on Dickinson hand-made paper in large clear type, bound in Burrows boards, deckle edges, uncut, in format, a small quarto. Each issue strictly limited to 250 copies, numbered, and 15 copies on Japanese vellum, numbered and signed by the editors.

Denton (Daniel). A Brief Description of New York. Edited by Felix Neumann. Size 6 x 9; pages 63, antique boards. (out of print.)

This volume was written during 1670 by one Daniel Denton, an officer of the law, in Jamaica, in Queens County, on Long Island, and is a vivid and clear description of New York city and of the surrounding country, (including the present State of New Jersey) of that period. The inhabitants, their customs, habits and conditions are also carefully noted, the Indians are mentioned quite exhaustively, and the whole forms a narrative of great historical interest.

"Aside from its physical peculiarities, the subject matter is of much interest to the collector of Americana or the student of the youth of his country."—*Reader Magazine.*

"The publishers are to be complimented on the excellent make up of the volume."—*N. Y. Times Sat. Review.*

"It is a vivid and clear description of New York City and the surrounding country including New Jersey, as it was in that period."—*Cumulative Book Index.*

"The introduction is an admirable piece of bibliographical writing in point of thoroughness, and adds to the value of the new edition, which presents a facsimile of the title page of the original."—*Outlook.*

*Wolley (Rev. Charles). A Two Years' Journal in New York. Edited by Prof. Edward Gaylord Bourne. Size 6 x 9, pages 75, two plates, antique boards, deckle edges (*postage .06*)   **$2.00**

The Rev. Charles Wolley (or Wooley) accompanied Sir Edmund Andros to New York as his chaplain in 1678. At the expiration of two years he returned to England and published, in 1701, his "Journal," to which much value is attached, particularly as concerns the Indians. His knowledge regarding the trade of New York at that date, and the prices of furs and other commodities, is of great interest.

An original copy is worth about $1,000.

"This reprint of his narrative is valuable as there are but few of the original copies in existence."—*N. Y. Press.*

"The introductions are ample and satisfactory."—*Amer. Hist. Review.*

"The introduction to the Journal is by Prof. Bourne, of Yale University, and leaves little to be desired."—*Baltimore Sun.*

*Alsop (George). A Character of the Province of Maryland. Edited by Newton D. Mereness, Ph. D. Size 6 x 9; pages 113, portrait of author and facsimiles, antique boards, deckle edges (*postage .08*)   **$2.00**

The work of an indented servant in that State and gives on the whole, a description of favorable circumstances of the then existing conditions. The work in the original is one of excessive rarity, and this reprint is in every way exact and correct in detail.

" . . . an admirable specimen of typography, and makes an interesting historical document accessible to the general public."—*N. Y. Sun.*

"The editing by Dr. Mereness leaves little to be desired."—*Baltimore Sun.*

"The booklet is of value to the student of our colonial history, and will give the reader a whiff of the spirit and atmosphere of the days of the Restoration."—*The Critic.*

*Miller (Rev. John). A Description of the Province and City of New York. Edited by Victor Hugo Paltsits. Size 6 x 9; pages 135, facsimiles and folding plans, antique boards, deckle edges (*postage .09*)   **$2.00**

This work was not printed at the time of its composition (1695). The original manuscript found its way from the archives of the Bishops of London to the hands of George Chalmers, the Scottish antiquary. It was sold afterwards to Thomas Rodd, a London bookseller, who first published it in 1843, and this was later used by Gowans in 1862. It is now in the British Museum. The text is transcribed *in loco*, and a sketch of the author given for the first time.

"Printing and binding are in every way worthy of what the publishers style 'the definitive edition.' "—*N. E. Hist. and Gen'g Register.*

" . . . a curious and interesting volume."—*Brooklyn Eagle.*

"By placing these old prints within the reach of modern students and readers, the enterprising publishers are doing an invaluable service to the literature of American history."—*The Dial.*

" . . . their elegant series of American historical reprints."—*The Nation.*

"The bibliographical and historical footnotes are very valuable."—*Literary Collector.*

*Budd (Thomas). Good Order Established in Pennsylvania and New Jersey. Edited by Frederick J. Shepard, size 6 x 9; pages 80, fac-simile, antique boards, deckle edges (*postage .06*) **$2.00**

Not only a very important early view of these States, but the original has the distinction of being the first book printed in America by William Bradford. Budd was a resident of Burlington, N. J., in 1678, and an extensive landowner. The book gives a good account of the country and its resources and would be today termed a treatise written for the use of emigrants. A translation of "The Dying Words of Ockanichon," an Indian who died at

Burlington, is appended. This latter tract recently sold, in the original, at auction for $1,450.00, and Budd for £125, in London.

"The publishers deserve thanks for their handsome reprint of a book which is accounted among the very rarest of Americana."—*Reader Magazine.*

"Contains a great deal of information, and Mr. Shepard's introduction is scholarly and full of interest."—*N. Y. Sun.*

*Thomas (Gabriel.) Pennsylvania and West-New Jersey in America. Edited by Cyrus Townsend Brady. Size 6 x 9; pages 83, antique boards, deckle edges (*postage .06*) $2.00

Little did this author realize the worth of his contribution, either as such or from a standpoint of financial value. At the date of its inception and composition, the writer is believed to have been a citizen of London, having previously resided in America for a period of about fifteen years, and the information contained in the book gives the result of his own experience and observation. In its general make-up the second portion of the book devoted to West-New-Jersey, is in every way similar to that preceding. Descriptions, exceedingly valuable to the student of contemporary history are lengthy and full of rich material, notices of the soil and climate and particularly the portions which refer to the native Indians, are of inestimable value. As to the scarcity of the original, little need be said. Its present day market valuation as a rare book is fully that of a thousand dollars, one having been recently offered for more than this amount by a prominent dealer.

"The original is extremely rare and the reprint, though limited, is timely."—*Amer. Hist. Review.*

"In typography and binding the volume is notable for modest elegance."—*Chicago Evening Post.*

All of the above reprints contain facsimiles of the original title pages, maps and illustrations. It is hoped that eventually there will be included some rare tracts or volumes dealing with many of the early States, each distinctive in itself, and attended biographically and bibliographically by competent authorities.

Other volumes to be announced later.

Narratives of Indian Captivities. A series of five volumes devoted to some of the scarcest and rarest works of this character. As a collection, the publishers once more put before the American public many accounts of the adventures, battles, imprisonments, and escapes of our forefathers, which though published and read in days long past, are now almost impossible to procure. . . Uniformity as to the number of copies of each work

prevails throughout the series, both on hand made paper and vellum, and each volume is numbered. The binding of the set is a uniform fine quality of cloth, the de luxe copies being untrimmed and with paper label.

*Gilbert (Benjamin). The Captivity and Sufferings of Benjamin Gilbert and his Family, 1780-83. Edited by Frank H. Severance. Size 8¼ x 5¾; pages 204, map and four plates, cloth, extra, deckle edges (*postage .13*)ʳ   **$3.50**
On Imperial Japanese vellum   **$5.00**

A most useful book to students of the Niagara region and its history, and of New York State as a whole, aside from offering much in the way of extraordinary adventure to the general reader. The work was written by William Walton, to whom the facts were told by the Gilberts after their release. Included is a facsimile of two of the original title pages, a remarkable woodcut from the first issue and a newly drawn map of the region traversed, also a complete index.

"Mr. Severance is just the man to edit a reprint of this work. Its publication should interest local people greatly."—*Niagara Falls Gazette.*

"Their journeyings and adventures are interesting and cast a curious light on the frontier life of the time."—*N. Y. Sun.*

"A straightforward, simple, direct narrative. . . . "—*Buffalo Express.*

*Eastburn (Robert). A Faithful Narrative During His Late Captivity. Edited by John R. Spears. Size 8¼ x 5¾, facsimile, cloth, extra, (*postage .07*)   **$2.00**
On Imperial Japanese vellum   **$3.50**

This is one of the rarest of Indian captivities in the original, being exceeded in that quality only by Dickenson's *God's Protecting Providence*, and Gyle's *Odd Adventures and Captivity.* The narrative is one of extreme importance because of its being an original authority relating to the war that destroyed the French power in North America. The excellent character of the author and his high standing among the pioneers and early settlers of Pennsylvania must also be taken into account.

"Mr. Spears has enhanced the value of the book by his illuminating introduction and his copious annotations."—*Chicago Evening Post.*

"Eastburn's hardships were severe but he was equal to them."—*Nation.*

"The narrative is printed with the old spelling and notes."—*N. Y. Times Sat. Review.*

*Leeth (John). A Short Biography of— With an Account of His Life Among the Indians. By Ewel Jeffries, edited by Reuben Gold Thwaites. Size 8¼ x 5¾, pages 70, facsimile, cloth extra (*postage .07*)   **$2.00**
On Imperial Japanese Vellum   **$3.50**

Leeth's narrative is from every viewpoint well worth the reprinting. The introduction by Dr. Thwaites is lengthy and lucid, giving all particulars concerning the old fur trader and his Indian experiences. The hero himself was in his seventy-seventh year when these recollections were reduced to writing by Jeffries and his memory was unusually accurate for a man of his humble walk in life. The story is on the whole an accurate matter of fact recital of the often thrilling personal experiences of a typical trader and hunter in the then Indian Territory of Pennsylvania and Ohio—his numerous expeditions, his intimate relations with the savages; and his captivity and life in their camps, chiefly during the stirring period between 1774 and 1790.

"The story of his adventures is a wonderful record of hardships and suffering, of indomitable bravery and rigid honesty.—*Chicago Evening Post.*

*How (Nehemiah). Narrative of his Captivity at Great Meadow Fort. Edited by Victor Hugo Paltsits. Size 8¼ x 5¾; pages 72, facsimiles, cloth, extra (*postage .06*)   **$2.00**
On Imperial Japanese Vellum   **$3.50**

The excessively rare original tract, consisting of twenty-four pages, was first published in Boston, one year after the death of How, which event occurred while he was a prisoner at Quebec. It is now reprinted for the first time vebatim et literatim et punctuatim, from a fine uncut copy (the Brinley) in the New York Public Library, with a lengthy and complete introduction, valuable footnotes and an index.

Mr. Paltsits has also supplied with the above, a genealogy of the author and brought to light many hidden facts which, though known, have not heretofore been authenticated, explaining and pointing out vagaries in New England and specially Vermont history, which will be of incalculable assistance to the future worker in this field. A facsimile of the orginal title-page is included. Nehemiah How was born in 1693 at Marlborough, Mass., and died while captive in Quebec, May 25, 1747. His narrative abounds in interest and is both lucid and accurately written. As a contemporary view of New England and southeastern Canada, it is of great value.

"The setting given the narrative in its new appearance is of the same excellence as the other volumes in this series of reprints.—*The Dial.*

"A diary of the twenty-eight pages, meager in historical material but worthy of a reprint because of its rarity."—*Amer. Hist. Review.*

Opinion in a letter from Prof. William F. Ganong, Smith College, Northampton, Mass.: "I have read it through with care and deep interest,—the latter arising in part from the narrative itself and in part from the way in which the subject is handled, and clarified by the editor. The whole work seems to me just a model of what such a work ought to be—not only in the editing, but also in the form and typography, including the very copious index."
—*Signed.*

*Johnston (Charles). Narrative of Incidents Attending his Capture. Edited by Edwin Erle Sparks, Ph. D. Size 8¼ x 5¾; pages 156, facsimile, cloth, extra (*postage .09*) $2.50
On Imperial Japanese Vellum $4.00

Although considerably shorter than many of the narratives offered from time to time by the early pioneers, this volume has many features which commend its perusal and which are of value and interest to the general reader as well as the student. During 1789, at the age of twenty-one years, Charles Johnston left a point near Petersburg, Virginia, for the State of Kentucky for the purpose of taking some depositions. His capture by the Indians took place during the summer of the year mentioned, and he was taken into the present State of Ohio and there kept prisoner until ransomed by a French Trader from Detroit. Eventually he made his way back to Virginia by way of New York. Some interesting international questions of that day touching upon the retention of American forts by the British, are fully and carefully treated. The sum paid for Johnson's release was eventually returned to the French trader by the United States Government. This book is fully annotated, the identifications of all proper names carefully attended to, and full explanations given by Professor Sparks, of the University of Chicago, author of "*The Expansions of the American People*", "*Formative Incidents in American Diplomacy*", etc., etc.

Other volumes in this series will be announced later, and will probably deal more especially with the western country as we know it today, the Rockies and the Pacific coast.

A descriptive circular on application.

Lincoln and Douglas Debates, in the Campaign of 1858 in Illinois. Size 10 x 7⅝; pages 415, buckram (*postage .22*) $3.50

Stephen A. Douglas, an exponent of views dissimilar and opposed, used all the force of splendid oratory and brilliant scholarship, but to no avail, as events have proven.

The speeches during the celebrated campaign in Illinois, and the two great speeches of Lincoln in Ohio, are masterpieces. The work is fully indexed with great care and the original edition of 1860 is now so scarce as to be practically unprocurable.

Haworth (Paul L.) The Hayes-Tilden Disputed Presidential Election of 1876. Size 8x5¾; pages 365. Buckram (*postage .12*)

Net $1.50

To the handling of this subject the author has devoted an enormous amount of the best work of a specially trained historical student's mind, and while his method is highly complete in a technical way, showing thorough scholarship, his style is also bright, picturesque, and interesting, showing thus ,not only that he has collected his materials with the highest degree of thoroughness, but also that he possesses the ability to co-ordinate the same and thus furnish to his readers something more than the mere building materials of history—a finished historical construction. The author's task was very difficult. It is practically safe to assert that up to ten years ago it would have been impossible, even with the best will in the world, to make so unbiased and thorough a study of the question as Mr. Haworth has done, and it would seem equally certain that at no time in the future will it be possible to secure such *personal* assistance as has been given to Mr. Haworth by a large number of parties directly connected in some way with one side or the other of this controversy.